Lecture Notes in Computer Science 13544

More information about this series at https://link.springer.com/bookseries/558

Ekaterina Komendantskaya (Ed.)

Mathematics
of Program Construction

14th International Conference, MPC 2022
Tbilisi, Georgia, September 26–28, 2022
Proceedings

 Springer

Editor
Ekaterina Komendantskaya
School of Mathematical and Computer Sciences
Heriot-Watt University
Edinburgh, UK

ISSN 0302-9743   ISSN 1611-3349 (electronic)
Lecture Notes in Computer Science
ISBN 978-3-031-16911-3   ISBN 978-3-031-16912-0 (eBook)
https://doi.org/10.1007/978-3-031-16912-0

Preface

Welcome to the proceedings of the 14th International Conference on Mathematics of Program Construction—MPC 2022!

The International Conference on Mathematics of Program Construction (MPC) aims to promote the development of mathematical principles and techniques that are demonstrably practical and effective in the process of constructing computer programs. Topics of interest range from algorithmics to support for program construction in programming languages and systems. Typical areas include type systems, program analysis and transformation, programming language semantics, security, and program logics. The notion of a 'program' is interpreted broadly, ranging from algorithms to hardware.

MPC 2022 welcomes theoretical contributions with relevance to the methods of program construction, reports on applications with solid mathematical basis, and programming pearls that present elegant and instructive examples of the mathematics of program construction.

The MPC series is a bi-annual conference; previous editions took place in Porto, Portugal (2019); Königswinter, Germany (2015); Madrid, Spain (2012); Québec City, Canada (2010); Marseille, France (2008); Kuressaare, Estonia (2006); Stirling, UK (2004); Dagstuhl, Germany (2002); Ponte de Lima, Portugal (2000); Marstrand, Sweden (1998); Kloster Irsee, Germany (1995); Oxford, UK (1992); and Twente, The Netherlands (1989).

The 14th installment of the conference was colocated with the Computational Logic Autumn Summit of 2022 (CLAS 2022), held during September 19–30, 2022, in Tbilisi, Georgia.

MPC 2022 featured invited talks, presentations of original research papers, and a discussion panel.

The program included three invited talks:

- Conor McBride, Strathclyde University, "Picking your way through Pascal's triangle".
- Daniela Petrisan, Université Paris Cité, "The semifree monad".
- Fabio Zanasi, University College London, "Lens Theoretic Foundations for Learning: from Semantics to Verification".

Research papers include nine original research papers, selected from 14 submissions including 13 complete submissions. Each submission was reviewed by at least three Program Committee members and went through an online discussion period undertaken by the Program Committee before a final decision was made. The selection was based only on the merit of each submission and regardless of scheduling or space constraints.

Research papers are grouped into three topics: (1) Semantics of Program Construction, (2) Programming Methods, and (3) Data Structures and Proofs.

The discussion panel "Mathematics of Program Construction Grand Challenge: Machine Learning" featured invited presenters speaking on

- Semantics for machine learning (Fabio Zanasi, University College London),
- Types and functional programming for machine learning (Nicholas Wu, Imperial College London), and
- Formalising machine learning in theorem provers (Reynold Affeldt, National Institute of Advanced Industrial Science and Technology, Japan).

We thank Besik Dundua and the local organizers of CLAS for hosting MPC 2022, and Springer for the longstanding, successful cooperation with the MPC series. We are grateful to the 19 members of the MPC 2022 Program Committee and the external reviewers for their timely and invaluable work. Many thanks to Matthew Daggitt, Heriot-Watt University, for serving as publicity chair of MPC 2022 and Alasdair Hill for designing the first version of the MPC 2022 webpage.

We are happy to note that the conference paper evaluation was successfully managed with the help of EasyChair.

August 2022   Ekaterina Komendantskaya

Organization

Program Chair

Ekaterina Komendantskaya   Heriot-Watt University, UK

Program Committee

Mohammad Abdulaziz	Technische Universität München, Germany
Aurore Alcolei	Università di Bologna, Italy
Henning Basold	Leiden University, The Netherlands
William Byrd	University of Alabama, USA
Jacques Carette	McMaster University, Canada
Andrea Costea	National University of Singapore, Singapore
Peter Hoefner	Australian National University, Australia
Johan Jeuring	Utrecht University, The Netherlands
Patricia Johann	Appalachian State University, USA
Ambrus Kaposi	Eötvös Loránd University, Hungary
Radu Mardare	University of Strathclyde, UK
Annabelle McIver	Macquarie University, Australia
Shin-Cheng Mu	Academia Sinica, Taiwan
Jose Oliveira	Universidade do Minho, Portugal
Grant Passmore	Imandra, USA
Philip Saville	University of Oxford, UK
Ana Sokolova	Universität Salzburg, Austria
Kathrin Stark	Princeton University, USA
Georg Struth	University of Sheffield, UK

Publicity Chair

Matthew Daggitt   Heriot-Watt University, UK

External Reviewers

Chris Chen
Yu-Ching Shen
Ian Shillito

Organization

Abstracts of Invited Talks

Picking Your Way Through Pascal's Triangle

Conor McBride

Strathclyde University
conor.mcbride@strath.ac.uk
www.strath.ac.uk/staff/mcbrideconordr/

Abstract. Every place in Pascal's triangle enumerates the paths to that place, zig-zagging downwards from the top, but we can do more than count them. Binomial coefficients make for remarkable dependent types: bit vectors indexed by their length and one-count can document selections from data structures, or the embedding of a term's support into its scope. They become all the more discriminating when you recognize that numerical indices are but the erasures of richer, individuating information. They compose in sequence categorically, and in parallel monoidally. Being made of bits, you can do Boolean logic with them, but with your eyes open as to their meaning. Working with Pascal's Triangle, rendered into types, has changed the way I see and organise data in general, and syntactic data in particular. I shall recount my path to this place, and seek to find the meaning in the turns of my journey.

The Semifree Monad

Daniela Petrisan

Université de Paris
petrisan@irif.fr
www.irif.fr/~petrisan/

Abstract. Weak distributive laws were considered recently in the work of Garner as a means of composing monads for which there is no strong distributive law. For example, the canonical weak distributive law exhibited in Garner's work between the powerset and the ultrafilter monad can be used to exhibit the Vietoris monad on compact Hausdorff spaces as a weak lifting of the powerset monad. Other weak distributive laws were considered in our work with Alexandre Goy. In particular we obtained a weak distributive law between the powerset monad and the distribution monad, which exhibits the convex powerset monad on barycentric algebras as a weak lifting of the powerset monad.

One essential ingredient in the theory of weak distributive laws is the notion o of semialgebras for a monad, that is, algebras for the underlying functor of the monad subject to the associativity axiom alone. In this talk I will discuss the algebraic nature of the semialgebras of a monad. If the underlying category has coproducts then semialgebras for a monad "M" are in fact the Eilenberg-Moore algebras for a suitable monad structure on the functor "id + M", which we call the semifree monad. Then I discuss how weak distributive laws between a monad "M" and "T" can be seen as strong distributive laws between the semifree monad on "M" and "T", subject to an additional condition. This is joint work with Ralph Sarkis.

Lens Theoretic Foundations for Learning: From Semantics to Verification

Fabio Zanasi

University College London
f.zanasi@ucl.ac.uk
www.zanasi.com/fabio/

Abstract. I will present recent and ongoing work on giving a semantic foundation to training algorithms in machine learning using the categorical formalisms of lenses. Lenses provide a much needed unifying perspective on various classes of such algorithms, as well as offering a different style of specifying and proving properties of training protocols. They also enable the study of machine learning for new classes of models such as Boolean circuits and polynomial circuits. In the last part of the talk I will also discuss how this foundation informs the development of new tools for the formal verification of machine learning algorithms.

References

1. Cruttwell, G.S.H., Gavranović, B., Ghani, N., Wilson, P., Zanasi, F.: Categorical foundations of gradient-based learning. In: Sergey, I. (eds.) Programming Languages and Systems. ESOP 2022. LNCS, vol. 13240, pp. 1 28. Springer, Cham. https://doi.org/10.1007/978-3-030-99336-8_1
2. Wilson, P.W., Zanasi, F.: Reverse derivative ascent: a categorical approach to learning Boolean. In: Proceedings of the 3rd International Conference on Applied Category Theory (ACT) (2020)
3. Wilson, P.W., Zanasi, F.: Categories of differentiable polynomial circuits for machine learning. In: Proceedings of the 5th International Conference on Applied Category Theory (ACT) (2022)

Contents

Breadth-First Traversal via Staging

Jeremy Gibbons[1], Donnacha Oisín Kidney[2], Tom Schrijvers[3],
and Nicolas Wu[2(⊠)]

[1] University of Oxford, Oxford, UK
[2] Imperial College London, London, UK
n.wu@imperial.ac.uk
[3] KU Leuven, Leuven, Belgium

Abstract. An effectful traversal of a data structure iterates over every element, in some predetermined order, collecting computational effects in the process. Depth-first effectful traversal of a tree is straightforward to define compositionally, since it precisely follows the shape of the data. What about breadth-first effectful traversal? An indirect route is to factorize the data structure into shape and contents, traverse the contents, then rebuild the data structure with new contents. We show that this can instead be done directly using staging, expressed using a construction related to free applicative functors. The staged traversals lend themselves well to fusion; we prove a novel fusion rule for effectful traversals, and use it in another solution to Bird's 'repmin' problem.

Keywords: Traversal · Staging · Applicative functor · Fusion

1 Introduction

This paper is about effectful traversals of data structures, in which the effects are modelled as applicative functors. This encompasses monadic effects (since every monad is also an applicative functor), but also generalizes to include monoidal aggregation, among other possibilities.

Applicative traversals capture the essence of the Iterator design pattern [9]. Informally, an applicative traversal processes a container data structure in a predetermined order, visiting each element precisely once, collecting computational effects as it goes (for example, in the state monad), and replacing each element with a new one while preserving the shape of the data structure.

For any polynomial datatype, it is completely straightforward to define an applicative traversal that follows the structure of the data. Indeed, the definition is so straightforward that it can be automated, or expressed as a single datatype-generic program. That straightforward traversal will be depth-first, completely traversing one child before moving on to the next. We give an example on lists in Sect. 2.1, and one on trees in Sect. 2.2.

But there are other possible traversal orders. In particular, what about breadth-first traversal of a tree? This is more awkward, because it goes against the grain of the tree, so to speak. One approach is to factorize the tree into shape

© The Author(s), under exclusive license to Springer Nature Switzerland AG 2022
E. Komendantskaya (Ed.): MPC 2022, LNCS 13544, pp. 1–33, 2022.
https://doi.org/10.1007/978-3-031-16912-0_1

(a tree of unit values) and contents (by breadth-first enumeration to a sequence of elements). One can then traverse the contents in isolation from the shape, then reassemble the unchanged shape and new contents into a new tree.

Executing breadth-first traversal in multiple passes in this way is a bit clumsy. Can we do the same thing in a single pass? We can! The key idea is to construct a *multi-phase computation*, with one phase per level of the tree. This multi-phase computation can be assembled in a single pass over the tree; then the phases of this computation are run one after the other. Although breadth-first traversal itself is not compositional (one cannot construct the breadth-first traversal of a tree from the traversals of its children), the multi-phase computation is compositional, because it is conveniently broken up into layers.

We present a novel approach to multi-phase computation in terms of applicative functors. In particular, we use a data representation due recently to Kidney and Wu [12], isomorphic to the *free applicative functor* on a given base functor but using a different applicative instance than that of the free applicative. Informally, we need to 'zip' together phases rather than concatenating them in order to combine computations.

We show that this approach also provides alternative solutions to other problems involving transforming multiple passes into one, but avoiding the need for laziness, such as breadth-first relabelling of a tree [11]. Examples include such as Bird's 'repmin' problem [2] and some other problems using circular definitions.

The paper is structured as follows. Section 2 relates background material on applicative functors and applicative traversal. Section 3 presents the indirect breadth-first approach via factorization into shape and contents. Our contribution starts in Sect. 4, which introduces two-phase computation, using the Day convolution of two functors, and discusses how to fuse traversals at multiple phases into a single multi-phase traversal. Section 5 generalizes this to arbitrarily many phases, by iterating Day convolution. Section 6 returns to breadth-first traversal and breadth-first relabelling, but now expressed compositionally in multi-phase terms and without needing laziness. Section 7 concludes. The key result about fusion of traversals used in Sect. 4 is proved in Appendix A.

We use Haskell as a vehicle of expression, but almost always read it in terms of sets and total functions rather than CPOs with strictness considerations. (The only divergence from that position is in discussing Bird's essentially lazy repmin solution, but our solution avoids this essential laziness.) The code in the paper is slightly simplified for presentation purposes, but the full details are available online [8]. We follow Haskell in using lowercase letters for polymorphic type parameters; but as a presentation convention, in prose though not in code, we use uppercase letters when discussing specific types. For example, *map* has the polymorphic type $(a \rightarrow b) \rightarrow [a] \rightarrow [b]$ (the type parameters a, b are implicitly universally quantified), but if applied to a specific function $f :: A \rightarrow B$ then we say that *map f* has type $[A] \rightarrow [B]$.

2   Applicative Functors

We focus on effects modelled as *applicative functors*, a slightly more general perspective than the more familiar monads. But we use the simpler categorically-inspired presentation, called the *monoidal* interface [14] rather than the more program-oriented one in the Haskell libraries:

> **class** *Functor f* $\Rightarrow$ *Applicative f* **where**
> $\quad unit :: f\ ()$
> $\quad (\otimes)\ :: f\ a \to f\ b \to f\ (a, b)$

Thus, there is a distinguished collection *unit* of unit values, and one can combine two collections into a collection of pairs. Categorically, an applicative functor is "strong lax-monoidal functor". Strength comes for free in a higher-order language like Haskell; and lax monoidality amounts to left- and right-unit and associativity properties, where $(\langle\$\rangle) :: Functor\ f \Rightarrow (a \to b) \to f\ a \to f\ b$ is the binary version the functorial mapping *fmap*.

$$
\begin{aligned}
unitl\ \langle\$\rangle\ (unit \otimes ys) &= ys \\
unitr\ \langle\$\rangle\ (xs \otimes unit) &= xs \\
assoc\ \langle\$\rangle\ (xs \otimes (ys \otimes zs)) &= (xs \otimes ys) \otimes zs
\end{aligned}
$$

that hold not on the nose, but only up to some conversions; we write

$$
\begin{aligned}
unitl &:: ((), a) \to a & unitl^{-1} &:: a \to ((), a) \\
unitr &:: (a, ()) \to a & unitr^{-1} &:: a \to (a, ()) \\
assoc &:: (a, (b, c)) \to ((a, b), c) & assoc^{-1} &:: ((a, b), c) \to (a, (b, c))
\end{aligned}
$$

for the obvious isomorphisms witnessing the (so-called 'strong') monoidal structure of the product.

While we are on the subject of isomorphisms for pairs, we will also make use of two involutions involving commutativity:

$$
\begin{aligned}
twist\ &:: (a, b) \to (b, a) \\
exch4\ &:: ((a, b), (c, d)) \to ((a, c), (b, d))
\end{aligned}
$$

The monoidal and the usual Haskell presentations of applicative functors are equivalent, and the interfaces interdefinable. In particular, we will still find the Haskell interface convenient for programming, and it can be implemented as follows:

$$
\begin{aligned}
pure &:: Applicative\ f \Rightarrow a \to f\ a \\
pure\ x &= fmap\ (const\ x)\ unit
\end{aligned}
$$

$$(\langle * \rangle) :: Applicative\ f \Rightarrow f\ (a \to b) \to f\ a \to f\ b \quad \text{-- left-associative}$$
$$fs\ \langle * \rangle\ xs = fmap\ (\lambda(f, x) \to f\ x)\ (fs \otimes xs)$$

$$(* \rangle) :: Applicative\ f \Rightarrow f\ a \to f\ b \to f\ b \quad\quad \text{-- left-associative}$$
$$xs\ * \rangle\ ys = fmap\ snd\ (xs \otimes ys)$$

This situation is analogous to the distinction between the presentation of monads in terms of bind ($\ggg$), which is more convenient for programming, and in terms of multiplication *join*, which is more categorically perspicuous.

Every monad is an applicative functor, with the following implementation:

instance *Monad m* $\Rightarrow$ *Applicative m* **where**
    unit   = *return* ()
    $xs \otimes ys = $ **do** $\{ x \leftarrow xs; y \leftarrow ys; return\ (x, y) \}$

—that is, ($\otimes$) can be seen as a form of sequencing. An illuminating applicative functor instance that does not arise from a monad is that of colists $[\,]^\omega$—that is, finite and infinite lists together—under zipping:

instance *Applicative* $[\,]^\omega$ **where**
    unit = *repeat* ()
    $(\otimes)$ = *zip*

Another is the constant applicative functor *Const A* for monoid *A*:

data *Const a b* = *Const* { *getConst* :: *a* }

instance *Monoid a* $\Rightarrow$ *Applicative* (*Const a*) **where**
    unit   = *Const mempty*
    $x \otimes y = Const\ (mappend\ (getConst\ x)\ (getConst\ y))$

2.1   Applicative Traversal

Applicative traversal is "the essence of the Iterator design pattern" [9], capturing computations that iterate over a data structure, in a predetermined order, processing each element in turn and collecting effects as they go:

class *Functor t* $\Rightarrow$ *Traversable t* **where**
    traverse :: *Applicative f* $\Rightarrow$ $(a \to f\ b) \to t\ a \to f\ (t\ b)$

For example, left-to-right traversal of (finite) lists just follows the shape of the list datatype:

```
instance Traversable [] where
  traverse f []      = pure []
  traverse f (x : xs) = (:) ⟨$⟩ f x ⟨*⟩ traverse f xs
```

Well-behaved traversals are those satisfying three axioms of *naturality, linearity,* and *unitarity* [10]. These essentially say that *traverse* is 'natural' in the applicative functor, and respects the compositional structure of applicative functors. This implies, among other consequences, that a well-behaved traversal preserves the shape of the data structure it traverses, and visits every element precisely once.

Formally, an *applicative morphism* $\phi : F \to G$ between applicative functors F and G is a polymorphic function $\phi :: \forall a . F\ a \to G\ a$ that respects the applicative structure. To be explicit, we write $(\otimes_F)$, $unit_F$ for the applicative operations for applicative functor F. Then for ϕ to be an applicative morphism, it must satisfy:

$$\phi\ unit_F \quad = unit_G$$
$$\phi\ (xs \otimes_F ys) = \phi\ xs \otimes_G \phi\ ys$$

for $xs :: F\ A$ and $ys :: F\ B$. Then the *naturality* axiom of a well-behaved traversal states that it respects applicative morphisms: for $f :: A \to F\ B$ and applicative morphism $\phi : F \to G$,

$$traverse\ (\phi \circ f) = \phi \circ traverse\ f$$

Applicative functors are closed under functor composition: the identity functor I is applicative, and if F and G are applicative then so is their composition $F \circ G$. The other two conditions on well-behaved traversals are that they should respect this compositional structure. To be explicit again, we subscript generic functions with the applicative functor. The *unitarity* axiom states that traversal with the identity function $id :: A \to I\ A$ is itself the identity:

$$traverse_I\ id = id$$

Together with the free theorem of the type $(A \to F\ B) \to T\ A \to F\ (T\ B)$ of *traverse*, we get more generally that traversal in the identity applicative functor—that is, traversal with a pure function $f :: A \to I\ B$—is just a map:

$$traverse_I\ f = fmap\ f$$

The *linearity* axiom states that traversal in the composition of applicative functors is a composition of traversals. That is, given applicative functors F and G, and traversal bodies $f :: A \rightarrow F\ B$ and $g :: B \rightarrow G\ C$, write ($\langle \circ \rangle$) for the obvious composition:

$$g \langle \circ \rangle f = \mathit{fmap}_F\ g \circ f :: A \rightarrow F\ (G\ C)$$

Then we have:

$$\mathit{traverse}_{F \circ G}\ (g \langle \circ \rangle f) = \mathit{traverse}_G\ g \langle \circ \rangle \mathit{traverse}_F\ f$$

Here we have equated $I\ A$ with A, and $(F \circ G)\ A$ with $F\ (G\ A)$. This isn't possible in Haskell; we would have to introduce *Identity* and *Compose* datatype wrappers, with corresponding injection and projection isomorphisms, and include those isomorphisms in the statements of the properties.

One more important result about traversals, a theorem rather than an axiom: the Representation Theorem for traversals [1] states that well-behaved traversals over an arbitrary traversable datatype are fully characterised by the corresponding list-based traversals over their contents, and so results about traversals in general follow from results about traversals over lists in particular. We will cover this theorem when we need it, in Sect. 4.

2.2   Trees

We will use the following datatype of trees throughout the paper:

```
data Tree a   = Node a (Forest a)
type Forest a = [ Tree a]
```

For example, here is a tree of integers:

```
t :: Tree Int
t = Node 3 [ Node 1 [ Node 1 []
                    , Node 5 []]
           , Node 4 [ Node 9 []
                    , Node 2 []]]
```

Depth-first traversal of a tree is easily captured as a *Traversable* instance:

```
instance Traversable Tree where
    traverse f (Node x ts) = Node ⟨$⟩ f x ⟨*⟩ traverseF f ts
        where traverseF f = traverse (traverse f)
```

This again follows the shape of the *Tree* datatype, which is mutually recursive with the *Forest* type. We will encounter several times this pattern of mutual recursion between the function on trees and the corresponding function on forests; here is another example, for computing the depths of a tree and a forest:

$$depth :: Tree\ a \rightarrow Int$$
$$depth\ (Node\ x\ ts) = 1 + depthF\ ts$$

$$depthF :: Forest\ a \rightarrow Int$$
$$depthF\ [\,] = 0$$
$$depthF\ ts = maximum\ (map\ depth\ ts)$$

The definition of traversal over trees is actually very similar in principle to the traversal of lists, as defined in Sect. 2.1. In fact, the outermost *traverse* in the definition of *traverseF* is that list instance of traversal. Moreover, each definition can in principle be derived automatically from the corresponding datatype definition.

But what about breadth-first traversal? It is not obvious how to do that structurally, as we have done for lists and for depth-first traversal of trees; in particular, it does not follow directly from the structure of the datatype definition.

3   Shape, Contents, Relabelling

An indirect approach to breadth-first traversal can be made by factoring a tree into its shape and contents [6]; here we see how.

Let us first consider breadth-first enumeration, returning just the list of elements in the tree. This is not compositional, because one cannot compute the breadth-first enumeration of a tree from the enumerations of its children. But the related "level-order enumeration", giving a list of lists, one list per level, is compositional:

$$levels :: Tree\ a \rightarrow [[a]]$$
$$levels\ (Node\ x\ ts) = [x] : levelsF\ ts$$

$$levelsF :: Forest\ a \rightarrow [[a]]$$
$$levelsF = foldr\ (lzw\ (+\!\!+))\ [\,] \circ map\ levels$$

Here, *lzw* (for "long zip with") is similar to *zipWith*, but returns a list as long as its longer argument [7]:

$$lzw :: (a \rightarrow a \rightarrow a) \rightarrow [a] \rightarrow [a] \rightarrow [a]$$
$$lzw\ f\ (x : xs)\ (y : ys) = f\ x\ y : lzw\ f\ xs\ ys$$
$$lzw\ f\ [\,] \qquad ys \qquad = ys$$
$$lzw\ f\ xs \qquad [\,] \qquad = xs$$

For example, with t as in Sect. 2, we have:

$$levels\ t = [\quad [3],$$
$$[1,4],$$
$$[1,5,9,2]$$
$$]$$

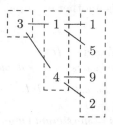

Given level-order enumeration, breadth-first enumeration is obtained by concatenation:

$$bf :: Tree\ a \rightarrow [a]$$
$$bf = concat \circ levels$$

so that $bf\ t = [3,1,4,1,5,9,2]$.

Now, enumeration is invertible, in the sense that one can reconstruct the tree given its shape (a tree of units) and its level-order enumeration (a list of elements). One way to define the inverse process is to pass the level-order enumeration around the tree, incrementally snipping bits off it. Here is a mutually recursive pair of functions to relabel a tree with a given list of lists, returning also the unused tails from the list of lists:

$$relabel :: (Tree\ (), [[a]]) \rightarrow (Tree\ a, [[a]])$$
$$relabel\ (Node\ ()\ ts, (x:xs):xss) = \textbf{let}\ (us, yss) = relabelF\ (ts, xss)$$
$$\textbf{in}\ (Node\ x\ us, xs:yss)$$

$$relabelF :: (Forest\ (), [[a]]) \rightarrow (Forest\ a, [[a]])$$
$$relabelF\ ([], xss) \quad = ([], xss)$$
$$relabelF\ (t:ts, xss) = \textbf{let}\ (u, yss)\ = relabel\ (t, xss)$$
$$(us, zss) = relabelF\ (ts, yss)$$
$$\textbf{in}\ (u:us, zss)$$

Assuming that the given list of lists is 'big enough'—that is, each list has enough elements for that level of the tree—the result is well-defined. Then *relabel* is determined by the equivalence

$$relabel\ (t, xss) = (u, yss) \iff$$
$$shape\ u = shape\ t \wedge length\ yss = length\ xss \wedge lzw\ (+\!\!+)\ (levels\ u)\ yss = xss$$

where *shape* discards the elements of a tree:

$$shape :: Tree\ a \rightarrow Tree\ ()$$
$$shape = fmap\ (const\ ())$$

In particular, if the given list of lists is the level-order enumeration of the tree, and so is exactly the right size, then *yss* will have no remaining elements, consisting entirely of empty levels:

$$relabel\ (shape\ t, levels\ t) = (t, replicate\ (depth\ t)\ [\,])$$

So we can factor a tree into its shape and contents, and reconstruct the tree from such data:

$$split :: Tree\ a \rightarrow (Tree\ (), [[a]])$$
$$split\ t = (shape\ t, levels\ t)$$

$$combine :: Tree\ () \rightarrow [[a]] \rightarrow Tree\ a$$
$$combine\ u\ xss = fst\ (relabel\ (u, xss))$$

This lets us traverse a tree in breadth-first order, by performing the traversal on the contents in isolation. We separate the tree into shape and contents, perform a list-based traversal, and reconstruct the tree:

$$bftSC :: Applicative\ f \Rightarrow (a \rightarrow f\ b) \rightarrow Tree\ a \rightarrow f\ (Tree\ b)$$
$$bftSC\ f\ t = combine\ (shape\ t) \langle\$\rangle\ traverse\ (traverse\ f)\ (levels\ t)$$

Incidentally, it is not necessary to have the enumeration of the tree conveniently partitioned into levels; one can also relabel the tree just from its breadth-first enumeration. The trick is to construct the appropriate partition of the breadth-first enumeration into levels. There is a clever cyclic program due to Geraint Jones [11] to do this at the same time as relabelling:

$$bflabel :: Tree\ () \rightarrow [a] \rightarrow Tree\ a$$
$$bflabel\ t\ xs = \textbf{let}\ (u, xss) = relabel\ (t, xs : xss)\ \textbf{in}\ u$$

Note that *xss* is defined cyclically, so it is crucial that this **let** has **letrec** semantics—that is, the variables bound on the left of the equals sign are in scope on the right as well as in the body. Informally, the output leftovers *xss* on one level also form the input elements to be used for relabelling all the lower levels. Given this definition, we have

$$bflabel\ (shape\ t)\ (bf\ t) = t$$

for any *t*. We can use this approach instead in the definition of breadth-first traversal:

$$bftL :: Applicative\ f \Rightarrow (a \rightarrow f\ b) \rightarrow Tree\ a \rightarrow f\ (Tree\ b)$$
$$bftL\ f\ t = bflabel\ (shape\ t) \langle\$\rangle\ traverse\ f\ (bf\ t)$$

However, both these implementations of breadth-first traversal are clunky and inefficient, because of having to factor into shape and contents. Also, breadth-first relabelling given only the enumeration is tricky: the program is cyclic, so doing it in a single pass seems to require laziness [13]. We will show that this impression is false: there are perfectly good ways of presenting it that make no use of laziness.

4   Fusing Traversals via Staged Computation

The circular function for breadth-first relabelling is tricky because it fuses two passes (splitting the input stream into levels, then applying these levels across the tree) into one, entangling the two together. There is a whole class of programs of this form: circular definitions, fusing together multiple passes into one. The classic example is Bird's 'repmin' problem [2]. Studying the structure of repmin will help us see what is going on with breadth-first relabelling.

4.1   The Repmin Problem

The repmin problem is to replace every element of a tree with the minimum element in that tree:

$$repmin :: Tree\ Int \rightarrow Tree\ Int$$
$$repmin\ t = replaceT\ t\ (minT\ t)\ \textbf{where}$$
$$minT :: Tree\ Int \rightarrow Int$$
$$minT\ (Node\ x\ [\,]) = x$$
$$minT\ (Node\ x\ ts) = min\ x\ (minF\ ts)$$

$$minF :: Forest\ Int \rightarrow Int$$
$$minF = minimum \circ map\ minT$$

$$replaceT :: Tree\ a \rightarrow b \rightarrow Tree\ b$$
$$replaceT\ (Node\ x\ ts)\ y = Node\ y\ (replaceF\ ts\ y)$$

$$replaceF :: Forest\ a \rightarrow b \rightarrow Forest\ b$$
$$replaceF\ ts\ y = [\,replaceT\ t\ y \mid t \leftarrow ts\,]$$

but to do so in one pass rather than two. Bird's technique is to define a composite function that computes the minimum in a tree and replaces all elements with a given element all in one go, and to feed the minimum output back in as the replacement input:

$$repmin_{RSB} :: Tree\ Int \rightarrow Tree\ Int$$
$$repmin_{RSB}\ t = \textbf{let}\ (u, m) = auxT\ t\ m\ \textbf{in}\ u$$
$$\textbf{where}$$
$$auxT :: Tree\ Int \rightarrow a \rightarrow (Tree\ a, Int)$$
$$auxT\ (Node\ x\ [\,])\ y = (Node\ y\ [\,], x)$$

$$auxT \; (Node \; x \; ts) \; y = (Node \; y \; us, min \; x \; z)$$
$$\textbf{where} \; (us, z) = auxF \; ts \; y$$

$$auxF :: Forest \; Int \to a \to (Forest \; a, Int) \quad \text{-- non-empty forest}$$
$$auxF \; ts \; y = (us, minimum \; ys)$$
$$\textbf{where} \; (us, ys) = unzip \; [\, auxT \; t \; y \mid t \leftarrow ts \,]$$

Note that the m in $repmin_{\text{RSB}}$ is defined cyclically, as with Jones's breadth-first relabelling, so that **let** must have **letrec** semantics.

But Bird's circular program making essential use of **letrec** semantics and laziness is not the only way to solve the repmin problem. Pettorossi and Skowron [15,16] show how to get the same results using only higher-order functions, and needing only call-by-value evaluation. Pettorossi's solution is as follows:

$$repmin_{\text{ADP}} :: Tree \; Int \to Tree \; Int$$
$$repmin_{\text{ADP}} \; t = \textbf{let} \; (u, m) = auxT \; t \; \textbf{in} \; u \; m$$
$$\quad \textbf{where}$$
$$\quad auxT :: Tree \; Int \to (a \to Tree \; a, Int)$$
$$\quad auxT \; (Node \; x \; [\,]) = (\lambda y \to Node \; y \; [\,], x)$$
$$\quad auxT \; (Node \; x \; ts) = (\lambda y \to Node \; y \; (us \; y), min \; x \; z)$$
$$\quad \quad \textbf{where} \; (us, z) = auxF \; ts$$

$$\quad auxF :: Forest \; Int \to (a \to Forest \; a, Int) \quad \text{-- non-empty forest}$$
$$\quad auxF \; ts = (\lambda y \to map \; (\$y) \; us, minimum \; ys)$$
$$\quad \quad \textbf{where} \; (us, ys) = unzip \; [\, auxT \; t \mid t \leftarrow ts \,]$$

Where Bird's $auxT$ takes a replacement value as an input, and returns an updated tree, Pettorossi's $auxT$ takes no such input, and returns instead a function from replacement value to updated tree. Where Bird's main function has a circular definition, feeding the output minimum back in as an input and returning only the updated tree, Pettorossi's main function is not circular (the **let** need not be treated as a **letrec**), and the output function is applied to the output minimum. Danvy et al. [4] say more about the relationship between these two approaches.

Pettorossi's approach neatly makes explicit the data dependencies, and therefore the sense in which the components of the solution are compositional, in a way that Bird's approach does not. Specifically, it is explicit in Pettorossi's program that the output minimum does not depend on the input replacement value— because there is no input replacement value upon which to depend. In contrast, the input replacement value y in Bird's $auxT$ is in scope for the definition of the output minimum; it takes some kind of program analysis to confirm that x, $min \; x \; z$, and $minimum \; ys$ are all independent of y, as required in order for the **letrec** to be productive and the result to be properly defined.

4.2   Fusing Traversals

The crucial ingredient in fitting this development into our framework is an appropriate fusion rule for traversals. Informally, two consecutive traversals over the same data structure with the same class of effects can be fused into a single traversal with a composite body. Formally, with applicative functor F, traversable data structure $t :: T\ A$, and traversal bodies $f :: A \to F\ B$ and $g :: A \to F\ C$, we have:

$$traverse\ f\ t \otimes traverse\ g\ t = fmap\ unzip\ (traverse\ (\lambda x \to f\ x \otimes g\ x)\ t)$$

where *unzip* separates a structure of pairs into a pair of structures:

$$unzip :: Functor\ t \Rightarrow t\ (a, b) \to (t\ a, t\ b)$$
$$unzip\ t = (fmap\ fst\ t, fmap\ snd\ t)$$

We will only use this rule in the special case in which f returns unit (that is, $B = ()$), or returns values that we discard. Then no unzipping is required:

$$traverse\ f\ t *\!\!> traverse\ g\ t = traverse\ (\lambda x \to f\ x *\!\!> g\ x)\ t$$

But neither fusion rule can hold in general, because of the order of effects: on the left, all the f-effects precede any of the g-effects, and on the right they are interleaved.

The interleaving would be irrelevant if F were *commutative*: that is, if

$$xs \otimes ys = fmap\ twist\ (ys \otimes xs)$$

for all $xs :: F\ A$, $ys :: F\ B$. But that condition is quite restrictive, ruling out in particular anything stateful. However, the interleaving is still irrelevant even when F is not commutative, provided more specifically that the f-effects commute with g-effects, in the sense that

$$f\ x \otimes g\ y = fmap\ twist\ (g\ y \otimes f\ x)$$

for all x, y. With this assumption we can prove both fusion rules using the Representation Theorem for applicative traversals [1]; the proof is given in Appendix A.

In particular, whenever f and g specify effects that occur in distinct phases of a two-phase computation, they will commute: it doesn't matter whether you say "do X now and Y later" or "do Y later and X now", because either way X is enacted before Y. So let us consider two-phase computations.

4.3 Day Convolution

The Day convolution [17] $Day\ F\ G$ of two functors F, G is given by:

```
data Day f g a where
    Day :: ((a, b) → c) → f a → g b → Day f g c
```

Thus, $Day\ f\ xs\ ys$ with $xs :: F\ A, ys :: G\ B$ represents a two-phase computation, with subcomputation xs happening in phase one generating effects in F, and ys in phase two generating effects in G. It is convenient to package this pair up with a function $f :: (A, B) \rightarrow C$ to combine the results from the two phases. This packaging is known as the "co-Yoneda trick", and it straightforwardly turns $Day\ F\ G$ into a functor:

> **instance** $Functor\ (Day\ f\ g)$ **where**
> $\quad fmap\ g\ (Day\ f\ xs\ ys) = Day\ (g \circ f)\ xs\ ys$

Moreover, $Day\ F\ G$ is applicative when F, G are applicative, with pointwise combination:

> **instance** $(Applicative\ f, Applicative\ g) \Rightarrow Applicative\ (Day\ f\ g)$ **where**
> $\quad unit \qquad\qquad\qquad\quad = Day\ unitr\ unit\ unit$
> $\quad Day\ f\ xs\ ys \otimes Day\ g\ zs\ ws = Day\ (cross\ f\ g \circ exch4)\ (xs \otimes zs)\ (ys \otimes ws)$

where

> $cross :: (a \rightarrow b) \rightarrow (c \rightarrow d) \rightarrow (a, c) \rightarrow (b, d)$
> $cross\ f\ g\ (x, y) = (f\ x, g\ y)$

And there are two ways to inject a computation, one for each phase:

> $phase1 :: (Applicative\ f, Applicative\ g) \Rightarrow f\ a \rightarrow Day\ f\ g\ a$
> $phase1\ xs = Day\ unitr\ xs\ unit$
>
> $phase2 :: (Applicative\ f, Applicative\ g) \Rightarrow g\ a \rightarrow Day\ f\ g\ a$
> $phase2\ xs = Day\ unitl\ unit\ xs$

Crucially for us, computations in different phases commute:

> $phase1\ xs \otimes phase2\ ys = fmap\ twist\ (phase2\ ys \otimes phase1\ xs)$

When the two phases share a class of effects, we can combine the two phases, running one after the other and post-processing the results:

> $runDay :: Applicative\ f \Rightarrow Day\ f\ f\ a \rightarrow f\ a$
> $runDay\ (Day\ f\ xs\ ys) = fmap\ f\ (xs \otimes ys)$

For example, we can send a two-part greeting in separate phases:

```
⟫⟩    runDay (phase1 (putStr "Hello ") *⟩
               phase2 (putStr "World"))
Hello World
```

It doesn't matter if we specify those two phases in the opposite order:

```
⟫⟩    runDay (phase2 (putStr "World") *⟩
               phase1 (putStr "Hello "))
Hello World
```

We can even interleave the specification of fragments from different phases:

```
⟫⟩    runDay (phase1 (putStr "Hel") *⟩
               phase2 (putStr "World") *⟩
               phase1 (putStr "lo "))
Hello World
```

4.4   Repmin in Two Phases

Returning now to the repmin problem, we have first to formulate it as an effectful computation. We could use the state monad, writing minimum values to the state in the first phase then reading the replacement value from the state in the second. But those two phases use the state in different ways: computing the minimum writes to the state without reading from it, and replacing tree elements reads from the state without writing to it. So a more precise expression of the two-phase solution would use two different classes of effect, writing and reading.

We therefore use the *Writer* and *Reader* monads respectively. For a monoid W, the writer monad *Writer W* is essentially pairing with the written value W:

$$runWriter :: Writer\ w\ a \rightarrow (a, w)$$

and provides an operation

$$tell :: Monoid\ w \Rightarrow Writer\ w\ ()$$

to 'write' a value. For arbitrary type R, the reader monad *Reader R* essentially comprises functions from the read value R:

$$runReader :: Reader\ r\ a \rightarrow (r \rightarrow a)$$

and provides an operation

$$ask :: Reader\ r\ r$$

to 'read' a value. We will also use the wrapper type *Min* to construct the monoid *Min Int*, with minimum as the binary operator and the least *Int* value as unit:

$$Min \quad :: Int \rightarrow Min\ Int$$
$$getMin :: Min\ Int \rightarrow Int$$

Therefore we work in *Day* (*Writer* (*Min Int*)) (*Reader* (*Min Int*)), the Day convolution of the two effects using a common value type. We introduce four abbreviations:

type *WInt* = *Writer* (*Min Int*)

$$tellMin :: Int \rightarrow WInt\ ()$$
$$tellMin\ x = tell\ (Min\ x)$$

type *RInt* = *Reader* (*Min Int*)

$$askMin :: RInt\ Int$$
$$askMin = fmap\ getMin\ ask$$

The core of the computation is the following function:

$$repminAux :: Tree\ Int \rightarrow Day\ WInt\ RInt\ (Tree\ Int)$$
$$repminAux\ t = phase1\ (minAux\ t) *\!\!\rangle\ phase2\ (replaceAux\ t)$$

where the first phase writes each element in turn:

$$minAux :: Tree\ Int \rightarrow WInt\ ()$$
$$minAux\ (Node\ x\ ts) = tellMin\ x *\!\!\rangle\ mapM\_\ minAux\ ts$$

and the second phase reads a fixed replacement value for each element:

$$replaceAux :: Tree\ Int \rightarrow RInt\ (Tree\ Int)$$
$$replaceAux\ (Node\ x\ ts) = Node\ \langle\$\rangle\ askMin\ \langle*\rangle\ (mapM\ replaceAux\ ts)$$

In fact, both phases are (depth-first) instances of *traverse* over trees—at least, if we allow the result returned in the first phase, which we discard anyway, to be a tree instead of void:

$$repminAux' :: Tree\ Int \rightarrow Day\ WInt\ RInt\ (Tree\ Int)$$
$$repminAux'\ t = phase1\ (minAux'\ t) *\!\!\rangle\ phase2\ (replaceAux'\ t)$$

$minAux' :: Tree\ Int \rightarrow WInt\ (Tree\ ())$
$minAux' = traverse\ (\lambda x \rightarrow tellMin\ x)$

$replaceAux' :: Tree\ Int \rightarrow RInt\ (Tree\ Int)$
$replaceAux' = traverse\ (\lambda x \rightarrow askMin)$

Now, *phase1* and *phase2* are applicative morphisms, so by the naturality axiom of traversal we have

$$phase1\ (traverse\ f) = traverse\ (phase1\ f)$$

and similarly for *phase2*. Therefore we can move the phase coercions inside the traversals:

$repminAux'' :: Tree\ Int \rightarrow Day\ WInt\ RInt\ (Tree\ Int)$
$repminAux''\ t = minAux''\ t *\!\!> replaceAux''\ t$

$minAux'' :: Tree\ Int \rightarrow Day\ WInt\ RInt\ (Tree\ ())$
$minAux'' = traverse\ (\lambda x \rightarrow phase1\ (tellMin\ x))$

$replaceAux'' :: Tree\ Int \rightarrow Day\ WInt\ RInt\ (Tree\ Int)$
$replaceAux'' = traverse\ (\lambda x \rightarrow phase2\ askMin)$

Finally, the two traversal bodies commute, because they are in different phases, so we can fuse the two traversals into one:

$repminAux''' :: Tree\ Int \rightarrow Day\ WInt\ RInt\ (Tree\ Int)$
$repminAux''' = traverse\ (\lambda x \rightarrow phase1\ (tellMin\ x) *\!\!> phase2\ askMin)$

To summarize the development:

$\quad phase1\ (traverse\ tellMin\ t) *\!\!> phase2\ (traverse\ (\lambda x \rightarrow askMin)\ t)$
$=\quad \{\ \text{naturality in applicative functor}\ \}$
$\quad traverse\ (phase1 \circ tellMin)\ t *\!\!> traverse\ (\lambda x \rightarrow phase2\ askMin)\ t$
$=\quad \{\ \text{fusion of traversals}\ \}$
$\quad traverse\ (\lambda x \rightarrow phase1\ (tellMin\ x) *\!\!> phase2\ askMin)$

So *repminAux'''* describes a one-pass traversal over the tree, generating a two-phase computation for later execution.

Now we turn to the question of extracting the *Tree Int* → *Tree Int* outer function from the above core. We can run a computation in the Day convolution of *Writer S* and *Reader S* for the same type *S* by extracting the writer and reader components in parallel, as follows:

$$parWR :: Day\ (Writer\ s)\ (Reader\ s)\ a \rightarrow a$$
$$parWR\ (Day\ f\ xs\ ys) = \textbf{let}\ ((x, s), y) = (runWriter\ xs, runReader\ ys\ s)$$
$$\textbf{in}\ f\ (x, y)$$

Note that this is circular, with s appearing on both sides of the local declaration, so the **let** must have **letrec** semantics. In particular,

$$repminWR_{\mathrm{RSB}} :: Tree\ Int \rightarrow Tree\ Int$$
$$repminWR_{\mathrm{RSB}}\ t = parWR\ (repminAux'''\ t)$$

is Bird's circular, lazy solution to the repmin problem.

Conversely, we can extract the writer component then the reader component sequentially:

$$seqWR :: Day\ (Writer\ s)\ (Reader\ s)\ a \rightarrow a$$
$$seqWR\ (Day\ f\ xs\ ys) = \textbf{let}\ (x, s) = runWriter\ xs$$
$$y\quad = runReader\ ys\ s$$
$$\textbf{in}\ f\ (x, y)$$

Now there is no circularity, and a plain non-recursive **let** suffices. In particular,

$$repminWR_{\mathrm{ADP}} :: Tree\ Int \rightarrow Tree\ Int$$
$$repminWR_{\mathrm{ADP}}\ t = seqWR\ (repminAux'''\ t)$$

is Pettorossi's non-circular, higher-order solution to the repmin problem. In a lazy language, clearly $parWR$ and $seqWR$ are equal, and so too therefore are $repminWR_{\mathrm{RSB}}$ and $repminWR_{\mathrm{ADP}}$.

Observe that in both the lazy and strict solutions the values xs and ys are nested tuples of values: the values in xs are all the unit, and the values in ys are all the minimum value. The function f picks the values out of ys and assembles them into the resulting tree; xs is ignored. A biased version

data $Day'\ f\ y\ a$ **where**
  $Day' :: f\ (b \rightarrow a) \rightarrow g\ b \rightarrow Day'\ f\ g\ a$

of Day convolution would avoid constructing the nested structure for xs in the first place.

5   Multiple Phases

We now generalize from two-phase computations to multiple (zero or more) phases [5]:

data *Phases f a* **where**
    Pure :: $a \rightarrow$ *Phases f a*
    Link :: $((a, b) \rightarrow c) \rightarrow f\ a \rightarrow$ *Phases f b* $\rightarrow$ *Phases f c*

Here, *Pure* produces a chain with no effectful phases, and *Link* adds one more effectful phase to the chain. It is basically a homogeneous iteration of Day convolution (*Link* constructs the Day convolution of *f* with *Phases f*), just as lists are essentially a homogeneous iteration of pairing (with cons pairing a list head with a tail). There is a single initial value as the base case; each additional link in the chain adds a combining function and a collection of values; and the types are all compatible "in the obvious way". For example, for some given base applicative functor *F*, we can link together components of types

    z :: *Char*
    ys :: *F Float*
    g :: (*Float*, *Char*) $\rightarrow$ *String*
    xs :: *F Bool*
    f :: (*Bool*, *String*) $\rightarrow$ *Int*

to form a chain

    example = *Link f xs* (*Link g ys* (*Pure z*)) :: *Phases F Int*

We will always have the *f* argument to *Phases* be at least a functor (justifying the phrase "a collection of" above), in which case *Phases f* is also a functor:

    instance *Functor f* $\Rightarrow$ *Functor* (*Phases f*) **where**
      fmap g (*Pure x*)   = *Pure* (*g x*)
      fmap g (*Link f xs ys*) = *Link* (*g* $\circ$ *f*) *xs ys*

That is, *example* is a symbolic representation of a collection of *Int*s.

5.1   Free Applicatives

Capriotti and Kaposi [3] show that the datatype *Phases* constructs the *free applicative functor* on a given functor argument. We won't dwell on what "free" means here; we will observe simply that *Phases f* can be given applicative structure when *f* is a functor:

    instance *Functor f* $\Rightarrow$ *Applicative* (*Phases f*) **where**   -- not used
      unit   = *Pure* ()
      Pure x $\otimes$ *ys*   = *fmap* (*x*,) *ys*
      Link f xs ys $\otimes$ *zs* = *Link* ($\lambda(x, (y, z)) \rightarrow (f\ (x, y), z)$) *xs* (*ys* $\otimes$ *zs*)

Informally, this defines $\otimes$ to concatenate two of these chains. Indeed, if we define the 'length' of such a chain to be the number of *Link* constructors:

$$chlen :: Phases\ f\ a \to Int$$
$$chlen\ (Pure\ x)\qquad = 0$$
$$chlen\ (Link\ f\ xs\ ys) = 1 + chlen\ ys$$

then $chlen\ (xs \otimes ys) = chlen\ xs + chlen\ ys$.

However, this canonical applicative structure on chains is not helpful when considering multiple-phase computations. Concatenation of chains amounts to a sequential scheduling of effects: $xs \otimes ys$ schedules all the phases of xs first, followed by all the phases of ys. It is more useful to schedule phases in parallel: $xs \otimes ys$ should mean "in phase 1, execute phase 1 of xs and then phase 1 of ys, in phase 2, execute phase 2 of xs and phase 2 of ys," and so on.

The corresponding product operation with these parallel semantics should 'zip' together two chains; and this should be a 'long zip', returning a chain as long as its longer argument—as we already used for breadth-first enumeration. In order to combine elements of the chain pointwise, we need the stronger assumption that the f argument is itself applicative and not merely a functor [12]:

$$\textbf{instance}\ Applicative\ f \Rightarrow Applicative\ (Phases\ f)\ \textbf{where}$$
$$unit = Pure\ ()$$
$$Pure\ x \otimes ys\qquad\qquad\qquad = fmap\ (x,)\ ys$$
$$xs \otimes Pure\ y\qquad\qquad\qquad = fmap\ (,y)\ xs$$
$$Link\ f\ xs\ ys \otimes Link\ g\ zs\ ws = Link\ (cross\ f\ g \circ exch4)\ (xs \otimes zs)\ (ys \otimes ws)$$

Now we have $chlen\ (xs \otimes ys) = max\ (chlen\ xs)\ (chlen\ ys)$.

Given that the chain is homogeneous and the functor argument is applicative, we can run each of the phases in a chain in turn to extract the collection of elements it represents:

$$runPhases :: Applicative\ f \Rightarrow Phases\ f\ a \to f\ a$$
$$runPhases\ (Pure\ x)\qquad = pure\ x$$
$$runPhases\ (Link\ f\ xs\ ys) = fmap\ f\ (xs \otimes runPhases\ ys)$$

Thus, *runPhases example* consists of values $f\ (x, g\ (y, z))$ where x, y are drawn pointwise from xs, ys (each of the first elements of xs, ys combined, then each of the second elements, and so on). In contrast, if we know no more about the functor argument, the only expansion we can give is to a nested collection of results: we could run the phases of *example* to yield an $F\ (F\ Int)$, containing values $f\ (x, g\ (y, z))$ where x, y are drawn from the cartesian product of xs, ys. On the other hand, if we knew further that the applicative argument were a monad, we could flatten the nesting to a single level.

5.2   Two Phases, More or Less

By design, *Phases f* is a generalization of the homogeneous Day convolution
Day f f. So of course we can inject the latter into the former:

> $inject :: Applicative\ f \Rightarrow Day\ f\ f\ a \rightarrow Phases\ f\ a$
> $inject\ (Day\ f\ xs\ ys) = Link\ f\ xs\ (Link\ unitr\ ys\ (Pure\ ()))$

And of course, $chlen\ (inject\ xs) = 2$ for any two-phase computation xs.

Analogous to *phase1* and *phase2*, we define one function that embeds a
computation into an arbitrary phase:

> $phase :: Applicative\ f \Rightarrow Int \rightarrow f\ a \rightarrow Phases\ f\ a$
> $phase\ 1 = now$
> $phase\ i = later \circ phase\ (i-1)$

where *now* embeds at phase one:

> $now :: Applicative\ f \Rightarrow f\ a \rightarrow Phases\ f\ a$
> $now\ xs = Link\ unitr\ xs\ (Pure\ ())$

and *later* shifts everything one phase later:

> $later :: Applicative\ f \Rightarrow Phases\ f\ a \rightarrow Phases\ f\ a$
> $later\ xs = Link\ unitl\ unit\ xs$

Note that we count phases from one, so that $chlen\ (phase\ i\ xs) = i$. Moreover,
inject $\circ$ *phase1* corresponds to *phase* 1. They are not quite equal as values of
type *Phases* (the chain length of the former is two, and of the latter is one), but
we do have

> $runPhases \circ inject \circ phase1 = runPhases \circ phase\ 1 = id$

5.3   The 'Sort-Tree' Problem

A related problem to repmin is the 'sort-tree' problem [2,16], which extracts the
elements of a tree as a list, sorts that list into ascending order, then relabels
the tree with the sorted list—but again does so in a single pass. (Bird called it
'sort-tips', because in his tree datatype the elements were all at the tips.)

We start with three phases, although only the first and last phase involve
traversing the tree:

$$sortTree :: Ord\ a \Rightarrow Tree\ a \rightarrow Tree\ a$$
$$sortTree\ t = evalState\ (runPhases\ (sortTreeAux\ t))\ [\,]$$

$$sortTreeAux :: Ord\ a \Rightarrow Tree\ a \rightarrow Phases\ (State\ [\,a])\ (Tree\ a)$$
$$sortTreeAux\ t = phase\ 1\ (traverse\ push\ t) *\!\!\!\!\rangle$$
$$phase\ 2\ (modify\ sort) *\!\!\!\!\rangle$$
$$phase\ 3\ (traverse\ (\lambda x \rightarrow pop)\ t)$$

The computation uses the state monad, where the state is a list of elements. We use the following operations provided by the state monad:

$$get \quad :: State\ s\ s$$
$$put \quad :: s \rightarrow State\ s\ ()$$
$$modify :: (s \rightarrow s) \rightarrow State\ s\ ()$$

The auxilliary function constructs a three-phase computation in that monad. The main function initializes the state to the empty list, runs the three phases, discards the final state (which will again be the empty list), and returns the final tree. The first phase of the auxilliary function traverses the tree, pushing the elements one by one onto the stored list:

$$push :: a \rightarrow State\ [\,a]\ ()$$
$$push\ x = modify\ (x:)$$

The second phase doesn't touch the tree; it just sorts the stored list. The third phase traverses the tree again, popping elements one by one off the stored list:

$$pop :: State\ [\,a]\ a$$
$$pop = \mathbf{do}\ \{\,x : xs \leftarrow get;\ put\ xs;\ return\ x\,\}$$

Note that the first phase pushes the tree elements from left to right, so the resulting list is in reverse order; but that is irrelevant as input to sorting.

As before, the specification of the three phases can be rearranged:

$$sortTreeAux'\ t = phase\ 2\ (modify\ sort) *\!\!\!\!\rangle$$
$$phase\ 1\ (traverse\ push\ t) *\!\!\!\!\rangle$$
$$phase\ 3\ (traverse\ (\lambda x \rightarrow pop)\ t)$$

and traversal commutes with staging:

$$sortTreeAux''\ t = phase\ 2\ (modify\ sort) *\!\!\!\!\rangle$$
$$traverse\ (\lambda x \rightarrow phase\ 1\ (push\ x))\ t *\!\!\!\!\rangle$$
$$traverse\ (\lambda x \rightarrow phase\ 3\ pop)\ t$$

and consecutive traversals with bodies in different phases fuse:

$$sortTreeAux''' \; t = phase \; 2 \; (modify \; sort) \; *\!\!>$$
$$traverse \; (\lambda x \to phase \; 1 \; (push \; x) \; *\!\!> \; phase \; 3 \; pop) \; t$$

Using *sortTreeAux'''* in place of *sortTreeAux* in *sortTree* solves the sort-tree problem with—clearly!—a single traversal over the tree.

6   Breadth-first Traversal in Stages

Finally, let us return to breadth-first traversal. The key insight is that we can specify such a traversal *compositionally*, by constructing a multi-stage computation with one phase per level of the tree. This is achieved by the auxilliary function *bftAux*:

$$bftAux :: Applicative \; f \Rightarrow (a \to f \; b) \to Tree \; a \to Phases \; f \; (Tree \; b)$$
$$bftAux \; f \; (Node \; x \; ts)$$
$$= Node \; \langle\$\rangle \; now \; (f \; x) \; \langle *\rangle \; later \; (traverse \; (bftAux \; f) \; ts)$$

Informally, the root label x is processed 'now', in phase one. A multi-stage computation is constructed for each child in *ts*, zipped together by levels using *traverse* for the list of children, then postponed until one phase 'later'. Finally, the resulting tree is assembled by applying the constructor *Node* to the results of processing the root now and the children later. Then *bft* is obtained by collapsing the chain of phases into a single computation:

$$bft :: Applicative \; f \Rightarrow (a \to f \; b) \to Tree \; a \to f \; (Tree \; b)$$
$$bft \; f = runPhases \circ bftAux \; f$$

It is instructive to compare *bftAux* above with the depth-first instance of *traverse* for trees that we had in Sect. 2.2—essentially:

$$dft :: Applicative \; f \Rightarrow (a \to f \; b) \to Tree \; a \to f \; (Tree \; b)$$
$$dft \; f \; (Node \; x \; ts) = Node \; \langle\$\rangle \; f \; x \; \langle *\rangle \; traverse \; (dft \; f) \; ts$$

which is recovered simply by deleting the staging annotations from *bftAux*.

In particular, we can relabel a tree in breadth-first order, without needing either queues [13] or cyclicity and laziness [11]:

$$bfl :: Tree \; a \to [b] \to Tree \; b$$
$$bfl \; t \; xs = evalState \; (bft \; (\lambda x \to pop) \; t) \; xs$$

where *pop* is as defined for the sort-tree problem in Sect. 5.3.

7   Discussion

We have presented a novel approach to multi-phase or staged computation. By this term, we mean computations split into separate phases, in order that intermediate phases may be extended; this is related to but distinct from the notion of staging as run-time code generation [19].

We have shown how multi-phase computation can be expressed using a construction related to free applicative functors, but combining structures by 'zipping' instead of 'concatenating' them. Two-phase computation is captured by Day convolution, which Rivas and Jaskelioff [17] showed to be the natural monoidal structure underlying applicative functors. Multi-stage computation is captured by iterated Day convolution, which is the same datatype as for free applicative functors [3] but with a different applicative instance. Among other examples, we have used these constructions to clarify Bird's and Pettorossi's solutions to the 'repmin' problem, doing away with the laziness inherent in Bird's solution; and to provide an implementation of breadth-first effectful traversal that avoids a clumsy factorization into shape and contents.

That implementation of breadth-first effectful traversal can be used in particular to implement breadth-first relabelling of a tree with a stream of fresh labels. Our multi-stage solution to that problem avoids the circular definition and inherent laziness in our earlier program [11]. Okasaki [13] discusses the same problem, providing a solution that requires a more sophisticated queue datatype in order to achieve linear-time execution. Okasaki states that "lazy evaluation is required. Without lazy evaluation, you [...] would need [...] a separate pass"; we have shown that neither a fancy queue datatype nor laziness are needed in order to avoid multiple passes. One might even say that Okasaki's queues are a form of staging too, postponing actions for later execution.

To be fair, one might argue about the extent to which any of these solutions to the repmin problem and its ilk have "eliminated multiple traversals". It is clear that the original input data structure is traversed only once; but there is a case to be made that a copy is created in the first pass and traversed in the second pass. Pettorossi's solution $repmin_{\text{ADP}}$ explicitly constructs a lambda abstraction that encodes a copy of the structure of the input tree, and then applies this function to the replacement value. One might say that Bird's solution $repmin_{\text{RSB}}$ constructs that same copy implicitly.

Anyway, we make no claims that these transformations improve running time or space usage. More broadly, we have not concerned ourselves with making these traversals take linear time; for example, bf in Sect. 3 is not linear, because of repeated concatenations of lists. This issue can be addressed by using difference lists, and more generally by Cayley representations [12], but is orthogonal to our main argument.

Day convolution as defined in Sect. 4 is heterogeneous: the two phases can use different classes of effect, which will of course entail different methods of 'running'. In contrast, the multi-stage computations defined as iterated Day convolution in Sect. 5 are homogeneous: all phases must use the same class of effects, which can then be combined using the applicative multiplication. This is analogous to situation with lists: ordinary pairs are heterogeneous, but lists (iterated pairs) are homogeneous. However, with suitably expressive typing facilities, one can define a datatype of heterogeneous lists, perhaps indexed by a type-level list of types; and in the same way, one could define heterogeneous multi-stage computations, indexed by a type-level list of applicative functors. But we know of no use for such a construction; nor is it clear how in general one would 'run' the heterogeneous collection of phases.

A minor point to note is that, while pure $Day\ f\ f$ computations have only one representation, those of $Phases\ f$ have infinitely many, one for each chain length: $pure\ x$, $phase\ 1\ (pure\ x)$, $phase\ 2\ (pure\ x)$, … This representational difference is not significant, and thus we consider $Phases\ f$ computations equal up to a pure "tail". In fact, $phases\ i$ is only an applicative morphism for this notion of equality. In case f is a *unital* applicative functor the representation could be normalised to eliminate pure tails. Following the notion of unital monads [18], a unital applicative functor is one for which it is possible to determine whether a given computation is in the image of *pure*.

Acknowledgements. We are very grateful to the members of IFIP Working Group 2.1 and of the Algebra of Programming research group at Oxford, for patient listening and helpful comments while this work was gestating. Thanks are especially due to Alberto Pettorossi for furnishing copies of his papers [15,16], and to Alexander Vandenbroucke for helpful comments.

This paper is dedicated to the memory of Richard Bird, who inspired us all.

A   Fusion of traversals

In this appendix we prove the fusion rule for traversals deployed in Sect. 4, using the Representation Theorem for traversals [1]. We take the opportunity to make the statement of the Representation Theorem more precise, using dependent types for indexing by size. Throughout the section, we fix an applicative functor F, and a traversable datatype T with corresponding *traverse* function (though of course they are arbitrary).

We will use the following gadgets for products of pure functions:

$cross :: (a \rightarrow b) \rightarrow (c \rightarrow d) \rightarrow (a, c) \rightarrow (b, d)$
$cross\ f\ g\ (x, y) = (f\ x, g\ y)$

$fork :: (a \rightarrow b) \rightarrow (a \rightarrow c) \rightarrow a \rightarrow (b, c)$
$fork\ f\ g\ x = cross\ f\ g\ (x, x)$

and their applicative counterparts for effectful functions:

$crossA :: Applicative\ f \Rightarrow (a \rightarrow f\ c) \rightarrow (b \rightarrow f\ d) \rightarrow (a, b) \rightarrow f\ (c, d)$
$crossA\ f\ g\ (x, y) = f\ x \otimes g\ y$

$forkA :: Applicative\ f \Rightarrow (a \rightarrow f\ b) \rightarrow (a \rightarrow f\ c) \rightarrow a \rightarrow f\ (b, c)$
$forkA\ f\ g\ x = crossA\ f\ g\ (x, x)$

The key property is for two effectful functions to commute, that is, for their effects not to interfere with each other:

Definition 1. *Given $f :: A \to F\ B$ and $g :: C \to F\ D$, say "f commutes with g" if*

$$g\ y \otimes f\ x = fmap\ twist\ (f\ x \otimes g\ y)$$

for all $x :: A, y :: C$.

Now for two consecutive traversals of the same data structure, if the two bodies commute with each other, then the two traversals can be fused into one:

Theorem 2 (Fusion rule for traversals). *If $f :: A \to F\ B$ commutes with $g :: A \to F\ C$, then*

$$forkA\ (traverse\ f)\ (traverse\ g) = fmap\ unzip \circ traverse\ (forkA\ f\ g)$$

The rest of this appendix proves Theorem 2.

A.1   Length-indexed vectors

We can make the statement of the Representation Theorem more precise than was possible in Haskell at the time the theorem was published [1], by using dependent types to be explicit about the size of a data structure. But the results still hold without the size indexing.

The traditional datatype definition of Peano naturals

> **data** $Nat = Z \mid S\ Nat$

introduces a new type Nat with new value inhabitants $Z, S\ N$; but it also introduces a new kind Nat with new type inhabitants $Z, S\ N$. For example, here is a new type $Four$ of kind Nat, serving as a type-level representation of the number four:

> **type** $Four = S\ (S\ (S\ (S\ Z)))$

We can use these type-level numbers to specify the size of a data structure. Here are length-indexed vectors:

> **data** $Vec :: Nat \to * \to *$ **where**
> $VNil$ $:: Vec\ Z\ a$
> $VCons :: (a, Vec\ n\ a) \to Vec\ (S\ n)\ a$

(the uncurried *VCons* is for later convenience). Vectors are of course traversable, as lists are:

```
instance Traversable (Vec n) where
    traverse f VNil            = pure VNil
    traverse f (VCons (x, xs)) = fmap VCons (f x ⊗ traverse f xs)
```

A.2 Size-indexed trees

In the same way, we can define size-indexed trees and forests:

```
data TreeI :: Nat → * → * where
    NodeI :: (a, ForestI n a) → TreeI (S n) a
data ForestI :: Nat → * → * where
    FNil  :: ForestI Z a
    FCons :: (TreeI m a, ForestI n a) → ForestI (Plus m n) a
```

Naturally, the size of a non-empty forest *FCons* (t, ts) is the sum of the sizes of t and ts, so we need type-level addition:

```
type family Plus (n :: Nat) (m :: Nat) :: Nat
type instance Plus Z     n = n
type instance Plus (S m) n = S (Plus m n)
```

And of course, trees are traversable too—in various ways. Here is the definition of depth-first traversal:

```
instance Traversable (TreeI n) where
    traverse f (NodeI (x, ts)) = fmap NodeI (f x ⊗ traverseF f ts) where
        traverseF :: Applicative f ⇒ (a → f b) → ForestI n a → f (ForestI n b)
        traverseF f FNil          = pure FNil
        traverseF f (FCons (t, ts)) = fmap FCons (traverse f t ⊗ traverseF f ts)
```

A.3 Make functions

Definition 3. *Define*

```
type Make t n a = Vec n a → t n a
```

Then, for a given size-indexed traversable datatype T with corresponding traversal function traverse, a make *function for T is a polymorphic function*

$$make :: Make\ T\ n\ a$$

that constructs a data structure from its contents, preserving those contents:

$$contents \circ make = contents$$

Here, *contents* returns the contents of a data structure as a list, in their order of traversal:

$$contents :: Traversable\ t \Rightarrow t\ a \rightarrow [a]$$
$$contents = getConst \circ traverse\ (\lambda x \rightarrow Const\ [x])$$

A.4 Representation Theorem

Note that what constitutes a make function for T depends on the corresponding *traverse* function, and in particular depends on the traversal order chosen for T. For example, given that we have defined traversal of trees to be depth-first, here is a make function of arity four for trees:

$$makeDF :: Make\ TreeI\ Four\ a$$
$$makeDF\ (VCons\ (w, (VCons\ (x, VCons\ (y, VCons\ (z, VNil)))))) =$$
$$NodeI\ (w, FCons\ (NodeI\ (x, FCons\ (NodeI\ (y, FNil), FNil)),$$
$$FCons\ (NodeI\ (z, FNil), FNil)))$$

Diagrammatically,

If we had defined traversal for trees instead to be breadth-first, this would not be a valid make function, because it would not preserve the order of elements.

The key insight is: for a given size-indexed traversable datatype and given definition of traversal, there is a unique corresponding make function, which uniquely relates data structures to the underlying vector of their contents, and traversal on the datatype to traversal on the underlying vector.

Theorem 4 (Representation Theorem). *For size-indexed traversable type T and data structure $t :: T \, N \, A$, there exists a unique make function $m :: (\forall a \,.\, Make \, T \, N \, a)$ and unique $xs :: Vec \, N \, A$ such that $t = m \, xs$ and contents $t = $ contents xs. Moreover, for any $f :: B \rightarrow F \, C$ and $ys :: Vec \, N \, B$,*

$$traverse \, f \, (m \, ys) = fmap \, m \, (traverse \, f \, ys)$$

where the traverse on the right-hand side is on vectors.

The earlier statement and proof of this theorem [1] was rigorous but not formal, relying on ellipsis ("*make $x_1 \ldots x_n$*") for referring to the arity; we have made it more formal by using size-indexed datatypes. But the adapted proof is essentially the same, so we do not repeat it here.

A.5 Commutativity

Obviously, the notion of "commuting with" is symmetric, because *twist* is an involution. Moreover, pairing preserves commutability:

Lemma 5. *If f commutes with g and with h, then f commutes with crossA $g \, h$.*

Proof. We have:

$crossA \, g \, h \, (y, z) \otimes f \, x$
$= \quad \{ \; crossA \; \}$
$(g \, y \otimes h \, z) \otimes f \, x$
$= \quad \{ \text{ associativity } \}$
$fmap \; assoc \, (g \, y \otimes (h \, z \otimes f \, x))$
$= \quad \{ \; f \text{ commutes with } h \; \}$
$fmap \; assoc \, (g \, y \otimes (fmap \; twist \, (f \, x \otimes h \, z)))$
$= \quad \{ \text{ naturality of } \otimes \}$
$fmap \; assoc \, (fmap \, (cross \; id \; twist) \, (g \, y \otimes (f \, x \otimes h \, z)))$
$= \quad \{ \text{ associativity } \}$
$fmap \; assoc \, (fmap \, (cross \; id \; twist) \, (fmap \; assoc^{-1} \, ((g \, y \otimes f \, x) \otimes h \, z)))$
$= \quad \{ \; assoc \circ cross \; id \; twist \circ assoc^{-1} = twist \circ assoc^{-1} \circ cross \; twist \; id \; \}$
$fmap \; twist \, (fmap \; assoc^{-1} \, (fmap \, (cross \; twist \; id) \, ((g \, y \otimes f \, x) \otimes h \, z)))$
$= \quad \{ \text{ naturality of } \otimes \}$
$fmap \; twist \, (fmap \; assoc^{-1} \, (fmap \; twist \, (g \, y \otimes f \, x) \otimes h \, z))$
$= \quad \{ \; f \text{ commutes with } g \; \}$
$fmap \; twist \, (fmap \; assoc^{-1} \, ((f \, x \otimes g \, y) \otimes h \, z))$
$= \quad \{ \text{ associativity } \}$
$fmap \; twist \, (f \, x \otimes (g \, y \otimes h \, z))$
$= \quad \{ \; crossA \; \}$
$fmap \; twist \, (f \, x \otimes crossA \, g \, h \, (y, z))$

(The step in the middle

$$assoc \circ cross\ id\ twist \circ assoc^{-1} = twist \circ assoc^{-1} \circ cross\ twist\ id$$

holds because both are the unique total function of type $((a, c), b) \to ((a, b), c)$. This proof would perhaps be clearer with appropriate string diagrams.)

Then traversal preserves commutability too:

Lemma 6. *If f commutes with g, then also traverse f commutes with g (and f commutes with traverse g, by symmetry of commutability).*

Proof. We prove that if f commutes with g then

$$g\ y \otimes traverse\ f\ xs = fmap\ twist\ (traverse\ f\ xs \otimes g\ y)$$

for $xs :: Vec\ N\ A$, $y :: B$, $f :: A \to F\ C$, $g :: B \to F\ D$, by induction on N. For the base case, we have:

$$
\begin{aligned}
&g\ y \otimes traverse\ f\ VNil \\
=\ &\{\ \text{definition of } traverse \text{ on } Vec\ \} \\
&g\ y \otimes pure\ VNil \\
=\ &\{\ \text{applicative interchange law: } us \otimes pure\ v = fmap\ (, v)\ us\ \} \\
&fmap\ (, VNil)\ (g\ y) \\
=\ &\{\ twist\ \} \\
&fmap\ twist\ (fmap\ (VNil,)\ (g\ y)) \\
=\ &\{\ fmap\ (u,)\ vs = pure\ u \otimes vs\ \} \\
&fmap\ twist\ (pure\ VNil \otimes g\ y) \\
=\ &\{\ \text{definition of } traverse \text{ on } Vec\ \} \\
&fmap\ twist\ (traverse\ f\ VNil \otimes g\ y)
\end{aligned}
$$

and for the inductive step:

$$
\begin{aligned}
&g\ y \otimes traverse\ f\ (VCons\ (x, xs)) \\
=\ &\{\ \text{definition of } traverse \text{ on } Vec\ \} \\
&g\ y \otimes (fmap\ VCons\ (f\ x \otimes traverse\ f\ xs)) \\
=\ &\{\ \text{naturality of } \otimes\ \} \\
&fmap\ (cross\ id\ VCons)\ (g\ y \otimes (f\ x \otimes traverse\ f\ xs)) \\
=\ &\{\ f \text{ and (by induction) } traverse\ f \text{ commute with } g\ \} \\
&fmap\ (cross\ id\ VCons \circ twist)\ ((f\ x \otimes traverse\ f\ xs) \otimes g\ y) \\
=\ &\{\ cross \text{ and } twist\ \} \\
&fmap\ (twist \circ cross\ VCons\ id)\ ((f\ x \otimes traverse\ f\ xs) \otimes g\ y) \\
=\ &\{\ \text{naturality of } \otimes\ \} \\
&fmap\ twist\ (fmap\ VCons\ (f\ x \otimes traverse\ f\ xs) \otimes g\ y) \\
=\ &\{\ \text{definition of } traverse \text{ on } Vec\ \} \\
&fmap\ twist\ (traverse\ f\ (VCons\ (x, xs)) \otimes g\ y)
\end{aligned}
$$

Therefore, two traversals with bodies that commute will fuse:

Lemma 7. *If f commutes with g, then traverse f fuses with traverse g on vectors:*

$$forkA \ (traverse \ f) \ (traverse \ g) \ xs = fmap \ unzip \ (traverse \ (forkA \ f \ g) \ xs)$$

for all xs :: Vec N A.

Proof. Proof by induction on N. For the base case:

$$
\begin{aligned}
&forkA \ (traverse \ f) \ (traverse \ g) \ VNil \\
=\ & \{ \ \text{definition of } forkA \ \} \\
&traverse \ f \ VNil \otimes traverse \ g \ VNil \\
=\ & \{ \ \text{definition of } traverse \ \text{on } Vec \ \} \\
&pure \ VNil \otimes pure \ VNil \\
=\ & \{ \ \text{applicative law} \ \} \\
&pure \ (VNil, VNil) \\
=\ & \{ \ \text{definition of } unzip \ \} \\
&pure \ (unzip \ VNil) \\
=\ & \{ \ \text{naturality of } pure \ \} \\
&fmap \ unzip \ (pure \ VNil) \\
=\ & \{ \ \text{definition of } traverse \ \text{on } Vec \ \} \\
&fmap \ unzip \ (traverse \ (forkA \ f \ g) \ VNil)
\end{aligned}
$$

For the inductive step, we use some abbreviations:

$$
\begin{aligned}
&assoc4 :: (a, ((b, c), d)) \to ((a, b), (c, d)) \\
&assoc4 = assoc \circ cross \ id \ assoc^{-1} \\[4pt]
&unassoc4 :: ((a, b), (c, d)) \to (a, ((b, c), d)) \\
&unassoc4 = cross \ id \ assoc \circ assoc^{-1} \\[4pt]
&twist4 :: (a, ((b, c), d)) \to (a, ((c, b), d)) \\
&twist4 = cross \ id \ (cross \ twist \ id) \\[4pt]
&exch4 :: ((a, b), (c, d)) \to ((a, c), (b, d)) \\
&exch4 = assoc4 \circ twist4 \circ unassoc4
\end{aligned}
$$

Then:

$$
\begin{aligned}
&forkA \ (traverse \ f) \ (traverse \ g) \ (VCons \ (x, xs)) \\
=\ & \{ \ \text{definition of } forkA \ \} \\
&traverse \ f \ (VCons \ (x, xs)) \otimes traverse \ g \ (VCons \ (x, xs)) \\
=\ & \{ \ \text{definition of } traverse \ \text{on } Vec \ \} \\
&fmap \ VCons \ (f \ x \otimes traverse \ f \ xs) \otimes fmap \ VCons \ (g \ x \otimes traverse \ g \ xs) \\
=\ & \{ \ \text{naturality of } \otimes \ \}
\end{aligned}
$$

$$fmap\,(cross\;VCons\;VCons)$$
$$((f\;x \otimes traverse\;f\;xs) \otimes (g\;x \otimes traverse\;g\;xs))$$
$-$ { associativity, twice }
$$fmap\,(cross\;VCons\;VCons \circ assoc4)$$
$$(f\;x \otimes ((traverse\;f\;xs \otimes g\;x) \otimes traverse\;g\;xs))$$
$=$ { f commutes with g, so $traverse\;f$ commutes with g }
$$fmap\,(cross\;VCons\;VCons \circ assoc4 \circ twist4)$$
$$(f\;x \otimes ((g\;x \otimes traverse\;f\;xs) \otimes traverse\;g\;xs))$$
$=$ { associativity, twice }
$$fmap\,(cross\;VCons\;VCons \circ assoc4 \circ twist4 \circ unassoc4)$$
$$((f\;x \otimes g\;x) \otimes (traverse\;f\;xs \otimes traverse\;g\;xs))$$
$=$ { $exch4$ }
$$fmap\,(cross\;VCons\;VCons \circ exch4)$$
$$((f\;x \otimes g\;x) \otimes (traverse\;f\;xs \otimes traverse\;g\;xs))$$
$=$ { definition of $forkA$, induction }
$$fmap\,(cross\;VCons\;VCons \circ exch4)$$
$$(forkA\;f\;g\;x \otimes fmap\;unzip\,(traverse\,(forkA\;f\;g)\;xs))$$
$=$ { naturality of $\otimes$ }
$$fmap\,(cross\;VCons\;VCons \circ exch4 \circ cross\;id\;unzip)$$
$$(forkA\;f\;g\;x \otimes traverse\,(forkA\;f\;g)\;xs)$$
$=$ { $unzip$ (see below) }
$$fmap\,(unzip \circ VCons)\,(forkA\;f\;g\;x \otimes traverse\,(forkA\;f\;g)\;xs)$$
$=$ { definition of $traverse$ on Vec }
$$fmap\;unzip\,(traverse\,(forkA\;f\;g)\,(VCons\,(x,xs)))$$

The penultimate step

$$unzip \circ VCons = cross\;VCons\;VCons \circ exch4 \circ cross\;id\;unzip$$

is basically the definition of $unzip$ on a $VCons$, where both sides have type

$$((a,b),\,Vec\;n\,(a,b)) \to (Vec\,(S\;n)\;a,\,Vec\,(S\;n)\;b)$$

Now Theorem 2 reduces to Lemma 7, by the Representation Theorem (Theorem 4).

Proof (of Theorem 2.) We have $t :: T\;N\;A$ for size-indexed traversable type T and arity N, a make function $m :: \forall a\;.\;Make\;T\;N\;a$ and contents $xs :: Vec\;N\;A$ such that $t = m\;xs$, and traversal bodies $f :: A \to F\;B$ and $g :: A \to F\;C$ that commute. Then:

$$forkA\,(traverse\;f)\,(traverse\;g)\;t$$
$=$ { Representation Theorem }
$$forkA\,(fmap\;m \circ traverse\;f)\,(fmap\;m \circ traverse\;g)\;xs$$

$$= \quad \{\text{ naturality of } forkA \}$$
$$fmap\,(cross\ m\ m)\,(forkA\,(traverse\ f)\,(traverse\ g)\ xs)$$
$$= \quad \{\text{ traverse fusion on vectors }\}$$
$$fmap\,(cross\ m\ m \circ unzip)\,(traverse\,(forkA\ f\ g)\ xs)$$
$$= \quad \{\ cross\ m\ m \circ unzip = unzip \circ m \text{ (see below) }\}$$
$$fmap\,(unzip \circ m)\,(traverse\,(forkA\ f\ g)\ xs)$$
$$= \quad \{\text{ Representation Theorem }\}$$
$$fmap\ unzip\,(traverse\,(forkA\ f\ g)\ t)$$

where the penultimate step

$$cross\ m\ m \circ unzip = unzip \circ m$$

is discharged as follows:

$$cross\ m\ m \circ unzip$$
$$= \quad \{\text{ definition of } unzip \}$$
$$cross\ m\ m \circ fork\,(fmap\ fst)\,(fmap\ snd)$$
$$= \quad \{\text{ fusing } cross \text{ and } fork \}$$
$$fork\,(m \circ fmap\ fst)\,(m \circ fmap\ snd)$$
$$= \quad \{\text{ naturality of } m \}$$
$$fork\,(fmap\ fst \circ m)\,(fmap\ snd \circ m)$$
$$= \quad \{\ fork \text{ fusion }\}$$
$$fork\,(fmap\ fst)\,(fmap\ snd) \circ m$$
$$= \quad \{\text{ definition of } unzip \}$$
$$unzip \circ m$$

References

1. Bird, R., Gibbons, J., Mehner, S., Voigtländer, J., Schrijvers, T.: Understanding idiomatic traversals backwards and forwards. In: Haskell Symposium. ACM (2013). https://doi.org/10.1145/2503778.2503781
2. Bird, R.S.: Using circular programs to eliminate multiple traversals of data. Acta Informatica **21**, 239–250 (1984). https://doi.org/10.1007/BF00264249
3. Capriotti, P., Kaposi, A.: Free applicative functors. In: Levy, P.B., Krishnaswami, N. (eds.) Mathematically Structured Functional Programming. EPTCS, vol. 153, pp. 2–30 (2014). https://doi.org/10.4204/EPTCS.153.2
4. Danvy, O., Thiemann, P., Zerny, I.: Circularity and lambda abstraction: from Bird to Pettorossi and back. In: Plasmeijer, R. (ed.) Implementation and Application of Functional Languages, p. 85. ACM (2013). https://doi.org/10.1145/2620678.2620687
5. Easterly, N.: Functions and newtype wrappers for traversing Trees: rampion/tree-traversals, January 2019. https://github.com/rampion/tree-traversals

6. Gibbons, J.: Breadth-first traversal, March 2015. https://patternsinfp.wordpress. com/2015/03/05/breadth-first-traversal/
7. Gibbons, J., Jones, G.: The under-appreciated unfold. In: International Conference on Functional Programming, pp. 273–279. Baltimore, Maryland, September 1998. https://doi.org/10.1145/289423.289455
8. Gibbons, J., Kidney, D.O., Schrijvers, T., Wu, N.: Code for "Breadth-First Traversal Via Staging". http://www.cs.ox.ac.uk/people/jeremy.gibbons/publications/ traversals.hs
9. Gibbons, J., dos Santos Oliveira, B.C.: The essence of the Iterator pattern. J. Funct. Programm. **19**(3,4), 377–402 (2009). https://doi.org/10.1017/S0956796809007291
10. Jaskelioff, M., Rypacek, O.: An investigation of the laws of traversals. In: Chapman, J., Levy, P.B. (eds.) Mathematically Structured Functional Programming. EPTCS, vol. 76, pp. 40–49 (2012). https://doi.org/10.4204/EPTCS.76.5
11. Jones, G., Gibbons, J.: Linear-time breadth-first tree algorithms: An exercise in the arithmetic of folds and zips. Computer Science Report No. 71, Dept of Computer Science, University of Auckland, May 1993. http://www.cs.ox.ac.uk/publications/ publication2363-abstract.html, also IFIP Working Group 2.1 working paper 705 WIN-2
12. Kidney, D.O., Wu, N.: Algebras for weighted search. In: Proceedings of the ACM on Programming Languages 5(ICFP), pp. 1–30 (2021). https://doi.org/10.1145/ 3473577
13. Okasaki, C.: Breadth-first numbering: lessons from a small exercise in algorithm design. In: Odersky, M., Wadler, P. (eds.) International Conference on Functional Programming, pp. 131–136. ACM (2000). https://doi.org/10.1145/351240.351253
14. Paterson, R.: Constructing applicative functors. In: Gibbons, J., Nogueira, P. (eds.) MPC 2012. LNCS, vol. 7342, pp. 300–323. Springer, Heidelberg (2012). https:// doi.org/10.1007/978-3-642-31113-0_15
15. Pettorossi, A., Skowron, A.: Higher order generalization in program derivation. In: Ehrig, H., Kowalski, R., Levi, G., Montanari, U. (eds.) TAPSOFT 1987. LNCS, vol. 250, pp. 182–196. Springer, Heidelberg (1987). https://doi.org/10.1007/ BFb0014981
16. Pettorossi, A., Skowron, A.: The lambda abstraction strategy for program derivation. Fundamenta Informaticae XII, pp. 541–562 (1989). https://doi.org/10.3233/ FI-1989-12407
17. Rivas, E., Jaskelioff, M.: Notions of computation as monoids. J. Funct. Program. **27**, e21 (2017). https://doi.org/10.1017/S0956796817000132
18. Rivas, E., Jaskelioff, M., Schrijvers, T.: A unified view of monadic and applicative non-determinism. Sci. Comput. Program. **152**, 70–98 (2018). https://doi.org/10. 1016/j.scico.2017.09.007
19. Taha, W.: A gentle introduction to multi-stage programming. In: Lengauer, C., Batory, D., Consel, C., Odersky, M. (eds.) Domain-Specific Program Generation. LNCS, vol. 3016, pp. 30–50. Springer, Heidelberg (2004). https://doi.org/10.1007/ 978-3-540-25935-0_3

Subtyping Without Reduction

Brandon Hewer[(✉)] and Graham Hutton

School of Computer Science, University of Nottingham, Nottingham, UK
brandon.hewer@nottingham.ac.uk

Abstract. Subtypes are useful and ubiquitous, allowing important properties of data to be captured directly in types. However, the standard encoding of subtypes gives no control over when the reduction of subtyping proofs takes place, which can significantly impact the performance of type-checking. In this article, we show how operations on a subtype can be represented in a more efficient manner that exhibits no reduction behaviour. We present the general form of the technique in Cubical Agda by exploiting its support by higher-inductive types, and demonstrate the practical use of the technique with a number of examples.

1 Introduction

Think of a subtype and some operations on it. We can give you two equivalent representations for the subtype that avoid the cost of subtyping proofs for the operations. The first representation provides an alternative internalisation for the subtyping condition, while the second does the same for the entire subtype. The purpose of this article is to introduce these two representations, explain how they compare, and formalise them in homotopy type theory.

Subtypes appear frequently in type theory, where a subtype of $A : \mathrm{Type}$ can be characterised by a dependent sum $\sum_{(a:A)} P(a)$ over a family of propositions $P : A \to \mathrm{Prop}$. For example, the even natural numbers can easily be seen as a subtype of the naturals by defining a family isEven : $\mathbb{N} \to \mathrm{Prop}$ which maps every even number to true, and every odd number to false. Another ubiquitous example is that of the (totally-ordered) finite sets Fin : $\mathbb{N} \to \mathrm{Type}$, which can be defined as subtypes of the natural numbers by means of the family $<: \mathbb{N} \to \mathbb{N} \to \mathrm{Prop}$.

Operations defined over subtypes must respect the subtyping condition. For example, addition restricts to an operation over even numbers because the addition of two even numbers is even. As a more complex example, the dependent sum over a family of finite types indexed by a finite type will always be finite for some sensible notion of 'finite'. In type theory, proving that an operation respects a subtyping condition involves computing a term of the respective proposition. For addition of even numbers, this means that given terms of the propositions isEven (m) and isEven (n), we would compute a term of isEven $(m + n)$.

In practice, computing subtyping proofs can be costly, and in a dependently typed setting this has performance consequences not just at runtime, but also during type checking. The impact of this problem can even be seen in simple

E. Komendantskaya (Ed.): MPC 2022, LNCS 13544, pp. 34–61, 2022.
https://doi.org/10.1007/978-3-031-16912-0_2

examples such as addition on finite sets. In particular, the addition operation
$+ : \text{Fin } m \to \text{Fin } n \to \text{Fin } (m+n)$ requires a proof that if $x < m$ and $y < n$ then
$x + y < m + n$, which typically proceeds by induction, and therefore the use of
$+$ may result in reduction taking place during type checking.

It is natural to see this issue as part of a much larger problem in type theory:
proofs whose content does not matter can drastically slow down type-checking as
a result of reduction behaviour. This problem is so prevalent that many dependently typed languages have special features for addressing it, such as Agda's
abstract definition mechanism. However, these language-specific features usually
come with their own problems, which we discuss later on.

Our subtyping technique differs from existing solutions as it does not require
special-purpose language extensions, and can be used in any implementation
of type-theory that supports quotient types. In addition, we retain important
computational properties that are absent in solutions such as Agda's abstract
definitions. More specifically, the article makes the following contributions:

- We introduce and formalise a general technique for translating a subtype with
  given operations into two representations that are isomorphic to the original
  subtype, but avoid the need to compute the proof of the subtyping condition
  for the operations;
- We discuss the differences between the two representations, compare their
  advantages and disadvantages, and provide practical examples of each;
- We describe a generalisation of our method for $\sum$-types in which the second
  component is an arbitrary type, rather than just a proposition.

All of our examples are written in Cubical Agda [13], and this is one of the
first articles to exploit the power of this system; a library that formalises all
of our results is available online [7]. The article is aimed at readers who are
familiar with functional programming and (dependent) type theory, but we do
not assume experience with homotopy type theory or Cubical Agda, and provide
explanations of the necessary concepts where appropriate.

2   Example: Even Numbers

In this section we introduce the basic type-theoretic encoding of even natural
numbers, which is used as the motivating example for the application of our
technique. In (Cubical) Agda we can define a recursive family of types that
witness whether a given natural number is even as follows:

```
isEven : ℕ → Type
isEven 0 = ⊤
isEven 1 = ⊥
isEven (suc (suc n)) = isEven n
```

Note that the definition uses Type rather than Prop, because in HoTT the definition of a subtype merely requires the subtyping condition to be a family of weak

propositions, i.e. *h-propositions*, a family of types for which any two inhabitants are propositionally equal. We can observe that isEven is such a family because the resulting type is always either the singleton type $\top$ or the empty type $\bot$.

We can also define isEven in a different but equivalent way as an inductive family, because a proof of evenness can be uniquely constructed from a proof that 0 is even and a proof that if n is even then so is $n+2$. We can then introduce these proofs as constructors even-z and even-ss of an inductive family:

```
data isEven : ℕ → Type where
    even-z : isEven 0
    even-ss : isEven n → isEven (suc (suc n))
```

This translation from a family of propositions to an inductive family is necessary for applying our technique. It is always possible for an arbitrary family $P : A \to$ Type, by defining an inductive family $\mathsf{Id}_P : A \to$ Type with a single constructor $\eta_P : (a : A) \to P\ a \to \mathsf{Id}_P\ a$. However, as illustrated above, we can often inline the definition of a propositional family as the constructors of an inductive family.

As with any type, we are also interested in the *operations* that can be used to construct terms of a subtype. Concretely, such an operation comprises a function that constructs a term of the underlying type, together with a proof that this term is an element of the subtype. We will often refer to the proof that an operation preserves a particular subtyping condition as a *closure property* of that condition. For example, one such operation on even numbers is addition, whose closure property we can construct in Agda as follows:

```
isEven+ : isEven m → isEven n → isEven (m + n)
isEven+ even-z q = q
isEven+ (even-ss p) q = even-ss (isEven+ p q)
```

We can think of isEven+ as a *non-canonical* constructor of isEven. Such constructors exhibit reduction behaviour by unfolding definitional equalities. In practice, the use of these constructors may have a significant impact on the performance of type-checking, due to an arbitrary number of reduction steps taking place.

3   Path Types

In this section we review *path types*, a key concept in homotopy type theory (HoTT) that will be used throughout the article. For any type A, the type of *paths* between two terms $x, y : A$ is written $x \equiv_A y$, or simply $x \equiv y$ when A is clear. The underlying definition of a path type varies in different models of HoTT. For example, in the Cohen, Coquand, Huber, and Mörtberg (CCHM) model [3], on which Cubical Agda is based, a path type on elements of A corresponds to a continuous function from the real interval $[0, 1]$ to A.

Readers unfamiliar with HoTT can think of the path type $x \equiv_A y$ as having the same behaviour as the inductively defined identity type. In particular, the eliminator for $\equiv_A$ is given by the J-rule, which states that for any $x : A$, and family $M : (y : A) \to x \equiv_A y \to$ Type, if we have a proof $t : M\,(x, \mathbf{refl})$ that M is inhabited for reflection on x, then for all $y : A$ and $p : x \equiv_A y$, we can construct a term $J_{M,t}\,(x, y, p) : M\,(x, y, p)$. Intuitively, the J-rule states that if the end-point y of the path p can vary, then we can substitute p for reflection on x.

4   Higher-Inductive Evenness

In this section we introduce our first approach to solving the above problem, which is based on the use of higher-inductive families. As an initial step, we might consider defining a new inductive family isEven?, by simply adding the proof that addition preserves evenness as a constructor:

```
data isEven? : ℕ → Type where
    even-z : isEven? 0
    even-ss : isEven? n → isEven? (suc (suc n))
    even-+ : isEven? m → isEven? n → isEven? (m + n)
```

However, isEven? and isEven are not isomorphic families, and hence cannot be used interchangeably. This is evident by observing that isEven? is not a family of propositions. For example, the type isEven? 0 is inhabited by the (provably) distinct terms even-z and even-+ 0 0.

Fortunately, there is a simple way to modify isEven? to obtain the desired isomorphism, by exploiting *higher-inductive* families [12]. These generalise inductive families by introducing the notion of *path constructors*, which internalise the idea of a (higher) quotient in type theory. While a data constructor for an inductive type A introduces a term of type A, a path constructor introduces a path of one of the iterated path types on A, e.g. $x \equiv y$ for terms $x, y : A$, or $p \equiv q$ for paths $p, q : x \equiv y$. In Cubical Agda, we can quotient our current definition of isEven? to obtain a family of propositions as follows:

```
data isEven! : ℕ → Type where
    η : isEven? n → isEven! n
    squash : (x y : isEven! n) → x ≡ y
```

That is, isEven! is given by *propositionally truncating* the family isEven?, where the path constructor squash asserts that all elements of isEven! n must be treated identically. As such, the eliminator for isEven! requires that the type being eliminated into is a proposition, thus ensuring all terms of isEven! n are mapped to provably equal terms. Formally, this means that for any family of h-propositions B : isEven! $n \to$ Type we can lift a function $f : (x : \text{isEven? } n) \to B\,(\eta\,x)$ on isEven? n to a function $g : (x : \text{isEven! } n) \to B\,x$ on isEven! n.

For example, we can use this eliminator to construct a function from isEven! n to isEven n. In this case, we begin by defining B to be the constant family choosing the proposition isEven n. The function g : isEven $n \to$ isEven? n maps each constructor of isEven n to its namesake, and f : isEven? $n \to$ isEven n behaves similarly while mapping η (even-+ p q) to isEven+ $(f\ p)\ (f\ q)$. Given that isEven n and isEven! n are provably propositions, our construction of a function in both directions is enough to establish an isomorphism.

Given two isomorphic types, it is natural to consider how they compare. Recall that isEven! encodes the proof that addition preserves evenness as a canonical constructor, which maps proofs p : isEven! m and q : isEven! n that m and n are even to a proof η (even-+ p q) : isEven! $(m+n)$ that their addition is even. Intuitively, we can understand this encoding as hiding the definitional equalities introduced by the function isEven+, and instead presenting them only as propositional equalities. Namely, while the equations

$$
\begin{aligned}
\text{isEven+ even-z } q \quad &= q \\
\text{isEven+ (even-ss } p)\ q &= \text{even-ss (isEven+ } p\ q)
\end{aligned}
$$

hold definitionally, i.e. they are the defining equations for isEven+, the equalities

$$
\begin{aligned}
\eta\,(\text{even-+ even-z } q) \quad &\equiv \eta\ q \\
\eta\,(\text{even-+ (even-ss } p)\ q) &\equiv \eta\,(\text{even-ss (even-+ } p\ q))
\end{aligned}
$$

only hold up to a path given in terms of the squash constructor. Consequently, our definition of isEven! realises our original goal of encoding the proof that addition preserves evenness in a way that exhibits no reduction behaviour.

At this point one might be concerned that the more involved definition of isEven! compared to isEven makes it more difficult to define functions on even numbers. In practice, common patterns arise that simplify the use of subtypes encoded by our technique, which we describe below using an example.

Given that isEven! and isEven are isomorphic families, one can always be replaced by the other by appropriately transporting along the isomorphism. However, when transporting from isEven! to isEven, an irreducible term of the form η (even-+ p q) may be mapped to a term that exhibits reduction behaviour. Therefore, it can often be preferable to more directly use the encoded family of propositions, rather than transport along the derived isomorphism.

For example, consider the function div2 : isEven! $n \to \mathbb{N}$ that divides an even natural number by two. Because $\mathbb{N}$ is not an h-proposition, div2 cannot be defined simply by applying the eliminator for isEven to a function div2? : isEven? $n \to \mathbb{N}$. Instead, there are several possible constructions for div2?, each of which makes intermediate use of the eliminator on isEven!. We highlight a few of these approaches below, which reveal common patterns for defining functions on the higher-inductive families arising from our technique.

One possible approach is to first eliminate isEven! n into an intermediate type B_n : Type that *is* an h-proposition. Then we can compose with a function $f_n : B_n \to \mathbb{N}$ for which the composition has the expected behaviour. For example, for div2 n we can take B_n as the h-proposition $\sum[\ k \in \mathbb{N}\ ]\ 2 * k \equiv n$, which when composed with the first projection is sufficient to construct div2.

Another approach arises by considering how to directly re-obtain the typical induction principle for evenness on our definition of isEven!. In particular, this requires constructing functions ¬isEven1 : isEven! 1 → ⊥ and even-pred : isEven! (suc (suc m)) → isEven! m. Because both of these functions eliminate into propositions, they can be constructed using the eliminator for isEven!.

A third option is to observe that div2? is constant over terms of isEven? and eliminates into an h-set. This 'coherently constant' function can hence be lifted to construct div2 by applying an alternative eliminator on isEven! [8]. The details of each of these constructions for div2 can be found in our Cubical Agda library.

5 Higher-Inductive Recursive Even Numbers

In this section we introduce our second approach to the problem identified in Sect. 2, based on the use of higher-induction recursion. Thus far, we have shown how to encode that addition preserves evenness in a manner that exhibits no reduction behaviour. This allows us to define addition on even numbers encoded by the sum type $\sum[\ n \in \mathbb{N}\ ]$ isEven! n. In particular, the second component of this pair can be constructed by applying the elimination rule for propositional truncation, and then using the constructor even-+ $p\ q$.

While the proof that addition preserves evenness no longer exhibits reduction behaviour, addition itself may still be unfolded. Therefore, we might consider whether there is an encoding of even numbers that encodes addition as a single canonical constructor. Indeed, by adapting the isomorphism between inductive families and inductive recursive types [6], we can extend our technique to achieve this aim. For even natural numbers, this translates to defining a higher-inductive type data Even : Type mutually with a recursive function toℕ : Even → ℕ. In Cubical Agda, the higher-inductive type Even can be defined by:

```
data Even where
    zero : Even
    2+_  : Even → Even
    _+E_  : Even → Even → Even
    eq : (x y : Even) → toℕ x ≡ toℕ y → x ≡ y
```

The three data constructors zero, 2+_ and _+E_ correspond to zero, the next even number, and the addition of two even numbers. As with isEven?, while every even number can be defined using these constructors, they are not defined in a *unique* way. For example, 0 can be encoded by both zero and zero +E zero. To restore uniqueness and establish an isomorphism with $\sum[\ n \in \mathbb{N}\ ]$ isEven! n, we again introduce an appropriate path constructor, eq, to quotient our type.

Intuitively, the eq path constructor asserts that two even numbers with the same numeric value must be treated identically. In order to define toℕ, we can recognise that it should behave in a similar manner to the first projection on the type $\sum[\ n \in \mathbb{N}\ ]$ isEven! n, i.e. by mapping every even number to its underlying value as a natural number. With this in mind, toℕ can be defined as follows:

```
toℕ zero = 0
toℕ (2+ x) = suc (suc (toℕ x))
toℕ (x +E y) = toℕ x + toℕ y
toℕ (eq x y p i) = p i
```

Readers unfamiliar with Cubical Agda may be surprised by the final equation: while eq appears to take three parameters, we are matching on four in toℕ. However, this is really an overloading of the pattern matching syntax, and combines the eliminator for the constructor eq with the eliminator for the path eq x y p. In Cubical Agda, which is based on the CCHM model of cubical type theory [3], we can think of this path as a continuous function from the interval $[0, 1]$, internally represented by I, to the type Even of even numbers. Therefore, for an element of the interval i : I, the term eq x y p i has type Even, as expected.

So far, we have claimed that the introduction of the path constructor eq is enough to establish an isomorphism between Even and $\sum[\,n \in \mathbb{N}\,]$ isEven n, but have not proved this. Indeed, the construction is significantly more involved than between isEven! and isEven. Crucially, however, we can construct an isomorphism between Even and $\sum[\,n \in \mathbb{N}\,]$ isEven n by constructing a bijection between them. In particular, this is equivalent to constructing an injection f : Even → $\mathbb{N}$ together with a family of functions h : isEven n → Even, such that f only constructs even numbers and the composition $f \circ h$ is the constant function returning n.

We begin this construction by defining f to be the recursive function toℕ, for which the proof of injectivity is simply the path constructor eq. The proof that toℕ only constructs even numbers follows by induction on a term of Even, and the case for the eq constructor is trivial because evenness is an h-proposition. We can then construct the family h by induction on terms of isEven n, mapping even-z to zero and even-ss p to $2+ (h\ p)$. Finally, the proof that toℕ $\circ$ h is the constant function returning n follows definitionally.

Readers familiar with HoTT might at this point wonder whether this construction only works for subtypes of h-sets, such as the natural numbers $\mathbb{N}$. In particular, we have only used the fact that eq is an injection, but to generalise this construction for any subtype we would require that it be an embedding. Surprisingly, a path constructor of this form, for an inductive-recursive definition, is enough to establish that the recursive function is an embedding, even for higher-groupoid structures. Indeed, a similar construction has been discussed for so-called 'univalent inductive-recursive universes' [11].

Formally, an *inductive-recursive universe* is an inductive type U : Type of 'codes', defined mutually with a recursive function El : U → Type which interprets each code as a type. Such a universe is *univalent* if it has a path constructor un : $(x\ y : U) \to$ El $x \simeq$ El $y \to x \equiv y$. It can be shown that un x y is always an equivalence, and hence El is an embedding. Our approach generalises this idea by considering recursive functions U → A for any type A, rather than just Type. Therefore, to generalise un we must replace the equivalence by a path; that is, we require a path constructor eq : $(x\ y : U) \to$ El $x \equiv$ El $y \to x \equiv y$. In a univalent setting such as Cubical Agda, if we take A to be Type, then the eq and un versions of the definition are equivalent.

6 Reflection

Now that we have introduced the basic ideas of our technique, it is useful to make some remarks about its monadic underpinnings, impact on performance, and how the two representations differ in terms of their construction.

Free Monads. We begin by outlining how free monads naturally underpin our technique, and play a central role in its formalisation and generalisation.

Our technique can be seen as first defining a domain-specific language (DSL) on a chosen subtype. More concretely, this means constructing a free monad on a dependent polynomial functor [9] which characterises the operations of the language. For example, our encoding of even numbers as an inductive-recursive type introduced a DSL with addition as a constructor. We could have further extended this type with any (strictly-positive) operation which constructs an even number, such as multiplication, and the isomorphism with the standard encoding of even numbers would remain constructible.

The above idea gives rise to the formalisation of our technique that is described in Sect. 8. Notably, this involves taking particular quotients of free monads which then allows us to construct a calculus on subtypes. In practice this simplifies the process of working with our approach, particularly in the case when constructing maps between two encoded subtypes.

Performance. The most significant impact of hiding reduction behaviour for operations on a subtype is the improvement in performance during type-checking. In particular, operations encoded as constructors of an inductive type will not be unfolded. Indeed, the performance cost of unnecessarily unfolding terms during type-checking is so prevalent that Agda provides two language features to address this problem. The key insight behind these features, and indeed our technique, is that even within the context of a total language the choice of when to reduce terms is an important practical consideration that can mean the difference between type-checking a proof in reasonable time and running out of memory before type-checking concludes. We discuss the differences between our technique and existing language features of Agda in Sect. 11.

Perhaps surprisingly, our encoding can also improve the performance of normalising specific terms. This is possible as a consequence of retaining additional information about how a term of a subtype is constructed. For example, consider the following function that proves that any positive power of two is even:

```
isEven-2^ : (n : ℕ) → isEven (2 ^ suc n)
isEven-2^ zero = even-ss even-zero
isEven-2^ (suc n) =
    let p = isEven-2^ n in isEven+ p (isEven+ p even-zero)
```

By replacing occurrences of isEven+ with the constructor even-+ and composing with η : isEven? n → isEven! n, we can similarly construct a function isEven!-2^ : $(n : \mathbb{N})$ → isEven! $(2 \,\hat{}\, \text{suc}\, n)$. Using these definitions we can construct two different proofs that the natural number 65536 is even, and crucially, these proofs are equal up to a heterogeneous path.

To compare performance, we normalised these proof terms in Cubical Agda's Emacs mode, as a working compiler for the language is not currently available. Using a Macbook Pro with a 2.7 GHz quad-core processor and 16 GB of memory, we were unable to normalise the first term for any tested amount of time (up to 30 min), while the second was normalised in under 30 s.

It is natural to wonder whether any 'useful' computation on even numbers would first require that we translate back to the standard representation of evenness, given by the recursive family isEven. However, as described in Sect. 4, the example of dividing any even number by two reveals that this is not the case. Interestingly, this can lead to significant performance benefits when normalising the result of dividing a large even number by two. For example, we tested a number of 'reasonable' definitions for div2' : isEven n → $\mathbb{N}$ and div2 : isEven! n → $\mathbb{N}$ and found that we were unable to reduce the time taken to normalise div2' (isEven-2^ 15) to below three minutes, whereas our implementation of div2 (isEven!-2^ 15) took less than fifteen seconds. We refer readers interested in our implementation of div2 to our Cubical Agda library.

A similar performance impact to utilising our technique can be found by instead making use of a strict Prop universe [5]. In particular, by defining the family of types isEven? introduced in Sect. 4 as a family of Props, it is then possible to construct a proof of the evenness of 65536 by instead defining isEven-2^ to construct a term of isEven? in a near identical fashion. At first glance, this may appear to be a simpler approach. However, one of the key characteristics of our approach is the preservation of computational content. In particular, this means that it interacts well with other constructions in HoTT. For example, if we were to define evenness as a family of strict Props, it would no longer be possible to show that the forgetful map from evens to naturals is an embedding, which is precisely the property we should expect from any subtype in HoTT.

Summary. We conclude by summarising our two approaches to encoding operations on a subtype. Both approaches give isomorphic representations, but differ in manner in which they are constructed.

Inductive families (IF) approach:

1. Given a subtype, select some closure properties on its subtyping condition;
2. Define the subtyping condition as an inductive family;
3. Extend the family with data constructors that encode the closure properties;
4. Extend the family with a path constructor which asserts that all subtyping proofs are equal.

Induction-recursion (IR) approach:

1. Given a subtype, select some operations on it;

2. Define the subtype as an inductive-recursive type;

3. Extend the inductive type with the operations, and extend the recursive function with their interpretations;

4. Extend the inductive type with a path constructor that asserts the function is injective, and trivially extend the function over the path constructor.

7 Example: Ordered Finite Sets

In this section we show how ordered finite sets can be represented using the inductive families version of our technique. In type theory, ordered finite sets are typically defined as an inductive family Fin : $\mathbb{N} \to$ Type with two constructors, zero : Fin (suc n) and suc : Fin $n \to$ Fin (suc n). This example illustrates that in order to obtain an extensible encoding, it is important to carefully choose the operations to be encoded by our technique. Moreover, while there remains a degree of creativity required to select operations on a subtype, we can identify desirable properties for our encoding. In particular, for the example of ordered finite sets, our focus will be on recovering the typical elimination principle by dependent pattern matching in Cubical Agda [2].

We can alternatively think of Fin n as a subtype of $\mathbb{N}$, with the subtyping condition on a natural number k given by $k < n$. This definition as a subtype is precisely the form our technique can be used with. Furthermore, the representation of Fin as a family of subtypes has several desirable properties over its definition as an inductive family. For example, the function to$\mathbb{N}$: $\sum[\, k \subset \mathbb{N}\,]\, k < n \to \mathbb{N}$ is trivially defined as the first projection, and the proof that this function is an embedding follows simply from the fact that $k < n$ is a proposition. Concretely, we can define the total order $\_<\_$ in Agda as the following inductive family:

```
data _<_ : N → N → Type where
  z<s : 0 < suc n
  s<s : m < n → suc m < suc n
```

Intuitively, we can observe that $\_<\_$ defines a family of propositions since the only way to prove that a number m is less than a number suc n is by applying the constructor s<s a total of m times to the constructor z<s.

We can now proceed by applying the next step of our technique. In particular, we can identify closure properties on the inductive family $\_<\_$ and extend its definition with constructors encoding them. As a general rule, we recommend prioritising closure properties that are both ubiquitous and for which the typical elimination principle can be 'easily' extended over. In order to highlight this idea, we shall give examples of such closure properties on $\_<\_$.

We begin by observing that the typical elimination principle for the inductive family $\_<\_$ can be constructed from proofs $\neg$m<0 : $m < 0 \to \bot$ and

<-suc-monic : suc m < suc $n \to m$ < n. Indeed, these proofs are precisely what is required to establish that the relation $\_ < \_$ is well-founded. As such, it will be sufficient to define the action of these functions on any additional closure properties we include in our definition of $\_ < \_$. For example, consider transitivity of the relation $\_ < \_$, which can typically be proven as follows:

```
trans< : m < n → n < o → m < o
trans< z<s (s<s q) = z<s
trans< (s<s p) (s<s q) = s<s (trans< p q)
```

We begin by encoding the proof of transitivity as a constructor trans< : $(n : \mathbb{N}) \to m < n \to n < o \to m < o$. We then extend the function ¬m<0 by defining ¬m<0 (trans< n p q) = ¬m<0 q, and in turn extend the function <-suc-monic:

```
<-suc-monic (trans< 0 p q)       = absurd (¬m<0 p)
<-suc-monic (trans< (suc n) p q) = trans< (<-suc-monic p) (<-suc-monic q)
```

Crucially, this construction allows us to recover the typical elimination principle for $\_ < \_$. As a second example, we consider the property that any natural number is less than its successor, which can typically be proven as follows:

```
n<sn : (n : ℕ) → n < suc n
n<sn zero = z<s
n<sn (suc n) = s<s (n<sn n)
```

We can encode this proof by a constructor n<sn : $(n : \mathbb{N}) \to n$ < suc n. Notably, our definition of ¬m<0 does not need to be extended since 0 never unifies with suc n, and we can extend <-suc-monic by simply mapping a term n<sn (suc n) to n<sn n.

While we have shown that the elimination principle for $\_ < \_$ can be preserved after extension with constructors trans< and n<sn, the new inductive family is of course not isomorphic to the original. However, by applying the next step of our technique, we quotient our new inductive family to obtain this isomorphism:

```
data _<_ : ℕ → ℕ → Type where
  z<s : 0 < suc n
  s<s : m < n → suc m < suc n
  n<sn : n < suc n
  trans< : m < n → n < o → m < o
  trunc : (p q : m < n) → p ≡ q
```

We also now require that ¬m<0 and <-suc-monic be extended over the path constructor, which is trivial as both functions eliminate into h-propositions.

It is important to highlight how the approach in this section differs from recovering the same elimination principle by simply transporting along the isomorphism between the alternative and original representations. In particular, by observing how the definition of <-suc-monic was extended over the inductive constructors trans< and n<sn, we can see that it does not 'expand' proofs built from these constructors into proofs built only from z<s and s<s. That is, in contrast to transporting along the induced isomorphism from the alternative definition of _<_ to the original definition, we preserve the efficient encodings of transitivity and the proof that every natural number is less than its successor.

The finite sets example can also be represented using our induction-recursion technique, with the details being available in our Cubical Agda library.

8   IF Formalisation

As discussed in Sect. 6, our encoding of a subtyping condition arises as a quotient of the free monad on a dependent polynomial functor. In this section, we give a formalisation of this idea using *indexed containers* [1, 10], which can be seen as an internalisation of dependent polynomial functors in type theory. In particular, we show how our technique arises as the free construction, over an indexed container, of an algebraic structure we call a *propositional monad*.

8.1   Indexed Containers

Indexed containers provide a generic means to capture and reason about strictly positive type families, and as such we can use them to capture collections of operations on a subtyping condition. Indexed containers can be represented in Agda as terms of the following record type:

```
record Container (I O : Type) : Type₁ where
  field
    Com : (o : O) → Type
    Res : ∀ {o} → Com o → Type
    next : ∀ {o} → (c : Com o) → Res o c → I
```

It is useful to think of such a container as a collection of trees, each with a single vertex, whose input edges are labelled by terms of I, and whose single output edge is labelled by a term of O. In this way, Com maps each $o : O$ to the type of trees whose output edge is labelled by o, Res maps a tree $c :$ Com o to the type of its input edges, and next maps an input edge $r :$ Res o c to its label from I.

Every $C :$ Container I O gives rise to a dependent polynomial functor $[\![C]\!]$: $(I \to$ Type$) \to O \to$ Type, by means of the following definition:

$$[\![C]\!] \, X \, o = \sum [\, c \in \text{Com} \, C \, o \,] \, (\forall \, r \to X \, (\text{next} \, C \, c \, r))$$

This family is termed the *extension* of C, and we can similarly formulate its *dependent extension* $[\![C]\!]_2 \, A \, B : O \to$ Type on all families $A : I \to$ Type, $B : \forall \, i \to A \, i \to$ Type, defined as follows:

$$[\![\, C \,]\!]_2 \; A \; B \; o = \textstyle\sum [\, (c \,,\, f) \in [\![\, C \,]\!] \; A \; o\,] \; (\forall \; r \to B \, \_ \, (f\, r))$$

Together with the notion of a container and its extension, our formalisation also uses the notion of a container morphism, captured by a record type:

record $\_ \Rightarrow \_$ $(C \; D : \mathsf{Container} \; I \; O)$: Type where
   field
      $\mathsf{Com}_1 : \forall \; o \to \mathsf{Com} \; C \; o \to \mathsf{Com} \; D \; o$
      $\mathsf{Res}_1 : \forall \; \{o\} \; (c : \mathsf{Com} \; C \; o) \to \mathsf{Res} \; D \; (\mathsf{Com}_1 \; o \; c) \to \mathsf{Res} \; C \; c$
      $\mathsf{Coh} : \forall \; o \; c \; r \to \mathsf{next} \; C \; c \; (\mathsf{Res}_1 \; c \; r) \equiv \mathsf{next} \; D \; (\mathsf{Com}_1 \; o \; c) \; r$

Every morphism $f \; : \; C \; \Rightarrow \; D$ can be extended to a morphism between the extensions of C and D. In particular, for every $B \; : \; I \; \to \; \mathsf{Type}$, we define $\langle \, f \, \rangle \; B : \forall \, o \to [\![\, C \,]\!] \; B \; o \to [\![\, D \,]\!] \; B \; o$ by mapping $o : O$ and $(c \,,\, g) : [\![\, C \,]\!] \; B \; o$ to:

$\mathsf{Com}_1 \; f \; o \; c \,,\, \lambda \; r \to \mathsf{subst} \; B \; (\mathsf{Coh} \; f \; o \; c \; r) \; (g \; (\mathsf{Res}_1 \; f \; c \; r)).$

8.2 Propositional Monads

We now introduce propositional monads, which will be used to formalise our technique. Given any $O : \mathsf{Type}$, a type family $M : (O \to \mathsf{Type}) \to O \to \mathsf{Type}$ is a propositional monad if there is a term of the following record type:

record $\mathsf{isPropMonad} \; M : \mathsf{Type_1}$ where
   field
      $\mathsf{isPropM} : \forall \; A \; o \to (x \; y : M \; A \; o) \to x \equiv y$
      $\mathsf{return} : \forall \; A \; o \to A \; o \to M \; A \; o$
      $\mathsf{bind} : \forall \; A \; B \; o \to M \; A \; o \to (\forall \; o \; \to A \; o \to M \; B \; o) \to M \; B \; o$

This definition of $\mathsf{isPropMonad}$ presents the structure of a monad on families of propositions. That is, return is the unit map of the monad, bind combines its multiplication map with its functorial action on morphisms, and isPropM asserts that M is a family of propositions. The monadic laws are not required in our definition, as they will always provably hold as a consequence of M being a family of h-propositions. For any type families $A \; B : O \to \mathsf{Type}$, we can construct both the functorial action of M on morphisms, and its monad multiplication map

$$\mathsf{join} : (B : O \to \mathsf{Type}) \to \forall \; o \to M \; (M \; B) \; o \to M \; B \; o$$

from bind and return in the usual way. Importantly, a term of type isPropMonad M is sufficient to prove the necessary monadic (and functorial) laws. Indeed, because M is a family of propositions, these laws trivially hold.

Given propositional monads $F\ G : (O \to \mathsf{Type}) \to O \to \mathsf{Type}$, a morphism from F to G is simply a morphism between the underlying type families, i.e. a family of functions $\alpha_B : (o : O) \to F\ B\ o \to G\ B\ o$ for every $B : O \to \mathsf{Type}$. If the family α_B exists, it will always be unique and respect the monadic structure. Both of these properties follow from appropriate application of the term

$$\mathsf{isPropM}\ G\ B : (o : O)\ (x\ y : G\ B\ o) \to x \equiv y$$

which states that for all $o : O$, the term $G\ B\ o$ is a proposition.

8.3   Free Propositional Monad

For every indexed container $C : \mathsf{Container}\ O\ O$, we can define the free propositional monad over C by truncating the free monad on C. In particular, this can be defined in Cubical Agda by the following higher inductive family:

```
data FreePM C (P : O → Type) : O → Type where
  η : (o : O) → P o → FreePM C P o
  fix : (o : O) → ⟦ C ⟧ (FreePM C P) o → FreePM C P o
  squash : (o : O) (x y : FreePM C P o) → x ≡ y
```

To show that $\mathsf{FreePM}\ C$ is a propositional monad, we begin by observing that $\mathsf{isPropM}$ is trivially given by the path constructor squash, and similarly return is given by the data constructor η. Given type families $P\ Q : O \to \mathsf{Type}$, a term $x : \mathsf{FreePM}\ C\ P\ o$, and a family of functions $g : \forall o \to P\ o \to \mathsf{FreePM}\ Q\ o$, the construction of $\mathsf{bind}\ P\ Q\ o\ x\ g : \mathsf{FreePM}\ C\ Q\ o$ follows by induction on x:

```
bind P Q o (η o p) g = g o p
bind P Q o (fix o (c , f)) g = fix o (c , λ r → bind P Q o (f r) g)
```

Importantly, we can also extend bind over the path constructor squash, because we are eliminating into a proposition.

We recall that this construction also gives us the functorial action of $\mathsf{FreePM}\ C$ on O-indexed type families. That is, for all type families $P\ Q : O \to \mathsf{Type}$, we can lift a family of functions $f : \forall o \to P\ o \to Q\ o$ to a family of functions $\mathsf{map}\ f : \forall o \to \mathsf{FreePM}\ C\ P\ o \to \mathsf{FreePM}\ C\ Q\ o$ between their corresponding free propositional monads. Similarly, we can define the monad multiplication map $\mathsf{joinFPM} : \forall o \to \mathsf{FreePM}\ C\ (\mathsf{FreePM}\ C\ P)\ o \to \mathsf{FreePM}\ C\ P\ o$.

The free propositional monad construction extends to a functor by lifting any morphism $\alpha : C \Rightarrow D$ to a family of functions $\mathsf{lift}\ \alpha\ P : \forall \{o\} \to \mathsf{FreePM}\ C\ P\ o \to \mathsf{FreePM}\ D\ P\ o$. In particular, we define lift inductively on the constructors of $\mathsf{FreePM}\ C\ P\ o$ by simply mapping $\eta\ o\ p$ to $\eta\ o\ p$ and $\mathsf{fix}\ o\ (c\ ,\ f)$ to:

```
fix o (⟨ α ⟩ (FreePM C B) (c , lift α ∘ f))
```

It is easy to extend lift over the path constructor squash because the proof that we are eliminating into a proposition is simply given by squash. The functorial laws follow from the proof that FreePM D P o is a proposition.

To show that FreePM C is the *free* propositional monad on C, we first require a unit of the free construction. In particular, this is a propositional monad morphism between $[\![\, C \,]\!]$ and FreePM C, which can be defined as follows:

$$\text{unit} : (B : O \to \text{Type}) \to \forall \, o \to [\![\, C \,]\!] \, B \, o \to \text{FreePM } C \, B \, o$$
$$\text{unit } B \, o \, (c \, , \, f) = \text{fix } o \, (s \, , \, \lambda \, r \to \eta \, (\text{next } C \, c \, r) \, (f \, r))$$

Furthermore, for all containers C D : Container O O for which there is a term δ : isPropMonad $[\![\, D \,]\!]$ witnessing that $[\![\, D \,]\!]$ is a propositional monad, and for every morphism $\alpha : C \Rightarrow D$ and family $B : O \to \text{Type}$, we can construct a unique family of functions fold α B : $\forall \, \{o\} \to \text{FreePM } C \, B \, o \to [\![\, D \,]\!] \, B \, o$. To define fold α B, we observe that the codomain is a proposition, and hence we can give its inductive definition on only the data constructors of FreePM C B o:

$$\text{fold } \alpha \, B \, (\eta \, o \, p) = \text{return } \delta \, B \, o \, p$$
$$\text{fold } \alpha \, B \, (\text{fix } o \, (c \, , \, f \,)) =$$
$$\quad \text{join } \delta \, B \, o \, (\langle \, \alpha \, \rangle \, ([\![\, D \,]\!] \, B) \, (c \, , \, \text{fold } \alpha \, B \circ f))$$

Importantly, for every $x : [\![\, C \,]\!] \, B \, o$, it is possible to construct a suitable path fold α B o (unit B o x) $\equiv \langle \, \alpha \, \rangle \, B \, o \, x$ witnessing the left adjunct (fold) interacts with the unit map in the expected way; fold α B is the unique such propositional monad morphism satisfying this condition, as its type is an h-prop.

We recall that the key result of our technique is the construction of an isomorphism between our alternative representation of a family of propositions P, i.e. FreePM C P, and P itself. Notably, as both P and FreePM C P are families of propositions, it suffices to construct a family of functions in both directions. The family from P to FreePM C P is trivially given by the data constructor η. In the other direction, it is not in general, possible to construct a family of functions from FreePM C P to P. Indeed, this is only the case when P is closed under the operations characterised by C, which means we can construct a C-algebra $\alpha : \forall \, o \to [\![\, C \,]\!] \, P \, o \to P \, o$ with P as the carrier. Given such an algebra, we can inductively construct the desired family, $f : \forall \, \{o\} \to \text{FreePM } C \, P \, o \to P \, o$, by mapping η o p to p and fix o $(c \, , \, g)$ to $\alpha \, o \, (c \, , \, \lambda \, r \to f \, (g \, r))$.

8.4   Example

To demonstrate how free propositional monads formalise the inductive families version of our technique, we provide an example whose construction follows the four step process in Sect. 6. In particular, we will consider a subtype of lists where adjacent elements are related by a *mere* relation, i.e. a family of h-propositions, which we denote $\_ \sim \_ : A \to A \to \text{Type}$. To do this, we begin by defining the following family of propositions on lists:

```
data isRelated : List A → Type where
  nil : isRelated []
  sing : (x : A) → isRelated (x :: [])
  ind : x ∼ y → isRelated (y :: xs) → isRelated (x :: y :: xs)
```

The constructors nil, sing and ind allow us to construct proofs of the subtyping condition for the empty list, singleton lists, and lists whose first two elements are related and whose tail respects the subtyping condition. Because _ ∼ _ is a mere relation, isRelated is a family of h-props. Notably, if _ ∼ _ is a total order, then a term of type isRelated xs corresponds to a proof that xs is sorted. However, for our purposes we will only require that _ ∼ _ be transitive. While this additional constraint will not be necessary to construct our alternative encoding of isRelated, it will be required to construct an isomorphism with the original definition.

The next step of our technique involves choosing closure properties on the subtyping condition isRelated. We will consider two such properties, namely that if _ ∼ _ is transitive then isRelated is closed under filtering of a list and (safe) removal of elements. That is, given functions

```
filter : (A → Bool) → List A → List A,
remove : (xs : List A) → Fin (length xs) → List A,
```

defined in the obvious way, we can construct the following two proof terms:

```
filterR : ∀ P xs → isRelated xs → isRelated (filter P xs)
removeR : ∀ xs i → isRelated xs → isRelated (remove xs i)
```

We now proceed by capturing these closure properties with an indexed container C : Container (List A) (List A). To do this, we begin by defining the commands, Com C : List A → Type, as the following inductive family:

```
data RelCom : List A → Type where
  filterC : ∀ P? xs → RelCom (filter P? xs)
  removeC : ∀ i xs → RelCom (remove i xs)
```

The next step is to define the inductive positions or 'responses', Res C : ∀ {xs} → RelCom xs → Type. Here, this is simply given by Res C xs c = ⊤ for all xs : List A and c : RelCom xs. Finally, we define next C : ∀ {xs} → (c : RelCom xs) → Res C xs c → List A by induction on the constructors of RelCom:

```
next C (filterC P? as) t = as
next C (removeC i as) t = as
```

From our definition of the container C, the alternative encoding of the inductive family isRelated is simply the free propositional monad FreePM C isRelated : List $A \to$ Type, which we denote by isRelatedF. Importantly, we can prove that for any list xs : List A, the h-props isRelatedF xs and isRelated xs are isomorphic. The construction of this family of isomorphisms follows from the proof that isRelated is indeed closed under the two operations we have encoded. That is, we can construct a C-algebra $\alpha : (xs : \text{List } A) \to [\![\ C \ ]\!]$ isRelated $xs \to$ isRelated xs, by constructing proofs that filtering and removal respect isRelated. Of course, this is only true when the relation $\_ \sim \_$ is transitive.

As is the intended purpose of our alternative encoding of isRelated, the family of propositions isRelatedF comes equipped with two canonical constructors:

filterF : $\forall$ $P?\to$ isRelatedF $xs \to$ isRelatedF (filter $P?$ xs),
removeF : $\forall$ $i \to$ isRelatedF $xs \to$ isRelatedF (remove xs i),

In particular, these constructors correspond to the proofs that isRelatedF is closed under filtering and removal. For example, filterF can be constructed as:

filterF $P?$ $xs =$ fix (filter $P?$ xs) (filterC $P?$ xs , λ $t \to xs$)

Importantly, as long as the arguments $P?$ and xs are in canonical form, then the proof that filterF preserves the subtyping condition will correspondingly be in canonical form. We can construct a similar term corresponding to removeF, and in this way the inductive family isRelatedF efficiently encodes closure of lists with related adjacent elements under filtering and element removal.

9   IR Formalisation

In this section, we will give a formalisation of our higher inductive-recursive encoding of subtypes. We call this encoding the *free subtype extension* on a container. This formalisation will again make use of indexed containers to capture collections of operations. We could also have encoded operations in terms of IR-codes [4], but these two approaches are equivalent [6] and the use of indexed containers simplifies many of our constructions. Once we have given a formalisation of the higher-inductive recursive encoding of subtypes, we then proceed by defining its eliminator and proving its equivalence to the higher-inductive family encoding of subtypes. We conclude this section by applying our formalisation to the practical example of ordered finite sets.

9.1   Fibers

In order to formalise our higher inductive-recursive encoding of subtypes in terms of indexed containers, we recall the definition of the *fiber* over a function. We can define the fiber over a function $f : A \to B$ as an inductive family:

data Fiber $f : B \to$ Type where
   fib : $(a : A) \to$ Fiber $f (f\ a)$

The inductive family Fiber f comes with eliminators unwrap $f\ b$: Fiber $f\ b \to A$ and unwrap-β $f\ b : (x :$ Fiber $f\ b) \to f$ (unwrap $f\ b\ x) \equiv b$, defined as follows:

   unwrap $f\ .(f\ a)$ (fib $a) = a$
   unwrap-β $f\ .(f\ a)$ (fib $a) =$ refl

There is a well-known equivalence between A-indexed type families and fibrations over A, i.e. $\sum [\ U \in$ Type $]$ $(U \to A)$. In particular, this equivalence maps an IR-definition, i.e. an inductive type U : Type defined mutually with a recursive function E : U $\to A$, to the fibers over E. The A-indexed type family corresponding to the fibers over E is precisely what is required when using indexed containers to formalise our higher-inductive recursive encoding of subtypes.

9.2   Free Subtype Extension

As with the previous approach, to formalise our inductive recursive encoding of subtypes we begin with an indexed container, C : Container $O\ O$, which corresponds to the operations that will be encoded as canonical constructors. We then proceed by mutually defining a higher-inductive datatype data FreeSTExt $C\ P$: Type together with a recursive function decode $C\ P$: FreeSTExt $C\ P \to O$, for every family $P : O \to$ Type. In particular, we define the type by

data FreeSTExt $C\ P$ where
   η : $\forall$ $o \to P\ o \to$ FreeSTExt $C\ P$
   fix : $\forall$ $o \to [\![\ C\ ]\!]$ (Fiber (decode $C\ P$)) $o \to$ FreeSTExt $C\ P$
   eq : $\forall$ $x\ y \to$ decode $C\ P\ x \equiv$ decode $C\ P\ y \to x \equiv y$

and the recursive function as follows:

   decode $C\ P$ $(\eta\ o\ p) = o$
   decode $C\ P$ (fix $o\ x) = o$
   decode $C\ P$ (eq $x\ y\ p\ i) = p\ i$

Intuitively, the eq path constructor of FreeSTExt $C\ P$ asserts that decode $C\ P$ is an injective function. In this manner, we can understand FreeSTExt $C\ P$ as being a subtype of O, and decode $C\ P$ as corresponding to the first projection or 'underlying' map on the typical representation of a subtype as a dependent pair. The fix constructor of FreeSTExt $C\ P$ extends the definition of the subtype given by η and eq with the operations characterised by the container C.

To construct functions out of the type FreeSTExt $C\ P$, we must prove that our constructions respect the path constructor eq. Concretely, for every eliminator

$f : (x : \mathsf{FreeSTExt}\ C\ P) \to B\ x$ this means that for all $x, y : \mathsf{FreeSTExt}\ C\ P$ and $p : \mathsf{decode}\ C\ P\ x \equiv \mathsf{decode}\ C\ P\ y$ we provide a construction for the path

$\quad\quad \mathsf{cong}\ f\ (\mathsf{eq}\ x\ y\ p) : \mathsf{PathP}\ (\lambda\ \mathsf{i} \to B\ (p\ i))\ (f\ x)\ (f\ y).$

It may at first seem that the eq path constructor, which appears to simply assert that $\mathsf{decode}\ C\ P$ is injective, is insufficient to capture higher subtypes. That is, injectivity of the underlying map is only enough when a subtype is an h-set. However, as we will show, the introduction of the eq path constructor is in fact sufficient to prove that $\mathsf{decode}\ C\ P$ is an embedding.

9.3 Decode Is an Embedding

A function $f : X \to Y$ is called an embedding if for all x, $y : X$, the action of f on the path space $x \equiv y$, i.e. $\mathsf{cong}\ f : x \equiv y \to f\ x \equiv f\ y$, is an equivalence. This is known to be equivalent to f having propositional fibers, i.e. $\mathsf{Fiber}\ f\ y$ is an h-prop for all $y : Y$. Importantly, this means that $\mathsf{decode}\ C\ P$ is an embedding precisely when $\mathsf{Fiber}\ (\mathsf{decode}\ C\ P)\ o$ is an h-prop for all $o : O$. In particular, this will simplify defining functions out of the free subtype extension into $\mathsf{Fiber}\ (\mathsf{decode}\ C\ P)\ o$, as it easy to show that the path constructor eq is respected when eliminating into an h-prop.

In order to show that $\mathsf{decode}\ C\ P$ is an embedding, it is sufficient to prove that the following two functions

$\quad\quad \mathsf{cong}\ (\mathsf{decode}\ C\ P) : x \equiv y \to \mathsf{decode}\ C\ P\ x \equiv \mathsf{decode}\ C\ P\ y,$
$\quad\quad \mathsf{eq}\ x\ y : \mathsf{decode}\ C\ P\ x \equiv \mathsf{decode}\ C\ P\ y \to x \equiv y,$

establish an isomorphism between $x \equiv y$ and $\mathsf{decode}\ C\ P\ x \equiv \mathsf{decode}\ C\ P\ y$. That is, we require constructions for both the left and right inverse:

$\quad\quad \mathsf{left} : \forall\ p \to \mathsf{cong}\ (\mathsf{decode}\ C\ P)\ (\mathsf{eq}\ x\ y\ p) \equiv p,$
$\quad\quad \mathsf{right} : \forall\ p \to \mathsf{eq}\ x\ y\ (\mathsf{cong}\ (\mathsf{decode}\ C\ P)\ p) \equiv p.$

The family of paths left is simply given by the action of $\mathsf{decode}\ C\ P$ on the path constructor eq. To construct the path right p for every path $p : x \equiv y$, it is sufficient to construct a path $\mathsf{eqRefl} : \mathsf{eq}\ x\ x\ \mathsf{refl} \equiv \mathsf{refl}$ by application of the J-eliminator on p. In order to construct the path eqRefl, we shall make use of one of the foundational concepts of cubical type theory, by constructing it as the lid of the cube shown in Fig. 1. In this figure, the variables $i, j, k : \mathsf{I}$ are terms of the interval that correspond to the dimensions of the cube, with i being the dimension from left to right, j from front to back, and k from bottom to top.

In Cubical Agda, the side faces of the cube can be constructed as a *partial element* of $\mathsf{FreeSTExt}\ C\ P$. For any $A : \mathsf{Type}$ and interval formula $\psi : \mathsf{I}$, the type $\mathsf{Partial}\ \psi\ A$ corresponds to the type of cubes in A for which for which the

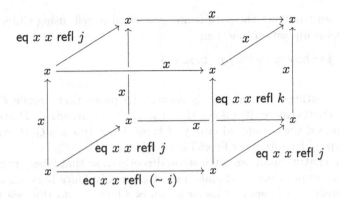

Fig. 1. A cube whose lid is eqRefl

formula ψ takes on the value i1 : I, where i1 is the maximum endpoint in the interval. Given the dimensions i, j, k of the cube, the formula which has value i1 only for the side faces is $i \vee \sim i \vee j \vee \sim j$. In this formula we use the connectives $\vee : I \to I \to I$ and $\sim : I \to I$, which together with $\wedge : I \to I \to I$ form a De Morgan algebra on the interval type whose laws are given definitionally. To express the side faces of our cube in Cubical Agda, we will construct the following term:

sides : $(i\ j\ k : I) \to$ Partial $(i \vee \sim i \vee j \vee \sim j)$ (FreeSTExt $C\ P$)

To do this, we will use a special form of pattern matching that allows us to individually consider when each of the disjuncts in our formula are i1. In particular, this will correspond to giving a construction for each side face. For example, the right-most face will consider the case $i = i1$ and will be given by a heterogeneous path over $\lambda\ k \to$ eq $x\ x$ refl $k = x$, between eq $x\ x$ refl : $x \equiv x$ and refl : $x \equiv x$. Concretely, we can can construct the side faces of our cube as follows:

sides $i\ j\ k\ (i = \text{i0}) =$ eq $x\ x$ refl j
sides $i\ j\ k\ (i = \text{i1}) =$ eq $x\ x$ refl $(j \vee k)$
sides $i\ j\ k\ (j = \text{i0}) =$ eq $x\ x$ refl $(\sim i \vee k)$
sides $i\ j\ k\ (j = \text{i1}) = x$

Here $(i = \text{i0})$, $(i = \text{i1})$, $(j = \text{i0})$ and $(j = \text{i1})$ correspond to the four face maps for the sides of the cube. To construct the lid, we also require a path corresponding to the base. Concretely, this is a heterogeneous path over $\phi = \lambda\ i \to$ eq $x\ x$ refl $(\sim i) \equiv x$ from eq $x\ x$ refl to itself, constructed as follows:

base : PathP ϕ (eq $x\ x$ refl) (eq $x\ x$ refl)
base $i\ j =$ eq (eq $x\ x$ refl $(\sim i)$) x refl j

Finally, we can construct the path from eq x x refl to refl, using Cubical Agda's homogeneous composition function:

eqRefl $i\,j$ = hcomp (sides $i\,j$) (base $i\,j$)

Crucially, as outlined earlier, this is enough to prove that decode C P is an embedding. Furthermore, it follows that the fibers of decode C P are propositions, and indeed the O-indexed family of types Fiber (decode C P) can be seen as the subtyping condition for FreeSTExt C P.

As an alternative proof, we can instead directly show that Fiber (decode C P) is a family of propositions, and make use of the equivalence between a function having propositional fibers and being an embedding. To do this, we first state the eta-law of the inductive family Fiber,

unwrap-η : $\forall$ $x \rightarrow$ PathP (Ψ x) (fib (unwrap x)) x
unwrap-η (fib a) = refl

where Ψ x i = Fiber f (unwrap-β x i). The next step involves defining two sides of a square, for all a : FreeSTExt C P and x : Fiber (decode C P) o:

sides $a\,x$: $(i\,j$: l) $\rightarrow$ Partial $(i \vee \sim i)$ (Ψ x j)
sides $a\,x\,i\,j$ $(i = $ i0) = fib (eq (unwrap x) a (unwrap-β x) j)
sides $a\,x\,i\,j$ $(i = $ i1) = unwrap-η x j

Finally, given any x, y : Fiber (decode C P) o, we can then construct a path $x \equiv y$ by induction on x, where we consider the single case $o = $ decode C P a and $x = $ fib a. We can then apply Cubical Agda's heterogeneous composition comp over the path Ψ y, to compute the lid of the square with sides given by sides a y and base given by fib (unwrap y).

The proof that the decode function has propositional fibers simplifies defining functions between free subtype extensions. Typically, to define a function f : FreeSTExt C P $\rightarrow$ FreeSTExt D P by induction on FreeSTExt C P, we need to show that f respects the path constructor eq. However, it is often simpler to define a family of functions g : $\forall$ o $\rightarrow$ Fiber (decode C P) o $\rightarrow$ Fiber (decode D P) o, and then construct f as unwrap $\circ$ g $\circ$ fib. To construct g, we can first induct on the single case of Fiber (decode C P) o, i.e. fib a for a : FreeSTExt C P, and then proceed by induction on a. Importantly, any construction we give by induction on a will respect the path constructor eq, as a consequence of eliminating into a h-prop. An important example is defining the functorial action of the free subtype extension on a container morphism $h : C \Rightarrow D$, which can be found online in our Cubical Agda library.

9.4   Equivalence Between IF and IR Approaches

The proof that decode C P has propositional fibers is central to our construction of an equivalence between our IF and IR encodings. In particular, it will facili-

tate the construction of a family of isomorphisms between the O-indexed families
FreePM C P and Fiber (decode C P), which correspond to the subtyping condition. Finally, we will construct an equivalence between the subtype encodings
themselves, i.e. FreeSTExt C P and $\sum[\, o \in O\,]$ FreePM C P o. Concretely, we
begin by constructing a family of functions IF→IR : $\forall\, \{o\} \to$ FreePM C P $o \to$
Fiber (decode C P) o, defined on the data constructors of FreePM C P o by:

   IF→IR (η o p) = fib (η o p)
   IF→IR (fix o (c , g)) = fib (fix o (c , λ $r \to$ IF→IR (g r)))

The action of IF→IR on the path constructor squash is given by the proof that
decode C P has propositional fibers. In the other direction, we construct a family
of functions IR→IF : $\forall\, \{o\} \to$ Fiber (decode C P) $o \to$ FreePM C P o by:

   IR→IF (fib (η o p)) = η o p
   IR→IF (fib (fix o (c , g))) = fix o (c , λ $r \to$ IR→IF (g r))

The proof that IF→IR and IR→IF witnesses a family of isomorphisms between
FreePM C P and Fiber (decode C P) follows simply from these families being h-
props. By univalence and function extensionality this is also enough to construct
a path between propositions FreePM C P and Fiber (decode C P). Moreover,
we can also prove the following function is an equivalence:

   IR→$\sum$IF : FreeSTExt C $P \to \sum[\, o \in O\,]$ FreePM C P o
   IR→$\sum$IF x = decode C P x , IR→IF x

In particular, it is sufficient to prove this function has contractible fibers. To
this end, we will first show IR→IF has propositional fibers, and then give a construction for $f : \forall\, y \to$ Fiber IR→IF y. We begin by observing that the function
$\pi_1 \circ$ IR→IF, i.e. the composition with the first projection, is definitionally equal
to decode C P, which we have already shown to have propositional fibers. It is
provable in HoTT that for any A B : Type and $C : B \to$ Type, if C is a family of propositions then given a function $f : A \to \sum[\, b \in B\,]$ C b, if $\pi_1 \circ f$ has
propositional fibers then so does f; the details can be found in our Cubical Agda
library. Given that FreePM C P is a family of propositions, it then follows that
IR→$\sum$IF has propositional fibers.

   To complete the proof that the fibers of IR→IF are contractible, it suffices to
construct a term Fiber IR→IF (o, x) for each $(o, x) : \sum[\, o \in O\,]$ FreePM C P o.
We proceed by induction on x, and note that our construction will respect
the path constructor squash as a consequence of eliminating into a h-prop,
i.e. Fiber IR→IF (o, x). For the case where $x = \eta$ o p, we construct the term
fib (η o p). If $x = $ fix o (c , g), we first construct the following path:

   $p : (o$, fix o $(c$, IR→IF $\circ$ IF→IR $\circ$ $g)) \equiv (o$, fix o $(c$, $g))$
   p $i = o$, squash o (fix o $(c$, IR→IF $\circ$ IF→IR $\circ$ $g))$ (fix o $(c$, $g))$

Finally, we transport the term fib (fix o $(c$, IF→IR ∘ $g))$ along p, in the family Fiber IR→IF, to construct a term of type Fiber IR→IF $(o$, fix o $(c$, $g))$ as required.

9.5   Example

We conclude this section by applying the formalisation of the IR encoding of subtypes to the same example used in Sect. 8.4 to illustrate the IF encoding of subtyping conditions. In particular, we will consider an encoding for the subtype of lists for which any two adjacent elements are related by a mere transitive relation _ ~ _ : A → A → Type. Furthermore, we will make use of the same indexed container C : Container (List A) (List A) as defined previously.

We can encode the given subtype on lists as the free subtype extension on C applied to isRelated _ ~ _, i.e. the type RelList = FreeSTExt C (isRelated _ ~ _). In this way, the subtyping condition is then encoded by the inductive family Fiber (decode C (isRelated _ ~ _)). In a similar manner to the example for the IF formalisation, and given lengthR = length ∘ decode C (isRelated _ ~ _), this encoding gives rise to the following canonical constructors:

> filterR : $(P?$: A → Bool) → RelList → RelList
> removeR : $(xs$: RelList) $(i$: Fin (lengthR $xs))$ → RelList

For example, we can construct filterR as follows:

> filterR $P?$ xs =
>   let ys = decode C (isRelated _~_) xs
>   in fix ys (filterC $P?$ ys , λ t → fib xs)

10   Generalising Our Technique

Our technique can be generalised in a natural manner, by considering an encoding for dependent sums whose second component is an arbitrary type, rather than just a proposition. The advantage of such an encoding for generalised dependent sums is the flexibility to control precisely when selected operations on a type are normalised. We begin this section with the motivating example of finite lists, and then provide a formalisation of the generalised approach for encoding arbitrary type families A : O → Type together with a collection of operations represented by a container C : Container O O.

As an alternative to the typical encoding of finite lists, we can instead first consider *vectors*, i.e. families of finite lists indexed by their length:

> data Vec $(A$: Type) : $\mathbb{N}$ → Type where
>   [] : Vec A 0
>   _::_ : A → Vec A n → Vec A (suc n)

Using vectors, we can encode finite lists of A as the sum over the family Vec A : $\mathbb{N} \to$ Type. That is, we define List $A = \sum [\, n \in \mathbb{N} \,]$ Vec A n, which can be shown to be equivalent to the typical presentation of lists. In particular, this representation requires that any operation that constructs a list must also compute its length, and therefore its length can be retrieved in constant time by projecting the first component. For example, concatenation of two lists is defined by addition of the first components, and application of the operation $\_++\_$: Vec A $m \to$ Vec A $n \to$ Vec A $(m + n)$ on the second components.

As an application of our generalised technique, we will consider encoding finite lists in such a manner that it is possible to control when the operation $\_++\_$ is normalised. We can first observe that the definition of List A using vectors does not fit the required scheme to apply the techniques we have described thus far, as for any $n > 0$ if A is not a proposition then neither is Vec A n. However, the first step of the generalisation to our IF approach follows in an identical fashion, i.e. by defining a new inductive family AVec A : $\mathbb{N} \to$ Type, with two constructors η : Vec A $n \to$ AVec A n and $\_++\_$: AVec A $m \to$ AVec A $n \to$ AVec A $(m + n)$. In particular, we intend for η to be an embedding from Vec A n into AVec A n, and for the constructor $\_++\_$ to encode the operation $\_++\_$.

In order to establish an equivalence between AVec A n and Vec A n, we can quotient AVec A n such that $\_++\_$ corresponds to concatenation of the *represented* vectors. To do this, it is necessary to be able to refer to the vectors being represented by terms of AVec A n in its own definition. This corresponds to mutually defining the family AVec A together with a family of functions vect : AVec A $n \to$ Vec A n that map a term of AVec A n to the vector it represents. Concretely, we define the quotiented family AVec A as follows:

```
data AVec A where
    η : Vec A n → AVec A n
    _++_ : AVec A m → AVec A n → AVec A (m + n)
    eq : (xs : Vec A m) (ys : Vec A n) → η (vect xs ++ vect ys) ≡ xs ++ ys
```

We then define the function vect as:

```
vect (η as) = as
vect (xs ++ ys) = vect xs ++ vect ys
vect (eq xs ys i) = vect xs ++ vect ys
```

Importantly, the path constructor eq is sufficient to construct a path of the type η (vect as) $\equiv as$ for all $n : \mathbb{N}$ and $as :$ AVec A n. Following from the definitional equality vect $(\eta\ as) = as$, this is enough to establish that the constructor η and the function vect witness a family of isomorphisms between Vec A and AVec A. Consequently, it is sufficient to establish an equivalence between the types $\sum [\, n \in \mathbb{N} \,]$ Vec A n and $\sum [\, n \in \mathbb{N} \,]$ AVec A n.

By encoding vectors using the type AVec A, we can precisely control when concatenation is normalised. In particular, it is possible to define a function normalise : AVec A n → AVec A n for this purpose, by composing vect with η. Indeed, this is similar to the approach of normalisation-by-evaluation, in which terms are evaluated and then reflected back into the syntax. In the case of our generalised encoding this reflection map is η and is an equivalence. More generally, we can use this approach to delay normalisation until after applying functions that do not require terms to be in a normalised form, e.g. the family of functions map : $(A \to B) \to$ AVec A $n \to$ AVec B n.

As can be observed with our finite lists example, in contrast to our definition of free propositional monads, the generalisation of our IF approach requires that we have a C-algebra α : $(o : O) \to$ ⟦ C ⟧ A $o \to A$ o before defining our new representation of A. The generalised IF approach proceeds by mutually defining a higher inductive family FreeRep C A α : $O \to$ Type and a recursive function rec α : ∀ $\{o\} \to$ FreeRep C A α $o \to A$ o. First, we define FreeRep C A α by:

```
data FreeRep C A α where
    η : ∀ o → A o → FreeRep C A α o
    fix : ∀ o → ⟦ C ⟧ (FreeRep C A α) o → FreeRep C A α o
    eq : ∀ o c g → η o (α o (c , rec C A α ∘ g)) ≡ fix o (c , g)
```

Then the function rec α is constructed as follows:

```
rec α (η o a) = a
rec α (fix o (c , g)) = α o (c , λ r → rec α (g r))
rec α (eq o c g i) = α o (c , λ r → rec α (g r))
```

We say that FreeRep C A α is a *freely represented family* for A over the container C. Given any $o : O$ and $x :$ FreeRep C A α o, we can extend the path constructor eq to a family of paths eq-η x : η o (rec α x) $\equiv x$ using the definition:

```
eq-η (η o a) = refl
eq-η (fix o (c , g)) = eq o c g
eq-η (eq o c g i) j = eq o c g (i ∧ j)
```

The functions rec α and η o establish an isomorphism between FreeRep C A α o and A o. Hence the inductive family FreeRep C A α gives an alternative representation of A, for which the operations encoded by C can be expressed in a manner that their computation is delayed until transporting along the isomorphism.

It is also possible to define an eliminator for FreeRep C A α into a family of types B : $O \to$ Type. This eliminator requires a C-algebra β : $(o : O) \to$ ⟦ C ⟧ B $o \to B$ o which has B as its carrier, and a family of functions f : $(o : O) \to A$ $o \to B$ o such that the following diagram commutes:

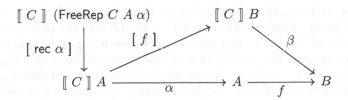

That is, under the image of $[\text{ rec } \alpha \text{ }]$, the family of functions f must be an algebra homomorphism between α and β. The construction of the eliminator itself is given in our Cubical Agda library. An interesting application for this idea is to define the functorial action of FreeRep C on morphisms between C-algebras. We remark that the correct notion of morphism between FreeRep C A α and FreeRep C B β is an algebra homomorphism between the algebras given by rec α and rec β. Again, our library gives the details.

The generalised IF approach can also be translated into a generalisation of the IR approach. In particular, for every type A and $\alpha : (o : O) \to [\![C]\!] \, A \, o \to A \, o$ we can mutually define a higher inductive type FreeRepIR C A α : Type,

> data FreeRepIR C A α where
> $\eta : \forall \, o \to A \, o \to$ FreeRepIR C A α
>   fix : $\forall \, o \to [\![C]\!]$ (Fiber $(\pi_1 \circ$ rec $\alpha)$) $o \to$ FreeRepIR C A α
>   eq : $\forall \, o \, c \, g \to \eta \, o \, (\alpha \, o \, (c \, , \, \mathsf{rec}\pi_2 \, \alpha \circ g)) \equiv$ fix $o \, (c \, , \, g)$

a function recπ_2 $\alpha : \forall \, \{o\} \to$ Fiber $(\pi_1 \circ$ rec $\alpha)$ $o \to A \, o$,

> recπ_2 α (fib x) $= \pi_1$ (rec α x)

and a function rec α : FreeRepIR C A $\alpha \to \sum [\, o \in O \,] \, A \, o$:

> rec α $(\eta \, o \, a) = o \, , \, a$
> rec α (fix $o \, (c \, , \, g)) = o \, , \, \alpha \, o \, (c \, , \, \mathsf{rec}\pi_2 \, \alpha \circ g)$
> rec α (eq $o \, c \, g \, i) = o \, , \, \alpha \, o \, (c \, , \, \mathsf{rec}\pi_2 \, \alpha \circ g)$

In a similar manner to the generalisation of the IF approach, the eq path constructor can be extended to a family of paths eq-η x : uncurry η (rec α $x) \equiv x$. In particular, this means that for all $o : O$, the functions rec α and uncurry η witness an isomorphism between FreeRepIR C A α and $\sum [\, o \in O \,] \, A \, o$.

11   Related Approaches

In this section we compare with two existing approaches in Agda to proofs whose content does not matter, *irrelevancy annotations* and *abstract definitions*, and with the use of the *Prop universe* in Coq and Agda.

In Agda, a term can be annotated as irrelevant in cases where its content will not be used in any proof-relevant constructions, and doing so prevents unfolding of the annotated term. The key distinction between our technique and irrelevancy annotations is the preservation of *computational content*. In particular, annotating proofs of the subtyping condition as irrelevant is problematic in a similar manner to that of using a strict universe of propositions, namely that we cannot then use the content of a proof in any proof-relevant context. For example, this means that we would be unable to use a proof that a natural number is even in order to construct the function div2 : isEven! $n \to \mathbb{N}$ that divides an even number by two, as discussed in Sect. 4.

Agda's abstract definition mechanism can be used to hide the implementation details of a subtype, and expose operations as irreducible terms. Abstract definitions are similar to our technique when defining a subtype X : Type within an abstract block, together with the first projection El : $X \to O$ and a term witnessing that the function El is an embedding. In particular, this is enough to construct paths corresponding to equational properties of operations on X outside of the block. However, abstract definitions still require explicit proofs of closure under the subtyping condition for operations within the abstract block. In contrast, our encoding only requires a proof that the encoded operations are coherent with respect to the subtyping condition in cases where we need to construct and transport along an isomorphism between our alternative representation of a subtype and its original definition. In this manner, encoding operations using our technique is similar to postulating them, with the important distinction that computational properties are preserved.

A third approach, provided in both Agda and Coq, is to use a universe of computationally irrelevant propositions, typically named Prop. Agda has a predicative hierarchy of Prop universes wherein pattern matching is restricted to only the absurd pattern on elimination into proof-relevant types, thereby preventing computational content from leaking. Meanwhile, Coq has a single impredicative Prop universe that also allows for matching on inductively defined propositions with a single constructor when eliminating into proof-relevant types. This is known as the singleton-elimination principle, and by application to the identity type in Coq it is possible to show the uniqueness of identity proofs, and is therefore inconsistent with univalence. As a closer analogue to Agda's Prop universe, Coq has an impredicative universe of definitionally proof-irrelevant propositions termed SProp that is consistent with univalence [5]. The primary drawback to using a definitionally proof-irrelevant Prop universe to prevent unnecessary reduction behaviour of terms is the inability to use proof content in any proof-relevant context. In contrast, our approach provides the advantage of preserving proof content, while preventing unnecessary reduction behaviour.

12   Conclusion

In this article we have presented a new technique that allows operations on a subtype to be represented in a manner that exhibits no reduction behaviour.

Our approach does not require special-purpose language extensions, can be used in any implementation of type theory that supports quotient types, and retains important computational properties. Interesting topics for further work include generalising our approach by introducing equational properties between operations as path constructors of the encoded subtype, generalising the equivalence between inductive-recursive types and inductive families to their higher counterparts by applying the transformation used in our technique, and developing a wider range of combinators for working with subtypes.

Furthermore, from the point of view of extensibility, it would be beneficial to identify a sufficient condition on a collection of operations such that the typical elimination principle for an encoded subtype can be recovered simply by dependent pattern matching in the sense of [2].

Acknowledgements. We would like to thank Nicolai Kraus for many interesting discussions, and the anonymous reviewers for their useful comments and suggestions. This work was funded by the EPSRC grant EP/P00587X/1, *Mind the Gap: Unified Reasoning About Program Correctness and Efficiency.*

References

1. Altenkirch, T., Ghani, N., Hancock, P., McBride, C., Morris, P.: Indexed containers. J. Funct. Program. **25** (2015)
2. Cockx, J., Devriese, D., Piessens, F.: Pattern matching without K. In: Proceedings of the 19th ACM SIGPLAN International Conference on Functional Programming, pp. 257–268 (2014)
3. Cohen, C., Coquand, T., Huber, S., Mörtberg, A.: Cubical type theory: a constructive interpretation of the univalence axiom. arXiv preprint arXiv:1611.02108 (2016)
4. Dybjer, P., Setzer, A.: Induction-recursion and initial algebras. Ann. Pure Appl. Log. **124**(1–3) (2003)
5. Gilbert, G., Cockx, J., Sozeau, M., Tabareau, N.: Definitional proof-irrelevance without K. Proc. ACM Program. Lang. **3**(POPL) (Jan 2019). https://doi.org/10.1145/3290316
6. Hancock, P., McBride, C., Ghani, N., Malatesta, L., Altenkirch, T.: Small induction recursion. In: Hasegawa, M. (ed.) TLCA 2013. LNCS, vol. 7941, pp. 156–172. Springer, Heidelberg (2013). https://doi.org/10.1007/978-3-642-38946-7_13
7. Hewer, B.: Subtyping Cubical Agda Library (2022). https://tinyurl.com/f8pezwxd
8. Kraus, N.: Ph.D. thesis, University of Nottingham (2015)
9. Malatesta, L., Altenkirch, T., Ghani, N., Hancock, P., McBride, C.: Small induction recursion, indexed containers and dependent polynomials are equivalent (2012)
10. Morris, P., Altenkirch, T.: Indexed containers. In: IEEE Symposium in Logic in Computer Science (2009)
11. Shulman, M.: Higher inductive-recursive univalence and type-directed definitions, June 2014. https://homotopytypetheory.org/2014/06/08/hiru-tdd/
12. Program, T.U.F.: Homotopy type theory: univalent foundations of mathematics. Technical report, Institute for Advanced Study (2013)
13. Vezzosi, A., Mörtberg, A., Abel, A.: Cubical Agda: a dependently typed programming language with univalence and higher inductive types. J. Funct. Program. **31** (2021)

Calculating Datastructures

Ralf Hinze[1] and Wouter Swierstra[2]([✉])

[1] TU Kaiserslautern, Kaiserslautern, Germany
`ralf-hinze@cs.uni-kl.de`
[2] Utrecht University, Utrecht, The Netherlands
`w.s.swierstra@uu.nl`

Abstract. Where do datastructures come from? This paper explores how to systematically derive implementations of *one-sided flexible arrays* from a simple reference implementation. Using the dependently typed programming language Agda, each calculation constructs an isomorphic—yet more efficient—datastructure using only a handful of laws relating types and arithmetic. Although these calculations do not generally produce novel datastructures they do give insight into how certain datastructures arise and how different implementations are related.

1 Introduction

There is a rich field of *program calculation*, deriving a program systematically from its specification. In this paper, we explore a slightly different problem: showing how efficient *datastructures* can be derived from an inefficient reference implementation. In particular, we consider how to derive implementations of *one-sided flexible arrays*, a datastructure that offers efficient indexing without being limited to store only a fixed number of elements. Although we do not claim to invent new datastructures by means of our calculations, we can demystify the definitions of familiar datastructures, providing a constructive rationalization identifying the key design choices that are made.

In contrast to program calculation, relating a program and its specification, the calculation of datastructures requires relating two different *types*. As it turns out, we show how to calculate efficient implementations that are *isomorphic* to our reference implementation. These calculations rely exclusively on familiar laws of types and arithmetic. Indeed, we have formalised these calculations in the dependently typed programming language and proof assistant Agda. While we present our derivations in quite some detail, we occassionally will refer to the accompanying source code for a more complete account; while not provable in the current type theory underlying Agda, we will occassionally assume the axiom of functional extensionality.

After defining the interface of flexible arrays (Sect. 2), we will define the Peano natural numbers (Sect. 3), leading to a first reference implementation of flexible arrays (Sect. 4). Starting from this reference implementation, we compute an isomorphic, yet inefficient, datastructure (Sect. 5). By shifting to a more efficient (binary) number representation (Sect. 6), we can define a similar reference

E. Komendantskaya (Ed.): MPC 2022, LNCS 13544, pp. 62–101, 2022.
https://doi.org/10.1007/978-3-031-16912-0_3

implementation (Sect. 7). Using this second reference implementation, we once again compute an isomorphic datastructure (Sect. 8)—but in this case several alternative choices exist (Sects. 9 & 10).

2   One-sided Flexible Arrays

Consider the following interface for one-sided flexible arrays:

$$
\begin{aligned}
&\mathbb{N} &&: Set \\
&Array &&: \mathbb{N} \to Set \to Set \\
&lookup &&: Array\,n\,elem \to (\{i : \mathbb{N} \mid i < n\} \to elem) \\
&tabulate &&: (\{i : \mathbb{N} \mid i < n\} \to elem) \to Array\,n\,elem \\
&nil &&: Array\,0\,elem \\
&cons &&: elem \to Array\,n\,elem \to Array\,(1 + n)\,elem \\
&head &&: Array\,(1 + n)\,elem \to elem \\
&tail &&: Array\,(1 + n)\,elem \to Array\,n\,elem
\end{aligned}
$$

An array of type $Array\,n\,elem$ stores n elements of type $elem$, for some natural number n. For the moment, we leave the type of natural numbers *abstract*. In what follows, we explore different implementations of arrays by varying the implementation of the natural number type.

We require flexible arrays to be isomorphic to functions from some finite set of indices to the $elem$ type. The $lookup$ function witnesses one direction of the isomorphism, $tabulate$ the other.

$$lookup\,(tabulate\,f) \equiv f \tag{1a}$$

$$tabulate\,(lookup\,a) \equiv a \tag{1b}$$

In what follows, we refer to functions with a finite domain, that is functions of the form $\{i : \mathbb{N} \mid i < n\} \to elem$, as *finite maps*.

In contrast to traditional fixed-size arrays, one-sided flexible arrays can be extended at the front using the $cons$ operation. Non-empty arrays can be shrunk with $tail$, discarding the first element. The following properties specify the interplay of indexing and the other operations that modify the size of the array.

$$lookup\,(cons\,x\,xs)\,0 \equiv x \tag{2a}$$

$$lookup\,(cons\,x\,xs)\,(1 + i) \equiv lookup\,xs\,i \tag{2b}$$

$$head\,xs \equiv lookup\,xs\,0 \tag{2c}$$

$$lookup\,(tail\,xs)\,i \equiv lookup\,xs\,(1 + i) \tag{2d}$$

To define any implementation of this interface, we first need to settle on the implementation of the natural number type. The most obvious choice is, of course, Peano's representation. Once we have this in place, we can explore different implementations of the $Array$ type.

3 Peano Numerals

To calculate an implementation of flexible arrays we proceed in two steps. First, we fix an indexing scheme by defining a type of natural numbers below some fixed, upper bound. Such an indexing scheme fixes the domain of our finite maps, $\{i \mid i < n\}$. Next, we calculate a more efficient representation of finite maps, yielding a datastructure rather than a function. This section details the ideas underlying the first step using the simplest representation of natural numbers; in Sect. 5, we explore the second step.

3.1 Number Type

The datatype of Peano numerals describes the set of natural numbers as the least set containing *zero* that is closed under a *succ*essor operation.

> **data** *Peano* : *Set* **where**
> *zero* : *Peano*
> *succ* : *Peano* → *Peano*

We use variable names such as k, m, and n to range over Peano numerals and use the Arabic numerals to denote *Peano* constants, writing 3 rather than *succ*(*succ*(*succ zero*)).

The operations doubling and incrementing natural numbers, needed in Sect. 6.1, illustrate how to define functions (by induction) in Agda.[1]

> _+1 _+2 : *Peano* → *Peano*
> n +1 = *succ* n
> n +2 = *succ*(*succ* n)
> _·2 : *Peano* → *Peano*
> *zero* ·2 = *zero*
> *succ* n ·2 = *succ*(*succ*(n ·2))

The underscores indicate that all three functions are written postfix.

3.2 Index Type

Having fixed the number type, we move on to define the type of valid indices in an *Array* of size n. Here we have several alternatives, each with its own advantages and disadvantages. The most obvious transcription of $\{i \mid i < n\}$ uses a *dependent pair* or Σ type to combine a natural number and a proof that it is within bounds:

---

[1] The single most important rule when reading Agda code is that *only* a space separates lexemes. For example, +1 is a single lexeme denoting the successor function, whereas $n + 1$ is a sequence of three lexemes. In general, an Agda identifier consists of an arbitrary sequence of non-whitespace Unicode characters. There are only a few exceptions to this rule: for example, parentheses, (and), and curly braces, { and }, must not form part of a name—for obvious reasons.

$Index : Peano \rightarrow Set$
$Index\, n = \Sigma[\, i \in Peano\,]\, i < n$

Here $<$ denotes the *strict* ordering on the naturals. While the definition is fairly straightforward, it is somewhat cumbersome to use in practice as any computation on indices involves manipulations of proofs. Before discussing alternative definitions, let us first explore some properties of the *Index* type.

$$Index\text{-}0 \; : \; Index\,(0) \quad\;\, \cong \perp$$
$$Index\text{-}1 \; : \; Index\,(1) \quad\;\, \cong \top$$
$$Index\text{-}{+} \; : \; Index\,(m+n) \cong (Index\,m \uplus Index\,n)$$
$$Index\text{-}{*} \; : \; Index\,(m*n) \cong (Index\,m \times Index\,n)$$
$$Index\text{-}{\uparrow} \; : \; Index\,(n \uparrow m) \cong (Index\,m \;\rightarrow\; Index\,n)$$

The formulas link arithmetic on numbers to operations on types, with the number 0 corresponding to the empty set (written $\perp$ in Agda), 1 to a singleton set (written $\top$), addition to disjoint union (written $\uplus$), multiplication to cartesian product (written $\times$), and, finally, exponentiation to the function space. We refer to these laws as *index transformations*.

For example, the sum rule *Index*-+ is witnessed by a mapping between indices for a pair of arrays and indices for a single array, as suggested below.

0	1	2	3	0	1	2	3	4	5	6

0	1	2	3	4	5	6	7	8	9	10

More instructively, the product rule, *Index*-*, is witnessed by a mapping between indices for a two-dimensional array and indices for a one-dimensional array.

	0	1	2	3	4	5	6
0	0	1	2	3	4	5	6
1	7	8	9	10	11	12	13
2	14	15	16	17	18	19	20
3	21	22	23	24	25	26	27

	0	1	2	3	4	5	6
0	0	4	8	12	16	20	24
1	1	5	9	13	17	21	25
2	2	6	10	14	18	22	26
3	3	7	11	15	19	23	27

In general, there is not a single *canonical* witness for an index transformation. The diagram on the left above exemplifies what is known as row-major order, but there is also column-major order, shown on the right. For now, we choose to ignore these specifics. However, when we start calculating datastructures the *choice* of isomorphism becomes tremendously important, a point we return to in Sect. 6.2.

Remark 1 (Categorical background). To provide some background, the type function *Index* is the object part of a functor from the preorder of natural numbers to the category of finite sets and total functions. (This is why the type is also known as *Fin* or *FinSet*.) The action of the functor on arrows embeds *Index m* into *Index n*, provided $m \preceq n$. In fact, the isomorphisms demonstrate that *Index* is simultaneously a *strong monoidal* functor of type $(\mathbb{N}, 0, +) \rightarrow (Set, \bot, \uplus)$ and a *strong monoidal* functor of type $(\mathbb{N}, 1, \cdot) \rightarrow (Set, \top, \times)$.   □

Returning to the issue of defining the *Index* type in Agda, we can use the isomorphisms above to determine the index set by pattern matching on the natural number n.

> *Index* : *Peano* → *Set*
> *Index* (*zero*)   = ⊥
> *Index* (*succ n*) = ⊤ ⊎ *Index n*

The zero rule *Index*-0 determines that the *Index*(0) type is uninhabited; whereas the rules for one and addition, *Index*-1 and *Index*-+, determine that *Index*(*succ n*) contains one more element than *Index n*.

For reasons of readability, we turn the definition of *Index* into idiomatic Agda, replacing the type function by an inductively defined indexed datatype.

> **data** *Index* : *Peano* → *Set* **where**
>   *izero* :   *Index* (*succ n*)
>   *isucc* : *Index n* → *Index* (*succ n*)

There are no constructors for *Index zero*, corresponding to the first equation of *Index*, and two constructors for *Index* (*succ n*), corresponding to *Index*'s second equation. The constructor names are almost identical to those of *Peano*. This is intentional: we want the constructors of *Index* to look *and* behave like their namesakes. The only difference is that the former carry vital type information about upper bounds. Reassuringly, all three definitions of index sets are equivalent. The straightforward, but rather technical proofs can be found in the accompanying material.

To illustrate working with indices, let us implement some index transformations that are needed later in Sect. 6.2.

> _·2+0 _·2+1 : *Index n* → *Index* (*n* ·2)
> (*izero*) ·2+0 = *izero*
> (*isucc i*) ·2+0 = *isucc* (*isucc* (*i* ·2+0))
> (*izero*) ·2+1 = *isucc izero*
> (*isucc i*) ·2+1 = *isucc* (*isucc* (*i* ·2+1))

The second operation combines doubling and increment. The "obvious" definition, $i \cdot 2 + 1 = isucc(i \cdot 2 + 0)$ does not work, as the expression on the right-hand side has type $Index(n \cdot 2 + 1)$ and not $Index(n \cdot 2)$, as required. On plain naturals we can separate doubling and increment; here we need to combine the operations to be able to establish precise upper bounds. We cannot expect Agda to automatically replicate the hand-written proof:

$$i \prec n \iff i + 1 \preceq n \iff (i + 1) \cdot 2 \preceq n \cdot 2 \iff i \cdot 2 + 1 \prec n \cdot 2.$$

In general, since *Index* combines data and proof, index transformations require more work than their vanilla counterparts on naturals.

Now that we have a precise understanding of the domain of our finite maps, we can start calculating an implementation of the interface specified in Sect. 2.

4   Functions as Datastructures

The simplest implementation of the *Array* type identifies arrays and finite maps:

$$Array : Peano \rightarrow Set \rightarrow Set$$
$$Array\ n\ elem\ =\ Index\ n \rightarrow elem$$

In this particular case, *lookup* and *tabulate* are manifest identities, rather than isomorphisms.

$$lookup : Array\ n\ elem \rightarrow (Index\ n \rightarrow elem)$$
$$lookup\ a\ =\ a$$
$$tabulate : (Index\ n \rightarrow elem) \rightarrow Array\ n\ elem$$
$$tabulate\ f\ =\ f$$

To complete this "implementation", however, we still need to define the remaining operations: *nil*, *cons*, *head*, and *tail*. The empty array *nil* is the unique function from the empty set, defined below using an absurd pattern, written (). For the other functions, the specification serves as the implementation, for example, (2a) and (2b) form the definition of *cons*, given that *lookup* is implemented as the identity function.

$$nil : Array\ zero\ elem$$
$$nil\,()$$
$$cons : elem \rightarrow Array\ n\ elem \rightarrow Array\ (succ\ n)\ elem$$
$$cons\ x\ xs\ (izero)\ =\ x$$
$$cons\ x\ xs\ (isucc\ i)\ =\ xs\ i$$
$$head : Array\ (succ\ n)\ elem \rightarrow elem$$
$$head\ xs\ =\ xs\ izero$$
$$tail : Array\ (succ\ n)\ elem \rightarrow Array\ n\ elem$$
$$tail\ xs\ i\ =\ xs\ (isucc\ i)$$

The proofs that the "implementation" satisfies the specification are consequently trivial: all the specified equivalences hold by definition.

While the "implementation" is exceptionally simple, it is also exceptionally slow: the running time of *lookup xs i* is not only determined by the index *i* but also by the number of operations used to build the array *xs*. For example, even though *tail(cons x xs)* is extensionally equal to *xs*, each lookup takes two additional steps as the index is first incremented by *tail* only to be subsequently decremented by *cons*. In other words, the run-time behaviour of *lookup* is sensitive to *how* the array has been constructed! To avoid this problem, we turn functions into datastructures, using this "implementation" above as our starting point. Finding a suitable datastructure is the topic of the coming section.

5 Lists Also Known as Vectors

Do you remember the *laws of exponents* from secondary school?

$$X^0 = 1 \qquad\qquad X^1 = X$$
$$X^{A+B} = X^A \cdot X^B \qquad\qquad X^{A \cdot B} = \left(X^B\right)^A$$

Quite amazingly, these equalities can be re-interpreted as isomorphisms between types, where B^A is the type of functions from A to B.

law-of-exponents-⊥ : $(\bot \to X)$ ≅ ⊤
law-of-exponents-⊤ : $(\top \to X)$ ≅ X
law-of-exponents-⊎ : $(A \uplus B \to X) \cong ((A \to X) \times (B \to X))$
law-of-exponents-× : $(A \times B \to X) \cong (A \to (B \to X))$

If we apply these isomorphisms from left to right, perhaps repeatedly, we can systematically eliminate function spaces. This process might be called *defunctionalization* or *trieification*, except that the former term is already taken.

Some background is perhaps not amiss. A trie is also known as a digital search tree. In a conventional search tree, the search path is determined on the fly by comparing a given key against the sign posts stored in the inner nodes. By contrast, in a digital search tree, the key *is* the search path. This idea is, of course, not limited to searching. The point of this paper is that it applies equally well to indexing: the index or position of an element within an array *is* a path into the datastructure that represents the array.

Remark 2 (Categorical background). A lot more can be said about trieification: functors of the form $A \to X$ are *contravariant* in A, and part of an adjoint situation, sending left adjoints (initial objects ⊥, coproducts ⊎, initial algebras) to right adjoints (terminal objects ⊤, products ×, final coalgebras) [2,15].   □

That's enough words for the moment, *calculemus*! We will now show how to derive an alternative implementation of the *Array* type. To trieify our type of finite maps,

trieify : ∀ *elem* → ∀ *n* → (*Index n* → *elem*) ≅ *Array n elem*

we proceed by induction on the size of the array n. For the derivation, we use Wim Feijen's proof format, which features explicit justifications for the calculational steps, written between angle brackets. While the notation may be familiar, it is worth pointing out that each of our calculations is a valid Agda term, constructing the desired isomorphism. The Agda type-checker verifies that each step provides the evidence to establish the desired isomorphism. The justification for each individual step can be rather verbose: for example, the first rewrite below is justified by an isomorphism between function spaces: *dom* ≅→≅ *cod* applies the isomorphism *dom* to the domain of its function argument and *cod* to its codomain.

$trieify\ elem\ zero\ =$
   proof
     $(Index\ zero\ \rightarrow\ elem)$
   $\cong\ \langle\ Index\text{-}zero \cong \rightarrow \cong\ \cong\text{-}reflexive\ \rangle$
     $(\bot\ \rightarrow\ elem)$
   $\cong\ \langle\ law\text{-}of\text{-}exponents\text{-}\bot\ \rangle$
     $\top$
   $\cong\ \langle\ use\text{-}as\text{-}definition\text{-}of\ Array\text{-}zero\ \rangle$
     $Array\ zero\ elem$
   ∎

The calculation suggests a defining equation: $Array\ zero\ elem\ =\ \top$, which expresses that there is exactly one array of size 0, namely the empty array. For non empty arrays, the calculation is almost just as straightforward.

$trieify\ elem\ (succ\ n)\ =$
   proof
     $(Index\ (succ\ n)\ \rightarrow\ elem)$
   $\cong\langle\ Index\text{-}succ \cong \rightarrow \cong\ \cong\text{-}reflexive\ \rangle$
     $(\top \uplus Index\ n\ \rightarrow\ elem)$
   $\cong\ \langle\ law\text{-}of\text{-}exponents\text{-}\uplus\ \rangle$
     $(\top\ \rightarrow\ elem) \times (Index\ n\ \rightarrow\ elem)$
   $\cong \hat{A}_\varrho\langle\ law\text{-}of\text{-}exponents\text{-}\top \cong \times \cong\ trieify\ elem\ n\ \rangle$
     $elem \times Array\ n\ elem$
   $\cong\ \langle\ use\text{-}as\text{-}definition\text{-}of\ Array\text{-}succ\ \rangle$
     $Array\ (succ\ n)\ elem$
   ∎

The final isomorphism expresses that an array of size $1 + n$ consists of an element followed by an array of size n. If we name the constructors appropriately, we obtain the familiar datatype of lists, indexed by length. This indexed type is also known as *Vector*.

variable $elem\ :\ Set$
data $Array\ :\ Peano \rightarrow Set \rightarrow Set$ **where**
  nil $:\ Array\ zero\ elem$
  $cons\ :\ elem \rightarrow Array\ n\ elem \rightarrow Array\ (succ\ n)\ elem$

Observe that the constructors of the interface, *nil* and *cons*, are now implemented by the constructors of the datatype.

If we *extract* the two components of the *trieify* isomorphism, we obtain the following definitions of *lookup* and *tabulate*.

$$lookup \; : \; Array \; n \; elem \to (Index \; n \to elem)$$
$$lookup \; (cons \; x \; xs) \; (izero) \;\;\; = \;\; x$$
$$lookup \; (cons \; x \; xs) \; (isucc \; i) \; = \;\; lookup \; xs \; i$$

$$tabulate \; : \; (Index \; n \to elem) \to Array \; n \; elem$$
$$tabulate \; \{\, zero \,\} \quad fm \; = \;\; nil$$
$$tabulate \; \{\, succ \; n \,\} \; fm \; = \;\; cons \; (fm \; izero) \; (tabulate \; (\lambda \; i \to fm \; (isucc \; i)))$$

Like *trieify*, both *lookup* and *tabulate* are defined by induction on the size. In the case of *lookup*, the size information remains implicit as Agda is able to recreate it from the explicit argument, namely, the argument list. For *tabulate*, no such information is available. Hence, we need to match on the implicit argument explicitly in its definition.

Unfortunately, Agda's extraction process is only semi-automatic, so we do not trust the resulting code. The proofs that *lookup* and *tabulate* are inverses are, however, entirely straightforward and can be found in the accompanying material.

The equations for *head* and *tail* are immediate consequences of the specification.

$$head \; : \; Array \; (succ \; n) \; elem \; \to \; elem$$
$$head \; (cons \; x \; xs) \; = \; x$$
$$tail \; : \; Array \; (succ \; n) \; elem \; \to \; Array \; n \; elem$$
$$tail \; (cons \; x \; xs) \;\;\; = \; xs$$

Thanks to our reference implementation, see Sect. 4, the proof of correctness is a breeze: we simply show that the "concrete" operations on vectors are equivalent to their "specification" on finite maps. Defining a shortcut for the *lookup* function, $[\![\_]\!]$, the proof obligations read as follows.

$$[\![nil]\!] \equiv FM.nil \tag{3a}$$
$$[\![cons \; x \; xs]\!] \equiv FM.cons \; x \, [\![xs]\!] \tag{3b}$$
$$head \; xs \equiv FM.head \, [\![xs]\!] \tag{3c}$$
$$[\![tail \; xs]\!] \equiv FM.tail \, [\![xs]\!] \tag{3d}$$
$$lookup \; xs \equiv FM.lookup \, [\![xs]\!] \tag{3e}$$
$$[\![tabulate \; f]\!] \equiv FM.tabulate \; f \tag{3f}$$

Here we have prefixed the operations of the reference implementation of Sect. 4 by *FM*, short for 'finite map'. Recalling that *FM.lookup* and *FM.tabulate* are both the identity function, Property (3e) means that *lookup* is indeed extensionally equal to the implementation using finite maps. Conversely, as (3f) shows, the *tabulate* is the right-inverse of *lookup*, which is unique.

The vector implementation of arrays does not suffer from history-sensitivity, *tail*(*cons x xs*) is now definitionally equal to *xs*, but thanks to the ivory tower number type, it is still too slow to be useful in practice. The cure is pretty obvious: we replace unary numbers by binary numbers—albeit with a twist.

6   Leibniz Numerals

Instead of working with Peano naturals, we could choose a different implementation of the natural number type. In this section, we will explore one possible implementation, *Leibniz numbers*, or binary numbers that have a unique representation of every Peano natural number.

6.1   Number Type

A Leibniz numeral is given by a sequence of digits with the most significant digit on the left. A digit is either 1 or 2.

> ***data** Leibniz* : *Set **where***
>   *0b* : *Leibniz*
>   *_1* : *Leibniz* → *Leibniz*
>   *_2* : *Leibniz* → *Leibniz*
> *Eau-de-Cologne* = *0b* 1 1 2 1 1 2 2 1 2 1 1 1

Agda's postfix syntax allows us to mimic standard notation for binary numbers: the expression $0b\,1\,1\,2\,1$ should be read as $(((0b\,1)\,1)\,2)\,1$.

To assign a meaning to a Leibniz numeral, we map it to a Peano numeral.

> $\mathcal{N}[\![\_]\!]$: *Leibniz* → *Peano*
> $\mathcal{N}[\![\,0b\,]\!]$ = 0
> $\mathcal{N}[\![\,n\,1\,]\!]$ = $\mathcal{N}[\![\,n\,]\!] \cdot 2 + 1$
> $\mathcal{N}[\![\,n\,2\,]\!]$ = $\mathcal{N}[\![\,n\,]\!] \cdot 2 + 2$
> *assert* : $\mathcal{N}[\![\,Eau\text{-}de\text{-}Cologne\,]\!] \equiv 4711$

For example, $\mathcal{N}[\![0b\,1\,1\,2\,1]\!]$ normalizes to 17. The meaning function makes it crystal clear that we implement a base-two positional number system, except that the digits 1 and 2 are used, rather than 0 and 1.

Thanks to this twist we avoid the problem of leading zeros: every natural number enjoys a *unique* representation; the Leibniz number system is *non-redundant*. Moreover, the meaning function establishes a one-to-one correspondence between the two number systems: *Leibniz* $\cong$ *Peano*. Speaking of number conversion, the other direction of the isomorphism can be easily implemented using the "pseudo-constructors" *zero* and *succ*.

> *zero* : *Leibniz*
> *zero* = *0b*
> *succ* : *Leibniz* → *Leibniz*
> *succ* (*0b*) = *0b* 1
> *succ* (*n* 1) = *n* 2
> *succ* (*n* 2) = (*succ n*) 1   -- carry

The binary increment exhibits the typical recursion pattern: the least significant digit is incremented, unless it is maximal, in which case a carry is propagated to the left. Using the meaning function it is straightforward to show that the implementation is correct.

$$zero\text{-}correct \; : \; \mathcal{N}[\![\, Leibniz.zero \quad]\!] \equiv Peano.zero$$
$$succ\text{-}correct \; : \; \mathcal{N}[\![\, Leibniz.succ\, n\,]\!] \equiv Peano.succ\, \mathcal{N}[\![\, n\,]\!]$$

The prefix "pseudo" indicates that the operations $zero$ and $succ$ are not full-fledged constructors: we cannot use them in patterns on the left-hand side of definitions. To compensate for this, we additionally offer a *Peano view* [21,31].

data *Peano-View* : *Leibniz* → *Set* **where**
  as-zero : *Peano-View zero*
  as-succ : $(i : Leibniz)$ → *Peano-View* $(succ\, i)$

The *view* function itself illustrates the use of view patterns.

$view$: $(n : Leibniz)$ → *Peano-View n*
$view\,(0b)$ = *as-zero*
$view\,(n\,1)$ **with** $view\,n$
... | *as-zero*   = *as-succ* $0b$
... | *as-succ m* = *as-succ* $(m\,2)$ -- borrow
$view\,(n\,2)$ = *as-succ* $(n\,1)$

In a sense, *view* combines two functions: the test for zero and the predecessor function, again following the typical recursion pattern: the least significant digit is decremented, unless it is minimal, in which case we borrow one from the left.

The semantics of such a view is defined by a mapping into the Peano numerals. The correctness criterion asserts that *view* does not change the value of its argument.

$\mathcal{V}[\![\, \_\,]\!]$: *Peano-View n* → *Peano*
$\mathcal{V}[\![\, as\text{-}zero \quad]\!] = 0$
$\mathcal{V}[\![\, as\text{-}succ\, n\,]\!] = \mathcal{N}[\![\, n\,]\!] + 1$
$view\text{-}correct \; : \; \mathcal{V}[\![\, view\, n\,]\!] \equiv \mathcal{N}[\![\, n\,]\!]$

Remark 3 (Agda). You may wonder why the type *Peano-View* is indexed by a Leibniz numeral. Why not simply define:

data *Peano-View* : *Set* **where**   -- too simple-minded
  as-zero : *Peano-View*
  as-succ : *Leibniz* → *Peano-View*

In contrast to the simple, unindexed datatype above, our indexed view type keeps track of the to-be-viewed value, which turns out to be vital for correctness proofs: if $view\,n$ yields *as-succ m* then we know that n definitionally equals $succ\,m$. The constructors of the unindexed datatype do not maintain this important piece of information, so the subsequent proofs do not go through.   □

As an intermediate summary, Leibniz numerals serve as a drop-in replacement for Peano numerals: the pseudo-constructors replace *zero* and *succ* on the right-hand side of equations; the view allows us to additionally replace them in patterns on the left-hand side.

6.2   Index Type

Of course, we would like to use binary numbers for indices, as well. Therefore we need to adapt the type of positions that specifies the domain of our finite maps. The following derivation is based on the *index transformations* but, as we have noted in Sect. 3, there are, in general, several options for the witnesses of these transformations. In other words, we have to make some design decisions! In particular, since we use a binary, *positional* number system we need to inject life into the *doubling* isomorphism:

$$Index\text{-}2\text{·}n \cong Index\text{-}n \uplus Index\text{-}n \; : \; Index\,(n\,{\cdot}2) \cong Index\,n \uplus Index\,n$$

There are two canonical choices, one based on appending and a second one based on zipping or interleaving.

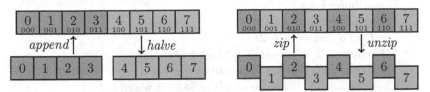

If the size is an exact power of two, halving separates the indices based on the most significant bit, whereas unzipping considers the least significant bit. (As an aside, do not be confused by the names: *append*, *zip* etc. are index transformations, not operations on arrays.) Both choices are viable, however, we choose to initially focus on the first alternative and return to the second in Sect. 12, but only briefly.

Zipping maps elements of the first summand to even indices and elements of the second to odd indices.

$$zip \; : \; Index\,n \uplus Index\,n \; \rightarrow \; Index\,(n\,{\cdot}2)$$
$$zip\,(inj_1\; i) \;=\; i\,{\cdot}2{+}0 \quad \text{-- even}$$
$$zip\,(inj_2\; i) \;=\; i\,{\cdot}2{+}1 \quad \text{-- odd}$$

Its inverse amounts to division by 2 with the remainder specifying the summand of the disjoint union.

$$unzip \; : \; Index\,(n\,{\cdot}2) \;\rightarrow\; Index\,n \uplus Index\,n$$
$$unzip\,\{\,succ\;n\,\}\,(izero) \qquad\quad = \; inj_1\; izero \quad \text{-- even}$$
$$unzip\,\{\,succ\;n\,\}\,(isucc\;izero) \;=\; inj_2\; izero \quad \text{-- odd}$$
$$unzip\,\{\,succ\;n\,\}\,(isucc\,(isucc\;i)) \; \textbf{with}\; unzip\;i$$
$$\dots \;\mid\; inj_1\; j \;=\; inj_1\,(isucc\;j)$$
$$\dots \;\mid\; inj_2\; k \;=\; inj_2\,(isucc\;k)$$

Given these prerequisites the calculation of

$$re\text{-}index \; : \; \forall\,n \;\rightarrow\; Peano.Index\,[\![\,n\,]\!] \cong Leibniz.Index\,n$$

proceeds by induction on the structure of Leibniz numerals. For the base case, there is little to do.

$$re\text{-}index\,(0b)\ =$$
$\quad\textbf{\textit{proof}}$
$\qquad Peano.Index\,[\![\,0b\,]\!]$
$\quad\cong\ \langle\ Peano.Index\text{-}zero\,\rangle$
$\qquad\bot$
$\quad\cong\ \langle\ use\text{-}as\text{-}definition\text{-}of\ Index\text{-}0\,\rangle$
$\qquad Leibniz.Index\ 0b$
$\quad\blacksquare$

The calculation for the first inductive case also works without any surprises.

$$re\text{-}index\,(n\ 1)\ =$$
$\quad\textbf{\textit{proof}}$
$\qquad Peano.Index\,[\![\,n\ 1\,]\!]$
$\quad\cong\ \langle\ Peano.Index\text{-}succ\,\rangle$
$\qquad\top\uplus Peano.Index\,([\![\,n\,]\!]\cdot 2)$
$\quad\cong\ \langle\ \cong\text{-}reflexive\cong\uplus\cong Index\text{-}2\cdot n\cong Index\text{-}n\uplus Index\text{-}n\,\rangle$
$\qquad\top\uplus Peano.Index\,[\![\,n\,]\!]\uplus Peano.Index\,[\![\,n\,]\!]$
$\quad\cong\ \langle\ \cong\text{-}reflexive\cong\uplus\cong (re\text{-}index\ n\cong\uplus\cong re\text{-}index\ n)\,\rangle$
$\qquad\top\uplus Leibniz.Index\ n\uplus Leibniz.Index\ n$
$\quad\cong\ \langle\ use\text{-}as\text{-}definition\text{-}of\ Index\text{-}1\,\rangle$
$\qquad Leibniz.Index\,(n\ 1)$
$\quad\blacksquare$

We plug in the definition of *Peano.Index*, apply the doubling isomorphism based on zipping, and finally invoke the induction hypothesis. The derivation for the final case follows exactly the same pattern, except that we unfold the definition of *Peano.Index* twice.

$$re\text{-}index\,(n\ 2)\ =$$
$\quad\textbf{\textit{proof}}$
$\qquad Peano.Index\,[\![\,n\ 2\,]\!]$
$\quad\cong\ \langle\ Peano.Index\text{-}succ\,\rangle$
$\qquad\top\uplus Peano.Index\,([\![\,n\,]\!]\cdot 2 +1)$
$\quad\cong\ \langle\ \cong\text{-}reflexive\cong\uplus\cong Peano.Index\text{-}succ\,\rangle$
$\qquad\top\uplus\top\uplus Peano.Index\,([\![\,n\,]\!]\cdot 2)$
$\quad\cong\ \langle\ \cong\text{-}reflexive\cong\uplus\cong (\cong\text{-}reflexive\cong\uplus\cong Index\text{-}2\cdot n\cong Index\text{-}n\uplus Index\text{-}n)\,\rangle$
$\qquad\top\uplus\top\uplus Peano.Index\,[\![\,n\,]\!]\uplus Peano.Index\,[\![\,n\,]\!]$
$\quad\cong\ \langle\ \cong\text{-}reflexive\cong\uplus\cong (\cong\text{-}reflexive\cong\uplus\cong (re\text{-}index\ n\cong\uplus\cong re\text{-}index\ n))\,\rangle$
$\qquad\top\uplus\top\uplus Leibniz.Index\ n\uplus Leibniz.Index\ n$
$\quad\cong\ \langle\ use\text{-}as\text{-}definition\text{-}of\ Index\text{-}2\,\rangle$
$\qquad Leibniz.Index\,(n\ 2)$
$\quad\blacksquare$

As usual, we introduce names for the summands of the disjoint unions, obtaining the following index type for Leibniz numerals. Note that these indices are not the same as the *Index* type we saw previously, indexed by a Peano number.

data *Index* : *Leibniz* → *Set* **where**

$$
\begin{array}{lll}
0b_1 : & Index\,(n\,1) & \text{-- } \top \\
\_1_1 : Index\,n \rightarrow & Index\,(n\,1) & \text{-- } \uplus Index\,n \\
\_2_1 : Index\,n \rightarrow & Index\,(n\,1) & \text{-- } \uplus Index\,n \\
0b_2 : & Index\,(n\,2) & \text{-- } \top \\
1b_2 : & Index\,(n\,2) & \text{-- } \uplus Index\,n \\
\_2_2 : Index\,n \rightarrow & Index\,(n\,2) & \text{-- } \uplus Index\,n \\
\_3_2 : Index\,n \rightarrow & Index\,(n\,2) & \text{-- } \uplus Index\,n \\
\end{array}
$$

A couple of remarks are in order. The index attached to the constructor names indicates the least significant digit of the upper bound. The constructors $0b_1$ and $0b_2$ say: "Operationally we are alike, both representing the zeroth index. However, we carry important type information, $0b_1$ lives below an odd upper bound, whereas $0b_2$ is below an even bound." The definition of the index set is perhaps not quite what we expected as it amalgamates two different number systems: the by now familiar 1-2 system and a variant that employs 0 and 1 as leading digits and 2 and 3 for non-leading digits.

Remark 4. As an aside, the 2-3 number system is also non-redundant. In general, any binary system that uses the digits $0, \ldots, a$ in the leading position and $a + 1$ and $a + 2$ for the other positions, enjoys the property that every natural number has a unique representation. □

To make the semantics of these indices precise, we extract the witness for the reverse direction of the *re-index*ing isomorphism (using *iz* and *is* as shorthands for *izero* and *isucc* on Peano indices).

$$
\begin{array}{ll}
\mathscr{I}[\![\_]\!] : Index\,n \rightarrow Peano.Index\,[\![\,n\,]\!] \\
\mathscr{I}[\![\,0b_1\,]\!] = iz \\
\mathscr{I}[\![\,i\,1_1\,]\!] = is\,(\mathscr{I}[\![\,i\,]\!]\cdot 2 + 0) \\
\mathscr{I}[\![\,i\,2_1\,]\!] = is\,(\mathscr{I}[\![\,i\,]\!]\cdot 2 + 1) \\
\mathscr{I}[\![\,0b_2\,]\!] = iz \\
\mathscr{I}[\![\,1b_2\,]\!] = is\,iz \\
\mathscr{I}[\![\,i\,2_2\,]\!] = is\,(is\,(\mathscr{I}[\![\,i\,]\!]\cdot 2 + 0)) \\
\mathscr{I}[\![\,i\,3_2\,]\!] = is\,(is\,(\mathscr{I}[\![\,i\,]\!]\cdot 2 + 1)) \\
\end{array}
$$

Just as we saw in Sect. 3, the expressions $n \cdot 2 + 1$ and $is\,(n \cdot 2 + 0)$ are quite different as they live below different upper bounds: if $j : Index\,a$, then $j \cdot 2 + 1 : Index(a \cdot 2)$, whereas $is(j \cdot 2 + 0) : Index(a \cdot 2 + 1)$. These types carry just enough information to avoid the infamous "index out of bounds" errors. While the definitions of *Index* and $\mathscr{I}[\![\_]\!]$ may seem quite bulky at first glance, they encode an essential invariant of the indices involved.

The same remark applies to the definition of *izero* and *isucc*.

$$izero \; : \; \forall \, \{\, n \,\} \; \rightarrow \; Index \, (succ \; n)$$
$$izero \, \{\, 0b \,\} \; = \; 0b_1$$
$$izero \, \{\, n\, 1 \,\} \; = \; 0b_2$$
$$izero \, \{\, n\, 2 \,\} \; = \; 0b_1$$

$$isucc \; : \; Index \; n \rightarrow Index \, (succ \; n)$$
$$isucc \, (0b_1) \; = \; 1b_2$$
$$isucc \, (i\, 1_1) \; = \; i\, 2_2$$
$$isucc \, (i\, 2_1) \; = \; i\, 3_2$$
$$isucc \, (0b_2) \; = \; izero \; 1_1$$
$$isucc \, (1b_2) \; = \; izero \; 2_1$$
$$isucc \, (i\, 2_2) \; = \; (isucc \; i) \; 1_1$$
$$isucc \, (i\, 3_2) \; = \; (isucc \; i) \; 2_1$$

The successor function maps an odd number to an even number, and vice versa, correspondingly incrementing the upper bounds. Consequently, arguments and results alternate between the two number systems. This is why $isucc(i2_2)$ yields $(isucc\, i)1_1$, rather than $i3_2$. The recursion pattern is interesting: if the argument is below an odd bound, *isucc* returns immediately; a recursive call is only made for indices that live below an even upper bound. We return to this observation in Sect. 8.

Using the meaning function we can establish the correctness of *izero* and *isucc*.

$$izero\text{-}correct \; : \; \mathscr{I}[\![\; izero \, \{\, n \,\} \;]\!] \equiv iz$$
$$isucc\text{-}correct \; : \; \mathscr{I}[\![\; isucc \; i \quad \;]\!] \equiv is \, \mathscr{I}[\![\; i \;]\!]$$

Both equations relate expressions of different types, for example, $\mathscr{I}[\![isucc\, i]\!]$: $\mathscr{N}[\![succ\, n]\!]$ whereas $is\,\mathscr{I}[\![i]\!]$: $\mathscr{N}[\![\, n\,]\!] + 1$. Fortunately, *succ-correct* tells us that both types are *propositionally* equal.[2]

You may have noticed that this section replicates the structure of Sect. 6.1. It remains to define an appropriate view on Leibniz indices.

> **data** *Index-View* : $Index \, (succ \; n) \rightarrow Set$ **where**
>   *as-izero* : $Index\text{-}View \, \{\, n \,\} \; izero$
>   *as-isucc* : $(i \; : \; Index \; n) \rightarrow Index\text{-}View \, (isucc \; i)$

The type *Index-View* is implicitly parametrized by a Leibniz numeral n and explicitly parametrized by a Leibniz index of type $Index \, (succ \; n)$. To use this view, we still need to define a function mapping (Leibniz) indices to their corresponding *Index-View*. To do so, we need to decide when a given index is zero,

---

[2] Agda correctly complains about a type mismatch as the types of the values on either side of the equation are not *definitionally* equal. This somewhat unfortunate situation can, however, be fixed with a hint of extensionality, adding *succ-correct* to Agda's definitional equality using a rewrite rule [6].

and compute the index's predecessor when it is not. The definition of the view function merits careful study.

$$iview : \{n : Leibniz\} \to (i : Index\,(succ\,n)) \to Index\text{-}View\,i$$
$$iview\,\{0b\}\,(0b_1) = as\text{-}izero$$
$$iview\,\{n\,1\}\,(0b_2) = as\text{-}izero$$
$$iview\,\{n\,1\}\,(1b_2) = as\text{-}isucc\,0b_1$$
$$iview\,\{n\,1\}\,(i\,2_2) = as\text{-}isucc\,(i\,1_1)$$
$$iview\,\{n\,1\}\,(i\,3_2) = as\text{-}isucc\,(i\,2_1)$$
$$iview\,\{n\,2\}\,(0b_1) = as\text{-}izero$$
$$iview\,\{n\,2\}\,(i\,1_1) \;\textbf{with}\; iview\,i$$

$$\cdots \qquad\qquad\quad |\; as\text{-}izero \;\;= as\text{-}isucc\,0b_2$$
$$\cdots \qquad\qquad\quad |\; as\text{-}isucc\,j = as\text{-}isucc\,(j\,2_2) \quad\text{-- borrow}$$
$$iview\,\{n\,2\}\,(i\,2_1) \;\textbf{with}\; iview\,i$$
$$\cdots \qquad\qquad\quad |\; as\text{-}izero \;\;= as\text{-}isucc\,1b_2$$
$$\cdots \qquad\qquad\quad |\; as\text{-}isucc\,j = as\text{-}isucc\,(j\,3_2) \quad\text{-- borrow}$$

Recall that the Peano view combines the test for zero and the predecessor function. The same is true of $iview$, except that arguments and results additionally alternate between the two number systems.

Finally, given the semantics of view patterns we can assert that $iview$ does not change the value of its argument.

$$\mathcal{W}[\![\_]\!] : \forall\,\{i : Index\,(succ\,n)\} \to Index\text{-}View\,i \to Peano.Index\,([\![\,n\,]\!]+1)$$
$$\mathcal{W}[\![\,as\text{-}izero\,]\!] = iz$$
$$\mathcal{W}[\![\,as\text{-}isucc\,i\,]\!] = is\,\mathcal{I}[\![\,i\,]\!]$$
$$iview\text{-}correct : (i : Index\,(succ\,n)) \to \mathcal{W}[\![\,iview\,i\,]\!] \equiv \mathcal{I}[\![\,i\,]\!]$$

7 Functions as Datastructures, Revisited

To showcase the use of our new gadgets we adapt the implementation of Sect. 4 to binary indices, setting $Array\,n\,elem = Index\,n \to elem$.

$$nil : Array\,0b\,elem$$
$$nil\,()$$

$$cons : elem \to Array\,n\,elem \to Array\,(succ\,n)\,elem$$
$$cons\,x\,xs\,i\;\textbf{with}\;iview\,i$$
$$\cdots\;|\;as\text{-}izero\;\;= x$$
$$\cdots\;|\;as\text{-}isucc\,j = xs\,j$$

$$head : Array\,(succ\,n)\,elem \to elem$$
$$head\,xs = xs\,izero$$

$$tail : Array\,(succ\,n)\,elem \to Array\,n\,elem$$
$$tail\,xs\,i = xs\,(isucc\,i)$$

As in the Peano case, "functions as datastructures" serve as our reference implementation for datastructures based on Leibniz numerals. With this specification in place, we can now try to discover a corresponding *datastructure*.

8   One-two Trees

Turning to the heart of the matter, let us trieify the type of finite maps based on binary indices.

$$trieify : \forall\, elem \to \forall\, n \to (Index\, n \to elem) \cong Array\, n\, elem$$

The strategy should be clear: as in Sect. 5, we eliminate the type of finite maps using the laws of exponents. The base case is identical to the one for lists.

> $trieify\, elem\,(0\,b) =$
> **proof**
> $(Index\,(0\,b) \to elem)$
> $\cong \langle\ Index\text{-}0 \cong\to\cong \cong\text{-}reflexive\ \rangle$
> $(\bot \to elem)$
> $\cong \langle\ law\text{-}of\text{-}exponents\text{-}\bot\ \rangle$
> $\top$
> $\cong \langle\ use\text{-}as\text{-}definition\text{-}of\, Array\text{-}0\ \rangle$
> $Array\,(0\,b)\, elem$
> ∎

The calculation for the inductive cases follows the same rhythm—we unfold the definition of *Index* and apply the laws of exponents—except that we additionally invoke the induction hypothesis.

> $trieify\, elem\,(n\,1) =$
> **proof**
> $(Index\,(n\,1) \to elem)$
> $\cong \langle\ Index\text{-}1 \cong\to\cong \cong\text{-}reflexive\ \rangle$
> $(\top \uplus Index\, n \uplus Index\, n \to elem)$
> $\cong \langle\ \cong\text{-}transitive\ law\text{-}of\text{-}exponents\text{-}\uplus$
> $(law\text{-}of\text{-}exponents\text{-}\top \cong \times \cong law\text{-}of\text{-}exponents\text{-}\uplus)\ \rangle$
> $elem \times (Index\, n \to elem) \times (Index\, n \to elem)$
> $\cong \langle\ (\cong\text{-}reflexive \cong \times \cong (trieify\, elem\, n \cong \times \cong trieify\, elem\, n))\ \rangle$
> $elem \times Array\, n\, elem \times Array\, n\, elem$
> $\cong \langle\ use\text{-}as\text{-}definition\text{-}of\, Array\text{-}1\ \rangle$
> $Array\,(n\,1)\, elem$
> ∎

The final step in the isomorphism above expresses that an array of size $n \cdot 2 + 1$ consists of an element followed by two arrays of size n. The isomorphism for arrays of size $n \cdot 2 + 2$ follows a similar pattern.

> $trieify\, elem\,(n\,2) =$
> **proof**
> $(Index\,(n\,2) \to elem)$
> $\cong \langle\ Index\text{-}2 \cong\to\cong \cong\text{-}reflexive\ \rangle$
> $(\top \uplus \top \uplus Index\, n \uplus Index\, n \to elem)$

$$\cong \langle \; \cong\text{-transitive law-of-exponents-}\uplus$$
$$(\text{law-of-exponents-}\top \cong \times \cong \text{law-of-exponents-}\uplus) \; \rangle$$
$$elem \times (\top \rightarrow elem) \times (Index\, n \uplus Index\, n \;\rightarrow\; elem)$$
$$\cong \langle \; \cong\text{-reflexive} \cong \times \cong (\text{law-of-exponents-}\top \cong \times \cong \text{law-of-exponents-}\uplus) \; \rangle$$
$$elem \times (elem \times (Index\, n \;\rightarrow\; elem) \times (Index\, n \;\rightarrow\; elem))$$
$$\cong \langle \; \cong\text{-reflexive} \cong \times \cong (\cong\text{-reflexive} \cong \times \cong$$
$$(\text{trieify elem}\, n \cong \times \cong \text{trieify elem}\, n)) \; \rangle$$
$$elem \times elem \times Array\, n\, elem \times Array\, n\, elem$$
$$\cong \langle \; \text{use-as-definition-of}\, Array\text{-}2 \; \rangle$$
$$Array\, (n\, 2)\, elem$$

∎

An array of size $n \cdot 2 + 2$ consists of two elements followed by two arrays of size n. All in all, we obtain the following datatype. Its elements are called *one-two trees*[3] for want of a better name.

variable *elem* : *Set*

data *Array* : *Leibniz* $\rightarrow$ *Set* $\rightarrow$ *Set* **where**
   Leaf   : *Array* 0 b *elem*
   $Node_1$: *elem* $\rightarrow$ *Array* n *elem* $\rightarrow$ *Array* n *elem* $\rightarrow$ *Array* (n 1) *elem*
   $Node_2$: *elem* $\rightarrow$ *elem* $\rightarrow$ *Array* n *elem* $\rightarrow$ *Array* n *elem* $\rightarrow$ *Array* (n 2) *elem*

As an aside, Agda like Haskell prefers curried data constructors over uncurried ones. The following equivalent definition that uses pairs shows more clearly that one-two trees are modelled after the 1-2 number system,

data *Array′* : *Leibniz* $\rightarrow$ *Set* $\rightarrow$ *Set* **where**
   Leaf   : *Array′* 0 b *elem*
   $Node_1$: $elem^1 \rightarrow (Array'\, n\, elem)^2 \rightarrow Array'\, (n\, 1)\, elem$
   $Node_2$: $elem^2 \rightarrow (Array'\, n\, elem)^2 \rightarrow Array'\, (n\, 2)\, elem$

where $A^1 = A$ and $A^2 = A \times A$.

Turning to the operations on one-two trees, we first extract the witnesses of the *trieify* isomorphism, obtaining human-readable definitions of *lookup* and *tabulate*.

$$lookup : Array\, n\, elem \rightarrow (Index\, n \rightarrow elem)$$
$$lookup\, (Node_1\, x_0 \quad l\, r)\, (0\, b_1) \; = \; x_0$$
$$lookup\, (Node_1\, x_0 \quad l\, r)\, (i\, 1_1) \; = \; lookup\, l\, i$$
$$lookup\, (Node_1\, x_0 \quad l\, r)\, (i\, 2_1) \; = \; lookup\, r\, i$$
$$lookup\, (Node_2\, x_0\, x_1\, l\, r)\, (0\, b_2) \; = \; x_0$$
$$lookup\, (Node_2\, x_0\, x_1\, l\, r)\, (1\, b_2) \; = \; x_1$$
$$lookup\, (Node_2\, x_0\, x_1\, l\, r)\, (i\, 2_2) \; = \; lookup\, l\, i$$
$$lookup\, (Node_2\, x_0\, x_1\, l\, r)\, (i\, 3_2) \; = \; lookup\, r\, i$$

---

[3] One-two trees are unconnected with 1-2 brother trees, an implementation of AVL trees.

The implementation of *lookup* nicely illustrates the central idea of tries, where the index serves as a path into the tree. The least significant digit selects the node component. If the component is a sub-tree, then *lookup* recurses. The diagrams below visualize the indexing scheme.

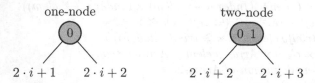

one-node   two-node

$2 \cdot i + 1 \qquad 2 \cdot i + 2 \qquad\qquad 2 \cdot i + 2 \qquad 2 \cdot i + 3$

A one-node corresponds to the digit 1, a two-node corresponds to 2. Conversely, the *tabulate* function computes the array corresponding to a given finite map.

$$
\begin{aligned}
&tabulate : (Index\ n \to elem) \to Array\ n\ elem \\
&tabulate\ \{0\,b\}\ f = Leaf \\
&tabulate\ \{n\,1\}\ f = Node_1\ (f\,0\,b_1) && (tabulate\ (\lambda\,i \to f(i\,1_1))) \\
&&& (tabulate\ (\lambda\,i \to f(i\,2_1))) \\
&tabulate\ \{n\,2\}\ f = Node_2\ (f\,0\,b_2)\ (f\,1\,b_2) && (tabulate\ (\lambda\,i \to f(i\,2_2))) \\
&&& (tabulate\ (\lambda\,i \to f(i\,3_2)))
\end{aligned}
$$

For example, $tabulate\{0b\,1121\}\,id$ yields the tree depicted below.

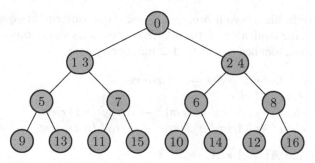

A couple of remarks are in order. By definition, one-two trees are not only *size-balanced*, they are also *height-balanced*—the height corresponds to the length of the binary representation of the size. The binary decomposition of the size fully determines the shape of the tree; all the nodes on one level have the same "shape"; the digits determine this shape from bottom to top. In the example above, $0b\,1\,1\,2\,1$ implies that the nodes on the third level (from bottom to top) are two-nodes, whereas the other nodes are one-nodes. There are 2^3 nodes on the bottom level, witnessing the weight of the most significant digit.

Turning to the size-changing operations, *cons* is based on the binary increment. Recall that *succ* alternates between odd and even numbers. Accordingly, *cons* alternates between one- and two-nodes.

$nil : Array\ zero\ elem$
$nil = Leaf$

$cons : elem \rightarrow Array\ n\ elem \rightarrow Array\ (succ\ n)\ elem$
$cons\ x_0\ (Leaf) \qquad\qquad = Node_1\ x_0\ Leaf\ Leaf$
$cons\ x_0\ (Node_1\ x_1 \qquad l\ r) = Node_2\ x_0\ x_1\ l\ r$
$cons\ x_0\ (Node_2\ x_1\ x_2\ l\ r) = Node_1\ x_0\ (cons\ x_1\ l)\ (cons\ x_2\ r)$

A one-node is turned into a two-node. Dually, a two-node becomes a one-node; the two surplus elements are pushed into the two sub-trees. Observe that the recursion pattern of *succ* dictates the recursion pattern of *cons*, that is, whether we stop or recurse. The definition of *isucc* dictates the layout of the data. For example, the first component of $Node_1$ becomes the second component of $Node_2$. You may want to view a two-node as a small buffer. Consing an element to a one-node allocates the buffer; consing a further element causes the buffer to overflow.

It is also possible to *derive* the implementation of *cons* from the specification (2a)–(2b). However, as the argument is based on positions and the *Index* type comprises seven constructors, the calculations are rather lengthy, but wholly unsurprising, so they have been relegated to Appendix A.

Figure 1 shows a succession of one-two trees obtained by consing 4, 3, 2, 1, and 0 (in this order) to $tabulate\{0b\,1\,2\,2\}\lambda i \rightarrow i + 5)$. In every second step, *cons* touches only the root node. However, every once in a while the entire tree is rewritten, corresponding to a cascading carry. In Fig. 1, this happens in the final step when a tree of size $0b\,2\,2\,2$ is turned into a tree of size $0b\,1\,1\,1\,1$.

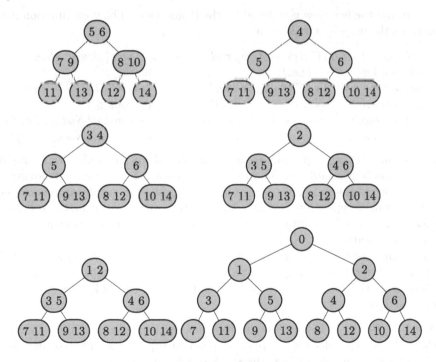

Fig. 1. One-two trees of shape $0b\,1\,2\,2$ up to $0b\,1\,1\,1\,1$.

Consequently, the *worst-case* running time of *cons* is $\Theta(n)$. However, like the binary increment, consing shows a more favourable behaviour if a sequence of operations is taken into account: *cons* runs in $\Theta(\log n)$ *amortized* time. This is less favourable than *succ*, which runs in constant amortized time. The reason is simple: for each carry *succ* makes one recursive call, whereas *cons* features two calls so a carry propagation takes time proportional to the weight of the digit. We return to this point in Sect. 10.

The operations *head* and *tail* basically undo the changes of *cons*.

$$
\begin{aligned}
&head \;:\; Array\,(succ\,n)\;elem \;\rightarrow\; elem \\
&head\,\{0b\}\;(Node_1\,x_0 \quad\;\; l\,r) \;=\; x_0 \\
&head\,\{n\,1\}\;(Node_2\,x_0\,x_1\,l\,r) \;=\; x_0 \\
&head\,\{n\,2\}\;(Node_1\,x_0 \quad\;\; l\,r) \;=\; x_0
\end{aligned}
$$

$$
\begin{aligned}
&tail \;:\; Array\,(succ\,n)\;elem \;\rightarrow\; Array\,n\;elem \\
&tail\,\{0b\}\;(Node_1\,x_0 \quad\;\; l\,r) \;=\; Leaf \\
&tail\,\{n\,1\}\;(Node_2\,x_0\,x_1\,l\,r) \;=\; Node_1\,x_1\,l\,r \\
&tail\,\{n\,2\}\;(Node_1\,x_0 \quad\;\; l\,r) \;=\; Node_2\,(head\,l)\,(head\,r)\,(tail\,l)\,(tail\,r)
\end{aligned}
$$

As an attractive alternative to these operations we also introduce a list view, analogous to the Peano view on binary numbers.

data *List-View* : *Peano-View n* $\rightarrow$ *Set* $\rightarrow$ *Set* **where**
   as-nil   : *List-View as-zero elem*
   as-cons : *elem* $\rightarrow$ *Array n elem* $\rightarrow$ *List-View* (*as-succ n*) *elem*

Observe that the list view is indexed by the Peano view. The view function itself illustrates the use of view patterns.

$$
\begin{aligned}
&list\text{-}view \;:\; \{\,n\;:\;Leibniz\,\} \;\rightarrow\; Array\,n\;elem \;\rightarrow\; List\text{-}View\,(view\,n)\;elem \\
&list\text{-}view\,\{\,n\;=\;0b\,\}\;(Leaf) &&= as\text{-}nil \\
&list\text{-}view\,\{\,n\;=\;n\,1\,\}\;(Node_1\,x_0\,l\,r)\;\textbf{with}\;view\,n\;|\;list\text{-}view\,l\;|\;list\text{-}view\,r \\
&\ldots\;|\;as\text{-}zero \quad\;\;|\;as\text{-}nil \quad\quad\;\;|\;as\text{-}nil \quad\quad = as\text{-}cons\,x_0\,r \\
&\ldots\;|\;as\text{-}succ\,m\;|\;as\text{-}cons\,x_1\,l'\;|\;as\text{-}cons\,x_2\,r' = as\text{-}cons\,x_0\,(Node_2\,x_1\,x_2\,l'\,r') \\
&list\text{-}view\,\{\,n\;=\;n\,2\,\}\;(Node_2\,x_0\,x_1\,l\,r) \quad\quad = as\text{-}cons\,x_0\,(Node_1\,x_1\,l\,r)
\end{aligned}
$$

The first and the last equation are straightforward, in particular, removing an element from a two-node yields a one-node. Following this logic, removing an element from a one-node gives a zero-node—except that our datatype does not feature this node type. Consequently, we need to borrow data from the sub-trees. To this end, a view is simultaneously placed on the size and the two sub-trees—a typical usage pattern.

The implementation of arrays using one-two trees can be shown correct with respect to our reference implementation in Sect. 7. The steps are completely analogous to the line of action in Sect. 5, but we have elided the details for reasons of space.

Remark 5 (Haskell). It is instructive to translate the Agda code into a language such as Haskell that does not support dependent types. The datatype definition is almost the same, except that the size index is dropped.

$\textbf{data}$ $\textit{Array}$ :: $\textit{Type}$ → $\textit{Type}$ $\textbf{where}$
   $\textit{Leaf}$ :: $\textit{Array elem}$
   $\textit{Node}_1$ :: $\textit{elem}$ → $\textit{Array elem}$ → $\textit{Array elem}$ → $\textit{Array elem}$
   $\textit{Node}_2$ :: $\textit{elem}$ → $\textit{elem}$ → $\textit{Array elem}$ → $\textit{Array elem}$ → $\textit{Array elem}$

If we represent the element of the index type by plain integers, then we need to translate the index patterns. This can be done in a fairly straightforward manner using guards and integer division.

$$
\begin{array}{lll}
\textit{lookup} :: \textit{Array elem} \;\to\; (\textit{Integer} \to \textit{elem}) \\
\textit{lookup} \,(\textit{Node}_1\; x_0 \quad l\, r)\, i \;\mid\; i \equiv 0 & = x_0 \\
\qquad\qquad\qquad\quad\;\mid\; i \; \textit{`mod'} \; 2 \equiv 1 & = \textit{lookup} \; l \; ((i-1) \; \textit{`div'} \; 2) \\
\qquad\qquad\qquad\quad\;\mid\; i \; \textit{`mod'} \; 2 \equiv 0 & = \textit{lookup} \; r \; ((i-2) \; \textit{`div'} \; 2) \\
\textit{lookup} \,(\textit{Node}_2\; x_0\; x_1\; l\, r)\, i \;\mid\; i \equiv 0 & = x_0 \\
\qquad\qquad\qquad\quad\;\mid\; i \equiv 1 & = x_1 \\
\qquad\qquad\qquad\quad\;\mid\; i \; \textit{`mod'} \; 2 \equiv 0 & = \textit{lookup} \; l \; ((i-2) \; \textit{`div'} \; 2) \\
\qquad\qquad\qquad\quad\;\mid\; i \; \textit{`mod'} \; 2 \equiv 1 & = \textit{lookup} \; r \; ((i-3) \; \textit{`div'} \; 2)
\end{array}
$$

A more sophisticated alternative is to replace each constructor of $\textit{Index}$ by a $\textit{pattern synonym}$ [27].

As the interface considered in this paper is rather narrow, there is no need to maintain the size of trees at run-time. However, if size information is needed, it can be computed on the fly,

$$
\begin{array}{ll}
\textit{size} :: \textit{Array elem} \to \textit{Integer} \\
\textit{size} \,(\textit{Leaf}) & = 0 \\
\textit{size} \,(\textit{Node}_1\; x_1 \quad l\, r) & = \textit{size} \; l * 2 + 1 \\
\textit{size} \,(\textit{Node}_2\; x_1\; x_2\; l\, r) & = \textit{size} \; l * 2 + 2
\end{array}
$$

in logarithmic time.   □

9   Braun Trees

The derivation of the Leibniz index type in Sect. 6.2 and its associated trie type in Sect. 8 are entirely straightforward. Too straightforward, perhaps? This section and the next highlight the decision points and investigate alternative designs.

9.1   Index Type, Revisited

The index type for $\textit{Peano numerals}$ enjoys an appealing property: its constructors look and behave like their Peano namesakes, indicated by the isomorphisms:

$$ \textit{Peano} \cong \top \uplus \textit{Peano} \qquad \textit{Index} \,(\textit{succ}\, n) \cong \top \uplus \textit{Index} \,(n)\,. $$

The same cannot be said of Leibniz indices. The indices below an even bound are based on 2-3 binary numbers, rather than the 1-2 system we started with.

$$ \textit{Leibniz} \cong \top \uplus \textit{Leibniz} \uplus \textit{Leibniz} \qquad \textit{Index} \,(n\, 2) \cong \top \uplus \top \uplus \textit{Index} \,(n) \uplus \textit{Index}(n) $$

Can we re-work the isomorphism on the right so that it has the *same shape* as the one on the left, with three constructors instead of four?

Let's calculate, revisiting the second inductive case.

$re\text{-}index\,(n\,2)\;=$
proof
  $Peano.Index\,[\![\,n\,2\,]\!]$
$\cong\;\langle\;\cong\text{-}transitive\;Index\text{-}succ\;(\cong\text{-}reflexive \cong \uplus \cong Index\text{-}succ)\;\rangle$
  $\top \uplus \top \uplus Peano.Index\,([\![\,n\,]\!]\cdot 2)$
$\cong\;\langle\;\cong\text{-}reflexive \cong \uplus \cong (\cong\text{-}reflexive \cong \uplus \cong Index\text{-}2\cdot n\cong Index\text{-}n\uplus Index\text{-}n)\;\rangle$
  $\top \uplus \top \uplus Peano.Index\,[\![\,n\,]\!] \uplus Peano.Index\,[\![\,n\,]\!]$

At this point, we have applied the induction hypothesis in the original derivation. An alternative is to first join the second and third summands of the disjoint union, applying the re-indexing law *Index-succ* backwards from right to left.

$\cong\;\langle\;\cong\text{-}reflexive \cong \uplus \cong \cong\text{-}symmetric\; \uplus\text{-}associative\;\rangle$
  $\top \uplus (\top \uplus Peano.Index\,[\![\,n\,]\!]) \uplus Peano.Index\,[\![\,n\,]\!]$
$\cong\;\langle\;\cong\text{-}reflexive \cong \uplus \cong (\cong\text{-}symmetric\;Index\text{-}succ \cong \uplus \cong \cong\text{-}reflexive)\;\rangle$
  $\top \uplus Peano.Index\,(Peano.succ\,[\![\,n\,]\!]) \uplus Peano.Index\,[\![\,n\,]\!]$
$\cong\;\langle\;(\cong\text{-}reflexive \cong \uplus \cong$
    $(\cong\text{-}congruence\;Peano.Index\,(symmetric\;succ\text{-}correct)$
    $\cong \uplus \cong \cong\text{-}reflexive))\;\rangle$
  $\top \uplus Peano.Index\,[\![\,Leibniz.succ\,n\,]\!] \uplus Peano.Index\,[\![\,n\,]\!]$
$\cong\;\langle\;\cong\text{-}reflexive \cong \uplus \cong (re\text{-}index\,(succ\,n) \cong \uplus \cong re\text{-}index\,n)\;\rangle$
  $\top \uplus Leibniz.Index\,(Leibniz.succ\,n) \uplus Leibniz.Index\,n$
$\cong\;\langle\;use\text{-}as\text{-}definition\text{-}of\;Index\text{-}2\;\rangle$
  $Leibniz.Index\,(n\,2)$
∎

Voilà Naming the anonymous summands, we arrive at the following, alternative index type for Leibniz numerals.

data $Index\;:\;Leibniz \rightarrow Set$ **where**
  $0b_1\;:\qquad\qquad\quad Index\,(n\,1)$
  $\_1_1\;:\;Index\,n\qquad \rightarrow Index\,(n\,1)$
  $\_2_1\;:\;Index\,n\qquad \rightarrow Index\,(n\,1)$
  $0b_2\;:\qquad\qquad\quad Index\,(n\,2)$
  $\_1_2\;:\;Index\,(succ\,n) \rightarrow Index\,(n\,2)$
  $\_2_2\;:\;Index\,n\qquad \rightarrow Index\,(n\,2)$

The datatype features two identical sets of constructors, one for indices below an odd upper bound and a second for indices below an even upper bound.

Having changed the index type, we need to adapt the operations on indices.

$$izero \; : \; Index \, (succ \; n)$$
$$izero \, \{ 0\,b \} \;\; = \;\; 0\,b_1$$
$$izero \, \{ n\,1 \} \;\; = \;\; 0\,b_2$$
$$izero \, \{ n\,2 \} \;\; = \;\; 0\,b_1$$
$$isucc \; : \; Index \; n \rightarrow Index \, (succ \; n)$$
$$isucc \, \{ n\,1 \} \, (0\,b_1) \;\; = \;\; izero \; 1_2$$
$$isucc \, \{ n\,1 \} \, (i\,1_1) \;\; = \;\; i\,2_2$$
$$isucc \, \{ n\,1 \} \, (i\,2_1) \;\; = \;\; (isucc \; i) \; 1_2$$
$$isucc \, \{ n\,2 \} \, (0\,b_2) \;\; = \;\; izero \; 1_1$$
$$isucc \, \{ n\,2 \} \, (i\,1_2) \;\; = \;\; i\,2_1$$
$$isucc \, \{ n\,2 \} \, (i\,2_2) \;\; = \;\; (isucc \; i) \; 1_1$$

If we ignore the subscripts, the first three clauses of the successor function are identical to the last three clauses. Operationally, the constructors 1_1 and 1_2 are treated in exactly the same way. This is precisely what we have hoped for! (At the risk of dwelling on the obvious, even though the definition of *isucc* seems repetitive, it is not: the proofs relating the indices to their upper bounds are quite different.)

9.2 Trie Type, Revisited

The new index type gives rise to a new trie type. We only need to adapt the trieification for the second inductive case: $n2$. As in the original derivation, the steps are entirely straightforward—nothing surprising here. ï̈ż£

$$trieify \; elem \, (n\,2) \;\; =$$
$$\quad \textbf{proof}$$
$$\qquad (Index \, (n\,2) \;\; \rightarrow \;\; elem)$$
$$\cong \langle \; Index\text{-}2 \cong \rightarrow \cong \; \cong\text{-}reflexive \; \rangle$$
$$\qquad (\top \uplus Index \, (succ \; n) \uplus Index \; n \;\; \rightarrow \;\; elem)$$
$$\cong \langle \; \cong\text{-}transitive \; law\text{-}of\text{-}exponents\text{-}\uplus$$
$$\qquad\qquad (law\text{-}of\text{-}exponents\text{-}\top \cong \times \cong law\text{-}of\text{-}exponents\text{-}\uplus) \; \rangle$$
$$\qquad elem \times (Index \, (succ \; n) \;\; \rightarrow \;\; elem) \times (Index \; n \;\; \rightarrow \;\; elem)$$
$$\cong \langle \; (\cong\text{-}reflexive \cong \times \cong (trieify \; elem \, (succ \; n) \cong \times \cong trieify \; elem \; n)) \; \rangle$$
$$\qquad elem \times Array \, (succ \; n) \; elem \times Array \; n \; elem$$
$$\cong \langle \; use\text{-}as\text{-}definition\text{-}of \; Array\text{-}2 \; \rangle$$
$$\qquad Array \, (n\,2) \; elem$$
$$\quad \blacksquare$$

Using this isomorphism, we obtain a variation of the 1–2 trees we constructed previously. Once again, we have three constructors, one for each constructor of the *Leibniz* data type; we have added a subscript attached to the node constructors to indicate the least significant digit of the upper bound (1 or 2). The pattern of computing such datastructures should now be familiar.

data $Array : Leibniz \rightarrow Set \rightarrow Set$ **where**
   $Leaf \quad : Array\,0b\;elem$
   $Node_1 : elem \rightarrow Array\,n \qquad elem \rightarrow Array\,n\;elem \rightarrow Array\,(n\,1)\;elem$
   $Node_2 : elem \rightarrow Array\,(succ\,n)\;elem \rightarrow Array\,n\;elem \rightarrow Array\,(n\,2)\;elem$

A moment's reflection reveals that we have rediscovered *Braun trees* [4,17]. Recall that the size of a Braun tree determines its shape: a Braun tree of odd size $(n1)$ consists of two sub-trees of the same size; in a Braun tree of even, non-zero size $(n2)$ the left sub-tree is one element larger. As an aside, the property that the size determines the shape is shared by all our implementations of flexible arrays. It is a consequence of the fact that the container types are based on *non-redundant* number systems.

Similar to one-two threes, erm, trees, Braun trees feature two constructors for non-empty trees. However, in contrast to one-two trees, indexing is the same for both constructors. This becomes apparent if we extract the witnesses from the *trieify* ismorphism.

$lookup : Array\,n\;elem \rightarrow (Index\,n \rightarrow elem)$
$lookup\,(Node_1\,x_0\,l\,r)\,(0b_1) \;=\; x_0$
$lookup\,(Node_1\,x_0\,l\,r)\,(i\,1_1) \;=\; lookup\,l\,i$
$lookup\,(Node_1\,x_0\,l\,r)\,(i\,2_1) \;=\; lookup\,r\,i$
$lookup\,(Node_2\,x_0\,l\,r)\,(0b_2) \;=\; x_0$
$lookup\,(Node_2\,x_0\,l\,r)\,(i\,1_2) \;=\; lookup\,l\,i$
$lookup\,(Node_2\,x_0\,l\,r)\,(i\,2_2) \;=\; lookup\,r\,i$

We make the same observation as for the successor function: if we ignore the subscripts, the first three clauses are identical to the last three clauses. In other words, the same indexing scheme applies to both varieties of inner nodes:

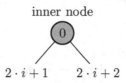

The definition of *tabulate* is similarly repetitive.

$tabulate : (Index\,n \rightarrow elem) \rightarrow Array\,n\;elem$
$tabulate\,\{0b\}\;f \;=\; Leaf$
$tabulate\,\{n\,1\}\;f \;=\; Node_1\,(f\,0b_1)\,(tabulate\,(\lambda\,i \rightarrow f(i\,1_1)))$
$\qquad\qquad\qquad\qquad\qquad (tabulate\,(\lambda\,i \rightarrow f(i\,2_1)))$
$tabulate\,\{n\,2\}\;f \;=\; Node_2\,(f\,0b_2)\,(tabulate\,(\lambda\,i \rightarrow f(i\,1_2)))$
$\qquad\qquad\qquad\qquad\qquad (tabulate\,(\lambda\,i \rightarrow f(i\,2_2)))$

For example, the call $tabulate\{0b1121\}id$ yields the Braun tree shown below.

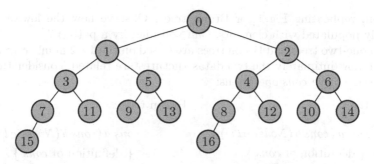

Here we observe the effect of the re-indexing isomorphism based on zipping or interleaving, see Sect. 6.2. Elements at odd positions are located in the left subtree, elements at even, non-zero positions in the right sub-tree.

There is, however, one problem with this definition. The $Node_2$ constructor has two subtrees: one of size n, the other of size $succ\,n$. As a result, the (implicit) Leibniz number passed implicitly to the *tabulate* function is not obviously decreasing: one call is passed n; the other is passed $succ\,n$. While the latter represents a smaller natural number, it is not a structurally smaller recursive call. As a result, Agda rejects this definition as it stands. There is a reasonably straightforward argument that we can make to guarantee termination—even if the recursion is not structural, it is well-founded: each recursive call is performed on a structurally smaller Peano number. In the remainder of this section, we will ignore such termination issues.

As before, the indexing scheme determines the implementation of the size-changing operations.

$$nil\ :\ Array\ zero\ elem$$
$$nil\ =\ Leaf$$

$$cons\ :\ elem \to Array\ n\ elem \to Array\ (succ\ n)\ elem$$
$$cons\ x_0\ (Leaf)\qquad\quad =\ Node_1\ x_0\ Leaf\ Leaf$$
$$cons\ x_0\ (Node_1\ x_1\ l\ r)\ =\ Node_2\ x_0\ (cons\ x_1\ r)\ l$$
$$cons\ x_0\ (Node_2\ x_1\ l\ r)\ =\ Node_1\ x_0\ (cons\ x_1\ r)\ l$$

$$head\ :\ Array\ (succ\ n)\ elem\ \to\ elem$$
$$head\,\{\,0\,b\}\ \ (Node_1\ x_0\ l\ r)\ =\ x_0$$
$$head\,\{\,n\,1\}\ (Node_2\ x_0\ l\ r)\ =\ x_0$$
$$head\,\{\,n\,2\}\ (Node_1\ x_0\ l\ r)\ =\ x_0$$

$$tail\ :\ Array\ (succ\ n)\ elem\ \to\ Array\ n\ elem$$
$$tail\,\{\,0\,b\}\ \ (Node_1\ x_0\ l\ r)\ =\ Leaf$$
$$tail\,\{\,n\,1\}\ (Node_2\ x_0\ l\ r)\ =\ Node_1\ (head\ l)\ r\ (tail\ l)$$
$$tail\,\{\,n\,2\}\ (Node_1\ x_0\ l\ r)\ =\ Node_2\ (head\ l)\ r\ (tail\ l)$$

Consider the definition of *cons*. Both recursive calls of *cons* are applied to the right sub-tree, additionally swapping left and right subtrees. Of course! Adding an element to the front requires re-indexing: elements that were at even positions before are now located at odd positions, and vice versa. Figure 2 shows *cons* in action, replicating Fig. 1 for Braun trees. Observe how the lowest level is gradually populated with elements. Can you identify a pattern?

Both one-two trees and Braun trees are based on the $1-2$ number system. To illustrate how intimately the two datastructures are related, consider the effect of two consecutive *cons* operations:

one-two trees:

$$cons\ a\,(cons\ b\,(Node_1\ c\,l\,r))$$
$$\equiv\ \ \{\ \text{definition of } cons\ \}$$
$$cons\ a\,(Node_2\ b\,c\,l\,r)$$
$$\equiv\ \ \{\ \text{definition of } cons\ \}$$
$$Node_1\ a\,(cons\ b\ l)\,(cons\ c\ r)$$

Braun trees:

$$cons\ a\,(cons\ b\,(Node_1\ c\,l\,r))$$
$$\equiv\ \ \{\ \text{definition of } cons\ \}$$
$$cons\ a\,(Node_2\ b\,(cons\ c\ r)\ l)$$
$$\equiv\ \ \{\ \text{definition of } cons\ \}$$
$$Node_1\ a\,(cons\ b\ l)\,(cons\ c\ r)$$

One-two trees may be characterized as *lazy Braun trees*: the first *cons* operation is in a sense delayed with the data stored in a two-node. The next *cons* forces the delayed call, issuing two recursive calls. By contrast, *cons* for Braun trees recurses immediately, but makes only a single call. However, after two steps— swapping the sub-trees twice—the net effect is the same. The strategy, lazy or

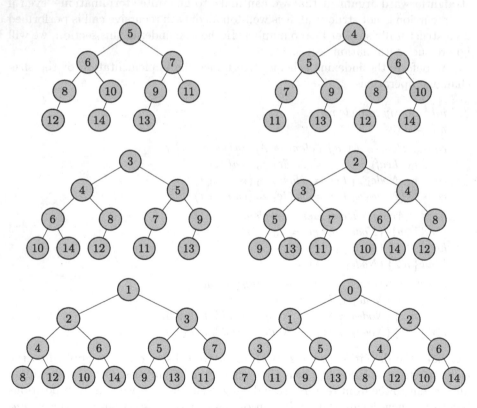

Fig. 2. Braun trees of shape $0\,b\,1\,2\,2$ up to $0\,b\,1\,1\,1\,1$.

eager, determines the performance: *cons* for Braun trees has a *worst-case* running time of $\Theta(\log n)$, whereas *cons* for one-two trees achieves the logarithmic time bound only in an *amortized* sense.

In this paper, we focus on one-sided flexible arrays. Braun trees are actually more flexible (pun intended) as they also support extension at the rear—they implement *two-sided flexible arrays*. Through the lens of the interface, *cons* and *snoc*[4] are perfectly symmetric. However, due to the layout of the data, their implementation for Braun trees is quite different. If an element is attached to the front, the positions, odd or even, of the original elements change: sub-trees must be swapped. By contrast, if an element is added to the rear, nothing changes: the sub-trees must stay in place. Depending on the size of the array, the position of the new element is either located in the left or in the right sub-tree, see Fig. 2. Staring at the sequence of trees, the position of the last element, the number 14, may appear slightly chaotic. Perhaps this is worth a closer look. Consider the diagram on the left below. The numbers indicate the order in which the positions on the lowest level are filled.

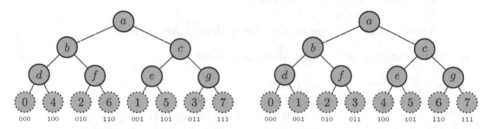

By contrast, the diagram on the right displays the "standard", left-to-right ordering. Comparing the diagrams, we observe that the positions of corresponding nodes are bit-reversals of each other, for example, position $0 = (110)_2$ on the left corresponds to $3 = (011)_2$ on the right. The reason is probably clear by now: the layout of Braun trees is based on zipping (indexing LSB first), whereas the "standard" layout is based on appending (indexing MSB first).

Turning to the implementation of *snoc*, the code is pretty straightforward since the data constructors carry the required size information: if the original size is odd, the element is added to the left sub-tree, if the size is even, it is added to the right sub-tree.

$$
\begin{aligned}
snoc &: Array\ n\ elem \rightarrow elem \rightarrow Array\ (succ\ n)\ elem \\
snoc\ (Leaf) \quad x_n &= Node_1\ x_n\ Leaf\ Leaf \\
snoc\ (Node_1\ x_0\ l\ r)\ x_n &= Node_2\ x_0\ (snoc\ l\ x_n)\ r \\
snoc\ (Node_2\ x_0\ l\ r)\ x_n &= Node_1\ x_0\ l\ (snoc\ r\ x_n\ )
\end{aligned}
$$

As the relative order of $x_0, l, r,$ and x_n must not be changed, each equation is actually forced upon us! (The power of dependent types is particularly tangible if the code is developed interactively.)

---

[4] It is customary to call the extension at the rear *snoc*, which is *cons* written backwards.

The implementation of *snoc* shows that the cases for $Node_1$ and $Node_2$ are not necessarily equal! This has consequences when porting the code to non-dependently typed languages such as Haskell—depending on the interface explicit size information may or may not be necessary.

Remark 6 (Haskell). Continuing the discussion of Remark 5, let us again translate Agda into Haskell code. The implementation of *snoc* has demonstrated that we cannot simply identify $Node_1$ and $Node_2$. For a Haskell implementation there are at least three options:

- we identify the constructors $Node_1$ and $Node_2$ but maintain explicit size information, either locally in each node or globally for the entire tree; or
- we identify the two constructors and recreate the size information on the fly—this can be done in $\Theta(\log^2 n)$ time [23]; or
- we faithfully copy the Agda code at the cost of some code duplication.

If we rather arbitrarily select the second option,

```
data Array :: Type → Type where
  Leaf :: Array elem
  Node :: elem → Array elem → Array elem → Array elem
```

the implementation of *lookup* is short and sweet,

```
lookup :: Array elem → (Integer → elem)
lookup (Node x₀ l r) i | i ≡ 0          = x₀
                       | i 'mod' 2 ≡ 1  = lookup l ((i - 1) 'div' 2)
                       | i 'mod' 2 ≡ 0  = lookup r ((i - 2) 'div' 2)
```

whereas the definition of *snoc* is more involved. ïż£

```
snoc Array a → a → Array a
snoc xs xₙ = put xs (size xs)
  where put (Leaf)      n     = Node xₙ Leaf Leaf
        put (Node a l r) n
            | n 'mod' 2 ≡ 1 = Node a (put l ((n - 1) 'div' 2)) r
            | n 'mod' 2 ≡ 0 = Node a l (put r ((n - 2) 'div' 2))
```

Unfortunately, the running time of *snoc* degrades to $\Theta(\log^2 n)$, as it is dominated by the initial call to *size*.   □

10   Random-Access Lists

Both one-two trees and Braun trees are based on the binary 1-2 number system: the types are tries for (two different) index sets; the operations are based on the arithmetic operations. Alas, as already noted, the operations on sequences do not quite achieve the efficiency of their arithmetic counterparts. While the binary increment runs in constant time (in an amortized sense), consing takes logarithmic time (amortized for one-two trees and worst-case for Braun trees).

The culprit is easy to identify: the *cons* operation makes two recursive calls for each carry (eagerly or lazily), whereas *incr* makes do with only one. There are two recursive calls as we introduced two recursive sub-trees when we invoked (an instance of) the sum law during triefication, see Sect. 8:

$$law\text{-}of\text{-}exponents\text{-}\uplus : (A \times 2 \to X) \cong (A \to X)^2$$

where $A \times 2 = A \uplus A$ and $A^2 = A \times A$. The isomorphism states that a finite map whose domain has an even size can be represented by two maps whose domains have half the size. If you know the laws of exponents by heart, then you may realize that this is not the only option. Alternatively, we could replace the finite map by a single map that yields pairs. The formal property is a combination of the product rule also known as currying, $law - of - exponents - \times$, and the sum rule:

$$law\text{-}of\text{-}exponents\text{-}sq : (A \times 2 \to X) \cong (A \to X^2)$$

Building on this isomorphism the triefication of the *original* index set of Sect. 6.2 proceeds as follows.

$trieify\ elem\ (n\ 1)\ =$
proof
  $(Index\ (n\ 1)\ \to\ elem)$
$\cong\ \langle\ Index\text{-}1 \cong \to \cong \cong\text{-}reflexive\ \rangle$
  $(\top \uplus (Index\ n \times 2)\ \to\ elem)$
$\cong\ \langle\ law\text{-}of\text{-}exponents\text{-}\uplus\ \rangle$
  $(\top \to elem) \times (Index\ n \times 2 \to elem)$
$\cong\ \langle\ law\text{-}of\text{-}exponents\text{-}\top \cong \times \cong law\text{-}of\text{-}exponents\text{-}sq\ \rangle$
  $elem \times (Index\ n \to\ elem^2)$
$\cong\ \langle\ \cong\text{-}reflexive \cong \times \cong trieify\ (elem^2)\ n\ \rangle$
  $elem \times Array\ n\ (elem^2)$
$\cong\ \langle\ use\text{-}as\text{-}definition\text{-}of\ Array\text{-}1\ \rangle$
  $Array\ (n\ 1)\ elem$
  ∎

A similar calculation yields $Array(n2)elem \cong elem \times elem \times Array\ n(elem^2)$ for the second inductive case.

All in all, we obtain the following datatype, which is known as the type of *binary, random-access lists*.

data $Array\ :\ Leibniz \to Set \to Set$ **where**
  $Nil\ :\ Array\ 0\ b\ elem$
  $One\ :\ elem\ \qquad\qquad \to\ Array\ n\ (elem \times elem)\ \to\ Array\ (n\ 1)\ elem$
  $Two\ :\ elem\ \to\ elem\ \to\ Array\ n\ (elem \times elem)\ \to\ Array\ (n\ 2)\ elem$

If we wish to emphasize that our new array type is modelled after the $1 - 2$ system, we might prefer the following equivalent definition:

> **data** $Array'$: $Leibniz \rightarrow Set \rightarrow Set$ **where**
> Nil : $Array'\ 0b\ elem$
> One : $elem^1 \rightarrow Array'\ n\,(elem^2) \rightarrow Array'\ (n\,1)\ elem$
> Two : $elem^2 \rightarrow Array'\ n\,(elem^2) \rightarrow Array'\ (n\,2)\ elem$

where $A^1 = A$ and $A^2 = A \times A$.

Two remarks are in order. First, our binary numbers are written with the most significant digit on the left. For the array types above, we have reversed the order of bits, as this corresponds to the predominant, left-to-right reading order. Second, our final implementation of arrays is a so-called *nested datatype* [3], where the element type changes at each level. Indeed, a random-access list can be seen as a standard list, except that it contains an element, a pair of elements, a pair of pairs of elements, and so forth. Nested datatypes are also known as non-uniform datatypes [19] or non-regular datatypes [26].

The rest is probably routine by now. As usual, we extract the witnesses of the *trieify* isomorphism, *lookup* and *tabulate*.

> $lookup$: $Array\ n\ elem \rightarrow (Index\ n \rightarrow elem)$
> $lookup\,(One\ x_0 \quad xs)\,(0\,b_1) = x_0$
> $lookup\,(One\ x_0 \quad xs)\,(i\,1_1) = proj_1\,(lookup\ xs\ i)$
> $lookup\,(One\ x_0 \quad xs)\,(i\,2_1) = proj_2\,(lookup\ xs\ i)$
> $lookup\,(Two\ x_0\ x_1\ xs)\,(0\,b_2) = x_0$
> $lookup\,(Two\ x_0\ x_1\ xs)\,(1\,b_2) = x_1$
> $lookup\,(Two\ x_0\ x_1\ xs)\,(i\,2_2) = proj_1\,(lookup\ xs\ i)$
> $lookup\,(Two\ x_0\ x_1\ xs)\,(i\,3_2) = proj_2\,(lookup\ xs\ i)$
>
> $tabulate$: $(Index\ n \rightarrow elem) \rightarrow Array\ n\ elem$
> $tabulate\,\{0b\}\ f = Nil$
> $tabulate\,\{n\,1\}\ f = One\,(f\,0\,b_1) \qquad (tabulate\,(\lambda\,i \rightarrow f(i\,1_1)\,, f(i\,2_1)))$
> $tabulate\,\{n\,2\}\ f = Two\,(f\,0\,b_2)\,(f\,1\,b_2)\,(tabulate\,(\lambda\,i \rightarrow f(i\,2_2)\,, f(i\,3_2)))$

The call $tabulate\{0b1121\}id$ yields the random-access list shown below.

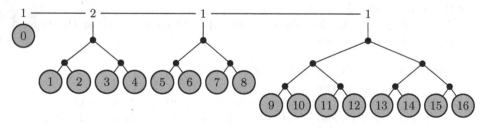

Now the elements appear sequentially from left to right. But wait! Isn't our indexing scheme based on interleaving rather than appending as set out in Sect. 6.2? This is probably worth a closer look. Let us define a variant of *lookup* that takes its two arguments in reverse order and works on the primed variants of our arrays, defined on the previous page.

$access\ :\ Index\ n \rightarrow Array'\ n\ elem \rightarrow elem$
$access\ i\ t\ =\ lookup\ t\ i$

If we compare the implementation of $access$ for one-two trees

$access\ (i\ 1_1)\ (Node_1\ x_0\ xs)\ =\ access\ i\ (proj_1\ xs)$

to the one for random-access lists, If we compare the implementation of $access$ for one-two trees

$access\ (i\ 1_1)\ (One\ x_0\ xs)\ =\ proj_1\ (access\ i\ xs)$

we make an interesting observation. The two projection functions are composed in a different order: $access\ i \cdot proj_1$ versus $proj_1 \cdot access\ i$. Of course! This reflects the change in the organisation of data: we have replaced a pair of sub-trees by a sub-tree of pairs. In more detail, the k-th tree of a random-access list corresponds to the k-th level of a one-two tree. As the access order is reversed, the corresponding sequences are bit-reversal permutations of each other. Consider, for example, the lowest level: 9 13 11 15 10 14 12 16 (one-two tree) is the bit-reversal permutation of 9 10 11 12 13 14 15 16 (random-access list).

It is time to reap the harvest. Since our new datastructure is list-like, $cons$ makes do with one recursive call.

$cons\ :\ elem\ \rightarrow\ Array\ n\ elem\ \rightarrow\ Array\ (succ\ n)\ elem$
$cons\ x_0\ (Nil)\qquad\qquad =\ One\ x_0\ Nil$
$cons\ x_0\ (One\ x_1\quad xs)\ =\ Two\ x_0\ x_1\ xs$
$cons\ x_0\ (Two\ x_1\ x_2\ xs)\ =\ One\ x_0\ (cons\ (x_1\ ,\ x_2)\ xs)$

The implementation is truly modelled after the binary increment. This entails, in particular, that $cons$ runs in constant amortized time. Figure 3 shows $cons$ in action, mirroring Figs. 1 and 2. The drawings nicely reflect that a 2 of weight 2^k is equivalent to a 1 of weight 2^{k+1}, see first and third diagram.

If we flip the equations for $cons$, we obtain implementations of $head$ and $tail$.

$head\ :\ Array\ (succ\ n)\ elem\ \rightarrow\ elem$
$head\ \{0b\}\ (One\ x_0\quad xs)\ =\ x_0$
$head\ \{n\ 1\}\ (Two\ x_0\ x_1\ xs)\ =\ x_0$
$head\ \{n\ 2\}\ (One\ x_0\quad xs)\ =\ x_0$

$tail\ :\ Array\ (succ\ n)\ elem\ \rightarrow\ Array\ n\ elem$
$tail\ \{0b\}\ (One\ x_0\quad xs)\ =\ Nil$
$tail\ \{n\ 1\}\ (Two\ x_0\ x_1\ xs)\ =\ One\ x_1\ xs$
$tail\ \{n\ 2\}\ (One\ x_0\quad xs)\ =\ Two\ (proj_1\ (head\ xs))\ (proj_2\ (head\ xs))\ (tail\ xs)$

Observe that we need to make the implicit size arguments explicit, so that Agda is able to distinguish between a singleton array, first equation, and an array that contains at least three elements, third equation. We leave the definition of a suitable list view as the obligatory exercise to the reader (the solution can be found in the accompanying material).

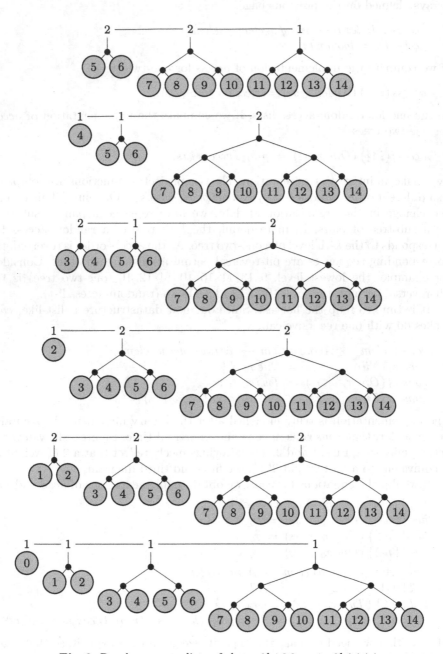

Fig. 3. Random-access lists of shape $0b\,1\,2\,2$ up to $0b\,1\,1\,1\,1$.

Remark 7 (Haskell). Translating the Agda code to Haskell poses little problems as Haskell supports nested datatypes,

```
data Array :: Type → Type where
  Nil  :: Array elem
  One :: elem →           Array (elem, elem) → Array elem
  Two :: elem → elem → Array (elem, elem) → Array elem
```

and the definition of recursive functions over them.

$$
\begin{aligned}
&lookup :: Array\ elem \ \rightarrow\ (Integer \ \rightarrow\ elem)\\
&lookup\ (One\ x_0 \quad xs)\ i\ |\ i \equiv 0 \qquad\qquad = x_0\\
&\qquad\qquad\qquad\quad |\ i\ 'mod'\ 2 \equiv 1 = fst\ (lookup\ xs\ ((i\text{-}1)\ 'div'\ 2))\\
&\qquad\qquad\qquad\quad |\ i\ 'mod'\ 2 \equiv 0 = snd\ (lookup\ xs\ ((i\text{-}2)\ 'div'\ 2))\\
&lookup\ (Two\ x_0\ x_1\ xs)\ i\ |\ i \equiv 0 \qquad\qquad = x_0\\
&\qquad\qquad\qquad\quad |\ i \equiv 1 \qquad\qquad = x_1\\
&\qquad\qquad\qquad\quad |\ i\ 'mod'\ 2 \equiv 0 = fst\ (lookup\ xs\ ((i\text{-}2)\ 'div'\ 2))\\
&\qquad\qquad\qquad\quad |\ i\ 'mod'\ 2 \equiv 1 = snd\ (lookup\ xs\ ((i\text{-}3)\ 'div'\ 2))
\end{aligned}
$$

Note that the definition is not typable in a standard Hindley-Milner system as the recursive call has type $Array(elem, elem) \rightarrow (Integer \rightarrow (elem, elem))$, which is a substitution instance of the declared type. The target language must support *polymorphic recursion* [22]. As typability in this system is undecidable [10], Haskell requires the programmer to provide an explicit type signature. □

Random-access lists outperform one-two trees and Braun trees. But, all that glitters is not gold: unlike their rival implementations, random-access lists do not support a *snoc* operation, extending the end of an array. For this added flexibility, we could "symmetrize" the design. The point of departure is a slightly weird number system that features two least significant digits, one at the front and another one at the rear. Inventing some syntax, $1\langle 2\langle 0\rangle 1\rangle 1$, for example, represents $1 + 2 \cdot (2 + 2 \cdot 0 + 1) + 1 = 8$. If we trieify a suitable index type based on this number system, we obtain so-called *finger trees* [5,16]. But that's a story to be told elsewhere.

11   Related Work

We are, of course, not the first to observe the connection between number systems and purely functional datastructures. This observation can be traced as far back as early work by Okasaki [24] and Hinze [11,13]. Indeed, Okasaki writes *"data structures that can be cast as numerical representations are surprisingly common, but only rarely is the connection to a number system noted explicitly"*. This paper tries to provide a framework for making this connection explicit.

Nor are not the first to propose such a framework. McBride's work on *orna-ments* describes how to embellish a data type with additional information—and even how to transport functions over one data type to work on its ornamented extension. Typical examples include showing how lists arise from decorating natural numbers with additional information; vectors arise from indexing lists with their length. Ko and Gibbons [18] have shown how these ideas can be applied to describe how binomial heaps arise as *ornaments* on binary numbers. Similarly, binary random-access lists can be implemented systematically in Agda by indexing with a slight variaton of the binary numbers used in this paper [29]. Instead of using the Leibniz numbers presented here, this construction uses a more traditional 'list of bits' to represent binary numbers. The resulting representation is no longer unique, leading to many different representations of zero—and the empty binary random access list accordingly. Without such unique a representation, the isomorphisms described in this paper do not hold. This situation is typical in *data refinement* [25], where isomorphisms may form too strong a requirement for certain derivations to hold.

The datastructures described in this paper are instances of so-called *Napierian functors* [9], more commonly know as *representable functors*. By design each of our datastructures is isomorphic to a functor of the form $P \to A$, for some (fixed) type of positions P. Indeed, this is the key *lookup-tabulate* isomorphism that we use to calculate the different datastructures throughout this paper. Gibbons's work on Napierian functors was driven by describing APL and enforcing size invariants in multiple dimensions. Although quad trees built from binary numbers are briefly mentioned, the different datastructures that can be calculated using positions built from binary numbers remains largely unexplored.

Nor are we the first to explore type isomorphisms. DiCosmo gives an overview of the field in his survey article [7]; Hinze and James have previously shown how to adapt an equational reasoning style to type isomorphisms, using a few principles from category theory. Recent work on *homotopy type theory* [30], where isomorphic types are guaranteed to be equivalent, might facilitate some of the derivations done in this paper, especially when establishing that operations such as *cons* are respected across isomorphic implementations [20].

There is a great deal of literature on datatype generic tries [12,14,15]. These tries exploit the same laws of exponentiation that we have used in this paper. Typically, these tries are used for memoising computations, trading time for space, whereas this paper uses the same laws in a novel context: the derivation of datastructures. These datatype generic tries have appeared in the context of dependent types when recognising languages [1,8] and memoising computations [28]—but their usage is novel in this context.

12 Conclusion

This paper has uncovered several well known datastructures in a new way. The key technology—tries, number representations, and type isomorphisms—have been known for decades, yet the connection between isomorphic implementations of datastructures has never been made this explicitly. In doing so, we open the door for further derivations and exploration. The traditional $0 - 1$ number system for binary numbers, for example, will lead to a derivation of zero-one trees, leaf-oriented Braun trees, or $0-1$ random-access lists. Providing a *generic* solution, however, where the shift in number representation automatically computes new datastructures, remains a subject for further work. Similarly, we have chosen to restrict ourselves to a single size dimension—an obvious question now arises how these results may be extended to handle matrices and richer nested datastructures.

Acknowledgements. We would like to thank Markus Heinrich for our discussions in the early stages of this work and his help in formalising several Agda proofs. Clare Martin and Colin Runciman gave invaluable feedback on an early draft.

A   Deriving Operations

The definition of *cons* for one-two trees can be systematically inferred using the abstraction function $[\![\_]\!] = lookup$ that maps one-two trees to finite maps. The types dictate that *cons* applied to a one-node returns a two-node, so we need to solve the equation

$$[\![cons\, x_0(Node_1\, x_1\, l\, r)]\!] \quad \equiv \quad [\![Node_2\, x_0'\, x_1'\, l'\, r']\!]$$

in the unknowns x_0', x_1', l', and r'. To determine the components of the two-node, we conduct a case analysis on the indices, the arguments of the finite maps. The index $i2_2$, for example, determines the third component, the left sub-tree. The derivation works towards a situation where we can apply the specification of *cons* (2b). (2b)

> ***proof***
> $\quad [\![cons\, x_0\, (Node_1\, x_1\, l\, r)]\!]\, (i\, ?)$
> $\equiv \langle\, by\text{-}definition\, \rangle$
> $\quad [\![cons\, x_0\, (Node_1\, x_1\, l\, r)]\!]\, (isucc\, (i\, 1_1))$
> $= \langle\, specification\text{-}cons\text{-}isucc\, x_1\, (Node_1\, x_1\, l\, r)\, (i\, 1_1)\ (2b)\, \rangle$
> $\quad [\![Node_1\, x_1\, l\, r]\!]\, (i\, 1_1)$
> $\equiv \langle\, by\text{-}definition\, \rangle$
> $\quad [\![l]\!]\, i$
> $\blacksquare$

We may conclude that $l' \equiv l$. The other cases are equally straightforward.
The equation for two-nodes

$$[\![cons\, x_0(Node_2\, x_1\, x_2\, l\, r)]\!] \quad \equiv \quad [\![Node_1\, x_0'\, l'\, r']\!]$$

is more interesting to solve. Consider the index $i'1_1$ that determines the second component, the left sub-tree of the one-node. We need to conduct a further case distinction on i'. Otherwise, Agda is not able to figure out the predecessor of $i'\,1_1$, that the equation $isucc\, i = i'1_1$ uniquely determines i for a given i'. For the case analysis we use a combined Peano view, on binary numbers and on binary indices, dealing with the inductive case first.

with *view n* | *iview i'*
... | *as-succ m* | *as-isucc i* =
proof
  $[\![\, cons\ x_0\ (Node_2\ x_1\ x_2\ l\ r)\,]\!]\ ((isucc\ i)\ 1_1)$
$\equiv \langle\ by\text{-}definition\ \rangle$
  $[\![\, cons\ x_0\ (Node_2\ x_1\ x_2\ l\ r)\,]\!]\ (isucc\ (i\,2_2))$
$\equiv \langle\ specification\text{-}cons\text{-}isucc\ x_0\ (Node_2\ x_1\ x_2\ l\ r)\ (i\,2_2)\ \ (2b)\ \rangle$
  $[\![\, Node_2\ x_1\ x_2\ l\ r\,]\!]\ (i\,2_2)$
$\equiv \langle\ by\text{-}definition\ \rangle$
  $[\![\, l\,]\!]\ i$
$\equiv \langle\ symmetric\ (specification\text{-}cons\text{-}isucc\ x_1\ l\ i)\ \ (2b)\ \rangle$
  $[\![\, cons\ x_1\ l\,]\!]\ (isucc\ i)$
∎

We conclude that $l' \equiv cons\ x_1\ l$. Again, the calculation is straightforward, except that it is not clear why the first element of l' has to be x_1. The answer is simple, the sub-case *as-isucc* fixes the tail of the sequence, its head is determined by the base case *as-izero*. Actually, there are two base cases, featuring almost identical calculations that only differ in the type arguments. (The "problem" can be traced back to the definition of *izero*, which is defined by case analysis on the size index).

... | *as-zero* | *as-izero* =
proof
  $[\![\, cons\ x_0\ (Node_2\ x_1\ x_2\ l\ r)\,]\!]\ (izero\ \{\,zero\,\}\ 1_1)$
$\equiv \langle\ by\text{-}definition\ \rangle$
  $[\![\, cons\ x_0\ (Node_2\ x_1\ x_2\ l\ r)\,]\!]\ (isucc\ \{\,0b\ 2\,\}\ (0b_2))$
$\equiv \langle\ specification\text{-}cons\text{-}isucc\ x_0\ (Node_2\ x_1\ x_2\ l\ r)\ 0b_2\ \ (2b)\ \rangle$
  $[\![\, Node_2\ x_1\ x_2\ l\ r\,]\!]\ 0b_2$
$\equiv \langle\ by\text{-}definition\ \rangle$
  x_1
$\equiv \langle\ symmetric\ (specification\text{-}cons\text{-}izero\ x_1\ l)\ \ (2a)\ \rangle$
  $[\![\, cons\ x_1\ l\,]\!]\ (izero\ \{\,zero\,\})$
∎
... | *as-succ m* | *as-izero* =
proof
  $[\![\, cons\ x_0\ (Node_2\ x_1\ x_2\ l\ r)\,]\!]\ (izero\ \{\,succ\ m\,\}\ 1_1)$
$\equiv \langle\ by\text{-}definition\ \rangle$
  $[\![\, cons\ x_0\ (Node_2\ x_1\ x_2\ l\ r)\,]\!]\ (isucc\ \{\,(succ\ m)\ 2\,\}\ (0b_2))$
$\equiv \langle\ specification\text{-}cons\text{-}isucc\ x_0\ (Node_2\ x_1\ x_2\ l\ r)\ 0b_2\ \ (2b)\ \rangle$
  $[\![\, Node_2\ x_1\ x_2\ l\ r\,]\!]\ 0b_2$
$\equiv \langle\ by\text{-}definition\ \rangle$
  x_1
$\equiv \langle\ symmetric\ (specification\text{-}cons\text{-}izero\ x_1\ l)\ \ (2a)\ \rangle$
  $[\![\, cons\ x_1\ l\,]\!]\ (izero\ \{\,succ\ m\,\})$
∎

The derivations confirm that $l' \equiv cons\ x_1\ l$.

On a final note, the steps flagged *by-definition* may be omitted as Agda is able to confirm the equalities automatically. But, of course, the equational proofs are targetted at human readers. An after-the-fact proof that *cons* is correct is actually a three-liner, plus a trivial three-liner for (2a) and a straightforward seven-liner for (2b), but would be wholly unsuitable as a *derivation*.

References

1. Abel, A.: Equational reasoning about formal languages in coalgebraic style (2016), submitted to the CMCS 2016 special issue (2016)
2. Altenkirch, T.: Representations of first order function types as terminal coalgebras. In: Abramsky, S. (ed.) TLCA 2001. LNCS, vol. 2044, pp. 8–21. Springer, Heidelberg (2001). https://doi.org/10.1007/3-540-45413-6_5
3. Bird, R., Meertens, L.: Nested datatypes. In: Jeuring, J. (ed.) MPC 1998. LNCS, vol. 1422, pp. 52–67. Springer, Heidelberg (1998). https://doi.org/10.1007/BFb0054285
4. Braun, W., Rem, M.: A logarithmic implementation of flexible arrays. Technical report, Eindhoven University of Technology (1983). memorandum M83/4
5. Claessen, K.: Finger trees explained anew, and slightly simplified (functional pearl). In: Proceedings of the 13th ACM SIGPLAN International Symposium on Haskell, pp. 31–38. Haskell 2020, New York, NY, USA. Association for Computing Machinery (2020). https://doi.org/10.1145/3406088.3409026
6. Cockx, J.: Type theory unchained: extending AGDA with user-defined rewrite rules. In: 25th International Conference on Types for Proofs and Programs (TYPES 2019). Schloss Dagstuhl-Leibniz-Zentrum für Informatik (2020)
7. Di Cosmo, R.: A short survey of isomorphisms of types. Math. Struct. Comput. Sci. **15**(5), 825–838 (2005)
8. Elliott, C.: Symbolic and automatic differentiation of languages. Proc. ACM Program. Lang. 5(ICFP) (2021). https://doi.org/10.1145/3473583
9. Gibbons, J.: APLicative programming with naperian functors. In: Yang, H. (ed.) ESOP 2017. LNCS, vol. 10201, pp. 556–583. Springer, Heidelberg (2017). https://doi.org/10.1007/978-3-662-54434-1_21
10. Henglein, F.: Type inference with polymorphic recursion. ACM Trans. Program. Lang. Syst. **15**(2), 253–289 (1993)
11. Hinze, R.: Functional Pearl: explaining binomial heaps. J. Funct. Program. **9**(1), 93–104 (1999). https://doi.org/10.1017/S0956796899003317
12. Hinze, R.: Generalizing generalized tries. J. Funct. Program. **10**(4), 327–351 (2000). https://doi.org/10.1017/S0956796800003713
13. Hinze, R.: Manufacturing datatypes. J. Funct. Program. **11**(5), 493–524 (2001). https://doi.org/10.1017/S095679680100404X
14. Hinze, R.: Type fusion. In: Johnson, M., Pavlovic, D. (eds.) AMAST 2010. LNCS, vol. 6486, pp. 92–110. Springer, Heidelberg (2011). https://doi.org/10.1007/978-3-642-17796-5_6
15. Hinze, R.: Adjoint folds and unfolds–an extended study. Sci. Comput. Program. **78**(11), 2108–2159 (2013). https://doi.org/10.1016/j.scico.2012.07.011
16. Hinze, R., Paterson, R.: Finger trees: a simple general-purpose data structure. J. Funct. Program. **16**(2), 197–217 (2006). https://doi.org/10.1017/S0956796805005769

17. Hoogerwoord, R.R.: A logarithmic implementation of flexible arrays. In: Bird, R.S., Morgan, C.C., Woodcock, J.C.P. (eds.) MPC 1992. LNCS, vol. 669, pp. 191–207. Springer, Heidelberg (1993). https://doi.org/10.1007/3-540-56625-2_14
18. Ko, H.s., Gibbons, J.: Programming with ornaments. J. Funct. Program. 27 (2016). https://doi.org/10.1017/S0956796816000307
19. Kubiak, R., Hughes, J., Launchbury, J.: Implementing projection-based strictness analysis. Technical report Department of Computing Science, University of Glasgow (1991)
20. Licata, D.: Abstract types with isomorphic types (2011). https://homotopytypetheory.org/2012/11/12/abstract-types-with-isomorphic-types/
21. McBride, C., McKinna, J.: The view from the left. J. Funct. Program. **14**(1), 69–111 (2004)
22. Mycroft, A.: Polymorphic type schemes and recursive definitions. In: Paul, M., Robinet, B. (eds.) Programming 1984. LNCS, vol. 167, pp. 217–228. Springer, Heidelberg (1984). https://doi.org/10.1007/3-540-12925-1_41
23. Okasaki, C.: Functional pearl: three algorithms on Braun trees. J. Funct. Program. **7**(6), 661–666 (1997)
24. Okasaki, C.: Purely Functional Data Structures. Cambridge University Press, Cambridge (1998)
25. Oliveira, J.N.: Transforming Data by Calculation, pp. 134–195. Springer, Berlin Heidelberg, Berlin, Heidelberg (2008). https://doi.org/10.1007/978-3-540-88643-3-4
26. Paterson, R.: Control structures from types, April 1994. ftp://santos.doc.ic.ac.uk/pub/papers/R.Paterson/folds.dvi.gz
27. Pickering, M., Érdi, G., Peyton Jones, S., Eisenberg, R.A.: Pattern synonyms. In: Proceedings of the 9th International Symposium on Haskell, pp. 80–91 (2016)
28. van der Rest, C., Swierstra, W.: A completely unique account of enumeration (2022). https://dl.acm.org/doi/abs/10.1145/3547636?af=R
29. Swierstra, W.: Heterogeneous binary random-access lists. J. Funct. Program. **30**, e10 (2020). https://doi.org/10.1017/S0956796820000064
30. Univalent Foundations Program, T.: Homotopy Type Theory: Univalent Foundations of Mathematics. Institute for Advanced Study (2013). https://homotopytypetheory.org/book
31. Wadler, P.: Views: A way for pattern matching to cohabit with data abstraction. In: Proceedings of the 14th ACM SIGACT-SIGPLAN Symposium on Principles of Programming Languages, pp. 307–313 (1987)

Flexibly Graded Monads and Graded Algebras

Dylan McDermott[1](✉) ⓘ and Tarmo Uustalu[1,2] ⓘ

[1] Department of Computer Science, Reykjavik University, Reykjavik, Iceland
{dylanm,tarmo}@ru.is
[2] Department of Software Science, Tallinn University of Technology, Tallinn, Estonia

Abstract. When modelling side-effects using a monad, we need to equip the monad with effectful operations. This can be done by noting that each algebra of the monad carries interpretations of the desired operations. We consider the analogous situation for graded monads, which are a generalization of monads that enable us to track quantitative information about side-effects. Grading makes a significant difference: while many graded monads of interest can be equipped with similar operations, the algebras often cannot. We explain where these operations come from for graded monads. To do this, we introduce the notion of flexibly graded monad, for which the situation is similar to the situation for ordinary monads. We then show that each flexibly graded monad induces a canonical graded monad in such a way that operations for the flexibly graded monad carry over to the graded monad. In doing this, we reformulate grading in terms of locally graded categories, showing in particular that graded monads are a particular kind of relative monad. We propose that locally graded categories are a useful setting for work on grading in general.

Keywords: Graded monad · Graded algebra · Flexible grading · Relative monad · Computational effect · Locally graded category

1 Introduction

Computational effects are often modelled, following Moggi [18,19], using (strong) monads. The structure of the monad is used to interpret sequencing of computations, but to interpret the constructs that cause effects we need additional data—usually a collection of *algebraic operations* in the sense of Plotkin and Power [21]. For example, finite nondeterminism can be modelled using the usual list monad on **Set**; nullary and binary nondeterministic choice are modelled as the empty list and concatenation of lists. *Presentations* of theories corresponding to monads are an important source of these algebraic operations. For a given presentation, an *algebra* consists of an object together with interpretations of its operations, subject to its equations. The corresponding monad T (if it exists) is defined to be such that the T-algebras are the algebras of the presentation. Every T-algebra therefore admits interpretations of the operations of the presentation,

E. Komendantskaya (Ed.): MPC 2022, LNCS 13544, pp. 102–128, 2022.
https://doi.org/10.1007/978-3-031-16912-0_4

and for free T-algebras these interpretations give rise to algebraic operations in the sense of Plotkin and Power. For example, if we start with the presentation of monoids with a constant and a binary operation and the unitality and associativity equations, then T will be the list monad; free T-algebras have lists as carriers, and the empty list and concatenation of lists provide the monoid structure of these free algebras.

We consider the analogous situation for the *graded* monads of Smirnov [22], Melliès [16] and Katsumata [9], focusing in particular on their application to tracking quantitative information about effects of programs [9,20]. (There are other applications, such as in process semantics [2,17], and in probability theory [3].) Instead of assigning a single object TX to each object X, a graded monad assigns an object TXe to each object X and *grade* e. The quantitative information is represented by e. For example, the grades could be natural numbers, upper-bounding the number of alternative outcomes from nondeterministic computations. We can model these computations using the graded list monad $T = \mathsf{List}$ where $TXe = \mathsf{List}Xe$ is the set of lists over X of length at most e.

At first glance, the situation with operations for graded monads seems similar to the situation for ordinary monads. The empty list $() \in \mathsf{List}X0$ and concatenation $\mathsf{List}Xe_1 \times \mathsf{List}Xe_2 \to \mathsf{List}X(e_1 + e_2)$ make $\mathsf{List}X$ into a *graded monoid*. We might expect that this graded monoid structure arises because List-algebras are graded monoids. But this is not the case, as we show below: graded monoids are not the algebras of the graded monad List, or indeed of *any* graded monad. The same phenomenon occurs also with other examples: the free algebras TX of a graded monad can often be equipped with some algebraic structure of interest, even when the general algebras cannot. (We also consider *graded arithmoids* as an example below.)

We explain this phenomenon via a new notion of *flexibly graded monad*. Flexibly graded monads should be thought of as more general than graded monads (though constructing a flexibly graded monad with the same algebras as a given graded monad relies on existence of certain colimits). The point is that flexibly graded monads often do capture these algebraic structures, for example, there *is* a flexibly graded monad $\mathsf{List}_{\mathsf{flex}}$ whose algebras are graded monoids. We show that every flexibly graded monad T induces a graded monad $\lfloor T \rfloor$; the latter may not have the same algebras as T, but does satisfy a universal property (Lemma 2) formulated in terms of algebras. Moreover, every free $\lfloor T \rfloor$-algebra forms a T-algebra. For example, we obtain List as the graded monad $\lfloor \mathsf{List}_{\mathsf{flex}} \rfloor$, and hence also the graded monoid structure of the free algebras $\mathsf{List}X$. This paper should be viewed as a step towards developing notions of presentation and algebraic operation for graded monads that can include, for example, the operations of a graded monoid. The graded presentations considered from the literature [2,12,17,22] are not flexible enough to present graded monoids. The appropriate notions of flexibly graded presentation and flexibly graded algebraic operation are discussed in the sequel paper [10].

As part of the development, we formulate graded monads in terms of *locally graded categories* of Wood [26]. (He used a different name, we use Levy's [13] terminology). These are a particular instance of enriched categories, and so they enable us to use constructions and results that apply to enriched categories in general. Still, here we use an explicit description of locally graded categories to avoid assuming knowledge of enriched category theory. We show that graded monads and flexibly graded monads are just instances of *relative monads* [1] on functors between locally graded categories; we rely heavily on general facts about relative monads in our other results. Locally graded categories also enable us to simplify some previous work (such as Fujii et al.'s [4], which uses *actegories* instead). For this reason, we propose that locally graded categories are a useful setting for work on grading in general.

Contributions. We begin by reviewing the existing notions of graded monad (Sect. 2) and locally graded category (Sect. 3). We then do the following.

- We define the appropriate notion of *relative monad* for locally graded categories, and develop some of the associated theory (Sect. 4). We show that graded monads are relative monads, and introduce our notion of *flexibly graded monad*. We show that flexibly graded monads capture algebraic structures we are interested in, such as graded monoids.
- We show that every flexibly graded monad T induces a graded monad ⌊T⌋ satisfying a universal property (Sect. 5). This construction canonically equips free ⌊T⌋-algebras with additional structure (for example, equips List$X$ with the structure of a graded monoid).
- We discuss the reverse direction: that of constructing a canonical flexibly graded monad ⌈T⌉ from a graded monad T (Sect. 6). We use this to show that graded monads do not capture certain algebraic structures (e.g. graded monoids), we characterize the existence of ⌈T⌉ in terms of existence of certain colimits.

2   Graded Monads

We begin by reviewing the existing notion of graded monad. The grades e are the objects of a category $\mathbb{E}$, one example being the poset $\mathbb{N}_\leq$ of natural numbers with their usual ordering. Various other examples can be found in the literature on graded monads.

Definition 1. *An $\mathbb{E}$-graded object of $\mathbb{C}$, where $\mathbb{E}$ and $\mathbb{C}$ are categories, is a functor $X : \mathbb{E} \to \mathbb{C}$. These form a category $[\mathbb{E}, \mathbb{C}]$, with natural transformations as morphisms.*

To assign suitable grades to the unit and Kleisli extension of a graded monad, we need a unit grade 1 and multiplication operator $(\cdot)$ on grades. For the rest of the paper, we suppose a monoidal category $(\mathbb{E}, 1, \cdot)$ that we assume to be small (for technical reasons) and strict (for convenience). For example, multiplication of natural numbers makes $\mathbb{N}_\leq$ into a strict monoidal category $\mathbb{N}_\leq^\times = (\mathbb{N}_\leq, 1, \cdot)$. We often omit the prefix $\mathbb{E}$- from $\mathbb{E}$-graded.

Definition 2 ([9,16,22]). *An* $\mathbb{E}$*-graded monad* T *on a category* $\mathbb{C}$ *consists of the following data:*

- *a graded object* $TX : \mathbb{E} \to \mathbb{C}$ *for each* $X \in |\mathbb{C}|$;
- *a unit morphism* $\eta_X : X \to TX1$ *for each* $X \in |\mathbb{C}|$;
- *a Kleisli extension operator* $(-)^\dagger$ *that maps every morphism* $f : X \to TYe$ *and grade* $d \in |\mathbb{E}|$ *to a morphism* $f_d^\dagger : TXd \to TY(d \cdot e)$.

Kleisli extension is required to be natural in d and e, and to satisfy the following unit and associativity laws.

$$
\begin{aligned}
f_1^\dagger \circ \eta_X &= f && \text{for each } f : X \to TYe \\
\mathrm{id}_{TXd} &= (\eta_X)_d^\dagger && \text{for each } X \in |\mathbb{C}|, d \in |\mathbb{E}| \\
(g_e^\dagger \circ f)_d^\dagger &= g_{d \cdot e}^\dagger \circ f_d^\dagger && \text{for each } f : X \to TYe, g : Y \to TZe', d \in |\mathbb{E}|
\end{aligned}
$$

2.1 Examples

We use the following three examples throughout the paper. In each case, we define a graded monad T, and then show that the T arises canonically from some class of (graded) algebraic structures. The latter fact provides a way of equipping the free algebras TX with the corresponding algebraic structure.

- The graded monad List (Definition 3) arises canonically from graded monoids (Definition 4), and so List$X$ forms a graded monoid. Despite this, graded monoids are not the algebras for any graded monad (Theorem 4).
- For each graded monoid M, the *graded writer monad* Wr^M (Definition 5) arises canonically from M-*actions* (Definition 6). Differently from the List example, Wr^M-algebras are exactly M-actions (Example 7).
- We define a graded monad Count for modelling computations that increment and decrement a counter (Definition 7). In this case, the corresponding algebraic structure is our notion of *graded arithmoid* (Definition 8), so Count$X$ forms a graded arithmoid for each set X. Graded arithmoids are not the algebras for Count or for any other graded monad (Theorem 5).

In this section, we define each of the graded monads, and the corresponding algebraic structure.

Graded Monoids and List. We begin with the example of the graded list monad.

Definition 3. *The* $\mathbb{N}_{\leq}^\times$*-graded monad* List *on* **Set** *maps each set X to the graded object* List$X$ *of lists over X of bounded length:* ListXe *is the set of lists of length at most $e \in \mathbb{N}$, and for $e \leq e' \in \mathbb{N}$ the function* List$X(e{\leq}e')$: List$Xe \to$ ListXe' *is the inclusion (where we write $e{\leq}e'$ for the unique element of $\mathbb{N}_{\leq}(e, e')$). The unit* $\eta_X : X \to$ List$X1$ *and Kleisli extension* $f_d^\dagger$: List$Xd \to$ List$Y(d \cdot e)$ *of* $f : X \to$ ListYe *are similar to those of the usual list monad on* **Set**: *they are defined by*

$$
\eta_X x = (x) \qquad f_d^\dagger(x_1, \ldots, x_k) = fx_1 +\!\!+ \cdots +\!\!+ fx_k
$$

where $(+\!\!+)$ *is concatenation of lists.*

For every set X, the graded object $\mathsf{List}X$ forms a *graded monoid* in the sense of the following definition, with

$$() \in \mathsf{List}X0 \qquad (\mathbin{+\!\!+}) : \mathsf{List}Xe_1 \times \mathsf{List}Xe_2 \to \mathsf{List}X(e_1 + e_2)$$

as unit and multiplication.

Definition 4. *We write $\mathbb{N}_{\leq}^+$ for the strict monoidal category $\mathbb{N}_{\leq}^+ = (\mathbb{N}_{\leq}, 0, +)$. A $\mathbb{N}_{\leq}^+$-graded monoid $\mathsf{A} = (A, u, m)$ on $\mathbf{Set}$ consists of a graded object $A : \mathbb{N}_{\leq} \to \mathbf{Set}$ (the carrier), a unit element $u \in A0$, and a family of multiplication functions $m_{e_1,e_2} : Ae_1 \times Ae_2 \to A(e_1 + e_2)$ natural in $e_1, e_2 \in \mathbb{N}_{\leq}$, such that multiplication is unital and associative:*

$$m_{0,e}(u, x) = x = m_{e,0}(x, u)$$
$$m_{e_1+e_2,e_3}(m_{e_1,e_2}(x, y), z) = m_{e_1,e_2+e_3}(x, m_{e_2,e_3}(y, z))$$

A homomorphism $h : \mathsf{A} \to \mathsf{A}'$ is a natural transformation $h : A \Rightarrow A'$ such that

$$h_0 u = u \qquad h_{e_1+e_2}(m_{e_1,e_2}(x, y)) = m_{e_1,e_2}(h_{e_1}x, h_{e_2}y)$$

(This definition can easily be generalized to grades other than natural numbers with addition and to monoidal categories other than **Set**, but for simplicity we consider only $\mathbb{N}_{\leq}^+$-graded monoids in **Set**.) An example is the following grading of the additive monoid of natural numbers:

$$Ne = \{0, \ldots, e\} \quad N(e \leq e')n = n \quad u = 0 \quad m_{e_1,e_2}(n_1, n_2) = n_1 + n_2$$

We give an informal explanation of why the algebras of the graded monad List are not graded monoids (for the proof, see Theorem 4). A List-*algebra* consists of a carrier $A : \mathbb{N}_{\leq} \to \mathbf{Set}$, and an operator $(-)^{\ddagger}$ that maps functions to functions as follows:

$$\frac{f : X \to Ae}{f_d^{\ddagger} : \mathsf{List}Xd \to A(d \cdot e)}$$

These are required to satisfy some laws; we defer the full definition to Sect. 4.1. Every graded monoid induces a List-algebra, by defining

$$f_d^{\ddagger}[x_1, \ldots, x_k] = m(fx_1, m(fx_2, \cdots m(fx_{k-1}, m(fx_k, u)) \cdots))$$

(where we omit the subscripts of m). If List-algebras were graded monoids, then this construction would be a bijection (by Corollary 1 below), so we should be able to recover m from $(-)^{\ddagger}$. This is not the case, intuitively because $f_d^{\ddagger}[x_1, \ldots, x_k]$ is an iterated multiplication of elements of A that all have the same grade, while the two arguments of m can have different grades. For a concrete example, we cannot recover the additive graded monoid structure on N above from

$$f_d^{\ddagger}[x_1, \ldots, x_k] = fx_1 + \cdots + fx_k$$

To see why, let N' be the smallest family of subsets $N'e \subseteq Ne$ closed under the inclusions $N(e' \leq e'')$ and under $(-)^{\ddagger}$, and such that $2 \in N'2$ and $3 \in N'3$. The

List-algebra structure on N restricts to N', so we can recover m only if m also restricts to N'. But it does not, because m sends $(2,3) \in N'2 \times N'3$ to $5 \notin N'5$.

M-actions and Wr^M. Our second example is the following.

Definition 5. *Every $\mathbb{N}_{\leq}^+$-graded monoid* $\mathsf{M} = (M, u, m)$ *induces a $\mathbb{N}_{\leq}^+$-graded writer monad Wr^M, with assignment on objects, unit, and Kleisli extension defined by*

$$\mathrm{Wr}^M X e = Me \times X \qquad \eta_X x = (u, x)$$
$$f_d^\dagger(p, x) = \mathrm{let}\,(q, y) = fx \text{ in } (m_{d,e}(p, q), y)$$

For every set X, the graded monoid M *acts* on $\mathrm{Wr}^M X$ via the multiplication of M. Precisely, if we define

$$\mathrm{act}_{e_1, e_2} : Me_1 \times \mathrm{Wr}^M X e_2 \to \mathrm{Wr}^M X(e_1 + e_2)$$
$$\mathrm{act}_{e_1, e_2}(p, (q, y)) = (m_{e_1, e_2}(p, q), y)$$

then $(\mathrm{Wr}^M X, \mathrm{act})$ is an M-action in the following sense.

Definition 6. *Let M be a $\mathbb{N}_{\leq}^+$-graded monoid. An M-action is a pair $\mathsf{A} = (A, \mathrm{act})$ of a graded object $A : \mathbb{N}_{\leq} \to \mathbf{Set}$ and a natural family of functions $\mathrm{act}_{e_1, e_2} : Me_1 \times Ae_2 \to A(e_1 + e_2)$ satisfying*

$$\mathrm{act}_{0,e}(u, x) = x \quad \mathrm{act}_{e_1+e_2, e_3}(m_{e_1, e_2}(p, q), x) = \mathrm{act}_{e_1, e_2+e_3}(p, \mathrm{act}_{e_2, e_3}(q, x))$$

A homomorphism $h : \mathsf{A} \to \mathsf{A}'$ of M-actions is a natural transformation $h : A \Rightarrow A'$ such that

$$h_{e_1+e_2}(\mathrm{act}_{e_1, e_2}(p, x)) = \mathrm{act}_{e_1, e_2}(p, h_{e_2} x)$$

Graded Arithmoids and Count. Our third example is computations that interact with a counter (which stores a natural number). These computations are able to either return a value, without changing the counter, or to do one of the following two operations.

- Increment: increase the value of the counter by 1, and then continue with a given computation.
- Test and decrement: if the value is 0, then continue with one computation, otherwise decrease the value by 1 and continue with another computation.

This can be seen as a special case of interaction with a stack of values drawn from a set V, in the case $V = 1$ (the stack is determined by its size, which is the value of the counter). Increment and decrement respectively correspond to push and pop. The graded monad is a graded version of Goncharov's stack monad [7], specialized to $V = 1$, and our notion of graded arithmoid (Definition 8 below) similarly arises by grading Goncharov's presentation of the stack monad.

We only consider finite computations, and in particular each computation can test the value of the counter only finitely many times (in other words, can interact with only a finite prefix of the stack, whose size depends on the computation). As a consequence, computations cannot always learn the exact value of the counter. This restriction is captured by the conditions involving ρ below.

Grades are integers, which provide an upper bound on the net amount the counter increases. (A negative upper bound $-e$ is equivalently a lower bound e on the amount the counter decreases by.) For example, if the counter is initially 6 and we run a computation of grade 3, then the final value will be at most 9 (but intermediate values can be greater than 9).

Definition 7. *We write $\mathbb{Z}_\leq$ for the poset of integers with their usual ordering, which forms a strict monoidal category $\mathbb{Z}_\leq^+ = (\mathbb{Z}_\leq, 0, +)$ using addition of integers. The $\mathbb{Z}_\leq^+$-graded monad* Count *on* **Set** *is defined as follows. Given a set X, the graded object* Count$X$ *is given by*

$$\text{Count}X e = \{t : \textstyle\prod_{i:\mathbb{N}} [0..i+e] \times X \mid$$
$$\exists \rho \in \mathbb{N}. \forall k, j \in \mathbb{N}, x \in X. t\,\rho = (j, x) \Rightarrow t(\rho + k) = (j + k, x)\}$$

where $[0..n] = \{0, 1, \ldots, n\}$ *(empty for negative n). Thus computations t are dependent functions that map each initial counter value i to a pair (j, x) of a final counter value j such that $j - i \leq e$ and a result x. (There are no such dependent functions if $e < 0$, i.e.* CountXe *is empty in this case.) The unit of the graded monad leaves the counter unchanged, and the Kleisli extension uses the final counter value of one computation as the initial counter value of another:*

$$\eta_X x = \lambda i.\,(i, x) \qquad f_d^\dagger t = \lambda i.\,\text{let}\,(j, x) = t\,i\,\text{in}\,f\,x\,j$$

The increment and decrement operations described above are captured by the following functions:

$\text{inc}_e : \text{Count}Xe \to \text{Count}X(e{+}1)$ $\text{dec}_e : \text{Count}Xe \times \text{Count}X(e{+}1) \to \text{Count}Xe$
$\text{inc}_e\,t = \lambda i.\,t(i+1)$ $\text{dec}_e(t_1, t_2) = \lambda i.\,\text{if}\,i{=}0\,\text{then}\,t_1 0\,\text{else}\,t_2(i{-}1)$

and these form *graded arithmoids* in the following sense.

Definition 8. *A* graded arithmoid *is a triple* $\mathsf{A} = (A, \text{inc}, \text{dec})$ *of a graded object* $A : \mathbb{Z}_\leq \to$ **Set** *and natural families of functions*

$$\text{inc}_e : Ae \to A(e+1) \qquad \text{dec}_e : Ae \times A(e+1) \to Ae$$

satisfying

$$\text{inc}_e(\text{dec}_e(x, y)) = y \qquad \text{dec}_e(x, \text{inc}_e x) = x$$
$$\text{dec}_e(\text{dec}_e(x, y), z) = \text{dec}_e(x, z)$$

A homomorphism $h : \mathsf{A} \to \mathsf{A}'$ *of graded arithmoids is a natural transformation* $h : A \Rightarrow A'$ *such that*

$$h_{e+1}(\text{inc}_e x) = \text{inc}_e(h_e x) \qquad h_e(\text{dec}_e(x, y)) = \text{dec}_e(h_e x, h_{e+1} y)$$

3 Locally Graded Categories

Locally graded categories are similar to ordinary categories, except that each morphism has a *grade e* in addition to a domain and codomain. An example of this situation appeared already in the definition of graded monad. While morphisms $f : X \Rightarrow Y$ in the ordinary category $[\mathbb{E}, \mathbb{C}]$ preserve the grades of elements (f sends elements of Xd to elements of Yd), Kleisli extensions $f^{\dagger} : TX \Rightarrow TY(- \cdot e)$ multiply by a grade e; in the locally graded category $\mathbf{GObj}_{\mathbb{E}}(\mathbb{C})$ of graded objects (Definition 10), $f^{\dagger}$ is a morphism from TX to TY *of grade e*.

Definition 9 ([26]). *A locally $\mathbb{E}$-graded category $\mathcal{C}$ consists of*

- *a collection $|\mathcal{C}|$ of* objects;
- *for each $X, Y \in |\mathcal{C}|$ and $e \in |\mathbb{E}|$, a set $\mathcal{C}(X, Y)e$ of* morphisms *from X to Y of grade e; we write $f : X -e\rightarrow Y$ to indicate $f \in \mathcal{C}(X, Y)e$;*
- *for each $X \in |\mathcal{C}|$, a morphism $\mathrm{id}_X : X -1\rightarrow X$;*
- *for each $f : X -e\rightarrow Y$ and $g : Y -e'\rightarrow Z$, a morphism $g \circ f : X -e \cdot e'\rightarrow Z$;*
- *for each $\zeta \in \mathbb{E}(e, e')$ and $f : X -e\rightarrow Y$, a morphism $\zeta^* f : X -e'\rightarrow Y$ (the* coercion *of f along ζ);*

such that composition is unital ($\mathrm{id}_Y \circ f = f = f \circ \mathrm{id}_X$) and associative (($h \circ g$) $\circ f = h \circ (g \circ f)$); coercions are functorial ($\mathrm{id}_e^* f = f$ and $\xi^*(\zeta^* f) = (\xi \circ \zeta)^* f$); and such that composition commutes with coercion (($\xi \cdot \zeta$)$^*(g \circ f) = \xi^* g \circ \zeta^* f$).

(In Wood's terminology [26, Definition 1.1], these are *large $\mathbb{E}^{\mathrm{op}}$-categories*.) We systematically use blackboard bold letters like $\mathbb{C}$ for ordinary categories and calligraphic letters like $\mathcal{C}$ for locally graded categories.

We define a locally graded category of graded objects, which we use throughout the paper, and then give some further examples.

Definition 10. *Let $\mathbb{C}$ be an ordinary category. The locally $\mathbb{E}$-graded category $\mathbf{GObj}_{\mathbb{E}}(\mathbb{C})$ is defined as follows.*

- *Objects $X \in |\mathbf{GObj}_{\mathbb{E}}(\mathbb{C})|$ are $\mathbb{E}$-graded objects of $\mathbb{C}$ (Definition 1).*
- *Morphisms $f : X -e\rightarrow Y$ are natural transformations $f : X \Rightarrow Y(- \cdot e)$.*
- *The identity id_X is the identity natural transformation $X \Rightarrow X$.*
- *The composition $g \circ f : X -e \cdot e'\rightarrow Z$ of $f : X -e\rightarrow Y$ and $g : Y -e'\rightarrow Z$ is*
$$X \xrightarrow{f} Y(- \cdot e) \xrightarrow{g- \cdot e} Z(- \cdot e \cdot e').$$
- *The coercion $\zeta^* f : X -e'\rightarrow Y$ of $f : X -e\rightarrow Y$ along $\zeta \in \mathbb{E}(e, e')$ is $X \xrightarrow{f} Y(- \cdot e) \xrightarrow{Y(- \cdot \zeta)} Y(- \cdot e').$*

Example 1. Just as monoids in **Set** are categories with one object, $\mathbb{N}_{\leq}^+$-graded monoids **A** in **Set** are locally $\mathbb{N}_{\leq}^+$-graded categories with one object (morphisms of grade e are elements of Ae).

Example 2. Using both the multiplicative and additive monoidal structures on $\mathbb{N}_{\leq}$, there is a locally $\mathbb{N}_{\leq}^{\times}$-graded category **GMon** that has $\mathbb{N}_{\leq}^{+}$-graded monoids as objects. Morphisms $f : \mathsf{A} - e \twoheadrightarrow \mathsf{A}'$ in **GMon** are homomorphisms $f : \mathsf{A} \to \mathsf{A}'(-\cdot e)$, where $\mathsf{A}'(-\cdot e)$ is the graded monoid $(A'(-\cdot e), u, m_{-\cdot e, -\cdot e})$ for $\mathsf{A}' = (A', u, m)$. Identities, composition, and coercions are as in $\mathbf{GObj}_{\mathbb{N}_{\leq}^{\times}}(\mathbf{Set})$.

We have similar locally graded categories for our other two examples. For a fixed $\mathbb{N}_{\leq}^{+}$-graded monoid M, the M-actions form a locally $\mathbb{N}_{\leq}^{+}$-graded category $\mathbf{GAct_M}$, in which morphisms $\mathsf{A} - e \twoheadrightarrow \mathsf{A}'$ in $\mathbf{GAct_M}$ are homomorphisms $\mathsf{A} \to \mathsf{A}'(-+e)$, where $\mathsf{A}'(-+e) = (A'(-+e), \mathrm{act}_{-,-+e})$. The graded arithmoids form a locally $\mathbb{Z}_{\leq}^{+}$-graded category **GArith** in which morphisms $\mathsf{A} - e \twoheadrightarrow \mathsf{A}'$ are similarly homomorphisms $\mathsf{A} \to \mathsf{A}'(-+e)$.

We also need to consider functors between locally graded categories, and natural transformations between these functors.

Definition 11 ([26]). *A functor $F : \mathcal{C} \to \mathcal{D}$ between locally graded categories consists of an object mapping $F : |\mathcal{C}| \to |\mathcal{D}|$ and a mapping of morphisms as on the left below; these are required to preserve identities, composition and coercion as on the right below.*

$$\frac{f : X - e \twoheadrightarrow Y}{Ff : FX - e \twoheadrightarrow FY} \qquad \begin{array}{c} F\mathrm{id}_X = \mathrm{id}_{FX} \\ F(g \circ f) = Fg \circ Ff \\ F(\zeta^* f) = \zeta^*(Ff) \end{array}$$

A natural transformation $\alpha : F \Rightarrow G$ between functors $F, G : \mathcal{C} \to \mathcal{D}$ consists of a morphism $\alpha_X : FX - 1 \twoheadrightarrow GX$ for each $X \in |\mathcal{C}|$, such that $\alpha_Y \circ Ff = Gf \circ \alpha_X$ for every $f : X - e \twoheadrightarrow Y$.

We of course have identity functors $\mathrm{Id}_{\mathcal{C}} : \mathcal{C} \to \mathcal{C}$, and functors $F : \mathcal{C}_1 \to \mathcal{C}_2$ and $G : \mathcal{C}_2 \to \mathcal{C}_3$ have a composition $G \cdot F : \mathcal{C}_1 \to \mathcal{C}_3$. There are also horizontal and vertical compositions of natural transformations.

Example 3. There is a forgetful functor $\mathbf{GMon} \to \mathbf{GObj}_{\mathbb{N}_{\leq}^{\times}}(\mathbf{Set})$ that sends each graded monoid A to its carrier A, and each morphism $f : \mathsf{A} - e \twoheadrightarrow \mathsf{A}'$ to itself. We similarly have forgetful functors $\mathbf{GAct_M} \to \mathbf{GObj}_{\mathbb{N}_{\leq}^{+}}(\mathbf{Set})$ and $\mathbf{GArith} \to \mathbf{GObj}_{\mathbb{Z}_{\leq}^{+}}(\mathbf{Set})$.

If $\mathcal{A}, \mathcal{A}'$ are two locally graded categories that can similarly be equipped with forgetful functors $U : \mathcal{A} \to \mathcal{C}$ and $U' : \mathcal{A}' \to \mathcal{C}$, we say that a functor $G : \mathcal{A} \to \mathcal{A}'$ is *over* $\mathcal{C}$ when $U' \cdot G = U$, i.e. when G preserves carriers and sends morphisms to themselves. For example, since addition of natural numbers is commutative, there is a functor $\mathbf{GMon} \to \mathbf{GMon}$ over $\mathbf{GObj}_{\mathbb{N}_{\leq}^{\times}}(\mathbf{Set})$ that swaps the arguments of the multiplication of each graded monoid.

Locally graded categories induce ordinary categories and vice versa. We use these constructions in our formulation of graded monads in terms of locally graded categories.

Definition 12. *Every locally graded category* C *has an* underlying *ordinary category* $\underline{C}$ *with the same objects; morphisms* $f : X \to Y$ *in* $\underline{C}$ *are morphisms* $f : X\,\text{–}1\!\!\to Y$ *in* C, *and these compose as in* C. *Every functor* $F : C \to D$ *between locally graded categories restricts to an ordinary functor* $\underline{F} : \underline{C} \to \underline{D}$.

In the other direction, *every ordinary category* $\mathbb{C}$ *induces a locally* $\mathbb{E}$-*graded category* $\mathbf{Free}_{\mathbb{E}}(\mathbb{C})$, *defined by:*

$$|\mathbf{Free}_{\mathbb{E}}(\mathbb{C})| = |\mathbb{C}| \qquad \mathbf{Free}_{\mathbb{E}}(\mathbb{C})(X,Y)e = \mathbb{E}(1,e) \times \mathbb{C}(X,Y)$$
$$\mathrm{id}_X = (\mathrm{id}_1, \mathrm{id}_X) \qquad (\xi', g) \circ (\xi, f) = (\xi \cdot \xi', g \circ f) \qquad \zeta^*(\xi, f) = (\zeta \circ \xi, f)$$

$\mathbf{Free}_{\mathbb{E}}(\mathbb{C})$ is free on $\mathbb{C}$ in the following sense. Let $H_{\mathbb{C}} : \mathbb{C} \to \mathbf{Free}_{\mathbb{E}}(\mathbb{C})$ be the ordinary functor defined on objects by $H_{\mathbb{C}}X = X$ and on morphisms by $H_{\mathbb{C}}f = (\mathrm{id}_1, f)$. Then every ordinary functor $F : \mathbb{C} \to \underline{D}$ induces a unique $F^{\sharp} : \mathbf{Free}_{\mathbb{E}}(\mathbb{C}) \to D$ such that $\underline{F^{\sharp}} \cdot H_{\mathbb{C}} = F$; this is given on objects by $F^{\sharp}X = FX$, and on morphisms $(\xi, f) : X\,\text{–}e\!\!\to Y$ by $F^{\sharp}(\xi, f) = \xi^*(Ff) : FX\,\text{–}e\!\!\to FY$.

We can view $\mathbf{Free}_{\mathbb{E}}(\mathbb{C})$ as a full sub-locally graded category of $\mathbf{GObj}_{j_{\mathbb{E}}}(\mathbb{C})$ as follows, assuming $\mathbb{C}$ has enough coproducts. Let X be an object of $\mathbb{C}$ (equivalently, an object of $\mathbf{Free}_{\mathbb{E}}(\mathbb{C})$). For each set A, we write $A \bullet X$ for the coproduct of A-many copies of X, if it exists. (This is the copower of X by A.) In particular, if $\mathbb{E}(1, e) \bullet X$ exists for every $e \in |\mathbb{E}|$, then we have a graded object $J_{\mathbb{C}}X = \mathbb{E}(1, -) \bullet X \in |\mathbf{GObj}_{j_{\mathbb{E}}}(\mathbb{C})|$; in this way, we can view every object X of $\mathbf{Free}_{\mathbb{E}}(\mathbb{C})$ as an object $J_{\mathbb{C}}X$ of $\mathbf{GObj}_{j_{\mathbb{E}}}(\mathbb{C})$. By the Yoneda lemma, morphisms $J_{\mathbb{C}}X\,\text{–}e\!\!\to Y$ in $\mathbf{GObj}_{j_{\mathbb{E}}}(\mathbb{C})$ are in bijection with morphisms $X \to Ye$ in $\mathbb{C}$:

$$\frac{\dfrac{\mathbb{E}(1, -) \bullet X \Rightarrow Y(- \cdot e) \text{ in } [\mathbb{E}, \mathbb{C}]}{\mathbb{E}(1, -) \Rightarrow \mathbb{C}(X, Y(- \cdot e)) \text{ in } [\mathbb{E}, \mathbf{Set}]}}{X \to Ye \text{ in } \mathbb{C}}$$

Intuitively, $J_{\mathbb{C}}X$ can be thought of as the graded object generated by assigning the grade 1 to each element of X.

Definition 13. *Let* $\mathbb{C}$ *be an ordinary category with coproducts of the form* $\mathbb{E}(1, e) \bullet X$. *We define* $J_{\mathbb{C}} : \mathbf{Free}_{\mathbb{E}}(\mathbb{C}) \to \mathbf{GObj}_{j_{\mathbb{E}}}(\mathbb{C})$ *to be unique such that* $\underline{J_{\mathbb{C}}} \cdot H_{\mathbb{C}}$ *is the ordinary functor* $(X \mapsto \mathbb{E}(1, -) \bullet X) : \mathbb{C} \to [\mathbb{E}, \mathbb{C}] = \mathbf{GObj}_{j_{\mathbb{E}}}(\mathbb{C})$.

Remark 1. We end this section by mentioning that, as shown by Wood [26, Theorem 1.6], locally graded category theory can be viewed as an instance of enriched category theory. Enriched category theory provides a useful source of concepts and results for grading; for example, the definition of the underlying ordinary category $\underline{C}$ is just an instance of the more general definition of the underlying category of an enriched category (cf. [11, Section 1.3]). In more detail, $[\mathbb{E}, \mathbf{Set}]$ forms a monoidal category $([\mathbb{E}, \mathbf{Set}], I, \otimes)$ with *Day convolution*:

$$I = \mathbb{E}(1, -) \qquad X \otimes Y = \int^{e_1, e_2 \in \mathbb{E}} \mathbb{E}(e_1 \cdot e_2, -) \times Xe_1 \times Ye_2$$

Locally graded categories $\mathcal{C}$ are $[\mathbb{E}, \mathbf{Set}]$-categories, with coercions making $\mathcal{C}(X, Y)$ into an object of $[\mathbb{E}, \mathbf{Set}]$, and identities and composition in $\mathcal{C}$ providing identity and composition morphisms in $[\mathbb{E}, \mathbf{Set}]$ (with composition in diagram order). Functors between locally graded categories are $[\mathbb{E}, \mathbf{Set}]$-functors between $[\mathbb{E}, \mathbf{Set}]$-categories, and similarly for natural transformations, so that the 2-categories of locally graded categories and of $[\mathbb{E}, \mathbf{Set}]$-categories are equivalent.

4   Flexibly and Rigidly Graded Monads

We next employ locally graded categories to define notions of flexibly graded monad and rigidly graded monad. Rigidly graded monads turn out to be exactly graded monads (Definition 2); we say 'rigidly' to more clearly distinguish between these and flexibly graded monads. Flexibly graded monads are intuitively more general than rigidly graded monads. There is a flexibly graded monad whose algebras are graded monoids, and one whose algebras are graded arithmoids.

Both notions arise as instances of the following definition of *relative monad* for locally graded categories. Relative monads are similar to monads, except that instead of having free algebras on every object, they only have free algebras on objects of the form JX where $J : \mathcal{J} \to \mathcal{C}$ is some functor (which should be thought of as a full sub-locally graded category of $\mathcal{C}$; every J we use below is fully faithful in the sense that the functions $(f \mapsto Jf) : \mathcal{J}(X, Y)e \to \mathcal{C}(JX, JY)e$ are bijective). Altenkirch et al. [1] give a definition of relative monad for ordinary categories; their definition generalizes easily to enriched categories (cf. Staton [23]), and the definition we give below arises from this via the discussion in Remark 1.

Definition 14. *Let $J : \mathcal{J} \to \mathcal{C}$ be a functor between locally graded categories. A J-relative monad T consists of an object mapping $T : |\mathcal{J}| \to |\mathcal{C}|$, a unit $\eta_X : JX \,{-}1{\to}\, TX$ for each $X \in |\mathcal{J}|$, and a Kleisli extension operator*

$$\frac{f : JX \,{-}e{\to}\, TY}{f^\dagger : TX \,{-}e{\to}\, TY}$$

which is required to be unital, associative, and natural, as follows:

$$
\begin{aligned}
f^\dagger \circ \eta_X &= f && \text{for each } f : JX \,{-}e{\to}\, TY \\
\mathrm{id}_{TX} &= \eta_X^\dagger && \text{for each } X \in |\mathcal{J}| \\
(g^\dagger \circ f)^\dagger &= g^\dagger \circ f^\dagger && \text{for each } f : JX \,{-}e{\to}\, TY, g : JY \,{-}e'{\to}\, TZ \\
(\zeta^* f)^\dagger &= \zeta^*(f^\dagger) && \text{for each } \zeta \in \mathbb{E}(e, e'), f : JX \,{-}e{\to}\, TY
\end{aligned}
$$

A morphism $\alpha : \mathsf{T} \to \mathsf{T}'$ of J-relative monads is a family of morphisms $\alpha_X : TX \,{-}1{\to}\, T'X$ in $\mathcal{C}$ such that $\alpha_X \circ \eta_X = \eta_X$ for all $X \in |\mathcal{J}|$ and such that $(\alpha_Y \circ f)^\dagger \circ \alpha_X = \alpha_Y \circ f^\dagger$ for all $f : JX \,{-}e{\to}\, TY$.

The object mapping of each J-relative monad T extends to a functor $T :$ $\mathcal{J} \to \mathcal{C}$ by defining $Tf = (\eta_Y \circ Jf)^\dagger$ for each $f : X -e\rightarrow Y$; under this definition, units, Kleisli extensions, and morphisms of relative monads are natural in the appropriate sense. The following two instances of the above definition are the ones that matter for us. Here $J_\mathbb{C}$ is as in Definition 13.

Definition 15. *Let $\mathbb{C}$ be an ordinary category with coproducts of the form $\mathbb{E}(1, e) \bullet X$. A flexibly $\mathbb{E}$-graded monad on $\mathbb{C}$ is a monad on the locally graded category $\mathbf{GObj}_\mathbb{E}(\mathbb{C})$, i.e. an $\mathrm{Id}_{\mathbf{GObj}_\mathbb{E}(\mathbb{C})}$-relative monad. A rigidly $\mathbb{E}$-graded monad on $\mathbb{C}$ is a $J_\mathbb{C}$-relative monad.*

We now prove our claim that graded monads can be formulated in terms of locally graded categories, by showing that they are just rigidly graded monads in the sense of the above definition. The following table compares the data the two definitions (Definition 2, Definition 15) ask for.

	Graded monad T	Rigidly graded monad T
Object mapping	$T : |\mathbb{C}| \to |[\mathbb{E}, \mathbb{C}]|$	$T : |\mathbf{Free}_\mathbb{E}(\mathbb{C})| \to |\mathbf{GObj}_\mathbb{E}(\mathbb{C})|$
Unit	$\eta_X : X \to TX1$	$\eta_X : \mathbb{E}(1, -) \bullet X \Rightarrow TX$
Kleisli extension	$\dfrac{f : X \to TYe}{f^\dagger : TX \Rightarrow TY(- \cdot e)}$	$\dfrac{f : \mathbb{E}(1, -) \bullet X \Rightarrow TY(- \cdot e)}{f^\dagger : TX \Rightarrow TY(- \cdot e)}$

The object mappings have identical types (since $|\mathbf{Free}_\mathbb{E}(\mathbb{C})| = |\mathbb{C}|$ and $|\mathbf{GObj}_\mathbb{E}(\mathbb{C})| = |[\mathbb{E}, \mathbb{C}]|$). The units and Kleisli extensions do not have identical types, but are in bijection via the Yoneda lemma (morphisms $X \to Ye$ are in bijection with natural transformations $\mathbb{E}(1, -) \bullet X \Rightarrow Y(- \cdot e)$).

Theorem 1. *There is a bijection between $\mathbb{E}$-graded monads on $\mathbb{C}$ and rigidly $\mathbb{E}$-graded monads on $\mathbb{C}$ for each $\mathbb{C}$ with coproducts of the form $\mathbb{E}(1, e) \bullet X$.*

From this point onwards, we view List, Wr^M and Count as rigidly graded monads.

Remark 2. We can also consider $K_\mathbb{C}$-relative monads, where $K_\mathbb{C} : \mathbb{C} \to [\mathbb{E}, \mathbb{C}]$ is the functor between ordinary categories defined by $K_\mathbb{C}X = \mathbb{E}(1, -) \bullet X$. These are similar to graded monads, but not the same. The Kleisli extension of a $K_\mathbb{C}$-relative monad has the form on the right below (equivalently, the form on the left below).

$$\frac{f : X \to TY1}{f^\dagger : TX \Rightarrow TY} \qquad \frac{f : \mathbb{E}(1, -) \bullet X \Rightarrow TY}{f^\dagger : TX \Rightarrow TY}$$

Compared to the table above, this is missing the quantification over e. The quantification over e is what locally graded categories (as opposed to ordinary categories) provide. This is why ordinary categories do not suffice when working with graded monads, and why we instead consider locally graded categories.

(where e appears as the grade of a morphism). (Fujii et al. [4] instead use categories equipped with an action of $\mathbb{E}$; the grade e then appears when applying the action. We discuss this approach further in Sect. 4.2 below.)

Turning to flexibly graded monads, their data are the following:

$$T : |\mathbf{GObj}_\mathbb{E}(\mathbb{C})| \rightarrow |\mathbf{GObj}_\mathbb{E}(\mathbb{C})|$$

$$\eta_X : X \Rightarrow TX$$

$$\frac{f : X \Rightarrow TY(- \cdot e)}{f^\dagger : TX \Rightarrow TY(- \cdot e)}$$

We use the following examples.

Example 4. We define a flexibly $\mathbb{N}_\leq^\times$-graded monad $\mathsf{List}_{\mathrm{flex}}$ on **Set**, whose algebras are $\mathbb{N}_\leq^+$-graded monoids (Theorem 2 below). Informally, $\mathsf{List}_{\mathrm{flex}}Xe$ is the set of lists over $X : \mathbb{N}_\leq \rightarrow$ **Set** whose total grade is at most $e \in \mathbb{N}$. To define $\mathsf{List}_{\mathrm{flex}}$ formally, let S_e be the poset of lists $\boldsymbol{n} = (n_1, \ldots, n_k)$ of natural numbers whose sum is at most $e \in \mathbb{N}$. (These lists may be empty, and any number of elements may be 0.) The ordering is pointwise, i.e. $\boldsymbol{n} \leq \boldsymbol{n}'$ if $\boldsymbol{n}$ and $\boldsymbol{n}'$ have the same length and $n_i \leq n_i'$ for all i. Then for each graded object $X : \mathbb{N}_\leq \rightarrow$ **Set**, we define a graded object $\mathsf{List}_{\mathrm{flex}}X : \mathbb{N}_\leq \rightarrow$ **Set** by

$$\mathsf{List}_{\mathrm{flex}}Xe = \mathrm{colim}_{\boldsymbol{n} \in S_e} \prod_i Xn_i \qquad \mathsf{List}_{\mathrm{flex}}X(e{\leq}e') = [\mathrm{in}_{\boldsymbol{n}}]_{\boldsymbol{n} \in S_e}$$

(Recall that we write $e{\leq}e'$ for the unique element of $\mathbb{N}_\leq(e, e')$; we also write in_i for the ith coprojection of a colimit.) Here we use the fact that if $e \leq e'$ then $S_e \subseteq S_{e'}$. For the unit $\eta_X : X \xrightarrow{-1} \mathsf{List}_{\mathrm{flex}}X$ (i.e. $\eta_X : X \Rightarrow \mathsf{List}_{\mathrm{flex}}X$), we use singleton lists, defining $\eta_{X,d}x = \mathrm{in}_{(d)}(x)$. Given $f : X \xrightarrow{-e} \mathsf{List}_{\mathrm{flex}}Y$ in $\mathbf{GObj}_\mathbb{E}(\mathbb{C})$ (i.e. $f : X \Rightarrow \mathsf{List}_{\mathrm{flex}}Y(- \cdot e)$), the Kleisli extension $f^\dagger : \mathsf{List}_{\mathrm{flex}}X \Rightarrow \mathsf{List}_{\mathrm{flex}}Y(- \cdot e)$ is defined by

$$f_d^\dagger(\mathrm{in}_{\boldsymbol{n}}(x_1, \ldots, x_k)) = \mathrm{in}_{\boldsymbol{m}_1 \cdots \boldsymbol{m}_k}(y_{11}, \ldots, y_{1\ell_1}, \ldots, y_{k1}, \ldots, y_{k\ell_k})$$
$$\text{where } \mathrm{in}_{\boldsymbol{m}_i}(y_{i1}, \ldots, y_{i\ell_i}) = f_{n_i}x_i$$

Here we use the fact that, if the sum of $\boldsymbol{n}$ is at most d, and the sum of each $\boldsymbol{m}_i$ is at most $n_i \cdot e$, then the sum of the concatenation $\boldsymbol{m}_1 \cdots \boldsymbol{m}_k$ is at most $\sum_i (n_i \cdot e) = (\sum_i n_i) \cdot e \leq d \cdot e$. Informally, $f^\dagger$ takes a list, applies f to each element, and then concatenates the results.

Example 5. Let M be a $\mathbb{N}_\leq^+$-graded monoid. There is a flexibly $\mathbb{N}_\leq^+$-graded writer monad $\mathsf{Wr}_{\mathrm{flex}}^\mathsf{M}$ defined on objects by $\mathsf{Wr}_{\mathrm{flex}}^\mathsf{M}X = M \otimes X$ where $\otimes$ is Day convolution (see Remark 1). This turns out to have the same algebras (namely M-actions) as the rigidly graded monad Wr^M (see Example 7 below), in contrast to the situation with $\mathsf{List}_{\mathrm{flex}}$ and List.

Example 6. We have a flexibly $\mathbb{Z}_\le^+$-graded monad $\mathsf{Count_{flex}}$ whose algebras are graded arithmoids (Theorem 3 below). For each graded object $X : \mathbb{Z}_\le \to \mathbf{Set}$, the graded object $\mathsf{Count_{flex}}X : \mathbb{Z}_\le \to \mathbf{Set}$ is defined by

$$\mathsf{Count_{flex}}Xe = \{t : \textstyle\prod_{i:\mathbb{N}} \coprod_{j:\mathbb{N}} X(e - (j - i)) \mid$$
$$\exists \rho \in \mathbb{N}. \forall k, j \in \mathbb{N}, x. t\,\rho = (j, x) \Rightarrow t(\rho + k) = (j + k, x)\}$$

The intuition is similar to that of Count above: a computation t takes an initial counter value i and returns a pair (j, x) of a final counter value j and result x. Note however that here the increase $j - i$ in the value of the counter may be greater than e; this is "corrected" by the fact that the grade of x is then negative. The unit and Kleisli extension are similar to those of Count:

$$\eta_{X,d}x = \lambda i. (i, x) \qquad f_d^\dagger t = \lambda i. \text{let } (j, x) = t\,i \text{ in } f_{d-(j-i)}\,x\,j$$

4.1 Eilenberg-Moore and Kleisli

Every relative monad T induces a locally graded category $\mathbf{EM}(\mathsf{T})$ of (Eilenberg-Moore) T-*algebras*, which is analogous to the usual Eilenberg-Moore category of a monad. We define $\mathbf{EM}(\mathsf{T})$, and prove a few basic properties; as for the definition of relative monad, these come directly from considering relative monads in enriched categories more generally (via Remark 1).

Definition 16. *Let* T *be a* J-*relative monad for some functor* $J : \mathcal{J} \to \mathcal{C}$ *between locally graded categories. A* T-*algebra* $\mathsf{A} = (A, (-)^\ddagger)$ *is a pair of a carrier* $A \in |\mathcal{C}|$ *and an* extension *operator*

$$\frac{f : JX -e\!\rightarrow A}{f^\ddagger : TX -e\!\rightarrow A}$$

which is required to satisfy the following equations:

$$\begin{array}{ll}
f^\ddagger \circ \eta_X = f & \text{for each } f : JX -e\!\rightarrow A \\
(g^\ddagger \circ f)^\ddagger = g^\ddagger \circ f^\dagger & \text{for each } f : JX -e\!\rightarrow TY, g : JY -e'\!\rightarrow A \\
(\zeta^* f)^\ddagger = \zeta^*(f^\ddagger) & \text{for each } \zeta \in \mathbb{E}(e, e'), f : JX -e\!\rightarrow A
\end{array}$$

These are the objects of a locally graded category $\mathbf{EM}(\mathsf{T})$. *Morphisms* $f : \mathsf{A}-e\!\rightarrow\mathsf{A}'$ *in* $\mathbf{EM}(\mathsf{T})$ *are morphisms* $f : A -e\!\rightarrow A'$ *in* $\mathcal{C}$ *such that* $f \circ g^\ddagger = (f \circ g)^\ddagger$ *for each* $g : JX -e'\!\rightarrow A$; *identities, composition and coercions are as in* $\mathcal{C}$. *The forgetful functor* $U_\mathsf{T} : \mathbf{EM}(\mathsf{T}) \to \mathcal{C}$ *sends* A *to* A, *and morphisms to themselves.*

We use this definition as our notion of algebra for rigidly and flexibly graded monads. Fujii et al. [4] define a notion of *graded algebra* for a graded monad T. When T is a rigidly graded monad, the T-algebras as defined as above are in bijection with graded algebras; see Sect. 4.2 below.

We characterize the algebras of the three flexibly graded monads defined above. First, we note that for every flexibly graded monad T, the T-algebras can be formulated equivalently as a pair of a carrier and a structure map (analogously to the standard definition of Eilenberg-Moore algebra), rather than in the extension form above. (This is an instance of a more general result, see Marmolejo and Wood [15].) The flexibly graded monad T has a *multiplication* $\mu : T \cdot T \Rightarrow T$, defined by $\mu_X = \mathrm{id}^{\dagger}_{TX}$. Each T-algebra A induces a morphism $a : TA - 1 \rightarrow A$ by $a = \mathrm{id}_A{}^{\ddagger}$, and this gives us a bijection between T-algebras A and pairs (A, a) of an object $A \in |\mathcal{C}|$ and a morphism $a : TA - 1 \rightarrow A$ compatible with the unit and multiplication of T (i.e. $a \circ \eta_A = \mathrm{id}_A$ and $a \circ \mu_A = a \circ Ta$).

As our first example, the flexibly $\mathbb{N}^{\times}_{\leq}$-graded monad $\mathsf{List}_{\mathrm{flex}}$ has graded monoids as algebras.

Theorem 2. *There exists an isomorphism* $\mathbf{GMon} \cong \mathbf{EM}(\mathsf{List}_{\mathrm{flex}})$ *over* $\mathbf{GObj}_{\mathbb{N}^{\times}_{\leq}}(\mathbf{Set})$.

Proof. Algebras A of $\mathsf{List}_{\mathrm{flex}}$ are, as above, in bijection with pairs (A, a) of a graded object A and morphism $a : \mathsf{List}_{\mathrm{flex}} A - 1 \rightarrow A$ (i.e. natural transformation $a : \mathsf{List}_{\mathrm{flex}} A \Rightarrow A$) compatible with the unit and multiplication of $\mathsf{List}_{\mathrm{flex}}$. Given (A, a), we define the multiplication and unit of a graded monoid (A, u, m) by

$$u = a_0(\mathrm{in}_{()}()) \qquad m_{e_1, e_2}(x_1, x_2) = a_{e_1 + e_2}(\mathrm{in}_{(e_1, e_2)}(x_1, x_2))$$

In the other direction, given a graded monoid (A, u, m), we define a as follows (omitting the subscripts of m):

$$a(\mathrm{in}_{(n_1, \ldots, n_k)}(x_1, \ldots, x_k)) = m(x_1, m(x_2, \cdots m(x_{k-1}, m(x_k, u)) \cdots))$$

Simple calculations show that these form a bijection between $\mathsf{List}_{\mathrm{flex}}$-algebras and graded monoids, and that a morphism $A - e \rightarrow A'$ in $\mathbf{GObj}_{\mathbb{E}}(\mathbb{C})$ is a morphism of algebras if and only if it is a morphism of the corresponding graded monoids.

As an example of this theorem, the free algebra $F_{\mathsf{List}_{\mathrm{flex}}} X$ forms the free graded monoid on $X : \mathbb{N}_{\leq} \rightarrow \mathbf{Set}$, with unit $u = \mathrm{in}_{()}()$ and multiplication

$$m_{d,e}(\mathrm{in}_n(x_1, \ldots, x_k), \mathrm{in}_m(x'_1, \ldots, x'_{\ell})) = \mathrm{in}_{nm}(x_1, \ldots, x_k, x'_1, \ldots, x'_{\ell})$$

Example 7. As our second example, the rigidly graded and flexibly graded writer monads have the same algebras: in both cases the algebras are M-actions, and there are isomorphisms $\mathbf{EM}(\mathsf{Wr}^{\mathsf{M}}_{\mathrm{flex}}) \cong \mathbf{GAct}_{\mathsf{M}} \cong \mathbf{EM}(\mathsf{Wr}^{\mathsf{M}})$ over $\mathbf{GObj}_{\mathbb{N}^{+}_{\leq}}(\mathbf{Set})$. An algebra for the flexibly graded monad $\mathsf{Wr}^{\mathsf{M}}_{\mathrm{flex}}$ is (as above) equivalently a pair of a graded object $A : \mathbb{N}_{\leq} \rightarrow \mathbf{Set}$ and a natural transformation $a : \mathsf{Wr}^{\mathsf{M}}_{\mathrm{flex}} A \Rightarrow A$ compatible with the unit and multiplication. These are equivalently M-actions by properties of Day convolution. For the rigidly graded monad Wr^{M}, algebras are again in bijection with M-actions, in particular, for each Wr^{M}-algebra A, we have functions $[A(\zeta + e_2)]_{\zeta \in \mathbb{N}_{\leq}(0,d)} : J_{\mathbf{Set}}(Ae_2)d \rightarrow A(d + e_2)$, and using these the graded monoid M acts on the carrier of A with $\mathrm{act}_{e_1, e_2} = ([A(\zeta + e_2)]_{\zeta})^{\ddagger}_{e_1}$.

Finally, for our third example we show that the flexibly $\mathbb{Z}_{\leq}^+$-graded monad Count$_{\text{flex}}$ has graded arithmoids as algebras.

Theorem 3. *There exists an isomorphism* $\textbf{GArith} \cong \textbf{EM}(\text{Count}_{\text{flex}})$ *over* $\textbf{GObj}_{\mathbb{Z}_{\leq}^+}(\textbf{Set})$.

Proof. Each algebra A of Count$_{\text{flex}}$ comes with a natural transformation $a :$ Count$_{\text{flex}}A \Rightarrow A$, and forms a graded arithmoid by defining

$$\text{inc}_e x = a_{e+1}(\lambda i.\,(i+1,x))$$
$$\text{dec}_e(x,y) = a_e(\lambda i.\,\text{if } i = 0 \text{ then } (0,x) \text{ else } (i-1,y))$$

Conversely, to make a graded arithmoid into a Count$_{\text{flex}}$-algebra, we define $a :$ Count$_{\text{flex}}A \Rightarrow A$ as follows. Let $\text{inc}_e^j : Ae \to A(e+j)$ be given by composing inc with itself j times. Given $t \in \text{Count}_{\text{flex}}Ae$, let ρ be a witness to the side-condition in the definition of Count$_{\text{flex}}Ae$, and set $(j_i, x_i) = t\,i$. We then define

$$a_e t = \text{dec}(\text{inc}^{j_0}x_0, \text{dec}(\text{inc}^{j_1}x_1, \cdots (\text{dec}(\text{inc}^{j_{\rho-1}}x_{\rho-1}, \text{inc}^{j_\rho}x_\rho)) \cdots))$$

(Here it does not matter which witness ρ is chosen because of the graded arithmoid law $\text{dec}_e(x, \text{inc}_e x) = x$. We can take for example the smallest such ρ.)

We frequently look at relative monads in terms of their algebras; this is justified by the fact that each relative monad is completely determined by its algebras. For example, List$_{\text{flex}}$ is (up to isomorphism) the only flexibly graded monad that has graded monoids as algebras. To make this precise, if $\alpha : \mathsf{T}' \to \mathsf{T}$ is a morphism of J-relative monads, then we let $\textbf{EM}(\alpha) : \textbf{EM}(\mathsf{T}) \to \textbf{EM}(\mathsf{T}')$ be the functor over $\mathcal{C}$ that sends $(A, (-)^{\ddagger})$ to $(A, (-)^{\ddagger'})$ where $f^{\ddagger'} = f^{\ddagger} \circ \alpha$. The following is a general fact about relative monads, specialized to locally graded categories:

Lemma 1. *Let* T *and* T' *be J-relative monads where $J : \mathcal{J} \to \mathcal{C}$. For every functor* $G : \textbf{EM}(\mathsf{T}) \to \textbf{EM}(\mathsf{T}')$ *over* $\mathcal{C}$, *there is a unique relative monad morphism* $\alpha : \mathsf{T}' \to \mathsf{T}$ *such that* $\textbf{EM}(\alpha) = G$.

The assignment $\alpha \mapsto \textbf{EM}(\alpha)$ is therefore a bijection between morphisms $\mathsf{T}' \to \mathsf{T}$ and functors $\textbf{EM}(\mathsf{T}) \to \textbf{EM}(\mathsf{T}')$ over $\mathcal{C}$. It follows that, if T' and T have the same algebras, in the sense that there exists an isomorphism $\textbf{EM}(\mathsf{T}) \cong \textbf{EM}(\mathsf{T}')$ over $\mathcal{C}$, then there also exists an isomorphism $\mathsf{T}' \cong \mathsf{T}$ of relative monads.

Remark 3. Lemma 1 relies on considering locally graded categories of algebras instead of the underlying ordinary categories: in general, there are ordinary functors $\underline{\textbf{EM}(\mathsf{T})} \to \underline{\textbf{EM}(\mathsf{T}')}$ over $\underline{\mathcal{C}}$ that are not of the form $\underline{\textbf{EM}(\alpha)}$. In particular, there are examples of this in which T and T' are rigidly graded monads.

If T is a J-relative monad (where $J : \mathcal{J} \to \mathcal{C}$), then the *free* T-*algebra* $F_{\mathsf{T}}X$ on $X \in |\mathcal{J}|$ has TX as carrier and Kleisli extension $(-)^{\dagger}$ as extension operator. Since X ranges over objects of $\mathcal{J}$, these alone do not provide a left adjoint to the forgetful functor $U_{\mathsf{T}} : \textbf{EM}(\mathsf{T}) \to \mathcal{C}$. Instead, the free algebras form the left J-*relative* adjoint $F_{\mathsf{T}} : \mathcal{J} \to \textbf{EM}(\mathsf{T})$ of $U_{\mathsf{T}} : \textbf{EM}(\mathsf{T}) \to \mathcal{C}$.

Definition 17 ([25]). *Let $J : \mathcal{J} \to \mathcal{C}$ be a functor between locally graded categories. A J-relative adjunction consists of functors $L : \mathcal{J} \to \mathcal{D}$ (the left adjoint) and $R : \mathcal{D} \to \mathcal{C}$ (the right adjoint), and a family of bijections*

$$\theta_{X,Y,e} : \mathcal{D}(LX, Y)e \cong \mathcal{C}(JX, RY)e$$

natural in X, Y, e in the sense that the following hold for all $f : LX -e{\twoheadrightarrow} Y$:

$$
\begin{aligned}
\theta_{X',Y,e'\cdot e}(f \circ Lg) &= \theta_{X,Y,e}f \circ Jg &&\text{for each } g : X' -e' {\twoheadrightarrow} X \\
\theta_{X,Y',e\cdot e'}(g \circ f) &= Rg \circ \theta_{X,Y,e}f &&\text{for each } g : Y -e' {\twoheadrightarrow} Y' \\
\theta_{X,Y,e'}(\zeta^* f) &= \zeta^*(\theta_{X,Y,e}f) &&\text{for each } \zeta \in \mathbb{E}(e, e')
\end{aligned}
$$

Each J-relative adjunction induces a J-relative monad, with object mapping $X \mapsto R(LX)$. Conversely, $\mathbf{EM}(\mathsf{T})$ forms a *resolution* of T, i.e. a J-relative adjunction that induces the relative monad T. This is the terminal resolution of T, analogously to the situation with ordinary monads. In fact, many of the usual properties of monads carry over to relative monads in general and to flexibly and rigidly graded monads in particular. Each relative monad also has an initial resolution, given by the Kleisli construction.

Definition 18. *Let T be a J-relative monad, where $J : \mathcal{J} \to \mathcal{C}$. The Kleisli locally graded category $\mathbf{Kl}(\mathsf{T})$ of T has the same objects as $\mathcal{J}$. The morphisms $f : X -e{\twoheadrightarrow} Y$ in $\mathbf{Kl}(\mathsf{T})$ are morphisms $f : JX -e{\twoheadrightarrow} TY$ in $\mathcal{C}$, the identity on X is $\eta_X : JX -1{\twoheadrightarrow} TX$, the composition of $f : JX -e{\twoheadrightarrow} TY$ and $g : JY -e'{\twoheadrightarrow} TZ$ is $g^\dagger \circ f : JX -e \cdot e'{\twoheadrightarrow} TZ$, and coercions are as in $\mathcal{C}$.*

In the special case where T is a rigidly graded monad, $\mathbf{Kl}(\mathsf{T})$ is (isomorphic to) the Kleisli locally graded category defined by Gaboardi et al. [5].

4.2 $\mathbb{E}$-actegories

Previous work on graded monads, in particular by Fujii et al. [4], uses $\mathbb{E}$-*actegories* instead of locally $\mathbb{E}$-graded categories. We outline the connection between the two settings, and show that our locally graded categories of T-algebras are in some sense the same as Fujii et al.'s actegories of graded algebras.

A strict $\mathbb{E}$-*actegory* is an ordinary category $\mathbb{C}$ equipped with a bifunctor $* : \mathbb{E} \times \mathbb{C} \to \mathbb{C}$ that is compatible with the monoidal structure of $\mathbb{E}$ strictly, i.e. up to equality. Every strict $\mathbb{E}$-actegory $(\mathbb{C}, *)$ induces a locally $\mathbb{E}$-graded category $\Psi(\mathbb{C}, *)$: objects are the same as $\mathbb{C}$, and morphisms $X -e{\twoheadrightarrow} Y$ in $\Psi(\mathbb{C}, *)$ are morphisms $X \to e * Y$ in $\mathbb{C}$. This construction extends to a 2-functor Ψ (with appropriate notions of 1- and 2-cell between actegories), and Ψ is 2-fully faithful (see [6,16]). In this way, we can view strict actegories as a special case of locally graded categories. An example of a locally graded category that arises in this way is $\mathbf{GObj}_{\mathbb{E}}(\mathbb{C})$: we can make $[\mathbb{E}, \mathbb{C}]$ into an actegory by defining $e * X = X(- \cdot e)$, and then $\mathbf{GObj}_{\mathbb{E}}(\mathbb{C})$ is exactly $\Psi([\mathbb{E}, \mathbb{C}], *)$.

Eilenberg-Moore locally graded categories $\mathbf{EM}(\mathsf{T})$ of rigidly graded monads also arise in this way. The ordinary category $\underline{\mathbf{EM}(\mathsf{T})}$ forms a strict $\mathbb{E}$-actegory by assigning to each grade $e \in |\mathbb{E}|$ and T-algebra A the T-algebra $e * A$ whose carrier is $A(- \cdot e)$, and whose extension operator is the restriction of that of A. The locally graded category $\Psi(\mathbf{EM(T)}, *)$ is then exactly $\mathbf{EM(T)}$. Moreover, the actegory $(\mathbf{EM(T)}, *)$ is isomorphic to Fujii et al.'s actegory of graded algebras. In this sense, the latter, viewed as a locally graded category, is just our $\mathbf{EM(T)}$.

Not all of the locally graded categories we define above arise in this way however: $\mathbf{Free}_{\mathbb{E}}(\mathbb{C})$ and $\mathbf{Kl(T)}$ do not. (Fujii et al. [4] define Kleisli actegories of graded monads; applying Ψ to these does not yield $\mathbf{Kl(T)}$.)

5   Rigidly Graded Monads from Flexibly Graded Monads

We turn to the relationship between flexibly and rigidly graded monads. In this section, we show that every flexibly graded monad induces a rigidly graded monad that is in some sense canonical. We use this construction to explain where the graded monoid structure on $\mathrm{List}\,X$ comes from. Throughout this section, we suppose an ordinary category $\mathbb{C}$ with coproducts of the form $\mathbb{E}(1, e) \bullet X$.

Let T be a flexibly $\mathbb{E}$-graded monad on $\mathbb{C}$. The *rigidly graded restriction* $\lfloor T \rfloor$ of T is the rigidly $\mathbb{E}$-graded monad $\lfloor T \rfloor$ on $\mathbb{C}$ defined by restricting the structure of T to objects of $\mathbf{Free}_{\mathbb{E}}(\mathbb{C})$ (viewed as a sub-locally graded category of $\mathbf{GObj}_{\mathbb{E}}(\mathbb{C})$ via the functor $J_{\mathbb{C}}$). Explicitly, $\lfloor T \rfloor$ is given on objects by $\lfloor T \rfloor X = T(J_{\mathbb{C}}X)$, and the unit and Kleisli extension are restrictions of those of T. This construction is functorial: every morphism $\alpha : T \to T'$ of flexibly graded monads restricts to a morphism $\lfloor \alpha \rfloor : \lfloor T \rfloor \to \lfloor T' \rfloor$ of rigidly graded monads, so we have a functor between the ordinary categories of flexibly $\mathbb{E}$-graded monads on $\mathbb{C}$ and rigidly $\mathbb{E}$-graded monads on $\mathbb{C}$:

$$\lfloor - \rfloor : \mathbf{FGMnd}_{\mathbb{E}}(\mathbb{C}) \to \mathbf{RGMnd}_{\mathbb{E}}(\mathbb{C})$$

We also have a functor $R_{\mathsf{T}} : \mathbf{EM(T)} \to \mathbf{EM}(\lfloor T \rfloor)$ over $\mathbf{GObj}_{\mathbb{E}}(\mathbb{C})$, which sends each T-algebra A to the $\lfloor T \rfloor$-algebra $R_{\mathsf{T}}A$ whose carrier is A, and whose extension operator $(-)^{\ddagger}$ is the restriction of that of A.

We record two crucial facts about $\lfloor T \rfloor$. The first is that the graded objects $\lfloor T \rfloor X$ form T-algebras. More specifically, the free $\lfloor T \rfloor$-algebra functor $F_{\lfloor T \rfloor}$ is equal to

$$\mathbf{Free}_{\mathbb{E}}(\mathbb{C}) \xrightarrow{J_{\mathbb{C}}} \mathbf{GObj}_{\mathbb{E}}(\mathbb{C}) \xrightarrow{F_{\mathsf{T}}} \mathbf{EM(T)} \xrightarrow{R_{\mathsf{T}}} \mathbf{EM}(\lfloor T \rfloor)$$

so in particular, $\lfloor T \rfloor X$ is the carrier of the T-algebra $F_{\mathsf{T}}(J_{\mathbb{C}}X)$. This is where, for example, the graded monoid structure on $\mathrm{List}\,X$ comes from; see Example 9 below.

The second fact is that $\lfloor T \rfloor$ is canonical, in that it satisfies the universal property expressed in the following lemma. Informally, the Eilenberg-Moore resolution of $\lfloor T \rfloor$ is as close as possible to the Eilenberg-Moore resolution of T. From this it follows that, if there is *any* rigidly graded monad T' with the same algebras as T, then T' is actually $\lfloor T \rfloor$ (Corollary 1).

Lemma 2. *Let* T *be a flexibly* $\mathbb{E}$*-graded monad on* $\mathbb{C}$*. For every rigidly* $\mathbb{E}$*-graded monad* T$'$ *on* $\mathbb{C}$ *and functor* R' : **EM**(T) → **EM**(T$'$) *over* $\mathbf{GObj}_{\mathbb{E}}(\mathbb{C})$*, there is a unique morphism* α : T$'$ → $\lfloor$T$\rfloor$ *of rigidly graded monads such that* $R' =$ **EM**$(\alpha) \cdot R_{\mathsf{T}}$.

$$\begin{array}{ccc}
\mathbf{EM}(\mathsf{T}) \xrightarrow{\;R_{\mathsf{T}}\;} \mathbf{EM}(\lfloor\mathsf{T}\rfloor) & & \lfloor\mathsf{T}\rfloor \\
\quad\searrow_{R'} \quad\downarrow^{\mathbf{EM}(\alpha)} & & \alpha\big\uparrow \\
\mathbf{EM}(\mathsf{T}') & & \mathsf{T}'
\end{array}$$

Proof. For each $X \in |\mathbb{C}|$, the T$'$-algebra $R'(F_{\mathsf{T}}(J_{\mathbb{C}}X))$ has carrier $\lfloor T \rfloor X = T(J_{\mathbb{C}}X)$, so $\eta_{J_{\mathbb{C}}X}{}^{\ddagger} : T'X -1\!\!\rightarrow \lfloor T \rfloor X$. Commutativity of the triangle above on $F_{\mathsf{T}}(J_{\mathbb{C}}X) \in \mathbf{EM}(\mathsf{T})$ implies $\alpha_X = \eta_{J_{\mathbb{C}}X}{}^{\ddagger}$, hence uniqueness of α. For existence, define $\alpha_X = \eta_{J_{\mathbb{C}}X}{}^{\ddagger}$.

Corollary 1. *Let* T *be a flexibly* $\mathbb{E}$*-graded monad on* $\mathbb{C}$*. If there exists a pair of a rigidly* $\mathbb{E}$*-graded monad* T$'$ *on* $\mathbb{C}$ *and isomorphism* R' : **EM**(T) $\cong$ **EM**(T$'$) *over* $\mathbf{GObj}_{\mathbb{E}}(\mathbb{C})$*, then* R_{T} : **EM**(T) → **EM**($\lfloor$T$\rfloor$) *is an isomorphism, and there is an isomorphism* T$'$ $\cong$ $\lfloor$T$\rfloor$ *of rigidly graded monads.*

Proof. The functor R' induces a morphism α : T$'$ → $\lfloor$T$\rfloor$ by Lemma 2. Another application of Lemma 2 shows that $R'^{-1} \cdot \mathbf{EM}(\alpha)$ is the inverse of R_{T}, so that R_{T} is an isomorphism. Since both R_{T} and R'^{-1} are isomorphisms, $\mathbf{EM}(\alpha)$ must be too, and then Lemma 1 implies α is an isomorphism T$'$ $\cong$ $\lfloor$T$\rfloor$.

Example 8. Corollary 1 implies that $\mathsf{Wr}^{\mathsf{M}} \cong \lfloor\mathsf{Wr}^{\mathsf{M}}_{\mathsf{flex}}\rfloor$, because Wr^{M} and $\mathsf{Wr}^{\mathsf{M}}_{\mathsf{flex}}$ have the same algebras (Example 7).

Example 9. The rigidly graded restriction of $\mathsf{List}_{\mathsf{flex}}$ is List. Indeed, the following defines an isomorphism ψ : $\mathsf{List} \cong \lfloor\mathsf{List}_{\mathsf{flex}}\rfloor$ of rigidly $\mathbb{N}^{\times}_{\leq}$-graded monads:

$$\psi_{X,e} : \quad \mathsf{List}Xe \to \mathrm{colim}_{n \in S_e} \prod_i \mathbb{E}(1, n_i) \bullet X$$
$$(x_1, \ldots, x_k) \mapsto \mathrm{in}_{\underbrace{(1,\ldots,1)}_{k}}(\mathrm{in}_{\mathrm{id}_1}x_1, \ldots, \mathrm{in}_{\mathrm{id}_1}x_k)$$

Recall from Theorem 2 that $\mathsf{List}_{\mathsf{flex}}$-algebras are graded monoids. Each graded object $\mathsf{List}X$ is isomorphic to the carrier of the free $\lfloor\mathsf{List}_{\mathsf{flex}}\rfloor$-algebra $F_{\lfloor\mathsf{List}_{\mathsf{flex}}\rfloor}X$, which as above forms a $\mathsf{List}_{\mathsf{flex}}$-algebra, and hence a graded monoid. One can calculate that this graded monoid structure is given by concatenation of lists. In summary, the graded monoid structure on $\mathsf{List}X$ arises by starting with the locally graded category **GMon** of graded monoids, constructing free graded monoids, which form the flexibly graded monad $\mathsf{List}_{\mathsf{flex}}$, and then showing that the restriction of $\mathsf{List}_{\mathsf{flex}}$ is List.

Lemma 2 provides a universal property for List. Every graded monoid induces a List-algebra via the following functor over $\mathbf{GObj}_{\mathbb{N}^{\times}_{\leq}}(\mathbf{Set})$:

$$R : \mathbf{GMon} \xrightarrow{\text{(Theorem 2)}} \mathbf{EM}(\mathsf{List}_{\mathsf{flex}}) \xrightarrow{R_{\mathsf{List}_{\mathsf{flex}}}} \mathbf{EM}(\lfloor\mathsf{List}_{\mathsf{flex}}\rfloor) \xrightarrow{\mathbf{EM}(\psi)} \mathbf{EM}(\mathsf{List})$$

For every rigidly $\mathbb{N}_{\leq}^{\times}$-graded monad T' and functor $R' : \mathbf{GMon} \to \mathbf{EM}(\mathsf{T}')$ over $\mathbf{GObj}_{\mathbb{N}_{\leq}^{\times}}(\mathbf{Set})$, there is a unique morphism $\alpha : \mathsf{T}' \to \mathsf{List}$ of rigidly graded monads such that $R' = \mathbf{EM}(\alpha) \cdot R$. Hence, while no rigidly graded monad has graded monoids as algebras (Theorem 4 below), List is as close as we can get.

Example 10. We have $\lfloor \mathsf{Count}_{\text{flex}} \rfloor \cong \mathsf{Count}$. To see this, note that $J_{\mathbf{Set}} X d = \emptyset$ for negative d, and $J_{\mathbf{Set}} X d \cong X$ otherwise. Hence, if $\lambda i.\,(j_i, x_i) \in \prod_{i:\mathbb{N}} \coprod_{j:\mathbb{N}} J_{\mathbf{Set}} X(e - (j - i))$, then, for each i, we must have $e - (j_i - i) \geq 0$, so $j_i \in [0..i + e]$.

This fact has analogous consequences to the list example above. It provides an explanation for where the graded arithmoid structure of the graded object $\mathsf{Count} X$ comes from. We also obtain a functor $\mathbf{GArith} \to \mathbf{EM}(\mathsf{Count})$ that provides a universal property for Count in terms of graded arithmoids.

6   Flexibly Graded Monads from Rigidly Graded Monads

We also consider going in the opposite direction: constructing a flexibly graded monad $\lceil \mathsf{T} \rceil$ from a given rigidly graded monad T. Ideally, we would like to construct $\lceil \mathsf{T} \rceil$ so that it has the same algebras as T. (This uniquely identifies $\lceil \mathsf{T} \rceil$ up to isomorphism by Lemma 1.) In general, there does not exist a $\lceil \mathsf{T} \rceil$ with this property, but we show below that there often does, by reducing existence of $\lceil \mathsf{T} \rceil$ to existence of certain colimits. Modulo existence of these colimits, flexibly graded monads are therefore more general than rigidly graded monads.

Throughout this section, we again suppose an ordinary category $\mathbb{C}$ with coproducts of the form $\mathbb{E}(1, e) \bullet X$.

Definition 19. *If it exists, the* flexibly graded extension *of a rigidly $\mathbb{E}$-graded monad T on $\mathbb{C}$ is a flexibly $\mathbb{E}$-graded monad $\lceil \mathsf{T} \rceil$ on $\mathbb{C}$ equipped with an isomorphism $Q_{\mathsf{T}} : \mathbf{EM}(\lceil \mathsf{T} \rceil) \cong \mathbf{EM}(\mathsf{T})$ over $\mathbf{GObj}_{\mathbb{E}}(\mathbb{C})$.*

Example 11. The flexibly graded extension of Wr^{M} is $\mathsf{Wr}^{\mathsf{M}}_{\text{flex}}$. The isomorphism $Q_{\mathsf{Wr}^{\mathsf{M}}} : \mathbf{EM}(\mathsf{Wr}^{\mathsf{M}}_{\text{flex}}) \cong \mathbf{EM}(\mathsf{Wr}^{\mathsf{M}})$ is defined in Example 7.

A basic result is that the rigidly graded restriction $\lfloor \lceil \mathsf{T} \rceil \rfloor$ is T itself, and $R_{\lceil \mathsf{T} \rceil} : \mathbf{EM}(\lceil \mathsf{T} \rceil) \to \mathbf{EM}(\lfloor \lceil \mathsf{T} \rceil \rfloor)$ is an isomorphism; this is immediate from Corollary 1. We show that, if $\lceil \mathsf{T} \rceil$ exists, then it is the free flexibly graded monad on T (Lemma 3 below). Existence of $\lceil \mathsf{T} \rceil$ for all T would imply that extensions would form an ordinary functor $\lceil - \rceil : \mathbf{RGMnd}_{\mathbb{E}}(\mathbb{C}) \to \mathbf{FGMnd}_{\mathbb{E}}(\mathbb{C})$ that is left adjoint to $\lfloor - \rfloor : \mathbf{FGMnd}_{\mathbb{E}}(\mathbb{C}) \to \mathbf{RGMnd}_{\mathbb{E}}(\mathbb{C})$. Moreover, since ϕ_{T} in the following lemma is an isomorphism, $\lceil - \rceil$ would then make $\mathbf{RGMnd}_{\mathbb{E}}(\mathbb{C})$ into a coreflective subcategory of $\mathbf{FGMnd}_{\mathbb{E}}(\mathbb{C})$.

Lemma 3. *Let T be a rigidly $\mathbb{E}$-graded monad on $\mathbb{C}$ that has a flexibly graded extension $\lceil \mathsf{T} \rceil$. There is a unique morphism $\phi_{\mathsf{T}} : \mathsf{T} \to \lfloor \lceil \mathsf{T} \rceil \rfloor$ of rigidly graded monads such that $\mathbf{EM}(\phi_{\mathsf{T}}) \cdot R_{\lceil \mathsf{T} \rceil} = Q_{\mathsf{T}}$. The unique ϕ_{T} is an isomorphism, and witnesses $\lceil \mathsf{T} \rceil$ as the free flexibly graded monad on T (with respect to $\lfloor - \rfloor$).*

Proof. By Corollary 1, the functor $R_{\lceil T \rceil} : \mathbf{EM}(\lceil T \rceil) \to \mathbf{EM}(\lfloor \lceil T \rceil \rfloor)$ is an isomorphism, so Lemma 1 implies that there is a unique ϕ_T such that $\mathbf{EM}(\phi_T) = Q_T \cdot R_{\lceil T \rceil}^{-1}$, and that ϕ_T is an isomorphism. To show that $\lceil T \rceil$ is free, suppose a flexibly $\mathbb{E}$-graded monad T' on $\mathbb{C}$ and morphism $\psi : T \to \lfloor T' \rfloor$ of rigidly graded monads. We show that there is a unique morphism $\hat{\psi} : \lceil T \rceil \to T'$ of flexibly graded monads such that $\psi = \lfloor \hat{\psi} \rfloor \circ \phi_T$. For every morphism $\hat{\psi} : \lceil T \rceil \to T'$ of flexibly graded monads we have

$$\psi = \lfloor \hat{\psi} \rfloor \circ \phi_T$$

$$\Leftrightarrow \quad \psi \circ \phi_T^{-1} = \lfloor \hat{\psi} \rfloor \qquad\qquad\qquad\qquad \phi_T \text{ is an isomorphism}$$

$$\Leftrightarrow \quad \mathbf{EM}(\phi_T^{-1}) \cdot \mathbf{EM}(\psi) = \mathbf{EM}(\lfloor \hat{\psi} \rfloor) \qquad\qquad \text{Lemma 1}$$

$$\Leftrightarrow \quad \mathbf{EM}(\phi_T^{-1}) \cdot \mathbf{EM}(\psi) \cdot R_{T'} = R_{\lceil T \rceil} \cdot \mathbf{EM}(\hat{\psi}) \qquad \text{Lemma 2}$$

$$\Leftrightarrow \quad Q_T^{-1} \cdot \mathbf{EM}(\psi) \cdot R_{T'} = \mathbf{EM}(\hat{\psi}) \qquad\qquad R_{\lceil T \rceil} \text{ is an isomorphism}$$

So the result follows from Lemma 1, using the last line to define $\hat{\psi}$.

Example 12. The rigidly $\mathbb{N}_{\leq}^{\times}$-graded monad List on **Set** has a flexibly graded extension $\lceil \mathsf{List} \rceil$, which can be constructed as follows. Recall from Example 4 that S_e is the poset of lists of natural numbers that sum to at most $e \in \mathbb{N}$. We define a family of full subposets $S'_e \subseteq S_e$ inductively by three rules: $(e) \in S'_e$; if $n_1, \ldots, n_k \in S'_e$ for $k \geq 0$, then the concatenation $n_1 n_2 \cdots n_k$ is in $S'_{k \cdot e}$; and if $k \in S'_e$ and $e \leq e'$, then $k \in S'_{e'}$. For example, $(2, 1, 1) \in S'_4$ but $(3, 1) \notin S'_4$. Then $\lceil \mathsf{List} \rceil$ is defined in exactly the same way as $\mathsf{List}_{\mathrm{flex}}$ (Example 4), except with S' instead of S. In particular, $\lceil \mathsf{List} \rceil Xe = \mathrm{colim}_{n \in S'_e} \prod_i Xn_i$. The unit, Kleisli extension, and functoriality of $\lceil \mathsf{List} \rceil$ are well-defined because of the three rules that define S'. The isomorphism $Q_{\mathsf{List}} : \mathbf{EM}(\lceil \mathsf{List} \rceil) \to \mathbf{EM}(\mathsf{List})$ sends a $\lceil \mathsf{List} \rceil$-algebra $(A, (-)^{\ddagger})$ to the List-algebra $(A, (-)^{\ddagger'})$, where $f^{\ddagger'} : \mathsf{List}X -e\!\!\to A$ is defined for $f : J_{\mathbb{C}}X -e\!\!\to A$ by

$$f^{\ddagger'}(x_1, \ldots, x_k) = f^{\ddagger}(\mathrm{in}_{(1,\ldots,1)}(\mathrm{in}_{\mathrm{id}_1} x_1, \ldots, \mathrm{in}_{\mathrm{id}_1} x_k))$$

The inclusions $S'_e \subseteq S_e$ induce a morphism $\alpha : \lceil \mathsf{List} \rceil \to \mathsf{List}_{\mathrm{flex}}$ of flexibly graded monads. This is not an isomorphism. For example, let $N : \mathbb{N}_{\leq} \to \mathbf{Set}$ be the graded object $Nn = \{0, \ldots, n\}$, where $N(n \leq n')$ is the inclusion $Nn \subseteq Nn'$. Then $\mathrm{in}_{(3,1)}(3, 1) \in \mathsf{List}_{\mathrm{flex}} N4$ is not in the image of $\alpha_{N,4}$, so $\alpha_{N,4}$ is not a bijection. In fact, there is no isomorphism $\lceil \mathsf{List} \rceil \cong \mathsf{List}_{\mathrm{flex}}$ *at all.* Existence of such an isomorphism would imply $\mathbf{GMon} \cong \mathbf{EM}(\mathsf{List}_{\mathrm{flex}}) \cong \mathbf{EM}(\lceil \mathsf{List} \rceil) \cong \mathbf{EM}(\mathsf{List})$ over $\mathbf{GObj}_{\mathbb{E}}(\mathbf{Set})$, and would therefore contradict the fact that no rigidly graded monad has graded monoids as algebras, which we prove as the following theorem.

Theorem 4. *There is no rigidly $\mathbb{N}_{\leq}^{\times}$-graded monad T on $\mathbf{Set}$ such that $\mathbf{GMon} \cong \mathbf{EM}(T)$ over $\mathbf{GObj}_{\mathbb{N}_{\leq}^{\times}}(\mathbf{Set})$.*

Proof. By Theorem 2, to give an isomorphism $\mathbf{GMon} \cong \mathbf{EM}(\mathsf{T})$ over $\mathbf{GObj}_{\mathbb{N}_{\leq}^{\times}}(\mathbf{Set})$ is equivalent to giving an isomorphism $\mathbf{EM}(\mathsf{List}_{\mathsf{flex}}) \cong \mathbf{EM}(\mathsf{T})$ over $\mathbf{GObj}_{\mathbb{N}_{\leq}^{\times}}(\mathbf{Set})$, so, by Corollary 1, it suffices to show that $R_{\mathsf{List}_{\mathsf{flex}}}$: $\mathbf{EM}(\mathsf{List}_{\mathsf{flex}}) \to \mathbf{EM}(\lfloor \mathsf{List}_{\mathsf{flex}} \rfloor)$ is not an isomorphism. We can calculate that $Q_{\mathsf{List}} \cdot \mathbf{EM}(\alpha) = \mathbf{EM}(\psi) \cdot R_{\mathsf{List}_{\mathsf{flex}}}$ where $\alpha : \lceil \mathsf{List} \rceil \to \mathsf{List}_{\mathsf{flex}}$ is as above, and ψ is the isomorphism $\mathsf{List} \cong \lfloor \mathsf{List}_{\mathsf{flex}} \rfloor$ from Example 9. Both Q_{List} and $\mathbf{EM}(\psi)$ are isomorphisms, but $\mathbf{EM}(\alpha)$ is not (by Lemma 1, since α is not an isomorphism). It follows that $R_{\mathsf{List}_{\mathsf{flex}}}$ is not an isomorphism either.

Remark 4. One may ask whether it would make any difference to weaken existence of an isomorphism $\mathbf{GMon} \cong \mathbf{EM}(\mathsf{T})$ commuting strictly with the forgetful functors, to existence of an equivalence commuting up to natural isomorphism with the forgetful functors. It does not, because existence of the latter implies existence of the former. We do not attempt to determine whether there exists an equivalence $\mathbf{GMon} \simeq \mathbf{EM}(\mathsf{T})$ that does not commute with the forgetful functors. Such an equivalence would not enable us to make the carrier of a given T-algebra into a graded monoid, so is not useful for what we are trying to achieve.

Example 13. The rigidly $\mathbb{Z}_{\leq}^{+}$-graded monad Count has a flexibly graded extension $\lceil \mathsf{Count} \rceil$, defined by

$$\lceil \mathsf{Count} \rceil X e = \{t : \textstyle\prod_{i:\mathbb{N}} \coprod_{j:\mathbb{N}} X(e - \max\{0, j - i\}) \mid$$
$$\exists \rho \in \mathbb{N}. \, \forall k, j \in \mathbb{N}, x.t \, \rho = (j, x) \Rightarrow t(\rho + k) = (j + k, x)\}$$

and with similar unit and Kleisli extension to $\mathsf{Count}_{\mathsf{flex}}$.

We construct the isomorphism $Q_{\mathsf{Count}} : \mathbf{EM}(\lceil \mathsf{Count} \rceil) \cong \mathbf{EM}(\mathsf{Count})$. Given a $\lceil \mathsf{Count} \rceil$-algebra $(A, (-)^{\ddagger})$, the corresponding Count-algebra $(A, (-)^{\ddagger'})$ is defined by $\int_{d}^{\dagger'} \iota = \int_{d}^{\dagger} \iota$, where on the left we view ι as an element of $\mathsf{Count} X d$, and on the right we view t as an element of $\lceil \mathsf{Count} \rceil (J_{\mathbf{Set}} X) d$. In the other direction, we construct $(-)^{\ddagger}$ from $(-)^{\ddagger'}$. First note that the latter can be seen as an operator

$$\frac{h : Z \to Ae}{h^{\ddagger''} : \mathsf{Count} Z \Rightarrow A(- + e)}$$

Given $f : X \Rightarrow A(- + e)$ and $t \in \lceil \mathsf{Count} \rceil X d$, let ρ be a witness to the side-condition on t in the definition of $\lceil \mathsf{Count} \rceil X d$, and set $(j_i, x_i) = t \, i$ and $m_i = \max\{0, j_i - i\}$. (It does not matter which ρ is chosen.) Define $g : [0..\rho] \to A(d+e)$ by

$$g \, i = (f_{d - m_i})_{m_i}^{\ddagger''} (\lambda i'. \, (\max\{0, i' + (j_i - i)\}, x_i))$$

so $g_0^{\ddagger''} : \mathsf{Count}[0..\rho]0 \to A(d + e)$, and then define $f_d^{\ddagger} t$ by

$$f_d^{\ddagger} t = g_0^{\ddagger''} (\lambda i. \, (i, \min\{i, \rho\}))$$

We show that graded arithmoids are not the algebras for any rigidly graded monad, using a similar argument to the argument for graded monoids above.

There is a morphism $\beta : \lceil \mathsf{Count} \rceil \to \mathsf{Count}_\mathrm{flex}$ of flexibly graded monads, given by

$$\beta_{X,e}(\lambda i.\,(j_i, x_i)) = \lambda i.\,(j_i, X(e - \max\{0, j_i - i\} \leq e - (j_i - i)) x_i)$$

This is not an isomorphism. To see this, define a graded set $Z : \mathbb{Z}_\leq \to \mathbf{Set}$ by $Zn = \{m \in \mathbb{Z} \mid m \leq n\}$. Then

$$(\lambda i.\,\text{if } i = 0 \text{ then } (0, 0) \text{ else } (i - 1, 1)) \in \mathsf{Count}_\mathrm{flex} Z0$$

is not in the image of $\beta_{Z,0}$. This implies the following theorem.

Theorem 5. *There is no rigidly $\mathbb{Z}_\leq^+$-graded monad T on $\mathbf{Set}$ such that* $\mathbf{GArith} \cong \mathbf{EM}(\mathsf{T})$ *over* $\mathbf{GObj}_{\mathbb{Z}_\leq^+}(\mathbf{Set})$.

Proof. By similar reasoning to the proof of Theorem 4, existence of such an isomorphism would imply that $\beta : \lceil \mathsf{Count} \rceil \to \mathsf{Count}_\mathrm{flex}$ is an isomorphism, which would be a contradiction.

6.1 Constructing Extensions

We turn to the problem of *constructing* the flexibly $\mathbb{E}$-graded monad $\lceil \mathsf{T} \rceil$ for a given rigidly $\mathbb{E}$-graded monad T on $\mathbb{C}$. It turns out that $\lceil \mathsf{T} \rceil$ exists exactly when certain (small) colimits exist in $\mathbf{EM}(\mathsf{T})$. We introduce the following class of (small) colimits in locally graded categories, which we use to construct $\lceil \mathsf{T} \rceil$.

Definition 20. *Let $\mathcal{D}$ be a locally $\mathbb{E}$-graded category, and let Y be an $\mathbb{E}$-graded object of $\underline{\mathcal{D}}$. The* internalization *of Y, if it exists, consists of an object $\mathrm{colim}^\mathbb{E} Y$ and natural family $(\lambda_d : Yd{-}d{\to}\mathrm{colim}^\mathbb{E} Y)_{d \in \mathbb{E}}$ of morphisms in $\mathcal{D}$, universal in the sense that, for every $e \in |\mathbb{E}|$, $Z \in |\mathcal{D}|$, and natural family $(f_d : Yd{-}d \cdot e{\to}Z)_{d \in \mathbb{E}}$, there is a unique $[f] : \mathrm{colim}^\mathbb{E} Y {-}e{\to} Z$ such that $f_d = [f] \circ \lambda_d$ for all $d \in |\mathbb{E}|$.*

Here *naturality* of a family $(f_d : Yd{-}d \cdot e{\to}Z)_{d \in \mathbb{E}}$ means $f_{d'} \circ Y\zeta = (\zeta \cdot e)^* f_d$ for all $\zeta \in \mathbb{E}(d, d')$. The universal property of $\mathrm{colim}^\mathbb{E} Y$ can be succinctly written as

$$\mathcal{D}(\mathrm{colim}^\mathbb{E} Y, Z)e \cong \int_{d \in \mathbb{E}} \mathcal{D}(Yd, Z)(d \cdot e) \qquad \text{naturally in } Z, e$$

where the naturality in Z is locally graded and the integral on the right is an end in $\mathbf{Set}$; the elements of the right-hand side are the natural families $(f_d : Yd{-}d \cdot e{\to}Z)_{d \in \mathbb{E}}$.

Example 14. Every graded object $X : \mathbb{E} \to \mathbb{C}$ of an ordinary category $\mathbb{C}$ induces a graded object $J_\mathbb{C}(X-)$ of $\mathbf{GObj}_\mathbb{E}(\mathbb{C})$. A natural family $(f_d : J_\mathbb{C}(Xd){-}d \cdot e{\to}Z)_{d \in \mathbb{E}}$ is a family of morphisms $\overline{f_{d,d'}} : \mathbb{E}(1, d') \bullet Xd \to Z(d' \cdot d \cdot e)$ natural in d, d'; by the Yoneda lemma, these are in bijection with natural transformations $X \Rightarrow Z(- \cdot e)$, i.e. morphisms $X{-}e{\to}Z$ in $\mathbf{GObj}_\mathbb{E}(\mathbb{C})$. Hence the internalization $\mathrm{colim}^\mathbb{E}(J_\mathbb{C}(X-))$ is just X equipped with the family λ corresponding to $\mathrm{id}_X : X{-}1{\to}X$.

More generally, let $F : \mathbf{Free}_{\mathbb{E}}(\mathbb{C}) \to \mathcal{D}$ be a functor. Then, for each $X : \mathbb{E} \to \mathbb{C}$, we have a graded object $F(X-) : \mathbb{E} \to \mathcal{D}$. If $\mathrm{colim}^{\mathbb{E}}(F(X-))$ exists for all X, then they form a functor $(X \mapsto \mathrm{colim}^{\mathbb{E}}(F(X-))) : \mathbf{GObj}_{\mathbb{E}}(\mathbb{C}) \to \mathcal{D}$. The latter is exactly the (pointwise) left Kan extension of F along $J_{\mathbb{C}}$ (in the enriched sense). We can therefore compute left Kan extensions along $J_{\mathbb{C}}$ as small colimits (even though $\mathbf{Free}_{\mathbb{E}}(\mathbb{C})$ might not be small). Example 14 above, where we take $F = J_{\mathbb{C}}$, shows that $\mathrm{Lan}_{J_{\mathbb{C}}} J_{\mathbb{C}}$ is the identity functor; in other words, that $J_{\mathbb{C}}$ is *dense*.

We can now construct $\lceil \mathsf{T} \rceil$ as follows. First construct the left Kan extension of the free T-algebra functor $F_{\mathsf{T}} : \mathbf{Free}_{\mathbb{E}}(\mathbb{C}) \to \mathbf{EM}(\mathsf{T})$ along $J_{\mathbb{C}}$, to obtain the left adjoint $\bar{F}_{\mathsf{T}} : \mathbf{GObj}_{\mathbb{E}}(\mathbb{C}) \to \mathbf{EM}(\mathsf{T})$ of the forgetful functor U_{T}. Then the composition $U_{\mathsf{T}} \cdot \bar{F}_{\mathsf{T}}$ forms a flexibly graded monad; this is $\lceil \mathsf{T} \rceil$. (Here we mean *left adjoint* in the usual enriched sense, in other words, the $\mathrm{Id}_{\mathbf{GObj}_{\mathbb{E}}(\mathbb{C})}$-relative left adjoint.)

Theorem 6. *A rigidly $\mathbb{E}$-graded monad T has a flexibly graded extension $\lceil \mathsf{T} \rceil$ if and only if $\mathrm{colim}^{\mathbb{E}}(F_{\mathsf{T}}(X-))$ exists in $\mathbf{EM}(\mathsf{T})$ for every $X : \mathbb{E} \to \underline{\mathbf{EM}(\mathsf{T})}$. When these exist, the functor*

$$\bar{F}_{\mathsf{T}} : X \mapsto \mathrm{colim}^{\mathbb{E}}(F_{\mathsf{T}}(X-)) : \mathbf{GObj}_{\mathbb{E}}(\mathbb{C}) \to \mathbf{EM}(\mathsf{T})$$

forms the left adjoint of U_{T}, and $\lceil \mathsf{T} \rceil$ is the flexibly graded monad induced by this adjunction.

Proof. The extension exists exactly when $U_{\mathsf{T}} : \mathbf{EM}(\mathsf{T}) \to \mathbf{GObj}_{\mathbb{E}}(\mathbb{C})$ is strictly monadic, and, by a general result about relative monads, this is the case exactly when U_{T} has a left adjoint. (If the left adjoint exists, the adjunction induces a flexibly graded monad $\lceil \mathsf{T} \rceil$, and functors $Q_{\mathsf{T}} : \mathbf{EM}(\lceil \mathsf{T} \rceil) \to \mathbf{EM}(\mathsf{T})$ and $Q_{\mathsf{T}}^{-1} : \mathbf{EM}(\mathsf{T}) \to \mathbf{EM}(\lceil \mathsf{T} \rceil)$ can be constructed and shown to be inverses using the fact that Eilenberg-Moore resolutions are terminal.) Consider the following:

$$\mathbf{EM}(\mathsf{T})(\bar{F}_{\mathsf{T}}X, \mathsf{A})e$$

$$\cong \int_{d \in \mathbb{E}} \mathbf{EM}(\mathsf{T})(F_{\mathsf{T}}(Xd), \mathsf{A})(d \cdot e) \qquad \text{universal property of } \mathrm{colim}^{\mathbb{E}}$$

$$\cong \int_{d \in \mathbb{E}} \mathbf{GObj}_{\mathbb{E}}(\mathbb{C})(J_{\mathbb{C}}(Xd), U_{\mathsf{T}}\mathsf{A})(d \cdot e) \qquad F_{\mathsf{T}} \text{ left } J_{\mathbb{C}}\text{-relative adjoint to } U_{\mathsf{T}}$$

$$\cong \mathbf{GObj}_{\mathbb{E}}(\mathbb{C})(\mathrm{colim}^{\mathbb{E}}_{d}(J_{\mathbb{C}}(Xd)), U_{\mathsf{T}}\mathsf{A})e \qquad \text{universal property of } \mathrm{colim}^{\mathbb{E}}$$

$$\cong \mathbf{GObj}_{\mathbb{E}}(\mathbb{C})(X, U_{\mathsf{T}}\mathsf{A})e \qquad \text{Example 14}$$

The first isomorphism exists when $\bar{F}_{\mathsf{T}}X$ does, the others always exist. Hence the left adjoint must necessarily be $\bar{F}_{\mathsf{T}}$.

Remark 5. To justify our use of the word "colimit" for the internalization $\mathrm{colim}^{\mathbb{E}} Y$ of $Y : \mathbb{E} \to \underline{\mathcal{D}}$, we note that, if we view $\mathcal{D}$ as an $[\mathbb{E}, \mathbf{Set}]$-category (using Remark 1), then internalizations are a special case of *weighted* colimits in $\mathcal{D}$. To be more specific, let $\mathbb{E}^{\mathrm{rev}}$ be the monoidal category $\mathbb{E}$ but with the arguments of the tensor swapped. By the universal property of free locally graded categories, there are unique functors W : $\mathbf{Free}_{\mathbb{E}^{\mathrm{rev}}}(\mathbb{E}^{\mathrm{op}}) \to \mathbf{GObj}_{\underline{\mathbb{E}}^{\mathrm{rev}}}(\mathbf{Set})$ and $Y^{\sharp}$: $\mathbf{Free}_{\mathbb{E}}(\mathbb{E}) \to \mathcal{D}$ such that $\underline{W} \cdot H_{\mathbb{E}^{\mathrm{op}}} = \mathrm{Hom}_{\mathbb{E}} : \mathbb{E}^{\mathrm{op}} \to [\mathbb{E}, \mathbf{Set}]$ and $\underline{Y^{\sharp}} \cdot H_{\mathbb{E}} = Y$. (Recall that $H_{\mathbb{C}} : \mathbb{C} \to \underline{\mathbf{Free}_{\mathbb{E}}(\mathbb{C})}$.) Then $\mathrm{colim}^{\mathbb{E}} Y$ is the colimit of $Y^{\sharp}$ weighted by W. This is a small colimit in $\mathcal{D}$, so it exists whenever $\mathcal{D}$ is cocomplete in the enriched sense. (Here the enriching category is not symmetric in general; for a definition of weighted colimit that does not assume symmetry, see [8].)

7   Related Work

Relative Monads. Relative monads were defined for ordinary categories by Altenkirch et al. [1], and generalized to $\mathbb{V}$-categories (for $\mathbb{V}$ symmetric monoidal) by Staton [23]. Our definitions of relative monad, algebra, and Kleisli (locally graded) category are generalizations of theirs. Our definition is not an instance of Lobbia's [14] generalization of relative monads to arbitrary 2-categories. Altenkirch et al. [1] studied the problem of extending a J-relative monad to a monad—as we do in Sect. 6. They defined a notion of well-behavedness for a functor J, which provides a sufficient condition for the extension to exist; when J is well-behaved, the extension $\lceil T \rceil$ of T has as underlying functor $\lceil T \rceil$ the left Kan extension of T along J. We cannot use this result to construct flexibly graded extensions, because $J_{\mathbb{C}}$ is not well-behaved (in the appropriate locally graded sense). Hence we give an alternative construction of $\lceil T \rceil$ (involving the Kan extension of F_{T} instead of T). In our case, the underlying functor of $\lceil T \rceil$ is not $\mathrm{Lan}_{J_{\mathbb{C}}} T$ in general ($\lceil \mathsf{List} \rceil$ is a counterexample).

Graded Monads. Graded monads were introduced independently by Smirnov [22], by Melliès [16], and by Katsumata [9]. A formal theory for graded monads was first developed using actegories by Fujii et al. [4] (based on Street's [24] formal theory of *lax functors*). Presentations of graded monads have been studied by various authors [2,12,17,22], but these are all rigid, in that they present algebras of rigidly graded monads (so are not general enough to capture graded monoids or graded arithmoids).

Locally Graded Categories. Locally graded categories were first introduced by Wood [26], who proved that they are enriched categories. We use the terminology of Levy [13]. They were also used in connection with grading by Melliès [16] and by Gaboardi et al. [5]. The latter in particular define the Kleisli locally graded category of a graded monad. The formulation of graded monads *within* locally graded category theory, which enables our development, is new here.

8   Conclusions

Graded monads cannot capture certain structures, such as graded monoids, as their algebras. This is the case even if their free algebras form instances of these structures. We show however that even when these structures are not captured exactly, we can often characterize the graded monad by a universal property, from which we can extract the structure of the free algebras. The proof of this involves the notion of flexibly graded monad. We introduce these primarily as a graded-monad-like tool for capturing these structures, though they may be useful in their own right as a generalization (modulo existence) of (rigidly) graded monads. We work within locally graded category theory, which provides a rich source of results for reasoning about grading.

As we state in the introduction, our primary motivation for this work is to develop a notion of presentation for graded monads that captures, for example, the operations of a graded monoid. This paper lays the groundwork for such a development, which we present in the sequel paper [10].

Acknowledgements. We thank Nathanael Arkor, Shin-ya Katsumata and Nicolas Wu for helpful discussions. Both authors were supported by the Icelandic Research Fund grants no. 196323-053 and 228684-051.

References

1. Altenkirch, T., Chapman, J., Uustalu, T.: Monads need not be endofunctors. Log. Methods Comput. Sci **11**(1), 3:1–3:40 (2015). https://doi.org/10.2168/lmcs-11(1: 3)2015

2. Dorsch, U., Milius, S., Schröder, L.: Graded monads and graded logics for the linear time - branching time spectrum. In: Fokkink, W., van Glabbeek, R. (eds.) Proc. of 30th Int. Conf. on Concurrency Theory, CONCUR 2019, Leibniz Int. Proc. in Informatics, vol. 140, pp. 36:1–36:16. Dagstuhl Publishing, Saarbrücken/Wadern (2019). https://doi.org/10.4230/lipics.concur.2019.36

3. Fritz, T., Perrone, P.: A probability monad as the colimit of spaces of finite samples. Theor. Appl. Categ. **34**(7), 170–220 (2019). http://www.tac.mta.ca/tac/volumes/ 34/7/34-07abs.html

4. Fujii, S., Katsumata, S., Melliès, P.-A.: Towards a formal theory of graded monads. In: Jacobs, B., Löding, C. (eds.) FoSSaCS 2016. LNCS, vol. 9634, pp. 513–530. Springer, Heidelberg (2016). https://doi.org/10.1007/978-3-662-49630-5_30

5. Gaboardi, M., Katsumata, S., Orchard, D., Sato, T.: Graded hoare logic and its categorical semantics. In: ESOP 2021. LNCS, vol. 12648, pp. 234–263. Springer, Cham (2021). https://doi.org/10.1007/978-3-030-72019-3_9

6. Garner, R.: An embedding theorem for tangent categories. Adv. Math. **323**, 668–687 (2018). https://doi.org/10.1016/j.aim.2017.10.039

7. Goncharov, S.: Trace semantics via generic observations. In: Heckel, R., Milius, S. (eds.) CALCO 2013. LNCS, vol. 8089, pp. 158–174. Springer, Heidelberg (2013). https://doi.org/10.1007/978-3-642-40206-7_13

8. Gordon, R., Power, A.: Algebraic structure for bicategory enriched categories. J. Pure Appl. Algebra **130**(2), 119–132 (1998). https://doi.org/10.1016/s0022-4049(97)00094-7

9. Katsumata, S.: Parametric effect monads and semantics of effect systems. In: Proceedings of 41st ACM SIGPLAN-SIGACT Symposium on Principles of Programming Languages, POPL 2014, pp. 633–645. ACM Press, New York (2014). https:// doi.org/10.1145/2535838.2535846

10. Katsumata, S., McDermott, D., Uustalu, T., Wu, N.: Flexible presentations of graded monads. Proc. ACM Program. Lang. **6**(ICFP), 123:1–123:29 (2022). https://doi.org/10.1145/3547654
11. Kelly, G.M.: Basic Concepts of Enriched Category Theory, London Math. Soc. Lecture Note Series, vol. 64. Cambridge University Press, Cambridge (1982), reprinted as: Reprints Theor. Appl. Categ. 10 (2005). http://www.tac.mta.ca/tac/reprints/articles/10/tr10abs.html
12. Kura, S.: Graded algebraic theories. In: FoSSaCS 2020. LNCS, vol. 12077, pp. 401–421. Springer, Cham (2020). https://doi.org/10.1007/978-3-030-45231-5_21
13. Levy, P.B.: Locally graded categories. Slides (2019). https://www.cs.bham.ac.uk/~pbl/papers/locgrade.pdf
14. Lobbia, G.: Distributive laws for relative monads. arXiv preprint arXiv:2007.12982 [math.CT] (2020). https://arxiv.org/abs/2007.12982
15. Marmolejo, F., Wood, R.J.: Monads as extension systems: No iteration is necessary. Theor. Appl. Categ. **24**(4), 84–113 (2010). http://www.tac.mta.ca/tac/volumes/24/4/24-04abs.html
16. Melliès, P.A.: Parametric monads and enriched adjunctions. Manuscript (2012). https://www.irif.fr/~mellies/tensorial-logic/8-parametric-monads-and-enriched-adjunctions.pdf
17. Milius, S., Pattinson, D., Schröder, L.: Generic trace semantics and graded monads. In: Moss, L.S., Sobociński, P. (eds.) Proceedings of 6th Conference on Algebra and Coalgebra in Computer Science, CALCO 2015, Leibniz Int. Proceedings in Informatics, vol. 35, pp. 253–269. Dagstuhl Publishing, Saarbrücken/Wadern (2015). https://doi.org/10.4230/lipics.calco.2015.253
18. Moggi, E.: Computational lambda-calculus and monads. In: Proceedings of 4th Annual Symposium on Logic in Computer Science, LICS 1989, pp. 14–23. IEEE Press, Los Alamitos, CA (1989). https://doi.org/10.1109/lics.1989.39155
19. Moggi, E.: Notions of computation and monads. Inf. Comput. **93**(1), 55–92 (1991). https://doi.org/10.1016/0890-5401(91)90052-4
20. Mycroft, A., Orchard, D., Petricek, T.: Effect systems revisited—control-flow algebra and semantics. In: Probst, C.W., Hankin, C., Hansen, R.R. (eds.) Semantics, Logics, and Calculi. LNCS, vol. 9560, pp. 1–32. Springer, Cham (2016). https://doi.org/10.1007/978-3-319-27810-0_1
21. Plotkin, G., Power, J.: Algebraic operations and generic effects. Appl. Categ. Struct. **11**, 69–94 (2003). https://doi.org/10.1023/a:1023064908962
22. Smirnov, A.: Graded monads and rings of polynomials. J. Math. Sci. **151**(3), 3032–3051 (2008). https://doi.org/10.1007/s10958-008-9013-7
23. Staton, S.: An algebraic presentation of predicate logic. In: Pfenning, F. (ed.) FoSSaCS 2013. LNCS, vol. 7794, pp. 401–417. Springer, Heidelberg (2013). https://doi.org/10.1007/978-3-642-37075-5_26
24. Street, R.: Two constructions on lax functors. Cah. Topol. Géom. Diff. Catég. 13(3), 217–264 (1972). http://www.numdam.org/item/CTGDC_1972__13_3_217_0
25. Ulmer, F.: Properties of dense and relative adjoint functors. J. Algebra 8(1), 77–95 (1968). https://doi.org/10.1016/0021-8693(68)90036-7
26. Wood, R.J.: Indicial Methods for Relative Categories. Ph.D. thesis, Dalhousie University (1976). http://hdl.handle.net/10222/55465

Folding over Neural Networks

Minh Nguyen[1]([✉])[iD] and Nicolas Wu[2][iD]

[1] University of Bristol, Bristol, UK
min.nguyen@bristol.ac.uk
[2] Imperial College London, London, UK
n.wu@imperial.ac.uk

Abstract. Neural networks are typically represented as data structures that are traversed either through iteration or by manual chaining of method calls. However, a deeper analysis reveals that structured recursion can be used instead, so that traversal is directed by the structure of the network itself. This paper shows how such an approach can be realised in Haskell, by encoding neural networks as recursive data types, and then their training as recursion scheme patterns. In turn, we promote a coherent implementation of neural networks that delineates between their structure and semantics, allowing for compositionality in both how they are built and how they are trained.

Keywords: Recursion schemes · Neural networks · Data structures · Embedded domain-specific languages · Functional programming

1 Introduction

Neural networks are graphs whose nodes and edges are organised into layers, generally forming a sequence of layers:

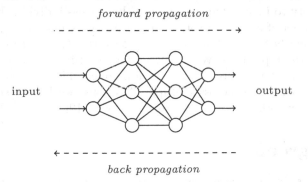

forward propagation

input   output

back propagation

Given input data (on the left), which is propagated through a series of transformations performed by each layer, the final output (on the right) assigns some particular meaning to the input. This process is called *forward propagation*. To improve the accuracy of neural networks, their outputs are compared with expected values, and the discrepencies are sent back in the reverse direction through each layer to appropriately update their parameters. This is *back propagation*.

How these notions are typically implemented is highly influenced by object-oriented and imperative programming design, where leading frameworks such as Keras [3] and PyTorch [16] can build on the extensive, existing support for machine learning in their host language. However, the design patterns of these paradigms tend to forgo certain appealing abstractions of neural networks; for example, one could perhaps view the diagram above as a composition of functions as layers, whose overall network structure is described by a higher-order function. Such concepts are more easily captured by functional languages, where networks can be represented as mathematical objects that are amenable to interpretation.

The relationship of neural networks with functional programming has been demonstrated several times, introducing support for compositional and type-safe implementation in various manners [2,4,14]. Using Haskell, this paper explores a categorical narrative that offers structure and compositionality in new ways:

- We illustrate how fully connected networks can be expressed as fixed-points of recursive data structures, and their operations of forward and back propagation as patterns of *folds* and *unfolds* over these structures. Neural network training (forward then back propagation) is then realised as a composition of fold and unfold (Sect. 3).
- We generalise our definition of neural networks into their types of layers by using coproducts, and provide an interface for modularly constructing networks using free monads (Sect. 4).
- We show how neural network training can be condensed into a single fold (Sect. 5).

We represent the ideas above with *structured recursion schemes* [9]. By doing so, we create a separation of concern between what the layers of a neural network do from how they comprise the shape of the overall network; this then allows compositionality to be developed in each of these areas individually.

A vast number of neural network architectures are sequentially structured [1, 8,21]. This paper hence uses fully connected networks [17] as a running example, being simple yet representative of this design. In turn, we believe the ideas presented are transferable to networks with more complex sequential structure, perhaps being sequential across multiple directions; we have tested this with convolutional networks [24] and recurrent networks [12] in particular.

2   Background

We begin by giving the necessary background to the recursion schemes used throughout this paper. First, consider the well-known recursive List type:

```
data List a = Nil | Cons a ( List a)
```

Folding and unfolding over a list are then defined as:

```
foldr :: (a → b → b) → b → List a → b        unfoldr :: (b → Maybe (a, b)) → b → List a
foldr f z Nil       = z                       unfoldr f b = case f b of
foldr f z (Cons x xs) = f x (foldr f z xs)      Just (a, b') → Cons a (unfoldr f b')
                                                Nothing      → Nil
```

Here, foldr recursively evaluates over a list of type [a] to an output of type b, by iteratively applying an accumulator function f (with some base value z). Conversely, unfoldr recursively builds a list of type [a] from a seed value b, by iteratively applying some generator function g.

Non-recursive Functors and Fix Points. The above useful patterns of recursion can be generalised to work over *arbitrary* nested data types, by requiring a common structure to recurse over – in particular, as a *functor* f:

```
class Functor f where
  fmap :: (k → l) → f k → f l
```

Additionally, f is required to be non-recursive, and recursion is instead represented abstractly in its type parameter k of f k. The function fmap can then support generic mappings to the recursive structure captured by k.

For example, the standard type List can be converted into a non-recursive functor ListF a:

```
data ListF a k = NilF | ConsF a k
instance Functor (ListF a) where
  fmap f NilF        = NilF
  fmap f (ConsF a k) = ConsF a (f k)
```

which is functorial over the new type parameter k, implicitly representing the recursive occurrence of ListF.

All explicit recursion is then instead relocated to the *fixed-point* type Fix f:

```
newtype Fix f = In (f (Fix f))
out :: Functor f ⇒ Fix f → f (Fix f)
out (In f) = f
```

The constructor In wraps a recursive structure of type f (Fix f) to yield the type Fix f, and the function out deconstructs this to reattain the type f (Fix f). Values of type Fix f hence encode the generic recursive construction of a functor f.

For example, the list [1, 2] in its Fix form would be represented as:

```
In (ConsF 1 (In (ConsF 2 (In NilF)))) :: Fix (ListF Int)
```

As NilF contains no parameter k, it encodes the base case (or least fixed-point) of the structure.

The ideas introduced so far provide us a setting for defining and using recursion schemes; this paper makes use of two in particular: catamorphisms (folds) and anamorphisms (unfolds).

Catamorphisms. A *catamorphism*, given by the function cata, generalises over folds of lists to arbitrary algebraic data types [11].

```
cata :: Functor f ⇒ (f a → a) → Fix f → a
cata alg = alg ∘ fmap (cata alg) ∘ out
```

The argument alg is called an *f-algebra* or simply *algebra*, being a function of type f a → a; this describes how a data structure of type f a is evaluated to an underlying value of type a. The type a is referred to as the algebra's *carrier type*.

Informally, cata recursively evaluates a structure of type Fix f down to an output of type a, by unwrapping the constructor of Fix via out, and then interpreting constructors of f with alg.

Anamorphisms. Conversely, an *anamorphism*, given by ana, generalises over unfolds of lists to arbitrary algebraic data types [13].

```
ana :: Functor f ⇒ (b → f b) → b → Fix f
ana coalg = In ∘ fmap (ana coalg) ∘ coalg
```

The argument coalg is called an *f-coalgebra* or simply *coalgebra*, being a function of type b → f b; this describes how a structure of type f b is constructed from an initial value of type b, where b is the carrier type of the coalgebra.

The function ana recursively generates a structure of type Fix f from a seed value of type b, by using coalg to replace occurrences of b with constructors of f, and then wrapping the result with the Fix constructor In.

3   Fully Connected Networks

We now consider how fully connected networks, one of the simplest types of neural networks, can be realised as an algebraic data type for structured recursion to operate over. These consist of a series of layers whose nodes are connected to all nodes in the previous and next layer:

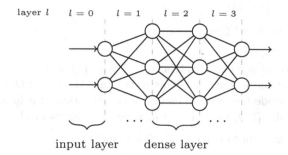

input layer   dense layer

The functor f chosen to represent this structure is the layer type, Layer:

```
data Layer k
  = InputLayer Values | DenseLayer Weights Biases k  deriving  Functor

type Values  = [Double]
type Biases  = [Double]
type Weights = [[Double]]
```

The case InputLayer is the first layer of the network and contains only the network's initial input Values. This is the base case of the functor.

The case DenseLayer is *any subsequent layer* (including the output layer), and contains as parameters a matrix Weights and vector Biases which are later used to transform a given input. Its argument k then represents its previous connected layer as a recursive parameter.

Notice that the dimensions of Weights and Biases in fact sufficiently describe a layer's internal structure:

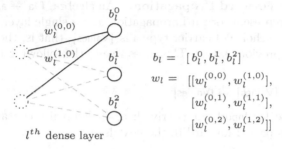

$$b_l = [b_l^0, b_l^1, b_l^2]$$
$$w_l = [[w_l^{(0,0)}, w_l^{(1,0)}],$$
$$[w_l^{(0,1)}, w_l^{(1,1)}],$$
$$[w_l^{(0,2)}, w_l^{(1,2)}]]$$

l^{th} dense layer

In the example layer l above, each jth node has a bias value b_l^j, and the edge to the jth node from the previous layer's i^{th} node has a weight value $w_l^{(i,j)}$. Hence, a weight matrix with dimensions $n \times m$ specifies n nodes in the current layer, with each node having m in-degrees. One could make this structure explicit by choosing a more precise type such as vectors [2], but we avoid this for simplicity.

By then incorporating Fix, an instance of a network is represented as a recursive nesting of layers of type Fix Layer. For example, below corresponds to the fully connected network shown at the beginning of Sect. 3:

```
fixNetwork :: Fix Layer
fixNetwork = In (DenseLayer w₃ b₃        -- l = 3, dims(w₃) = 2 × 3
            (In (DenseLayer w₂ b₂        -- l = 2, dims(w₂) = 3 × 3
            (In (DenseLayer w₁ b₁        -- l = 1, dims(w₁) = 3 × 2
            (In (InputLayer a₀ ))))))    -- l = 0, dims(a₀) = 2
```

A comparison can be drawn between the above construction and that of lists, where DenseLayer and InputLayer are analogous to Cons and Nil. Of course, there are less arduous ways of constructing such values, and a monadic interface for doing this is later detailed in Sect. 4.

The type Fix Layer then provides a base for encoding the operations of neural networks – forward and back propagation – as recursion schemes.

3.1   Forward Propagation as a Catamorphism

The numerous end-user applications that neural networks are well-known for, such as facial recognition [10] and semantic parsing [25], are all done via *forward propagation*: given unstructured input data, this is propagated through a sequence of transformations performed by each network layer; the final output can then be interpreted meaningfully by humans, for example, as a particular decision or some classification of the input.

One may observe that forward propagation resembles that of a fold: given an input, the layers of a neural network are recursively collapsed and evaluated to an output value (analogous to folding a list whose elements are layers). We can implement this notion using a generalised fold – a *catamorphism* – over the type Fix Layer; to do so simply requires a suitable algebra to fold with.

An Algebra for Forward Propagation. An algebra, f a → a, specialised to our context will represent forward propagation over a single layer. The functor f is hence Layer. The choice of carrier type a is [Values], that is, the accumulation of outputs of all previous layers. This gives rise to the following type signature:

$$alg_{fwd} \ :: \ Layer \ [Values] \ \rightarrow \ [Values]$$

Defining the case for InputLayer is trivial: a singleton list containing only the initial input a_0 is passed forward to the next layer.

$$alg_{fwd} \ (InputLayer \ a_0) \ = \ [a_0]$$

Defining the case for DenseLayer is where any numerical computation is involved:

$$alg_{fwd} \ (DenseLayer \ w_l \ b_l \ (a_{l-1} : as)) \ = \ (a_l : a_{l-1} : as)$$
$$\textbf{where } a_l = \sigma(w_l * a_{l-1} + b_l)$$

Above, the output a_{l-1} of the previous layer is used as input for the current l^{th} layer, letting the next output a_l be computed; this is given by multiplying a_{l-1} with weights w_l, adding on biases b_l, and applying some normalization function σ (we assume the correct operators $*$ and $+$ for matrices or vectors, given fully in Sect. A.1). The output a_l is then prepended to the list of previous outputs.

Having defined forward propagation over a single layer, recursively performing this over an entire neural network is done by applying cata alg_{fwd} to a value of type Fix Layer, yielding each of its layers' outputs:

$$cata \ alg_{fwd} \ :: \ Fix \ Layer \ \rightarrow \ [Values]$$

This decoupling of non-recursive logic (alg_{fwd}) from recursive logic (cata) provides a concise description of how a layer transforms its input to its output, without concerning the rest of the network structure.

A Better Algebra for Forward Propagation. The initial input to a neural network is currently stored as an argument of the InputLayer constructor:

```
-- currently
data Layer k = InputLayer Values | DenseLayer Weights Biases k
```

However, this design is somewhat simplistic. Rather, a neural network should be able to exist independently of its input value like so:

```
data Layer k = InputLayer | DenseLayer Weights Biases k
```

and have its input be provided externally instead. To implement this, we will have alg$_{fwd}$ evaluate a layer to a *continuation* of type Values $\rightarrow$ [Values] that awaits an input before performing forward propagation:

alg$_{fwd}$ :: Layer (Values $\rightarrow$ [Values]) $\rightarrow$ (Values $\rightarrow$ [Values])

In the case of InputLayer, this returns a function that wraps some provided initial input into a singleton list:

alg$_{fwd}$ InputLayer $= \lambda a_0 \rightarrow [a_0]$

For DenseLayer, its argument "forwardPass" is the continuation built from forward propagating over the previous layers:

alg$_{fwd}$ (DenseLayer w_l b_l forwardPass)
$= (\lambda(a_{l-1} : as) \rightarrow \text{let } a_l = \sigma(w_l * a_{l-1} + b_l) \text{ in } (a_l : a_{l-1} : as))$ $\circ$ forwardPass

This is composed with a new function that takes the previous outputs $(a_{l-1} : as)$ and prepends the current layer's output a_l, as defined before.

Folding over a neural network with the above algebra will then return the composition of each layer's forward propagation function:

cata alg$_{fwd}$ :: Fix Layer $\rightarrow$ (Values $\rightarrow$ [Values])

Given an initial input, the type Values $\rightarrow$ [Values] returns a list of all the layers' resulting outputs.

3.2 Back Propagation as an Anamorphism

Using a neural network to extract meaning from input data, via forward propagation above, is only useful if the network produces accurate outputs in the first place; this is determined by the "correctness" of its Weights and Biases parameters. Learning these parameters is called *back propagation*: given the *actual* output of forward propagation, it proceeds in the reverse direction of the network by updating each layer's parameters with respect to a *desired* output.

One could hence view back propagation as resembling an unfold, which recursively constructs an updated neural network from right to left. Dually to Sect. 3.1, we can encode this as a generalised unfold – an *anamorphism* – over the type Fix Layer; to do so simply requires an appropriate coalgebra to unfold with.

A Coalgebra for Back Propagation. A coalgebra, b $\rightarrow$ f b, will represent back propagation over a single layer. As before, f is Layer. The choice of carrier type b is slightly involved, as it should denote the information to be passed backwards through each layer, letting their weights and biases be correctly updated.

In particular, to update the lth layer requires knowledge of:

(i) Its original input a_{l-1} and output a_l.

(ii) The next layer's weights w_{l+1} and *delta value* δ_{l+1}, the latter being the output error of that layer. If there is no next layer, the *desired output* of the entire network is needed instead.

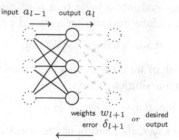

This is all captured by the type BackProp below, where as is the list of all layers' inputs and outputs produced from forward propagation:

```
type Deltas    = [Double]
data BackProp = BackProp { as            :: [Values]
                         , w_{l+1}       :: Weights
                         , δ_{l+1}       :: Deltas
                         , desiredOutput :: Values }
```

The choice of carrier type b, in coalgebra b → Layer b, is then (Fix Layer, BackProp):

```
coalg_bwd :: (Fix Layer, BackProp) → Layer (Fix Layer, BackProp)
```

As well as containing the information that is passed back through each layer, it also contains the *original network* of type Fix Layer. Defining coalg_bwd thus consists of pattern matching against values of Fix Layer, determining the network structure to be generated.

When matching against In InputLayer, there are no parameters to update and so InputLayer is trivially returned:

```
coalg_bwd (In (InputLayer), _) = InputLayer
```

When matching against In DenseLayer, the layer's output error and updated parameters must be computed:

```
coalg_bwd (In (DenseLayer w_l b_l prevLayer), backProp_{l+1})
  = let (δ_l, w_l^{new}, b_l^{new}) = backward w_l b_l backProp_{l+1}
        backProp_l = BackProp { w_{l+1} = w_l,
                                δ_{l+1} = δ_l,
                                as      = tail (as backProp_{l+1}) }
    in DenseLayer w_l^{new} b_l^{new} (prevLayer, backProp_l)

backward :: Weights → Biases → BackProp → (Deltas, Weights, Biases)
```

Above assumes the auxiliary function backward (given fully in Sect. A.2): this takes as arguments the old parameters w_l and b_l, and the back propagation values backProp$_{l+1}$ computed by the *next* layer; it then returns an output error δ_l and updated weights w_l^{new} and biases b_l^{new}.

Next, backProp$_l$ constructs the data to be passed to the *previous* layer: this stores the old weights, the newly computed delta, and the tail of the outputs as;

the last point ensures the head of *as* is always the original output of the layer being updated. Finally, a new DenseLayer is returned with updated parameters.

Having implemented back propagation over a single layer, recursively updating an entire network, Fix Layer, is then done by calling ana coalg$_{\text{bwd}}$ (provided some initial value of type BackProp):

ana coalg$_{\text{bwd}}$ :: (Fix Layer, BackProp) → Fix Layer

This can be incorporated alongside forward propagation to define the more complete procedure of neural network *training*, as shown next.

3.3   Training Neural Networks with Metamorphisms

Transforming an input through a neural network to an output (forward propagation), and then optimising the network parameters according to a desired output (back propagation), is known as *training*; the iteration of this process prepares a network to be reliably used for real-world applications.

Training can hence be viewed as the composition of forward and back propagation, which in our setting, is a catamorphism (fold) followed by an anamorphism (unfold), also known as a *metamorphism* [6]. We encode this below as train: given an initial input a_0, a corresponding desired output, and a neural network nn, this performs a single network update:

train :: (Values, Values) → Fix Layer → Fix Layer
train (a_0, desiredOutput) nn = (ana coalg$_{\text{bwd}}$ ∘ h ∘ cata alg$_{\text{fwd}}$) nn
    where h :: (Values → [Values]) → (Fix Layer, BackProp)
        h forwardPass = **let** as = forwardPass a_0
                    in (nn, BackProp as [] [] desiredOutput)

First, forward propagation is performed by applying cata alg$_{\text{fwd}}$ to nn, producing a function of type Values → [Values].

The intermediary function h then maps the *output* of forward propagation, forwardPass :: Values → [Values], to the *input* of back propagation, which has type (Fix Layer, BackProp). Here, forwardPass is applied to the initial input a_0 to yield the outputs as of all layers, which are returned alongside the desired output and original network nn.

Lastly, back propagation is performed by ana coalg$_{\text{bwd}}$. From the seed value of type (Fix Layer, BackProp), it generates a network with new weights and biases.

Updating a neural network over many inputs and desired outputs is then simple, and can be defined by folding with train; this is shown in Sect. 5.3.

4   Neural Networks à la Carte

Below shows how one would use the previous implementation to represent a fully connected neural network, consisting of an input layer and two dense layers.

fixNetwork :: Fix Layer
fixNetwork = In (DenseLayer w_2 b_2 (In (DenseLayer w_1 b_1 (In InputLayer))))

Such values of type Fix Layer can be rather cumbersome to write, and require all of their layers to be declared non-independently at the same time. A further orthogonal issue is that each kind of layer, DenseLayer and InputLayer, exclusively belongs to the type Layer of fully connected networks; in reality, the same kinds of layers are commonly reused in many different network designs, but the current embedding does not support modularity in this way.

We resolve these matters by taking influence from the *data types à la carte* approach [18], and incorporate free monads and coproducts in our recursion schemes. The result allows neural networks to be defined modularly as coproducts of their types of layers, and then constructed using monadic do-notation:

```
freeNetwork :: Free (InputLayer :+: DenseLayer) a
freeNetwork = do
  denselayer w₂ b₂
  denselayer w₁ b₁
  inputlayer
```

This then enables sections of networks to be independently defined in terms of the layers they make use of, and then later connected:

```
                              network₂ :: DenseLayer ⊂ f ⇒ Free f ()
                              network₂ = do denselayer w₂ b₂
freeNetwork = do
  network₂
  network₁                    network₁ :: (InputLayer ⊂ f, DenseLayer ⊂ f) ⇒ Free f a
                              network₁ = do denselayer w₁ b₁
                                            inputlayer
```

4.1   Free Monads and Coproducts

Free Monads. The type Fix f currently forces neural networks to be declared in one go. Free monads, of the type Free f a, instead provide a monadic interface for writing elegant, composable constructions of functors f:

```
--     Fix f   = In (f (Fix f))
data Free f a = Op (f (Free f a)) | Pure a

instance Functor f ⇒ Monad (Free f) where
  return a     = Pure a
  Pure a >>= k = k a
  Op f   >>= k = Op (fmap (>>=) k)
```

Identical to In of Fix f, the constructor Op of Free f a also encodes the generic recursion of f; the constructor Pure then represents a return value of type a. The key property of interest, is that monadically binding with (>>=) in the free monad corresponds to extending its recursive structure at the most nested level.

Using this, a fully connected network would have type Free Layer a, and an example of one input layer and two dense layers can be constructed like so:

```
freeNetwork' :: Free Layer a
```

```
freeNetwork′ = do
  Op (DenseLayer w₂ b₂ (Pure ()))
  Op (DenseLayer w₁ b₁ (Pure ()))
  Op InputLayer
```

Coproducts. To then promote modularity in the kinds of layers, the constructors of Layer are redefined with their own types:

```
data DenseLayer a = DenseLayer Weights Biases a deriving Functor
data InputLayer a = InputLayer deriving Functor
```

A type that contains these two layers can be described using the *coproduct* type f :+: g, being the coproduct of two functors f and g:

```
data (f :+: g) a = L (f a) | R (g a) deriving Functor
```

For example, a fully connected network would correspond to the free monad whose functor is the coproduct InputLayer :+: DenseLayer:

```
type FullyConnectedNetwork a = Free (InputLayer :+: DenseLayer) a
```

This supports reusability of layers when defining different variations of networks. As a simple example, one could represent a convolutional network by extending FullyConnectedNetwork with a convolutional layer (Sect. B.1):

```
type ConvolutionalNetwork a = Free (InputLayer :+: DenseLayer :+: ConvLayer) a
```

To then instantiate and pattern match against coproduct values, the type class sub ⊂ sup is used, stating that sup is a type signature that contains sub.

```
class (Functor sub, Functor sup) ⇒ sub ⊂ sup where
  inj :: sub a → sup a
  prj :: sup a → Maybe (sub a)
```

When this constraint holds, there must be a way of *injecting* a value of type sub a into sup a, and a way of *projecting* from sup a back into a value of type Maybe (sub a). These can be used to define "smart constructors" for each layer, as seen before in freeNetwork:

```
denselayer :: (DenseLayer ⊂ f) ⇒ Weights → Biases → Free f ()
denselayer w b = Op (inj (DenseLayer w b (Pure ())))

inputlayer :: (InputLayer ⊂ f) ⇒ Free f a
inputlayer = Op (inj InputLayer)
```

The above provides an abstraction for injecting layers into the type Free f where f is a coproduct of those layers.

4.2   Training Neural Networks with Free Monads

We next turn to reimplementing the recursion schemes cata and ana to support free monads and coproducts – this then involves minor revisions to how the algebra and coalgebra for forward and back propagation are represented.

Forward Propagation with Free Monads. The free monadic version of cata is known as eval, and evaluates a structure of Free f a to a value of type b:

```
eval  ::  Functor f ⇒ (f b → b) → (a → b) → Free f a → b
eval alg gen (Pure x) = gen x
eval alg gen (Op f)   = (alg ∘ fmap (eval alg gen)) f
```

Above carries out the same procedure as cata, but also makes use of a *generator* gen :: a → b; the generator's purpose is to interpret values of type a in Free f a into a desired carrier type b for alg :: f b → b. We remark that eval can in fact be defined in terms of cata, and is thus also a catamorphism.

Some minor changes are then made to the forward propagation algebra: as each layer now has its own type, defining alg_{fwd} for each of these requires ad-hoc polymorphism. The type class AlgFwd f is hence introduced which layers f can derive from to support forward propagation:

```
class Functor f ⇒ AlgFwd f where
  algfwd  ::  f (Values → [Values]) → (Values → [Values])
```

The algebra alg_{fwd} for constructors InputLayer and DenseLayer are unchanged:

```
instance AlgFwd InputLayer where
  algfwd InputLayer  = λa₀ → [a₀]
instance AlgFwd DenseLayer where
  algfwd (DenseLayer wₗ bₗ forwardPass)
    = (λ(aₗ₋₁ : as) → let aₗ = σ(wₗ * aₗ₋₁ + bₗ) in (aₗ : aₗ₋₁ : as)) ∘ forwardPass
```

Using alg_{fwd} with eval is then similar to as with cata:

```
eval algfwd genfwd  ::  AlgFwd f ⇒ Free f a → (Values → [Values])
  where genfwd  ::  a → (Values → [Values])
        genfwd = const (λx → [x])
```

This recursively evaluates a neural network of type Free f a to yield its forward propagation function. Here, the generator gen_{fwd} is chosen as const $(\lambda x \to [x])$, mapping the type a in Free f a to the desired carrier Values → [Values].

Back Propagation with Free Monads. The free monadic version of ana is known as build (which can also be defined in terms of ana), and generates a structure of Free f a from a seed value of type b:

```
build  ::  Functor f ⇒ (b → f b) → b → Free f a
build coalg = Op ∘ fmap (ana f) ∘ coalg
```

Similar to AlgFwd f, the type class CoalgBwd f is defined from which derived instances f implement back propagation via its $coalg_{bwd}$ method:

```
class Functor f ⇒ CoalgBwd f where
  coalgbwd  ::  (Free f a, BackProp) → f (Free f a, BackProp)
```

Here, the coalgebra's carrier now has the neural network to be updated as the type Free f rather than Fix f. Also note that unlike AlgFwd f whose instances correspond to *individual layers*, the instances of f derived for CoalgBwd f correspond to the *entire network* to be constructed.

For fully connected networks, f would be (InputLayer :+: DenseLayer):

instance CoalgBwd (InputLayer :+: DenseLayer) **where**

Defining coalg$_\text{bwd}$ is then the familiar process of pattern matching on the structure of the original network (Sect. 3.2), determining the updated network to be generated. Rather than directly matching on values of (InputLayer :+: DenseLayer) a, we make use of *pattern synonyms* [23] for a less arduous experience:

pattern InputLayer' ← (prj → Just InputLayer)
pattern DenseLayer' w_l b_l prevLayer ← (prj → Just (DenseLayer w_l b_l prevLayer))

Here, matching a layer against the pattern synonym InputLayer' would be equivalent to it passing it to prj below:

prj :: InputLayer ⊂ f ⇒ f a → Maybe (InputLayer a)

and then successfully pattern matching against Just InputLayer. A similar case holds for DenseLayer'.

The coalgebra coalg$_\text{bwd}$ for InputLayer' and DenseLayer' are then the same as with Fix, but now the updated layers are injected into a coproduct:

coalg$_\text{bwd}$ (Op InputLayer', _) = inj InputLayer
coalg$_\text{bwd}$ (Op (DenseLayer' w_l b_l prevLayer), backProp$_{l+1}$) =
   let $(w_l^{new}, b_l^{new}, \delta_l) = \ldots$
      backProp$_l$ $= \ldots$
  in   inj (DenseLayer w_l^{new} b_l^{new} (prevLayer, backProp$_l$))

Using coalg$_\text{bwd}$ with build instead of ana is also familiar, but now generates neural networks of the type Free f:

build coalg$_\text{bwd}$ :: AlgBwd f ⇒ (Free f a, BackProp) → Free f b

Training with Free Monads. Finally, eval and build can be combined to redefine the function train, now incorporating free monads and coproducts:

train :: (AlgFwd f, CoalgBwd f) ⇒ (Values, Values) → Free f a → Free f a
train (a_0, desiredOutput) nn = (build coalg$_\text{bwd}$ ∘ h ∘ eval alg$_\text{fwd}$ gen$_\text{fwd}$) nn

This maps a network of type Free f a, where f implements forward and back propagation, to an updated network; the intermediary function h used is unchanged.

5   Training with Just Folds

Currently, we encode forward then back propagation as a fold followed by an unfold. Rather than needlessly traversing the structure of a neural network twice, it is desirable to combine this work under a *single traversal*. This can be made possible by matching the recursion patterns used for each propagation. We show this by encoding back propagation as a *fold* instead (Sect. 5.1), which can then be performed alongside forward propagation under a single fold (Sect. 5.2).

5.1 Back Propagation as a Fold

Back propagation begins from the end of a neural network and progresses towards the start, the reason being that each layer is updated with respect to the next layer's computations. An anamorphism may seem like a natural choice of recursive pattern for this: it generates the outermost constructor (final layer) first, and then recurses by generating nested constructors (thus progressing towards the input layer). This is in contrast to cata which begins evaluating from the most nested constructor and then progresses outwards.

However, just as unfold can be defined in terms of fold, coalg$_{bwd}$ can be redefined as a back propagation *algebra* alg$_{bwd}$ for folding with:

class AlgBwd g f **where**
    alg$_{bwd}$ :: g (BackProp → Free f a) → (BackProp → Free f a)

In AlgBwd g f, the parameter g is the specific layer that is back propagated over, and f is the entire network to be constructed. The algebra alg$_{bwd}$ then has as its carrier type the continuation BackProp → Free f a, which given back propagation values from the next layer, will update the current and all previous layers.

Defining alg$_{bwd}$ for InputLayer returns a function that always produces an Input-Layer (injected into the free monad).

instance InputLayer ⊂ f ⇒ AlgBwd InputLayer f **where**
    alg$_{bwd}$ InputLayer = const (inject InputLayer)

    inject = Op ∘ inj

Defining alg$_{bwd}$ for DenseLayer returns a function that uses the backProp$_{l+1}$ value from the next layer to first update the current layer.

instance DenseLayer ⊂ f ⇒ AlgBwd DenseLayer f **where**
    alg$_{bwd}$ (DenseLayer w_l b_l backwardPass) = λ backProp$_{l+1}$ →
      let $(w_l^{new}, b_l^{new}, \delta_l)$ = ...
          backProp$_l$ = ...
      in   inject (DenseLayer w_l^{new} b_l^{new} (backwardPass backProp$_l$))

The computed backProp$_l$ value is then passed to the continuation "backwardPass" of type BackProp → Free f a, invoking back propagation on all the *previous* layers.

Folding back propagation over an entire network, via eval alg$_{bwd}$, will then compose each layer's BackProp → Free f a function, resulting in a chain of promises between layers to update their previous layer:

eval alg$_{bwd}$ gen$_{bwd}$ ::
(AlgBwd f f, InputLayer ⊂ f) ⇒ Free f a → (BackProp → Free f a)
    where gen$_{bwd}$ :: a → (BackProp → Free f a)
            gen$_{bwd}$ _ = const (inject InputLayer)

Here, the constraint AlgBwd f f says we can evaluate a network f to return a function that updates that same network. The generator gen$_{bwd}$ simply interprets the type a of Free f a to the desired carrier.

5.2   Training as a Single Fold

Having implemented forward and back propagation as algebras, it becomes possible to perform both in the same fold; this circumstance is given rise to by the 'banana split' property of folds [13], stating that any pair of folds over the same structure can always be combined into a single fold that generates a pair.

To do this, the function pairGen is defined to take two generators of types b and c, and return a generator for (b, c). Similarly, the function pairAlg takes two algebras with carrier types b and c, and returns an algebra of carrier type (b, c).

```
pairGen  ::  (a → b) → (a → c) → a → (b, c)
pairGen gen_b gen_c a = (gen_b a, gen_c a)

pairAlg  ::  Functor f ⇒ (f b → b) → (f c → c) → f (b, c) → (b, c)
pairAlg alg_b alg_c f_{bc} = (alg_b (fmap fst f_{bc}), alg_c (fmap snd f_{bc}))
```

These are incorporated below to redefine the function train, by first pairing the algebras and generators for forward and back propagation:

```
train  ::  (InputLayer ⊂ f, AlgFwd f, AlgBwd f f) ⇒ (Values, Values) → Free f a →
Free f a
train (a_0, desiredOutput) nn =
  let alg_train = pairAlg alg_fwd alg_bwd
      gen_train = pairGen gen_fwd gen_bwd
```

Folding over a neural network with these produces a function forwardPass of type Values → [Values] and a function backwardPass of type BackProp → Free f a:

```
(forwardPass, backwardPass) = eval alg_train gen_train nn
```

The intermediary function h is then defined to take the future output of forwardPass and initialise a BackProp value as input for backwardPass.

```
h  ::  [Values]  → BackProp
h as = BackProp as [] [] desiredOutput
```

Finally, passing an initial input a_0 to the composition of forwardPass, h, and backwardPass, returns an updated network:

```
in   (backwardPass ∘ h ∘ forwardPass) a_0
```

5.3   Example: Training a Fully Connected Network

We now show that our construction of fully connected networks is capable of learning. As an example, we will aim to model the sine function, such that the desired output of the network is the sine of a provided input value.

The network we construct is seen below on the right, where a single input value is propagated through three intermediate layers, and then the output layer produces a single value. Its implementation is given by fcNetwork, where rand-Mat2D m n represents a randomly valued matrix of dimension m×n.

```
type FullyConnectedNetwork = (InputLayer :+: DenseLayer)
```

```
fcNetwork :: Free FullyConnectedNetwork a
fcNetwork = do
    denselayer (randMat2D 1 3) (randVec 1)  -- l₄
    denselayer (randMat2D 3 3) (randVec 3)  -- l₃
    denselayer (randMat2D 3 3) (randVec 3)  -- l₂
    denselayer (randMat2D 3 1) (randVec 3)  -- l₁
    inputlayer                              -- l₀
```

To perform consecutive updates to the network over many inputs and desired outputs, one can define this as a straightforward list fold:

```
trainMany :: (InputLayer ⊂ f, AlgFwd f, AlgBwd f f)
          ⇒ [(Values, Values)] → Free f a → Free f a
trainMany dataset nn = foldr  train  nn dataset
```

An example program using this to train the network is given below:

```
main n_samples = do
  g ← getStdGen
  let initialInputs   = take n_samples (randoms g)
      desiredOutputs = map sine  initialInputs
      nn             = trainMany (zip initialInputs desiredOutputs) fcNetwork
```

Figure 1 shows the change in the output error of the neural network as more samples are trained with, comparing total sample sizes of 800 and 1400. The error produced when classifying samples can be seen to gradually converge, where the negative curvature denotes the network's ability to progressively produce more accurate values. The higher magnitude in correlation coefficient on the right indicates a stronger overall rate of learning for the larger sample size.

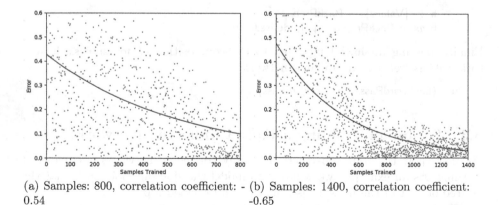

(a) Samples: 800, correlation coefficient: - (b) Samples: 1400, correlation coefficient: 0.54   -0.65

Fig. 1. Training a fully connnected neural network

6 Summary

This paper discussed a new narrative that offers structure and generality in describing neural networks, showing how they can be represented as recursive data structures, and their operations of forward and back propagation as recursion schemes. We demonstrated modularity in three particular ways: a delineation between the structure and semantics of a neural network, and compositionality in both neural network training and the types of layers in a network. Although only fully connected networks have been considered, we believe the ideas shown are transferrable to network types with more complex, sequential structure across multiple directions, and we have explored this externally with convolutional (Sect. B.1) and recurrent (Sect. B.2) networks in particular.

There are a number of interesting directions that are beyond the scope of this paper. One of these is performance, in particular, establishing to what extent we trade off computational efficiency in order to achieve generality in our approach. It is hoped that some of this can be offset by the performance gains of "fusion properties" [22] which the setting of structured recursion may give rise to; further insight would be needed as to the necessary circumstance for our implementation to exploit this. A second direction is to explore the many useful universal properties that recursion schemes enjoy, such as having unique solutions and being well-formed [13]; these may offer a means for equationally reasoning about the construction and evaluation of neural networks.

6.1 Related Work

It has been long established that it is typically difficult to state and prove laws for arbitrary, explicitly recursive functions, and that structured recursion [11,19,20] can instead provide a setting where properties of termination and equational reasoning can be readily applied to programs [13]. Neural networks are not typically implemented using recursion, and are instead widely represented as directed graphs of computation calls [7]; the story between neural networks and recursion schemes hence has limited existing work. A particularly relevant discussion is presented by Olah [14] who corresponds the representation of neural networks to type theory in functional programming. This makes a number of useful intuitions, such as networks as chains of composed functions, and tree nets as catamorphisms and anamorphisms.

Neural networks have seen previous exploration in Haskell. Campbell [2] uses dependent types to implement recurrent neural networks, enabling type-safe composition of network layers of different shapes; here, networks are represented as heterogeneous lists of layers, and forward and back propagation over layer types as standard type class methods.

There is also work in the functional programming community on structured approaches towards graph types. Erwig [5] takes a compositional view of graph, and defines graph algorithms in terms of folds that can facilitate program transformations and optimizations via fusion properties. Oliveira and Cook [15] use parametric higher-order abstract syntax (PHOAS), and develop a language for representing structured graphs generically using fix points; operations on these graphs are then implemented as generalized folds.

Lastly, a categorical approach to deep learning has also been explored by Elliot [4], in particular towards automatic differentiation which is central in computing gradients during back propagation. They realise an intersection between category theory and computing derivatives of functions, and present a generalisation of automatic differentiation by replacing derivative values with an arbitrary cartesian category.

Acknowledgements. We are sincerely grateful to the anonymous reviewers for their helpful suggestions and discussion, to Alessio Zakaria for aiding the 'unfolding' of the ideas in this paper, and for the constant support of the Bristol Programming Languages Research group. This work was partly funded by EPSRC Grant EP/S028129/1.

Appendix A. Elaborated code

A.1 Forward Propagation

Below gives the full implementation of alg_{fwd} in Sect. 3.1 for forward propagation.

```
type Values = [Double]
algfwd :: Layer [Values] → [Values]
algfwd (DenseLayer wₗ bₗ (aₗ₋₁ : as))
  = (aₗ : aₗ₋₁ : as)
  where aₗ = σ(wₗ * aₗ₋₁ + bₗ)

-- vector addition
⊕ᵥ :: [Double] → [Double] → [Double]
xs ⊕ᵥ ys  = zipWith (+) xs ys

-- matrix-vector multiplication
⊗ₘᵥ :: [[Double]] → [Double] → [Double]
xss ⊗ₘᵥ ys = map (sum ∘ zipWith (*) ys) yss

-- sigmoid function
σ :: [Double] → [Double]
σ = map (λx → 1/(1 + e⁻ˣ))
```

Input   Output

A.2 Back Propagation

Below gives the full implementation of backward, used during back propagation.

```
backward :: Weights → Biases → BackProp → (Deltas, Weights, Biases)
backward wₗ bₗ (BackProp (aₗ : aₗ₋₁ : as) wₗ₊₁ δₗ₊₁ desiredOutput) =
    let δₗ  = case δₗ₊₁ of
                [] → (aₗ ⊖ᵥ desiredOutput)   ⊗ᵥ σ'(aₗ₋₁)  -- compute δₗ for final layer
                _  → ((transpose wₗ₊₁) ⊗ₘᵥ δₗ₊₁) ⊗ᵥ σ'(aₗ₋₁)  -- compute δₗ for any other layer
        wₗⁿᵉʷ = wₗ ⊖ₘ (aₗ₋₁ ⊙ δₗ)
        bₗⁿᵉʷ = bₗ ⊖ᵥ δₗ
    in (δₗ, wₗⁿᵉʷ, bₗⁿᵉʷ)

    -- vector multiplication
```

```
⊗ᵥ :: [Double] → [Double] → [Double]
xs ⊗ᵥ ys = zipWith (*) xs ys

-- vector subtraction
⊖ᵥ :: [Double] → [Double] → [Double]
xs ⊖ᵥ ys = zipWith (-) xs ys

-- matrix subtraction
⊖ₘ :: [[Double]] → [[Double]] → [[Double]]
xss ⊖ₘ yss = zipWith (⊖ᵥ) xs ys

-- outer product
⊚ :: [Double] → [Double] → [[Double]]
xs ⊚ ys = map (λx → map (x *) ys) xs

-- inverse then differential sigmoid function
σ' :: [Double] → [Double]
σ' = map (λx → let y = log(x/(1 - x)) in y * (1 - y))
```

Appendix B. Training convolutional and recurrent networks

B.1 Training a Convolutional Neural Network

Convolutional neural networks are used primarily to classify images. To demonstrate the ability of a convolutional network implementation to learn, we choose to classify matrix values as corresponding to either an image displaying the symbol 'X' or an image displaying the symbol 'O'.

A diagram of the neural network used can be seen in Fig. 2 where dimensions are given in the form (width × height × depth) × number of filters. An input image of dimensions $(7 \times 7 \times 1)$ is provided to the network, resulting in an output vector of length two where each value corresponds to the probability of the image being classified as either an 'X' or an 'O' symbol.

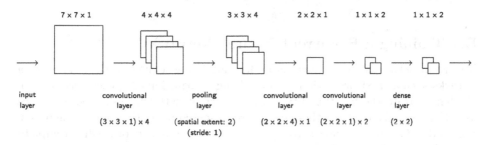

Fig. 2. Convolutional network

The network above is constructed by convNetwork, whose type ConvNetwork is the coproduct of five possible layer types found in a convolutional network:

```
type ConvNetwork = (InputLayer :+: DenseLayer :+: ConvLayer :+: PoolLayer :+: ReLuLayer)

convNetwork :: Free ConvNetwork a
convNetwork = do
```

```
denselayer (randMat2D 2 2)  (zeroMat1D 2)
convlayer (randMat4D 2 2 1 2) (zeroMat2D 2 1)
convlayer (randMat4D 2 2 4 1) (zeroMat2D 1 1)
poollayer 2 1
convlayer (randMat4D 3 3 1 4) (zeroMat2D 1 1)
inputlayer
```

In Fig. 3, we see the change in error as the amount of trained samples increases, using sample sizes of 300 and 600. The negative curvature demonstrates the convolutional neural network is successful in learning to classify the provided images. Two distinct streams of blue dots can also be observed in each graph, which represent the different paths of error induced by both of the sample types. The negative correlation coefficient is stronger in magnitude when using a sample size of 600, showing a better rate of convergence for the larger data set.

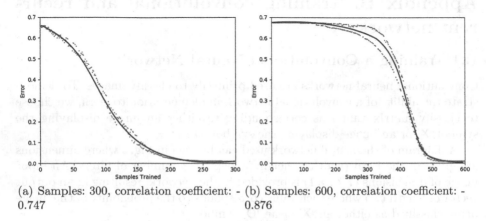

(a) Samples: 300, correlation coefficient: - (b) Samples: 600, correlation coefficient: -
0.747   0.876

Fig. 3. Training a convolutional neural network (Color figure online)

B.2 Training a Recurrent Neural Network

Recurrent networks are primarily used for classifying sequential time-series data in tasks such as text prediction, hand writing recognition or speech recognition. To demonstrate the functionality of our recurrent network implementation, we use DNA strands as data—these can be represented using the four characters a, t, c, and g. Given a strand of five DNA characters, our network will attempt to learn the next character in the sequence.

A diagram of the recurrent network used is shown in Fig. 4, consisting of two layers of five cells. We omit its corresponding implementation, but note that training over this network structure is represented by a catamorphism over layers where the algebra is a catamorphism over the cells of the layer.

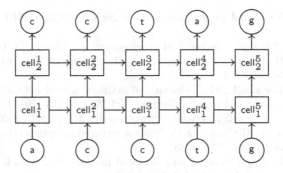

Fig. 4. Recurrent network

In Fig. 5, we see the change in error as the amount of trained samples increases, using sample sizes of 300 and 600. The negative curvature shown is less noticeable than the tests performed on previous networks, but still present. In contrast to the previous results, the correlation coefficient for the larger sample size of 600 is lower in magnitude than for the sample size of 300, perhaps showing convergence early on; achieving more conclusive results would require a more informed approach to the architecture and design of recurrent networks.

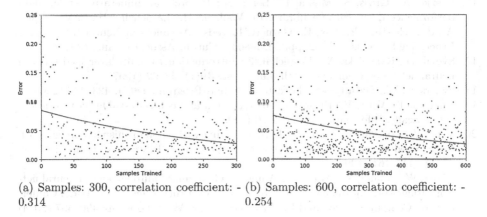

(a) Samples: 300, correlation coefficient: - (b) Samples: 600, correlation coefficient: -
0.314   0.254

Fig. 5. Training a recurrent neural network

References

1. Bebis, G., Georgiopoulos, M.: Feed-forward neural networks. IEEE Potentials **13**(4), 27–31 (1994)
2. Campbell, H.: Grenade (2017). https://github.com/HuwCampbell/grenade
3. Chollet, F., et al.: Keras (2015). https://github.com/fchollet/keras
4. Elliott, C.: The simple essence of automatic differentiation. Proc. ACM Program. Lang. **2**(ICFP), 1–29 (2018)

5. Erwig, M.: Functional programming with graphs. ACM SIGPLAN Not. **32**(8), 52–65 (1997)
6. Gibbons, J.: Streaming representation-changers. In: Kozen, D. (ed.) MPC 2004. LNCS, vol. 3125, pp. 142–168. Springer, Heidelberg (2004). https://doi.org/10.1007/978-3-540-27764-4_9
7. Guresen, E., Kayakutlu, G.: Definition of artificial neural networks with comparison to other networks. Procedia Comput. Sci. **3**, 426–433 (2011)
8. Hinton, G.E.: Deep belief networks. Scholarpedia **4**(5), 5947 (2009)
9. Hinze, R., Wu, N., Gibbons, J.: Unifying structured recursion schemes. ACM SIGPLAN Not. **48**(9), 209–220 (2013)
10. Khashman, A.: Application of an emotional neural network to facial recognition. Neural Comput. Appl. **18**(4), 309–320 (2009)
11. Malcolm, G.: Data structures and program transformation. Sci. Comput. Program. **14**(2–3), 255–279 (1990)
12. Medsker, L.R., Jain, L.: Recurrent neural networks. Des. Appl. **5**, 64–67 (2001)
13. Meijer, E., Fokkinga, M., Paterson, R.: Functional programming with bananas, lenses, envelopes and barbed wire. In: Hughes, J. (ed.) FPCA 1991. LNCS, vol. 523, pp. 124–144. Springer, Heidelberg (1991). https://doi.org/10.1007/3540543961_7
14. Olah, C.: Neural networks, types, and functional programming. https://colah.github.io/posts/2015-09-NN-Types-FP/
15. Oliveira, B.C., Cook, W.R.: Functional programming with structured graphs. In: Proceedings of the 17th ACM SIGPLAN International Conference on Functional Programming, pp. 77–88 (2012)
16. Paszke, A., Gross, S., Massa, F., Lerer, A.: Pytorch: an imperative style, high-performance deep learning library. In: Wallach, H., Larochelle, H., Beygelzimer, A., d' Alché-Buc, F., Fox, E., Garnett, R. (eds.) Advances in Neural Information Processing Systems, vol. 32, pp. 8024–8035. Curran Associates, Inc. (2019)
17. Svozil, D., Kvasnicka, V., Pospichal, J.: Introduction to multi-layer feed-forward neural networks. Chemom. Intell. Lab. Syst. **39**(1), 43–62 (1997)
18. Swierstra, W.: Data types à la carte. J. Funct. Program. **18**(4), 423–436 (2008)
19. Uustalu, T., Vene, V.: Primitive (co) recursion and course-of-value (co) iteration, categorically. Informatica **10**(1), 5–26 (1999)
20. Vene, V., Uustalu, T.: Functional programming with apomorphisms (corecursion). In: Proceedings of the Estonian Academy of Sciences: Physics, Mathematics, vol. 47, pp. 147–161 (1998)
21. Wang, W., Huang, Y., Wang, Y., Wang, L.: Generalized autoencoder: a neural network framework for dimensionality reduction. In: Proceedings of the IEEE Conference on Computer Vision and Pattern Recognition Workshops, pp. 490–497 (2014)
22. Wu, N., Schrijvers, T.: Fusion for Free. In: Hinze, R., Voigtländer, J. (eds.) MPC 2015. LNCS, vol. 9129, pp. 302–322. Springer, Cham (2015). https://doi.org/10.1007/978-3-319-19797-5_15
23. Wu, N., Schrijvers, T., Hinze, R.: Effect handlers in scope. In: Proceedings of the 2014 ACM SIGPLAN Symposium on Haskell, pp. 1–12 (2014)
24. Yamashita, R., Nishio, M., Do, R.K.G., Togashi, K.: Convolutional neural networks: an overview and application in radiology. Insights Imaging **9**(4), 611–629 (2018). https://doi.org/10.1007/s13244-018-0639-9
25. Yih, W.T., He, X., Meek, C.: Semantic parsing for single-relation question answering. In: Proceedings of the 52nd Annual Meeting of the Association for Computational Linguistics (Volume 2: Short Papers), pp. 643–648 (2014)

Towards a Practical Library for Monadic Equational Reasoning in Coq

Ayumu Saito[1] and Reynald Affeldt[2]($\boxtimes$) (iD)

[1] Tokyo Institute of Technology, School of Computing, Department of Mathematical and Computing Science, Tokyo, Japan
[2] National Institute of Advanced Industrial Science and Technology (AIST), Tokyo, Japan
reynald.affeldt@aist.go.jp

Abstract. Functional programs with side effects represented by monads are amenable to equational reasoning. This approach to program verification has been experimented several times using proof assistants based on dependent type theory. These experiments have been performed independently but reveal similar technicalities such as how to build a hierarchy of interfaces and how to deal with non-structural recursion. As an effort towards the construction of a reusable framework for monadic equational reasoning, we report on several practical improvements of Monae, a Coq library for monadic equational reasoning. First, we reimplement the hierarchy of effects of Monae using a generic tool to build hierarchies of mathematical structures. This refactoring allows for easy extensions with new monad constructs. Second, we discuss a well-known but recurring technical difficulty due to the shallow embedding of monadic programs. Concretely, it often happens that the return type of monadic functions is not informative enough to complete formal proofs, in particular termination proofs. We explain library support to facilitate this kind of proof using standard Coq tools. Third, we augment Monae with an improved theory about nondeterministic permutations so that our technical contributions allow for a complete formalization of quicksort derivations by Mu and Chiang.

1 Introduction

Pure functional programs, being referentially transparent, are suitable for equational reasoning. To reason about programs with side effects, one can use monads and their rich algebraic properties. In monadic equational reasoning, effects are defined by interfaces with a set of equations; these interfaces can be combined and extended to represent the combination of several effects. A number of programs using combined effects (state, nondeterminism, probability, etc.) have been verified this way (e.g., [14, 22–26]), and some of them have been formally verified with proof assistants such as Coq and Agda (e.g., [4, 24–26]).

The application to monadic equational reasoning of different proof assistants raises common issues. The construction of the hierarchy of monad interfaces

© The Author(s), under exclusive license to Springer Nature Switzerland AG 2022
E. Komendantskaya (Ed.): MPC 2022, LNCS 13544, pp. 151–177, 2022.
https://doi.org/10.1007/978-3-031-16912-0_6

is such an issue. There exist several approaches such as canonical structures (e.g., [4]) or type classes (e.g., [24]). The construction of a hierarchy of interfaces nevertheless requires care because it is known that large hierarchies suffer scalability issues due to the complexity of type inference (as discussed, e.g., in [12]). In the context of monadic equational reasoning, shallow embedding is the privileged way to represent monadic functions. This is the source of other issues, which are well-known. For example, when needed, induction w.r.t. syntax requires the use of reflection (see, e.g., [4, Sect. 5.1]). Non-structural recursion is another issue related to the use of a shallow embedding. General approaches and tools have been developed to deal with non-structural recursion in proof assistants but they are still cumbersome to use.

The Coq library MONAE is an effort to provide a tool for formal verification of monadic equational reasoning. It already proved useful by uncovering errors in pencil-and-paper proofs (e.g., [4, Sect. 4.4]), leading to new fixes for known errors (e.g., [3]), and providing clarifications for the construction of monads used in probabilistic programs (e.g., [2, Sect. 6.3.1]).

Before explaining our contribution in this paper, let us illustrate concretely the main ingredients of monadic equational reasoning in a proof assistant using MONAE.

Example of Proof by monadic equational reasoning Let us assume that we are given a type `monad` for monads, where `Ret` denotes unit and $\gg=$ denotes the bind operator ($\gg$ is defined by `m` $\gg$ `k` = `m` $\gg=$ `(fun _ ` $\Rightarrow$ ` k)`). We can use this type to define a generic function that repeats a computation `mx` (the computation `skip` is `Ret tt`):

```
Fixpoint rep {M : monad} n (mx : M unit) :=
  if n is n.+1 then mx ≫ rep n mx else skip.
```

Let us also assume that we are given a type `stateMonad T` for monads with a state of type `T` equipped with the usual `get` and `put` operators. We can use this type to define a `tick` function (`succn` is the successor function of natural numbers and ∘ is function composition):

```
Definition tick {M : stateMonad nat} : M unit := get ≫= (put ∘ succn).
```

Let us use monadic equational reasoning to prove "tick fusion" [25, Sect. 4.1] (in a state monad; `addn` is the addition of natural numbers):

```
Lemma tick_fusion n : rep n tick = get ≫= (put ∘ addn n).
```

Despite the side effect, this proof can be carried out by equational reasoning using standard monadic laws. Computations in any monad satisfy the following laws:

```
bindA    ∀ A B C (m : M A) (f : A → M B) (g : B → M C),
           (m ≫= f) ≫= g = m ≫= (fun a ⇒ f a ≫= g)
bindretf ∀ A B (a : A) (f : A → M B), Ret a ≫= f = f a
bindmret ∀ A (m : M A), m ≫= Ret = m
```

Computations in a state monad moreover satisfy the following laws:

INITIAL GOAL	rep n tick $=$ get $\gg\!\!=$ (put $\circ$ addn n)	
BASE CASE	rep 0 tick $=$ get $\gg\!\!=$ (put $\circ$ addn 0)	
	get $\gg\!\!=$ put $=$ get $\gg\!\!=$ (put $\circ$ addn 0)	(by getputskip)

INDUCTIVE CASE	rep n.+1 tick $=$ get $\gg\!\!=$ (put $\circ$ addn n.+1)	
$\left.\begin{array}{l}\text{(get} \gg\!\!= \text{(put} \circ \text{succn))} \gg\!\!= \\ \text{(get} \gg\!\!= \text{(put} \circ \text{addn n))}\end{array}\right\}$	$=$ get $\gg\!\!=$ (put $\circ$ addn n.+1)	(by inductive hyp.)
$\left.\begin{array}{l}\text{get} \gg\!\!= \text{(fun x} \Rightarrow \text{(put} \circ \text{succn) x} \gg\!\!= \\ \text{(get} \gg\!\!= \text{(put} \circ \text{addn n)))}\end{array}\right\}$	$=$ get $\gg\!\!=$ (put $\circ$ addn n.+1)	(by bindA)
(put $\circ$ succn) m $\gg\!\!=$ (get $\gg\!\!=$ (put $\circ$ addn n)) $=$ (put $\circ$ addn n.+1) m		(by extensionality)
((put $\circ$ succn) m $\gg$ get) $\gg\!\!=$ (put $\circ$ addn n) $=$ (put $\circ$ addn n.+1) m		(by bindA)
(put m.+1 $\gg$ Ret m.+1) $\gg\!\!=$ (put $\circ$ addn n) $=$ (put $\circ$ addn n.+1) m		(by putget)
put m.+1 $\gg$ (Ret m.+1 $\gg\!\!=$ (put $\circ$ addn n)) $=$ (put $\circ$ addn n.+1) m		(by bindA)
put m.+1 $\gg$ (put $\circ$ addn n) m.+1 $=$ (put $\circ$ addn n.+1) m		(by bindretf)
put (n + m.+1) $=$ (put $\circ$ addn n.+1) m		(by putput)
put (n + m.+1) $=$ put (n + m.+1)		(by addSnnS)

Fig. 1. Intermediate goals displayed by Coq when executing the proof script for tick fusion

putput	$\forall$ s s', put s $\gg$ put s' = put s'
putget	$\forall$ s, put s $\gg$ get = put s $\gg$ Ret s
getputskip	get $\gg\!\!=$ put = skip
getget	$\forall$ A (k : T $\rightarrow$ T $\rightarrow$ M A),
	get $\gg\!\!=$ (fun s $\Rightarrow$ get $\gg\!\!=$ k s) = get $\gg\!\!=$ fun s $\Rightarrow$ k s s

The following proof script (written with the SSREFLECT dialect of the Coq proof language [31]) shows that tick fusion can be proved by induction (using the `elim` tactic) and a sequence of rewritings involving mostly monadic laws (see Fig. 1 for the intermediate goals displayed by Coq or [25, Sect. 4.1] for a pencil-and-paper proof):

```
Lemma tick_fusion n : rep n tick = get ≫= (put ∘ addn n).
Proof.
elim: n ⇒ [|n ih]; first by rewrite /= -getputskip.
rewrite /= /tick ih bindA; bind_ext ⇒ m.
by rewrite -bindA putget bindA bindretf putput /= addSnnS.
Qed.
```

This example illustrates the main ingredients of a typical formalization of monadic equational reasoning: monadic functions (such as `rep` and `tick`) are encoded as functions in the language of the proof assistant (this is a shallow embedding), and monadic equational reasoning involves several monads with inheritance relations (here the state monad satisfies more laws than a generic monad).

Our contribution in this paper is to improve several practical aspects of MONAE [21]. More specifically, we address the following issues:

– In monadic equational reasoning, monadic effects are the result of the combination of several interfaces. The formalization of these interfaces and their combination in a coherent and reusable hierarchy requires advanced techniques. MONAE provides the largest hierarchy [4] we are aware of by using the methodology of *packed classes* [12]. However, when this methodology is implemented manually as in [4], it is verbose and the extension of the hierarchy is error-prone. In this work, we reimplement and extend this hierarchy using a more scalable and robust approach (Sect. 2).

– As we observe in the above example, monadic functions are written with the language of the proof assistant. Though this shallow embedding is simple and natural, in practice it is also the source of inconveniences when proving lemmas in general and when proving termination in particular. Indeed, contrary to a standard functional programming language, a type-based proof assistant requires termination proofs for every function involved. However, it happens that in practice the tooling provided by proof assistants to deal with non-structurally recursive functions is insufficient in the context of monadic equational reasoning. We explain how one can enrich the return type of monadic functions using dependent types to deal with such proofs (Sect. 3); we also propose *dependently-typed assertions* for that purpose (Sect. 4).

– Last, we demonstrate the usefulness of the two previous technical contributions by completing an existing formalization of quicksort by Mu and Chiang (Sect. 5). The original motivation by Mu and Chiang [24] was to demonstrate program derivation using the non-determinism monad and refinement but they left a few postulates unproved in their Agda formalization (see Table 1). We explain how to provide the remaining formal proofs and, as a by-product, we furthermore enrich MONAE with, in particular, a theory of nondeterministic permutations.

2   An Extensible Implementation of Monad Interfaces

We explain how we formalize a hierarchy of interfaces for monads used in monadic equational reasoning. This hierarchy is a conservative extension and complete reimplementation of previous work [2–4]. In previous work, the hierarchy in question was hand-written and its extension was error-prone (see Sect. 6). To allow for easy and flawless extensions, we use a generic tool called HIERARCHY-BUILDER [11] for the formalization of hierarchies of mathematical structures. The first version of this tool handled hierarchies of structures whose carrier has a type T : Type; it has recently[1] been extended to allow carriers with a functional type, and this section is an application of this new feature. As illustrations, we will use HIERARCHY-BUILDER to formalize the plus-array monad and revise a prior formalization of monad transformers.

2.1   HIERARCHY-BUILDER in a nutshell

HIERARCHY-BUILDER extends Coq with commands to define hierarchies of mathematical structures. It is designed so that hierarchies can evolve (for example by splitting a structure into smaller structures) without breaking existing

---

[1] HIERARCHY-BUILDER version 1.1.0 (2021-03-30).

code. These commands are compiled to packed classes [12] but the technical details (Coq modules, records, coercions, implicit arguments, canonical structures instances, notations, etc.) are hidden to the user. The main concept is the one of *factory*. This is a record defined by the command `HB.factory` that packs a carrier, operations, and properties. This record usually corresponds to the standard definition of a mathematical structure. *Mixins* (defined by the command `HB.mixin`) are factories used as the default definition for a mathematical structure. *Structures* (defined by the command `HB.structure`) are essentially sigma-types with a carrier paired with one or more factories. A mixin usually extends a structure, so it typically takes as parameters a carrier and other structures.

A *builder* is a function that shows that a factory is sufficient to build a mixin. Factories (including mixins) can be instantiated (command `HB.instance`) with concrete objects. Instances are built with `.Build` functions that are automatically generated for each factory. To write a builder, one uses the command `HB.builders` that opens a Coq section starting from a factory and ending with instances of mixins.

In addition to commands to build hierarchies, HIERARCHY-BUILDER also checks their validity by detecting missing interfaces (see Sect. 6) or *competing inheritance paths* [1].

2.2 Functors and Natural Transformations

Our hierarchy starts with the definition of functors on the category **Set** of sets. The domain and codomain of functors are fixed to the type `Type` of Coq, which can be interpreted as the universe of sets in set-theoretic semantics. Using HIERARCHY-BUILDER, we define functors by the mixin `isFunctor` (line 1). The carrier is a function `F` of type `Type` $\rightarrow$ `Type` (line 1) that represents the action on objects and the operator `actm` (line 2) represents the action on morphisms.

```
1   HB.mixin Record isFunctor (F : Type → Type) := {
2     actm : ∀ A B, (A → B) → F A → F B ;
3     functor_id : FunctorLaws.id actm ;    (* actm id = id *)
4     functor_o : FunctorLaws.comp actm }.   (* actm (g o h) = actm g o actm h *)
5   #[short(type=functor)]
6   HB.structure Definition Functor := {F of isFunctor F}.
```

The operator `actm` satisfies the functor laws (lines 3 and 4; `FunctorLaws.id` and `FunctorLaws.comp` are definitions whose meaning is indicated as comments). Line 5 prepares a notation for the type of functors. The structure of functors is defined at line 6 as the functions that satisfy the `isFunctor` mixin. Given a functor `F` and a morphism `f`, we note `F # f` the action of `F` on `f`.

We can now create instances of the type `functor`. For example, we can equip `idfun`, the standard identity function of Coq, with the structure of functor by using the `HB.instance` command (line 5 below). It is essentially a matter of proving that the functor laws are satisfied (lines 3, 4):

```
1   Section functorid.
2   Let id_actm (A B : Type) (f : A → B) : idfun A → idfun B := f.
3   Let id_id : FunctorLaws.id id_actm. Proof. by []. Qed.
```

```
4  Let id_comp : FunctorLaws.comp id_actm. Proof. by []. Qed.
5  HB.instance Definition _ := isFunctor.Build idfun id_id id_comp.
6  End functorid.
```

As a consequence of this declaration, we can use the HIERARCHY-BUILDER notation [the functor of idfun] to invoke the functor corresponding to idfun. Since it is often used, we introduce the notation FId for this purpose. Similarly, we provide an instance so that [the functor of F ∘ G] denotes the composition of two functors F and G, where ∘ is the standard function composition of Coq.

We now define natural transformations. Given two functors F and G, we formalize the components of natural transformations as a family of functions f, each of type ∀ A, F A → G A (short notation: F ⤳ G) that satisfies the following predicate:

```
Definition naturality (F G : functor) (f : F ⤳ G) :=
  ∀ A B (h : A → B), (G # h) ∘ f A = f B ∘ (F # h).
```

Natural transformations are defined by means of the mixin (line 1) and the structure (line 4) below.

```
1  HB.mixin Record isNatural (F G : functor) (f : F ⤳ G) := {
2     natural : naturality F G f }.
3  #[short(type=nattrans)]
4  HB.structure Definition Nattrans (F G : functor) := {f of isNatural F G f}.
5  Notation "f ⟹ g" := (nattrans f g) : monae_scope.
```

Hereafter, we use the notation F ⟹ G (declared at line 5) of natural transformations from the functor F to the functor G.

2.3   Formalization of Monads

We now formalize monads. A monad extends a functor with two natural transformations: the unit ret (line 2 below) and the multiplication join (line 3). They satisfy three laws (lines 7–9). Furthermore, we add to the mixin an identifier for the bind operator (line 4) and an equation that defines bind in term of unit and multiplication (line 6). Note however that this does not mean that the creation of a new instance of monads requires the (redundant) definition of the unit, multiplication, *and* bind (this will be explained below).

```
1   HB.mixin Record isMonad (F : Type → Type) of Functor F := {
2     ret : FId ⟹ [the functor of F] ;
3     join : [the functor of F ∘ F] ⟹ [the functor of F] ;
4     bind : ∀ A B, F A → (A → F B) → F B ;
5     bindE : ∀ A B (f : A → F B) (m : F A),
6        bind A B m f = join B (([the functor of F] # f) m) ;
7     joinretM : JoinLaws.left_unit ret join ;    (* join ∘ ret (F A) = id *)
8     joinMret : JoinLaws.right_unit ret join ;   (* join ∘ F # ret A = id *)
9     joinA : JoinLaws.associativity join }.       (* @join A ∘ F # @join A =
10                                                      @join A ∘ @join (F A) *)
11  #[short(type=monad)]
12  HB.structure Definition Monad := {F of isMonad F &}.
```

The fact that a monad extends a functor can be observed at line 1 with the of keyword; also, when declaring the structure at line 12, the & mark indicates inheritance w.r.t. all the mixins on which the structure depends on. Hereafter, we use Ret as a notation for (@ret _ _) (the modifier @ in Coq disables implicit arguments) and ≫= as a notation for bind.

The above definition of monads is not the privileged interface to define new instances of monads. We also provide factories with a smaller interface from which the above mixin is recovered. For example, here is the factory to build monads from the unit and the multiplication:

```
HB.factory Record isMonad_ret_join (F : Type → Type) of isFunctor F := {
  ret : FId ⟹ [the functor of F] ;
  join : [the functor of F ∘ F] ⟹ [the functor of F] ;
  joinretM : JoinLaws.left_unit ret join ;
  joinMret : JoinLaws.right_unit ret join ;
  joinA : JoinLaws.associativity join }.
```

This corresponds to the textbook definition of a monad, since it does not require the simultaneous definition of the unit, the multiplication, *and* bind. We use the HB.builders command (Sect. 2.1) to show that this lighter definition is sufficient to satisfy the isMonad interface.

Similarly, there is a factory to build monads from the unit and bind only:

```
HB.factory Record isMonad_ret_bind (F : Type → Type) of isFunctor F := {
  ret : FId ⟹ [the functor of F] ;
  bind : ∀ A B, F A → (A → F B) → F B ;
  fmapE : ∀ A B (f : A → B) (m : F A),
    ([the functor of F] # f) m = bind A B m (ret B ∘ f) ;
  bindretf : BindLaws.left_neutral bind ret ; (* ret ≫= f = f *)
  bindmret : BindLaws.right_neutral bind ret ; (* m ≫= ret = m *)
  bindA : BindLaws.associative bind }. (* (m ≫= f) ≫= g =
                                          m ≫= (fun x ⇒ f x ≫= g) *)
```

This new definition of monad is an improvement compared to the original formalization [1, Sect. 2.1] because there is now an explicit type of natural transformations (for ret and join) and because HIERARCHY-BUILDER guarantees that monads instantiated by factories do correspond to the same type monad. See [21, file monad_model.v] for many instances of the monad structure handled by the isMonad_ret_bind factory.

2.4   Extending the Hierarchy with New Monad Interfaces

Like we extended the type of functor to the type of monad in the previous section, we can extend the type of monad to the type of nondeterminism monad (by extending the interface of monad with a nondeterministic choice operator and more laws), the type of state monad, the type of exception monad, etc. We actually ported all monads from our previous work [4] using HIERARCHY-BUILDER; doing this port helped us identify and fix at least one type inference problem (see Sect. 6). In this section, we explain in particular the plus-array monad which is a new addition that we will use in Sect. 5.4 to formalize in-place quicksort.

The array monad. The array monad extends a basic monad with a notion of indexed array (see, e.g., [24, Sect. 5.1]). It provides two operators to read and write indexed cells. Given an index i, aget i returns the value stored at i and aput i v stores the value v at i. These operators satisfy the following laws (where S is the type of the cells' contents):

aputput	$\forall$ i v v', aput i v $\gg$ aput i v' = aput i v'
aputget	$\forall$ i v A (k : S $\rightarrow$ M A),
	aput i v $\gg$ aget i $\ggeq$ k = aput i v $\gg$ k v
agetputskip	$\forall$ i, aget i $\ggeq$ aput i = skip
agetget	$\forall$ i A (k : S $\rightarrow$ S $\rightarrow$ M A),
	aget i $\ggeq$ (fun v $\Rightarrow$ aget i $\ggeq$ k v) =
	aget i $\ggeq$ fun v $\Rightarrow$ k v v
agetC	$\forall$ i j A (k : S $\rightarrow$ S $\rightarrow$ M A),
	aget i $\ggeq$ (fun u $\Rightarrow$ aget j $\ggeq$ (fun v $\Rightarrow$ k u v)) =
	aget j $\ggeq$ (fun v $\Rightarrow$ aget i $\ggeq$ (fun u $\Rightarrow$ k u v))
aputC	$\forall$ i j u v, (i $\neq$ j) $\vee$ (u = v) $\rightarrow$
	aput i u $\gg$ aput j v = aput j v $\gg$ aput i u
aputgetC	$\forall$ i j u A (k : S $\rightarrow$ M A), i $\neq$ j $\rightarrow$
	aput i u $\gg$ aget j $\ggeq$ k =
	aget j $\ggeq$ (fun v $\Rightarrow$ aput i u $\gg$ k v)

For example, aputput means that the result of storing the value v at index i and then storing the value v' at index i is the same as the result of storing the value v'. The law aputget means that it is not necessary to get a value after having stored it provided this value is directly passed to the continuation. Other laws can be interpreted similarly.

The extension of the array monad can be simply implemented by extending a basic monad with the following mixin (note that the type of indices is an eqType, i.e., a type with decidable equality, as required by the laws of the array monad):

```
HB.mixin Record isMonadArray (S : Type) (I : eqType) (M : Type → Type)
    of Monad M := {
  aget : I → M S ;
  aput : I → S → M unit ;
  aputput : ∀ i s s', aput i s ≫ aput i s' = aput i s';
  aputget : ∀ i s (A : Type) (k : S → M A), aput i s ≫ aget i ≫= k =
    aput i s ≫ k s ;
  (* other laws omitted to save space,
      see [21, file hierarchy.v] for details *) }.
#[short(type=arrayMonad)]
HB.structure Definition MonadArray (S : Type) (I : eqType) :=
  { M of isMonadArray S I M & }.
```

The plus monad We define the plus monad following [26] and [24, Sect. 2]. It extends a basic monad with two operators: failure and nondeterministic choice. These operators satisfy three groups of laws: (1) failure and choice form a monoid, (2) choice is idempotent and commutative, and (3) failure and choice interact with bind according to the following laws (where [~] is a notation for nondeterministic choice):

```
left_zero            ∀ A B (f : A → M B), fail A ⫸ f = fail B
right_zero           ∀ A B (m : M A), m ⫸ fail B = fail B
left_distributivity  ∀ A B (m1 m2 : M A) (f : A → M B),
                       m1 [~] m2 ⫸ f = (m1 ⫸ f) [~] (m2 ⫸ f)
right_distributivity ∀ A B (m : M A) (f1 f2 : A → M B),
                       m ⫸ (fun x ⇒ f1 x [~] f2 x) =
                       (m ⫸ f1) [~] (m ⫸ f2)
```

We take advantage of monads already available in MONAE [2] to implement the plus monad with a minimal amount of code while staying conservative. Indeed, we observe that the needed operators and most laws are already available in MONAE. The monads `failMonad` and `failROMonad` (which inherits from `failMonad` and comes from [3], see Fig. 2) introduce the failure operator, and the `left_zero` and `right_zero` laws. The monad `altMonad` introduces nondeterministic choice and the `left_distributivity` law. The monad `altCIMonad` (which extends `altMonad`) introduces commutativity and idempotence of nondeterministic choice. Finally, `nondetMonad` and `nondetCIMonad` (which is the combination of `altCIMonad` and `nondetMonad`) are combinations of `failMonad` and `altMonad`; these monads are coming from [4]. In other words, only the right-distributivity law is missing.

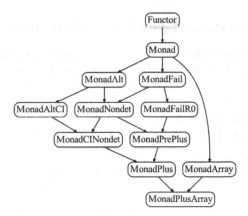

Fig. 2. The hierarchy of monad interfaces discussed in this paper. It is part of a larger hierarchy that can be found online [21].

We therefore implement the `plusMonad` by extending above monads with the right-distributivity law as follows. First, we define the intermediate prePlusMonad by adding right-distributivity to the combination of nondetMonad and failROMonad[2]. Below, alt is the identifier behind the notation [~].

```
HB.mixin Record isMonadPrePlus (M : Type → Type)
  of MonadNondet M & MonadFailRO M :=
  { alt_bindDr : BindLaws.right_distributive (@bind [the monad of M]) alt }.
#[short(type=prePlusMonad)]
HB.structure Definition MonadPrePlus := {M of isMonadPrePlus M & }.
```

Second, plusMonad is defined as the combination of nondetCIMonad and prePlusMonad:

```
#[short(type=plusMonad)]
HB.structure Definition MonadPlus := {M of MonadCINondet M & MonadPrePlus M}.
```

The plus-array monad Finally, we can combine the array and the plus monads to obtain the plusArrayMonad [24, Sect. 5]:

```
#[short(type=plusArrayMonad)]
HB.structure Definition MonadPlusArray (S : Type) (I : eqType) :=
  { M of MonadPlus M & isMonadArray S I M}.
```

To instantiate the interface of the plus-array monad the basic idea is to define aget to be the function fun i a ⇒ [set (a i, a)] and aput to be the function fun i s a ⇒ [set (tt, insert i s a)], where [set _] is a notation for single-ton sets and insert i s a is fun j ⇒ if i == j then s else a j. One of course needs to instantiate the interfaces of Fig. 2 (except MonadCINondet, MonadPlus, and MonadPlusArray that are just joined interfaces). See [21, file monad_model.v] for details.

2.5   Monad Transformers Using HIERARCHY-BUILDER

As another illustration of the ease to add monad constructs using HIERARCHY-BUILDER, we explain how we formalize monad transformers. This improves the formalization of monad transformers from previous work [3, Sections 3.3–3.4] with more readable formal definitions and more robust type inference.

Given two monads M and N, a monad morphism is a function M ⤳ N that satisfies the laws of monad morphisms [7, Def. 19][16, Def. 7]:

```
HB.mixin Record isMonadM (M N : monad) (e : M ⤳ N) := {
  monadMret : MonadMLaws.ret e ; (* e ∘ Ret = Ret *)
  monadMbind : MonadMLaws.bind e (* e (m ≫= f) = e m ≫= (e ∘ f) *) }.
```

An important property of monad morphisms is that they are natural transformations, so that we define the type of monad morphism using the interfaces of monad morphisms and natural transformations (Sect. 2.2):

---

[2] The existence of this intermediate interface is further justified by its use in the definition of the interface of the backtrackable state monad [14].

```
#[short(type=monadM)]
HB.structure Definition MonadM (M N : monad) :=
  {e of isMonadM M N e & isNatural M N e}.
```

However, since the laws of monad morphisms imply naturality, a monad morphism can be defined directly by a factory with *only* the laws of monad morphisms:

```
HB.factory Record isMonadM_ret_bind (M N : monad) (e : M ~~~> N) := {
  monadMret : MonadMLaws.ret e ;
  monadMbind : MonadMLaws.bind e }.
```

Like for monads in Sect. 2.3, we are again in the situation where the textbook definition ought better be sought in factories.

A monad transformer t is a function from monad to monad such that for any monad M there is a monad morphism from M to t M [7, Sect. 3.3][16, Def. 9]:

```
HB.mixin Record isMonadT (t : monad → monad) := {
  Lift : ∀ M, monadM M (t M) }.
#[short(type=monadT)]
HB.structure Definition MonadT := {t of isMonadT t}.
```

Going one step further, we define *functorial monad transformers* [16, Def. 20]. A functorial monad transformer is a monad transformer t with an `hmap` operator of type ∀ M N : monad, (M ⟹ N) → t M ⟹ t N (i.e., `hmap` preserves natural transformations) with additional properties. First, `hmap` respects identities of natural transformations (line 4) and (vertical) composition of natural transformations (line 6).

```
1  HB.mixin Record isFunctorial (t : monad → monad) := {
2    hmap : ∀ {M N : monad}, (M ⟹ N) → t M ⟹ t N ;
3    functorial_id : ∀ M : monad,
4      hmap [the _ ⟹ _ of NId M] = [the _ ⟹ _ of NId (t M)] ;
5    functorial_o : ∀ (M N P : monad) (t : M ⟹ N) (s : N ⟹ P),
6      hmap (s \v t) = hmap s \v hmap t }.
7  #[short(type=functorial)]
8  HB.structure Definition Functorial := {t of isFunctorial t}.
```

See [21, file `monad_lib.v`] for the definitions of the identity natural transformation NId and of vertical composition \v. Second, `hmap` preserves monad morphisms (lines 2–5) and the `Lift` operator of the monad transformer is natural (line 7):

```
1  HB.mixin Record isFMT (t : monad → monad) of MonadT t & Functorial t := {
2    fmt_ret : ∀ M N (e : monadM M N),
3      MonadMLaws.ret (hmap [the functorial of t] e) ;
4    fmt_bind : ∀ M N (e : monadM M N),
5      MonadMLaws.bind (hmap [the functorial of t] e) ;
6    natural_hmap : ∀ (M N : monad) (n : M ⟹ N),
7      hmap [the functorial of t] n \v Lift [the monadT of t] M =
8      Lift [the monadT of t] N \v n }.
9  HB.structure Definition FMT := {t of isFMT t & }.
```

Using the above formal definitions, we have been able to produce several instances of monad transformers (state, exception, environment, continuation, etc.) and functorial monad transformers, and revise a formalization of Jaskelioff's modular monad transformers [16]; see [21, directory `impredicative_set`].

3 Difficulties with the Termination of Monadic Functions

In the context of monadic equational reasoning, we observe that we often run into difficulties when proving properties of monadic functions because their type is not informative enough. This happens in particular when proving termination. For example, in their derivations of quicksort, Mu and Chiang postulate the termination of several functions using the Agda pragma `{-# TERMINATING #-}`, which is not safe in general [5]. Before discussing practical solutions in the next section (Sect. 4), we provide in this section background information about the standard Coq tooling to prove termination in Sect. 3.1 and explain concrete examples of difficulties in Sect. 3.2.

3.1 Background: Standard Coq Tooling to Prove Termination

Functions defined in a proof assistant based on dependent types need to terminate to preserve logical consistency.

The `Equations` command In Coq, the `Equations` command [29,30] provides support to prove the termination of functions whose recursion is not structural. For example, functional quicksort can be written as follows (the type `T` can be any ordered type [20]):

```
Equations? qsort (s : seq T) : seq T by wf (size s) lt :=
| [::] ⇒ [::]
| h :: t ⇒ qsort (partition h t).1 ++ h :: qsort (partition h t).2.
```

The function call `partition h t` returns a pair of lists (say, `ys` and `zs`) that partitions the list `t` w.r.t. the pivot `h` (the notations `.1` and `.2` are for taking the first and second projection of a pair). The annotation `by wf (size s) lt` indicates that the relation between the sizes of lists is well-founded (`lt` is the comparison for natural numbers). Once the `Equations?` declaration of `qsort` is processed, Coq asks for a proof that the arguments are indeed decreasing, that is, proofs of `size ys < size s` and `size zs < size s`. Under the hood, Coq uses the accessibility predicate [8, Chapter 15].

At first sight, the approach using `Equations` is appealing: the syntax is minimal and, as a by-product, it automatically generates additional useful lemmas, e.g., in the case of `qsort`, one equation for each branch (`qsort_equation_{1,2}`) and a lemma capturing the fixpoint equation (`qsort_elim`).

The `Program/Fix` approach The `Program/Fix` approach is more primitive and verbose than the `Equations` approach, but it is also more flexible and robust to changes because it relies on less automation. It is a combination of the `Program` command for dependent type programming [31, Chapter Program] and of the `Fix` definition from the `Coq.Init.Wf` module for well-founded fixpoint of the standard library. For the sake of explanation, let us show how to define functional quicksort using this approach.

First, one defines an intermediate function `qsort'` similar to the declaration that one would write with the `Equations` command except that its recursive calls are to a parameter function (`f` below). This parameter function takes as an additional argument a proof that the measure (here the size of the input list) is decreasing. These proofs appear as holes (`_` syntax) to be filled next by the user[3]:

```
Program Definition qsort' (s : seq T)
  (f : ∀ s', (size s' < size s) → seq T) : seq T :=
  if s isn't h :: t then [::] else
  let: (ys, zs) := partition h t in f ys _ ++ h :: f zs _.
```

Second, one defines the actual `qsort` function using `Fix`. This requires a (trivial) proof that the order chosen for the measure is well-founded:

```
Definition qsort : seq T → seq T :=
  Fix (@well_founded_size _) (fun _ ⇒ _) qsort'.
```

The `Program`/`Fix` approach does not generate any helper lemmas, it is essentially the manual version of the `Equations` approach but it is more widely applicable as we will see in Sect. 5.4.

3.2   Limitations of Coq Standard Tooling to Prove Termination

We now illustrate some limitations of Coq standard tooling with a monadic function that computes permutations nondeterministically. The function `perm` below (written in Agda) is not the most obvious definition for this task but it is a good fit to specify quicksort and it is used as such by Mu and Chiang to perform program derivation [24, Sect. 3].

```
split : {{_ : MonadPlus M}} → List A → M (List A × List A)
split [] = return ([] , [])
split (x :: xs) = split xs >>=
  λ {(ys, zs) → return (x :: ys, zs) || return (ys, x :: zs)}

{-# TERMINATING #-}
perm : {{_ : MonadPlus M}} → List A → M (List A)
perm [] = return []
perm (x :: xs) = split xs >>=
  λ { (ys , zs) → liftM2 (_++[ x ]++_) (perm ys) (perm zs) }
```

The function `split` splits a list nondeterministically. The notation || corresponds to nondeterministic choice (in MONAE, this is the notation [˜] that we already saw in Sect. 2.4). The function `perm` uses `split` and `liftM2`, a generic monadic function that lifts a function `h : A -> B -> C` to a monadic function of type `M A -> M B -> M C`.

---

[3] The `Program` command can be configured by the user so that Coq provides proofs automatically.

First, we observe that since `split` is structurally recursive, it can be encoded directly in Coq as a `Fixpoint` (using the `altMonad` of Sect. 2.4)[4]:

```
Fixpoint splits {M : altMonad} A (s : seq A) : M (seq A * seq A) :=
  if s isn't x :: xs then Ret ([::], [::])
  else splits xs >>= (fun '(ys, zs) =>
    Ret (x :: ys, zs) [~] Ret (ys, x :: zs)).
```

Applying the `Equations` approach to define `perm` (we call it `qperm` in Coq for the sake of clarity) does not fail immediately but the termination proof cannot be completed. Here follows the definition of `qperm`:

```
Equations? qperm (s : seq A) : M (seq A) by wf (size s) lt :=
| [::] => Ret [::]
| x :: xs =>
  splits xs >>= (fun '(ys, zs) =>
    liftM2 (M := M) (fun a b => a ++ x :: b) (qperm ys) (qperm zs)).
```

As expected, Coq asks the user to prove that the size of the list is decreasing. The first generated subgoal is:

```
qperm: ∀ s : seq A, size s < (size xs).+1 → M (seq A)
x: A
xs: seq A
ys, zs: seq A
=============================================================
size ys < (size xs).+1
```

There is no way to prove this goal since there is no information about the list `ys` (the same is true for `zs`). The same problem happens with the `Program/Fix` approach.

4   Add Dependent Types to Return Types for Formal Proofs

The difficulty explained in the previous section is no surprise to the practitioner. It is known that such formal proofs can be completed by enriching the return type of functions with appropriate dependent types. However, in practice this is bothersome enough so that one is tempted to resort to axioms/postulates (e.g., [24]). In face of such a technical difficulty, we advocate the following pragmatic approach: use a standard dependent type if available and instrumented (Sect. 4.1), otherwise use a *dependently-typed assertion* (Sect. 4.2).

4.1   Add Dependent Types to Called Functions to Prove Termination

The first idea is to use standard dependent types to augment the return type of functions so that the `Equations` approach succeeds.

---
[4] Since Coq already has a `split` tactic, we call the function `splits`.

Let us explain how to prove the termination of the qperm function of Sect. 3.2. The splits function is defined such that its return type is M (seq A * seq A). We add information about the size of the returned lists by providing another version of splits whose return type is M ((size s).-bseq A * (size s).-bseq A), where s is the input list and n.-bseq A is the type of lists of size less than or equal to n. This type of "bounded-size lists" comes from the MATHCOMP library [20].

```
Fixpoint splits_bseq {M : altMonad} A (s : seq A)
  : M ((size s).-bseq A * (size s).-bseq A) :=
  if s isn't x :: xs then Ret ([bseq of [::]], [bseq of [::]])
  else splits_bseq xs >>= (fun '(ys, zs) =>
  Ret ([bseq of x :: ys], widen_bseq (leqnSn _) zs) [~]
  Ret (widen_bseq (leqnSn _) ys, [bseq of x :: zs])).
```

The body of this definition is the same as the original one provided one ignores the notations and lemmas about bounded-size lists. The notation [bseq of [::]] is for an empty list seen as a bounded-size list. The lemma widen_bseq captures the fact that a m.-bseq T list can be seen as a n.-bseq T list provided that $m \leq n$:

```
Lemma widen_bseq T m n : m ≤ n → m.-bseq T → n.-bseq T.
```

Since leqnSn n is a proof of $n \leq n.+1$, we understand that widen_bseq (leqnSn _) turns a n.-bseq A list into a n.+1.-bseq A list. The notation [bseq of x :: ys] is a MATHCOMP idiom that triggers automation canonical structures to build a n.+1.-bseq A list using the fact that ys is itself a n.-bseq A list.

Since there is a coercion from lists to bounded-size lists, we can define qperm like in Sect. 3.2 but using splits_bseq instead of splits:

```
Equations? qperm (s : seq A) : M (seq A) by wf (size s) lt :=
| [::] ⇒ Ret [::]
| x :: xs → splits_bseq xs >>= (fun '(ys, zs) →
  liftM2 (M := M) (fun a b ⇒ a ++ x :: b) (qperm ys) (qperm zs)).
```

The proofs required by Coq now contain in their local context the additional information that the lists ys and zs are of type (size xs).-bseq A, which allows for completing the termination proof.

The nonderministic computation of permutations using nondeterministic selection is another example of the use of bounded-size lists [14, Sect. 4.4] (see [21, file fail_lib.v]).

This use of bounded-size lists to prove termination is reminiscent of *sized types* which have already been shown to be useful to guarantee the termination of programs such as quicksort [6]. However, as of today, it appears that users of the Coq proof assistant still need a support library to prove termination manually since there are indications that sized types for Coq might not be practical [9].

4.2   Add Dependent Types with a Dependently-Typed Assertion

The approach explained in the previous section is satisfactory when the needed type is already available and instrumented in some standard library. Otherwise, one needs to define a new, potentially ad hoc type, instrument it with lemmas, possibly with a new notation, etc. Yet, we can reach a similar result without this boilerplate using *dependently-typed assertions*.

For the fail monad M, it is customary to define assertions as follows. A computation `guard b` of type `M unit` fails or skips according to a boolean value b:

```
Definition guard {M : failMonad} b : M unit := if b then skip else fail.
```

An assertion `assert p a` is a computation of type `M A` that fails or returns a according to whether `p a` is true or not (`pred` is the type of boolean predicates in MATHCOMP):

```
Definition assert {M : failMonad} A (p : pred A) a : M A :=
  guard (p a) ≫ Ret a.
```

Similarly, we define a dependently-typed assertion that fails or returns a value *together with a proof* that the predicate is satisfied:

```
Definition dassert {M : failMonad} A (p : pred A) a : M { a | p a } :=
  if Bool.bool_dec (p a) true is left pa then Ret (exist _ _ pa)
  else fail.
```

We illustrate the alternative approach of using `dassert` with a non-trivial property of the `qperm` function: the fact that it preserves the size of its input (this is a postulate in [24]). This statement uses the generic `preserves` predicate:

```
Definition preserves {M : monad} A B (f : A → M A) (g : A → B) :=
  ∀ x, (f x ≫ fun y ⇒ Ret (y, g y)) = (f x ≫ fun y ⇒ Ret (y, g x)).
Lemma qperm_preserves_size {M : prePlusMonad} A :
  preserves (@qperm M A) size.
```

In the course of proving `qperm_preserves_size` (by strong induction of the size of the input list), we run into the following subgoal:

```
s : seq A
ns : size s < n
m:=fun '(ys, zs) ⇒ liftM2 (fun a b ⇒ a ++ p :: b) (qperm ys) (qperm zs)
=====================
splits s ≫ (fun x ⇒ m x ≫ (fun y ⇒ Ret (y, size y))) =
splits s ≫ (fun x ⇒ m x ≫ (fun y ⇒ Ret (y, (size s).+1)))
```

If we use the extensionality of bind to make progress (by applying the tactic `bind_ext ⇒ -[a b].`), we add to the local context two lists a and b that correspond to the output of `splits`:

```
s : seq A
ns : size s < n
m:=fun '(ys, zs) ⇒ liftM2 (fun a b ⇒ a ++ p :: b) (qperm ys) (qperm zs)
a, b : seq A
=====================
m (a, b) ≫ (fun y ⇒ Ret (y, size y)) =
m (a, b) ≫ (fun y ⇒ Ret (y, (size s).+1))
```

As in Sect. 3.2, we cannot make progress because there is no size information about a and b. Instead of introducing a new variant of splits, we use dassert and bind to augment the return type of splits with the information that the concatenation of the returned lists is of the same size as the input (definition dsplitsT below):

```
Definition dsplitsT A n :=
  {x : seq A * seq A | size x.1 + size x.2 == n}.
Definition dsplits
    {M : nondetMonad} A (s : seq A) : M (dsplitsT A (size s)) :=
  splits s >>= dassert [pred n | size n.1 + size n.2 == size s].
```

The equivalence between splits and dsplits can be captured by an application of fmap (fmap f is a notation for _ # f, the functor is inferred automatically) that projects the witness of the dependent type (sval returns the witness of a dependent pair):

```
Lemma dsplitsE {M : prePlusMonad} A (s : seq A) :
  splits s = fmap (fun x => ((sval x).1, (sval x).2)) (dsplits s) :> M _.
```

We can locally introduce dsplits using the lemma dsplitsE to complete the proof of qperm_preserves_size. Once dassert is inserted in the code, we can use the following lemma to lift the assertions to the local proof context:

```
Lemma bind_ext_dassert
    {M : failMonad} A (p : pred A) a B (m1 m2 : _ → M B) :
  (∀ x h, p x → m1 (exist _ x h) = m2 (exist _ x h)) →
  dassert p a >>= m1 = dassert p a >>= m2.
```

This leads us to a local proof context where the sizes of the output lists are related to the input list s with enough information to complete the proof:

```
s : seq A
ns : size s < n
m:=fun '(ys, zs) => liftM2 (fun a b => a ++ p :: b) (qperm ys) (qperm zs)
a, b : seq A
ab : size a + size b == size s
====================
m (a, b) >>= (fun y => Ret (y, size y)) =
m (a, b) >>= (fun y => Ret (y, (size s).+1))
```

See [21, file example_iquicksort.v] for the complete script.

Although we use here a dependently-typed assertion to prove a lemma, we will see in Sect. 5.4 an example of termination proof where dassert also comes in handy. Nevertheless, dassert requires to work with a monad that provides at least the failure operator.

5   A Complete Formalization of Quicksort Derivation

In this section, we apply the library support we explained so far to prove postulates left by Mu and Chiang in their formalization of quicksort derivations [24].

Beforehand we need to complete our theory of computations of nondeterministic permutations (Sect. 5.1). Then we will explain the key points of specifying and proving functional quicksort (Sect. 5.3) and in-place quicksort (Sect. 5.4). These proofs rely on the notion of refinement (Sect. 5.2).

5.1   Formal Properties of Nondeterministic Permutations

The specifications of quicksort by Mu and Chiang rely on the properties of nondeterministic permutations as computed by `qperm` (Sect. 3.2). The shape of this function makes proving its properties painful, intuitively because of two non-structural recursive calls and the interplay with the properties of `splits`. As a matter of fact, Mu and Chiang postulate many properties of `qperm` in their Agda formalization, e.g., its idempotence (here stated using the Kleisli symbol):

```
Lemma qperm_idempotent {M : plusMonad} (E : eqType) :
  qperm >=> qperm = qperm :> (seq E → M (seq E)).
```

The main idea to prove these postulates is to work with a simpler definition of nondeterministic permutations, namely `iperm`, defined using nondeterministic insertion:

```
Fixpoint insert {M : altMonad} A (a : A) (s : seq A) : M (seq A) :=
  if s isn't h :: t then Ret [:: a] else
  Ret (a :: h :: t) [~] fmap (cons h) (insert a t).
Fixpoint iperm {M : altMonad} A (s : seq A) : M (seq A) :=
  if s isn't h :: t then Ret [::] else iperm t >= insert h.
```

Since `insert` and `iperm` each consist of one structural recursive call, their properties can be established by simple inductions, e.g., the idempotence of `iperm`:

```
Lemma iperm_idempotent {M : plusMonad} (E : eqType) :
  iperm >=> iperm = iperm :> (seq E → M _).
```

The equivalence between `iperm` and `qperm` can be proved easily by first showing that the recursive call to `iperm` can be given the same shape as `qperm`:

```
Lemma iperm_cons_splits (A : eqType) (s : seq A) u :
  iperm (u :: s) = do a ← splits s; let '(ys, zs) := a in
                   liftM2 (fun x y ⇒ x ++ u :: y) (iperm ys) (iperm zs).
```

We can use this last fact to show that `iperm` and `qperm` are equivalent

```
Lemma iperm_qperm {M : plusMonad} (A : eqType) : @iperm M A = @qperm M A.
```

Thanks to `iperm_qperm`, all the properties of `iperm` can be transported to `qperm`, providing formal proofs for several postulates from [24] (see Table 1).

5.2 Program Refinement

The rest of this paper uses a notion of program refinement introduced by Mu and Chiang [24, Sect. 4]. This is about proving that two programs obey the following relation:

```
Definition refin {M : altMonad} A (m1 m2 : M A) : Prop := m1 [~] m2 = m2.
Notation "m1 ⊆ m2" := (refin m1 m2).
```

As the notation symbol indicates, it represents a relationship akin to set inclusion, which means that the result of m1 is included in that of m2. We say that m1 *refines* m2. The refinement relation is lifted as a pointwise relation as follows:

```
Definition lrefin {M : altMonad} A B (f g : A → M B) := ∀ x, f x ⊆ g x.
Notation "f ⊆̇ g" := (lrefin f g).
```

Table 1. Admitted facts in [24] and their formalization in [21] (Lemmas xyz-spec require the TERMINATING pragma as a consequence of the function xyz being postulated as terminating.)

Definition/lemma in [24]	Status	Coq equivalent in [21] or in this paper
file Implementation.agda		
ext	postulate	standard axiom of functional extensionality
file Monad.agda		
write-write-swap	postulate	not used
writeList-++	postulate	writeList_cat (array_lib.v)
writeList-writeList-comm	postulate	writeListC (array_lib.v)
file Nondet.agda		
return?perm	postulate	refin_qperm_ret (fail_lib.v)
perm-idempotent	postulate	Sect. 5.1
perm-snoc	postulate	qperm_rcons (fail_lib.v)
sorted-cat3	postulate	Sect. 5.3
perm-preserves-length	postulate	Sect. 4.2
perm-preserves-all	postulate	Sect. 5.3
perm	TERMINATING	Sect. 4.1
mpo-perm	TERMINATING	commutation of computations (Sect. 5.3)
partl/partl-spec	TERMINATING	partl (example_iqsort.v), solved by currying
partl'/partl'-spec	TERMINATING	qperm_partl (example_iqsort.v)
mpo-partl'	TERMINATING	commutation of computations (Sect. 5.3)
qsort/qsort-spec	TERMINATING	Sect. 3.1
file IPartl.agda		
ipartl/ipartl-spec	TERMINATING	Sect. 5.4, solved by currying
introduce-swap [24, eqn 11]	postulate	refin_writeList_rcons_aswap (array_lib.v)
introduce-read	postulate	not used
file IQSort.agda		
iqsort/iqsort-spec	TERMINATING	Sect. 4.2
introduce-read	postulate	writeListRet (array_lib.v)
introduce-swap [24, eqn 13]	postulate	refin_writeList_cons_aswap (array_lib.v)

5.3 A Complete Formalization of Functional Quicksort

We explain how we formalize quicksort as a function as Mu and Chiang did [24], proving in Coq the few axioms they left in their Agda formalization.

What we actually prove is that the sort algorithm implemented by the `qsort` function of Sect. 3.1 refines an algorithm that is obviously correct. The algorithm in question is `slowsort`: a function that filters only the sorted permutations of all permutations derived by `qperm`, which is obviously correct as a sorting algorithm:

```
Definition slowsort {M : plusMonad} T : seq T → M (seq T) :=
  qperm >=> assert sorted.
```

Using the refinement relation, the specification that `qsort` should meet can be written as follows:

```
Lemma qsort_spec : Ret ∘ qsort ⊆ slowsort.
```

The axioms left by Mu and Chiang that we prove are either about termination or about equational reasoning. As for the former, we have explained the termination of `qperm` and `qsort` in Sect. 4. As for the axioms about equational reasoning, the main[5] one is `perm-preserves-all` which is stated as follows (using the Agda equivalent of the `preserves` predicate we saw in Sect. 4.2):

```
postulate
  perm-preserves-all : {{_ : MonadPlus M}} {{_ : Ord A}}
                     → (p : A → Bool) → perm preserves (all p)
```

This lemma says that all the permutations that result from `perm` preserve the fact that all the elements satisfy p or not. In Coq, we proved the equivalent (using `guard`) rewrite lemma `guard_all_qperm`:

```
Lemma guard_all_qperm
  {M : plusMonad} T B (p : pred T) s (f : seq T → M B) :
  qperm s >>= (fun x ⇒ guard (all p s) >> f x) =
  qperm s >>= (fun x ⇒ guard (all p x) >> f x).
```

The proof of `guard_all_qperm` is not trivial: it is carried out by strong induction, requires the intermediate use of the dependently-typed version of `splits` (Sect. 4.1), and more crucially because it relies on the fact that `guard` commutes with computations in the plus monad. This latter fact is captured by the following lemma:

```
Definition commute {M : monad} A B (m : M A) (n : M B) C
    (f : A → B → M C) : Prop :=
  m >>= (fun x ⇒ n >>= (fun y ⇒ f x y)) =
  n >>= (fun y ⇒ m >>= (fun x ⇒ f x y)).
Lemma commute_plus_guard
  {M : plusMonad} b B (n : M B) C (f : unit → B → M C) :
  commute (guard b) n f.
```

Its proof uses induction on syntax as explained in [4, Sect. 5.1].

Our formalization is shorter than Mu and Chiang's. It is not really fair to compare the total size of both formalizations in particular because the proof

---
[5] There is another axiom `sorted-cat3`, but its proof is easy using lemmas from MATH-COMP.

style in Agda is verbose (all the intermediate goals are spelled out). Yet, with the SSREFLECT dialect of Coq, we manage to keep each intermediate lemmas under the size of 15 lines. For example, the intermediate lemma `slowsort'-spec` in Agda is about 170 lines, while our proof in Coq is written in 15 lines (see `partition_slowsort_spec` [21]), which arguably is more maintainable.

5.4   A Complete Formalization of In-Place Quicksort

We now explain how we formalize the derivation of in-place quicksort by Mu and Chiang [24]. The first difficulty is to prove termination, which Mu and Chiang postulate (see Table 1).

Let us first explain the original Agda implementation. The partition step is performed by the function `ipartl`, which uses the array monad (Sect. 2.4):

```
{-# TERMINATING #-}
ipartl : {{_ : Ord A}} {{_ : MonadArr A M}} →
A → N → (N × N × N) → M (N × N)
ipartl p i (ny, nz, 0) = return (ny, nz)
ipartl p i (ny, nz, suc k) = read (i + ny + nz) >>= λ x →
 if x ≤ᵇ p then swap (i + ny) (i + ny + nz) >> ipartl p i (ny + 1, nz, k)
            else ipartl p i (ny, nz + 1, k)
where open Ord.Ord {{...}}
```

The call `ipartl p i (ny, nz, nx)` partitions the subarray ranging from index `i` (included) to `i + ny + nz + nx` (excluded) and returns the sizes of the two partitions. For the sake of explanation, we can think of the contents of this subarray as a list `ys ++ zs ++ xs`; `ys` and `zs` are the two partitions and `xs` is yet to be partitioned; `ny` and `nz` are the sizes of `ys` and `zs`. At each iteration, the first element of `xs` (i.e., the element at index `i + ny + nz`) is read and compared with the pivot `p`. If it is smaller or equal, it is swapped with the element following `ys` and partition proceeds with a `ys` enlarged by one element. (The `swap` function uses the read/write operators of the array monad to swap two cells of the array.) Otherwise, partition proceeds with a `zs` enlarged by one element.

The quicksort function `iqsort` takes an index and a size; it is a computation of the unit type. The code selects a pivot (line 5), calls `ipartl` (line 6), swaps two cells (line 7) and then recursively calls itself on the partitioned arrays:

```
1  {-# TERMINATING #-}
2  iqsort : {{_ : Ord A}} {{_ : MonadArr A M}} → N → N → M N
3  iqsort i 0 = return tt
4  iqsort i (suc n) =
5    read i >>= λ p →
6    ipartl p (i + 1) (0 , 0 , n) >>= λ { (ny , nz) →
7    swap i (i + ny) >>
8    iqsort i ny >> iqsort (i + ny + 1) nz }
```

We encode this definition in Coq and prove its termination as explained in Sect. 4.2. First, observe that the termination of the function `ipartl` need not be postulated: its curried form is accepted by Agda and Coq because the recursion is structural. Let us define `iqsort` in Coq using the `Program`/`Fix` approach (Sect. 3.1). The direct definition fails for the same reasons as explained in Sect. 3: it turns out that the termination proof requires more information about the relation between the input and the output of `ipartl` than the mere fact that it is a pair of natural numbers. We therefore introduce a dependently-typed version of `ipartl` that extends its return type to a dependent pair of type `dipartlT`:

```
Definition dipartlT y z x :=
  {n : nat * nat | (n.1 ≤ x + y + z) ∧ (n.2 ≤ x + y + z)}.
```

The parameters `x`, `y`, and `z` are the sizes of the lists input to `ipartl`; this dependent type ensures that the sizes returned by the partition function are smaller than the size of the array being processed. The dependently-typed version of `ipartl` is obtained by means of `dassert` (Sect. 4.2)[6]:

```
Definition dipartl
    {M : plusArrayMonad T Z_eqType} p i y z x : M (dipartlT y z x) :=
  ipartl p i y z x ≫=
  dassert [pred n | (n.1 ≤ x + y + z) ∧ (n.2 ≤ x + y + z)].
```

Using `dipartl` instead of `ipartl` allows us to complete the definition of `iqsort` (the notation `%:Z` is for injecting natural numbers into integers):

```
Program Definition iqsort' {M : plusArrayMonad E Z_eqType} ni
    (f : ∀ mj, mj.2 < ni.2 → M unit) : M unit :=
  match ni.2 with
  | 0 ⇒ Ret tt
  | n.+1 ⇒ aget ni.1 ≫= (fun p ⇒
            dipartl p (ni.1 + 1) 0 0 n ≫= (fun nynz ⇒
            let ny := nynz.1 in let nz := nynz.2 in
            aswap ni.1 (ni.1 + ny%:Z) ≫
            f (ni.1, ny) _ ≫ f (ni.1 + ny%:Z + 1, nz) _))
  end.
```

See [21, file `example_iquicksort.v`] for the complete termination proof. Note that our in-place quicksort is a computation in the plus-array monad which is the only array monad that provides the failure operator in our hierarchy. Anyway, the following refinement proof requires the plus-array monad. We have not been able to use the `Equations` approach here; it seems that the default setting does not give us access to the proof that we introduced through dependent types.

The specification of in-place quicksort uses the same `slowsort` function as for functional quicksort (Sect. 5.3):

```
Lemma iqsort_slowsort {M : plusArrayMonad E Z_eqType} i xs :
  writeList i xs ≫ iqsort (i, size xs) ⊆ slowsort xs ≫= writeList i.
```

The function `writeList i xs` writes all the elements of the `xs` list to the array starting from the index `i`. This is just a recursive application of the `aput` operator we saw in Sect. 2.4:

---

[6] The type `Z_eqType` is the type of integers equipped with decidable equality. This is a slight generalization of the original definition that is using natural numbers.

```
Fixpoint writeList {M : arrayMonad T Z_eqType} i s : M unit :=
  if s isn't x :: xs then Ret tt else aput i x ≫ writeList (i + 1) xs.
```

Most of the derivation of in-place quicksort is explained by Mu and Chiang in their paper [24]. In fact, we did not need to look at the accompanying Agda code except for the very last part which is lacking details [24, Sect. 5.3]. Our understanding is that the key aspect of the derivation (and of the proof of iqsort_slowsort) is to show that the function ipartl refines a simpler function partl that is a slight generalization of partition used in the definition of functional quicksort (Sect. 3.1). In particular, this refinement goes through an intermediate function that fusions qperm (Sect. 4.1) with partl; this explains the importance of the properties of idempotence of qperm whose proof we explained in Sect. 5.1.

6   Related Work

The hierarchy of interfaces we build in Sect. 2 is a reimplementation and an extension of previous work [3,4]. The latter was built using packed classes written manually. The use of HIERARCHY-BUILDER is a significant improvement: it is less verbose and easier to extend as seen in Sects. 2.4 and 2.5. It is also more robust. Indeed, we discovered that previous work [3, Fig. 1] lacked an intermediate interface, which required us to insert some type constraints for type inference to succeed (see [15] for details). HIERARCHY-BUILDER detects such omissions automatically. Type classes provide an alternative approach for the implementation of a hierarchy of monad interfaces and it has been used to a lesser extent in some related work (e.g., [24]).

The examples used in this paper stem from the derivations of quicksort by Mu and Chiang [24]. Together with their paper, the authors provide an accompanying formalization in Agda. It contains axiomatized facts (see Table 1) that are arguably orthogonal to the issue of quicksort derivation but that reveals issues that need to be addressed to improve formal monadic equational reasoning in practice. In this paper, we explained in particular how to complete their formalization, which we actually rework from scratch, favoring equational reasoning and the creation of reusable lemmas; in other words, our formalization is not a port.

To complete Mu and Chiang's formalization, we needed in particular to formalize a thorough theory of nondeterministic permutations (see Sect. 5.1) It turns out that this is a recurring topic of monadic equational reasoning. They are written in different ways depending on the target specification: using nondeterministic selection [14, Sect. 4.4], using nondeterministic selection and the function unfoldM [22, Sect. 3.2], using nondeterministic insertion [23, Sect. 3], or using liftM2 [24, Sect. 3]. The current version of MONAE has now a formalization of each.

Sakaguchi provides a formalization of the quicksort algorithm in Coq using the array state monad [27, Sect. 6.2]. His formalization is primarily motivated by the generation of efficient executable code. This makes for an intricate definition of quicksort (for example, all the arguments corresponding to indices are bounded). Though his framework does not prevent program verification [27, Sect. 4], it seems difficult to reuse it for monadic equational reasoning (the type of monads is specialized to state/array and there is no hierarchy of monad interfaces).

This paper is focusing on monadic equational reasoning but this is not the only way to verify effectful programs using monads in Coq. For example, Jomaa et al. have been using a Hoare monad to verify properties of memory isolation [17]. They are therefore only dealing with the effects of state and exception. Maillard et al. have been developing a framework to verify programs with effects using Dijkstra monads [19]. Their Dijkstra monads are based on specification monads and are built using monad morphisms. Verification of a monadic computation amounts to type it in Coq with the appropriate Dijkstra monad. Christiansen et al. have been verifying effectful Haskell programs in Coq [10] and Letan et al. have been exploring verification in Coq of impure computations using a variant of the free monad [18].

The formalization of monads we explained in Sect. 2 is specialized to the category **Set** of sets. MONAE also features a formalization of (concrete) categories that has been used to formalize the geometrically convex monad [2, Sect. 5]. Both are connected in the sense that a monad over the category corresponding to the type `Type` of Coq (seen as a Grothendieck universe) can be used to instantiate the `isMonad` interface. Yet, as far as this paper is concerned, this generality is not useful.

7   Conclusion

In this paper, we reported on practical advances about formalization of monadic equational reasoning, illustrated by a complete formalization of functional quicksort and in-place quicksort. For that purpose, we improved an existing Coq library called MONAE. To ease the addition of new monad constructs, we reimplemented the hierarchy of interfaces of MONAE using HIERARCHY-BUILDER and illustrated this extension with the plus-array monad and monad transformers. We observed that the shallow embedding of monadic functions is a source of a recurring technical issue making some proofs (in particular, termination proofs) bothersome; we argued that appropriate library extensions using dependent types are useful in practice to complement Coq's standard tooling. We applied these techniques to the formal verification of quicksort derivations by Mu and Chiang that we were able to formalize without admitted facts.

As for future work, we plan to further enrich the hierarchy of interfaces and to apply MONAE to other formalization experiments (e.g., [26, 28]). We also plan to investigate the use of MONAE as a back-end for the formal verification of Coq programs, for example as generated automatically from OCaml [13].

Acknowledgements. The authors would like to thank Cyril Cohen and Enrico Tassi for their assistance with HIERARCHY-BUILDER, Kazuhiko Sakaguchi and Takafumi

Saikawa for their comments, the members of the Programming Research Group of the Department of Mathematical and Computing Science at the Tokyo Institute of Technology for their input, and the anonymous reviewers for many comments that improved this paper. The second author acknowledges the support of the JSPS KAKENHI grants 18H03204 and 22H00520.

References

1. Affeldt, R., Cohen, C., Kerjean, M., Mahboubi, A., Rouhling, D., Sakaguchi, K.: Competing inheritance paths in dependent type theory: a case study in functional analysis. In: Peltier, N., Sofronie-Stokkermans, V. (eds.) IJCAR 2020. LNCS (LNAI), vol. 12167, pp. 3–20. Springer, Cham (2020). https://doi.org/10.1007/978-3-030-51054-1_1
2. Affeldt, R., Garrigue, J., Nowak, D., Saikawa, T.: A trustful monad for axiomatic reasoning with probability and nondeterminism. J. Funct. Program. **31**, e17 (2021). https://doi.org/10.1017/S0956796821000137
3. Affeldt, R., Nowak, D.: Extending equational monadic reasoning with monad transformers. In: 26th International Conference on Types for Proofs and Programs (TYPES 2020). Leibniz International Proceedings in Informatics, vol. 188, pp. 2:1–2:21. Schloss Dagstuhl, June 2021. https://doi.org/10.4230/LIPIcs.TYPES.2020.2, https://arxiv.org/abs/2011.03463
4. Affeldt, R., Nowak, D., Saikawa, T.: A hierarchy of monadic effects for program verification using equational reasoning. In: Hutton, G. (ed.) MPC 2019. LNCS, vol. 11825, pp. 226–254. Springer, Cham (2019). https://doi.org/10.1007/978-3-030-33636-3_9
5. Agda: Agda's documentation v2.6.2.1 (2021). https://agda.readthedocs.io/en/v2.6.2.1/
6. Barthe, G., Grégoire, B., Riba, C.: Type-based termination with sized products. In: Kaminski, M., Martini, S. (eds.) CSL 2008. LNCS, vol. 5213, pp. 493–507. Springer, Heidelberg (2008). https://doi.org/10.1007/978-3-540-87531-4_35
7. Benton, N., Hughes, J., Moggi, E.: Monads and effects. In: Barthe, G., Dybjer, P., Pinto, L., Saraiva, J. (eds.) APPSEM 2000. LNCS, vol. 2395, pp. 42–122. Springer, Heidelberg (2002). https://doi.org/10.1007/3-540-45699-6_2
8. Bertot, Y., Castéran, P.: Interactive Theorem Proving and Program Development–Coq'Art: The Calculus of Inductive Constructions. Texts in Theoretical Computer Science. An EATCS Series. Springer, Cham (2004). https://doi.org/10.1007/978-3-662-07964-5
9. Chan, J., Li, Y., Bowman, W.J.: Is sized typing for Coq practical? (2019). https://arxiv.org/abs/1912.05601
10. Christiansen, J., Dylus, S., Bunkenburg, N.: Verifying effectful Haskell programs in Coq. In: 12th ACM SIGPLAN International Symposium on Haskell (Haskell 2019), Berlin, Germany, 18–23 August 2019, pp. 125–138. ACM (2019). https://doi.org/10.1145/3331545.3342592
11. Cohen, C., Sakaguchi, K., Tassi, E.: Hierarchy builder: algebraic hierarchies made easy in Coq with Elpi (system description). In: 5th International Conference on Formal Structures for Computation and Deduction (FSCD 2020), June 29-July 6, 2020, Paris, France (Virtual Conference). LIPIcs, vol. 167, pp. 34:1–34:21. Schloss Dagstuhl - Leibniz-Zentrum für Informatik (2020). https://doi.org/10.4230/LIPIcs.FSCD.2020.34

12. Garillot, F., Gonthier, G., Mahboubi, A., Rideau, L.: Packaging mathematical structures. In: Berghofer, S., Nipkow, T., Urban, C., Wenzel, M. (eds.) TPHOLs 2009. LNCS, vol. 5674, pp. 327–342. Springer, Heidelberg (2009). https://doi.org/10.1007/978-3-642-03359-9_23

13. Garrigue, J.: Proving the correctness of OCaml typing by translation into Coq. In: The 17th Theorem Proving and Provers meeting (TPP 2021), November 2021. presentation

14. Gibbons, J., Hinze, R.: Just do it: simple monadic equational reasoning. In: 16th ACM SIGPLAN International Conference on Functional Programming (ICFP 2011), Tokyo, Japan, 19–21 September 2011. pp. 2–14. ACM (2011). https://doi.org/10.1145/2034773.2034777

15. Hierarchy Builder: Hierarchy builder wiki–missingjoin. https://github.com/math-comp/hierarchy-builder/wiki/MissingJoin (2021)

16. Jaskelioff, M.: Modular monad transformers. In: Castagna, G. (ed.) ESOP 2009. LNCS, vol. 5502, pp. 64–79. Springer, Heidelberg (2009). https://doi.org/10.1007/978-3-642-00590-9_6

17. Jomaa, N., Nowak, D., Grimaud, G., Hym, S.: Formal proof of dynamic memory isolation based on MMU. Sci. Comput. Program. **162**, 76–92 (2018). https://doi.org/10.1016/j.scico.2017.06.012

18. Letan, T., Régis-Gianas, Y.: FreeSpec: specifying, verifying, and executing impure computations in Coq. In: 9th ACM SIGPLAN International Conference on Certified Programs and Proofs (CPP 2020), New Orleans, LA, USA, 20–21 January 2020, pp. 32–46. ACM (2020). https://doi.org/10.1145/3372885.3373812

19. Maillard, K., et al.: Dijkstra monads for all. Proc. ACM Program. Lang. 3(ICFP), 104:1 104:29 (2019). https://doi.org/10.1145/3341708

20. MathComp: The mathematical components repository (2022). https://github.com/math-comp/math-comp. version 1.14.0. See `sreflect/order.v` for ordered types. See https://github.com/math-comp/math-comp/blob/251c8ec2490ff645a6afa45dd1ec238b9f71a554/mathcomp/ssreflect/tuple.v#L460-L499 for the bseq type

21. Monae: Monadic effects and equational reasoning in Coq (2021). https://github.com/affeldt-aist/monae, version 0.4.1

22. Mu, S.: Calculating a backtracking algorithm: an exercise in monadic program derivation. Technical report, Academia Sinica (2019). TR-IIS-19-003

23. Mu, S.: Equational reasoning for non-determinism monad: a case study of Spark aggregation. Technical report, Academia Sinica (2019). TR-IIS-19-002

24. Mu, S.-C., Chiang, T.-J.: Declarative pearl: deriving monadic quicksort. In: Nakano, K., Sagonas, K. (eds.) FLOPS 2020. LNCS, vol. 12073, pp. 124–138. Springer, Cham (2020). https://doi.org/10.1007/978-3-030-59025-3_8

25. Oliveira, B.C.D.S., Schrijvers, T., Cook, W.R.: MRI: Modular reasoning about interference in incremental programming. J. Funct. Program. **22**, 797–852 (2012). https://doi.org/10.1017/S0956796812000354

26. Pauwels, K., Schrijvers, T., Mu, S.-C.: Handling local state with global state. In: Hutton, G. (ed.) MPC 2019. LNCS, vol. 11825, pp. 18–44. Springer, Cham (2019). https://doi.org/10.1007/978-3-030-33636-3_2

27. Sakaguchi, K.: Program extraction for mutable arrays. Sci. Comput. Program. **191**, 102372 (2020). https://doi.org/10.1016/j.scico.2019.102372

28. Schrijvers, T., Piróg, M., Wu, N., Jaskelioff, M.: Monad transformers and modular algebraic effects: what binds them together. In: 12th ACM SIGPLAN International Symposium on Haskell (Haskell 2019), Berlin, Germany, 18–23 August 2019, pp. 98–113. ACM (2019). https://doi.org/10.1145/3331545.3342595

29. Sozeau, M.: Equations–a function definitions plugin (2009). https://mattam82. github.io/Coq-Equations/. last stable release: 1.3 (2021)
30. Sozeau, M., Mangin, C.: Equations reloaded: high-level dependently-typed functional programming and proving in coq. Proc. ACM Program. Lang. **3**(ICFP), 86:1-86:29 (2019). https://doi.org/10.1145/3341690
31. The Coq Development Team: The Coq Proof Assistant Reference Manual. Inria (2022). https://coq.inria.fr. Version 8.15.1

Semantic Preservation for a Type Directed Translation Scheme of Featherweight Go

Martin Sulzmann[1]([⊠]) [iD] and Stefan Wehr[2] [iD]

[1] Karlsruhe University of Applied Sciences, Karlsruhe, Germany
martin.sulzmann@h-ka.de
[2] Offenburg University of Applied Sciences, Offenburg, Germany
stefan.wehr@hs-offenburg.de

Abstract. Featherweight Go (FG) is a minimal core calculus that includes essential Go features such as overloaded methods and interface types. The most straightforward semantic description of the dynamic behavior of FG programs is to resolve method calls based on run-time type information. A more efficient approach is to apply a type-directed translation scheme where interface-values are replaced by dictionaries that contain concrete method definitions. Thus, method calls can be resolved by a simple lookup of the method definition in the dictionary. Establishing that the target program obtained via the type-directed translation scheme preserves the semantics of the original FG program is an important task.

To establish this property we employ logical relations that are indexed by types to relate source and target programs. We provide rigorous proofs and give a detailed discussion of the many subtle corners that we have encountered including the need for a step index due to recursive interfaces and method definitions.

1 Introduction

Type directed translation is the process of elaborating a source into some target program by making use of type information available in the source program. Source and target may be from the same language as found in the case of compiler transformations, e.g. consider [16]. The target may be a more elementary language compared to the source, e.g. consider [7,13]. In all cases it is essential to establish that the target program resulting from the translation preserves the meaning of the source program.

Here, we consider a type directed translation method applied to Featherweight Go. Featherweight Go (FG) is a minimal core calculus that includes the essential features of Go such as method overloading and interfaces. Earlier work by Griesmer and co-authors [6] specifies static typing rules and a run-time method lookup semantics for FG. In our own prior work [26], we give a type directed translation that elaborates methods calls to method lookup in dictionaries that will be passed around in place of interfaces. We could establish correctness of our translation but the result was somewhat limited as semantic

E. Komendantskaya (Ed.): MPC 2022, LNCS 13544, pp. 178–197, 2022.
https://doi.org/10.1007/978-3-031-16912-0_7

preservation only holds under the assumption that source and target programs terminate.

In this work, we significantly extend our earlier semantic preservation result and establish the following properties.

- If the source program terminates so will the target program and the resulting values are equivalent.
- If the source program diverges so will the target program.
- If the source program panics due to a failed run-time type check, the target program will panic as well.

These results require non-trivial extensions and adaptations of our earlier proof method and type-indexed relation to connect source to target values. The upcoming Sect. 2 gives an overview and highlights the changes from [26] to achieve the above results.

In summary, we make the following contributions.

- We introduce a family of syntactic, step-indexed logical relations to establish semantic preservation for terminating, diverging and panicking source programs (Sect. 5)
- We provide for rigorous proofs of our results (Sect. 5).

Section 3 specifies Featherweight Go (FG). The type directed translation of FG including a description of the target language is given in Sect. 4. Both sections are adopted from our earlier work [26]. Related work is covered in Sect. 6. Section 7 concludes.

2 Overview

Translation by Example. We consider a type directed translation scheme that transforms a FG program into some target program. The target language is an untyped lambda-calculus extended with recursive let-bindings, constructors, and pattern matching. Here, we use Haskell-style notation.

For example, the FG program on the left translates to the target program on the right. For simplicity, we leave out some details (marked by . . .).

```
type Int struct {val int}
type Eq interface {eq(that Eq) bool}
func (this Int) eq(that Eq) bool {...}        eqInt this that = ...
func main() {                                 main =
  var i Eq = Int{1}                             let j = (1,eqInt)
  var _ bool = i.eq(i) }                        in case j of (x,eq) -> eq x j
```

The FG program on the left contains a struct Int, an interface Eq, and a definition for method eq for receiver type Int (line 3). Our example only contains one definition of the eq method. In general, FG methods can be overloaded on the receiver type. Hence, in the translation on the right, the function name eqInt uniquely identifies the definition of eq for receiver type Int.

Interfaces give a name to a set of method signatures. They are types, and so interface type Eq effectively describes all receiver types implementing the eq method. Type Int implements this eq method and therefore Int{1} is (also) of type Eq. Hence, the method call i.e.q(i) type checks.

The FG semantics performs a run-time type lookup to resolve method calls such as i.e.q(i). In the translation, an interface is represented as a pair that consists of the value that implements the interface and a dictionary of method definitions for this specific value. For example, i at type Eq translates to the pair (1,eqInt). Assuming that we represent the FG variable i as j in the target, the method call i.e.q(i) translates to **case** j **of** (x,eq) -> eq x j, where we only require a pattern match to access the underlying value and the concrete method definition. See Sect. 4 for details of the type-directed translation.

Semantic Preservation via Logical Relations. To establish that the translation is meaning preserving we need to relate source to target expressions. One challenge is that evaluation steps are not in sync. For example, FG method calls reduce in a single step whereas the translated code first performs a pattern match to obtain the method definition followed by another step to execute the call.

Earlier work:

$$\frac{\forall k_1, k_2, v, V \ . \ k - (k_1 + k_2) > 0 \ \wedge \ e \longrightarrow^{k_1} v \ \wedge \ E \longrightarrow^{k_2} V}{\implies \quad v \equiv_{APLAS} V \in [\![t]\!]_{k-(k_1+k_2)}}$$
$$e \approx_{APLAS} E \in [\![t]\!]_k$$

This work:

TERMINATE
$$\frac{\forall k' < k, v \ . \ e \longrightarrow^{k'} v \implies \exists V.E \longrightarrow^* V \wedge v \equiv V \in [\![t]\!]_{k-k'}}{e \approx E \in [\![t]\!]_k}$$

DIVERGE
$$\frac{\forall k' < k, e' \ . \ e \longrightarrow^{k'} e' \wedge \mathsf{diverge}(e') \implies \mathsf{diverge}(E)}{e \approx_\uparrow E \in [\![t]\!]_k}$$

PANIC
$$\frac{\forall k' < k, e' \ . \ e \longrightarrow^{k'} e' \wedge \mathsf{panic}(e') \implies \mathsf{panic}(E)}{e \approx_\ell E \in [\![t]\!]_k}$$

Fig. 1. Improvements compared to earlier work

In our earlier work [26], we introduce a logical relation $e \approx_{APLAS} E \in [\![t]\!]_k$ to express that source and target expressions behave the same. See top of Fig. 1. The relation is indexed by type t and a step index k where we assume that step indices are natural numbers starting with 0. Source expression e and target expression E are in a relation: if the sum of evaluation steps to reduce e to some source value v and E to some target value V is less than k, then the values must be in a relation.[1] Thus, the number of reduction steps in the source and target do not need to be in sync. If we need more than k steps, or if only the source expression yields a value within k steps, or if one of the expressions diverges or panics, the relation $e \approx_{APLAS} E \in [\![t]\!]_k$ holds vacuously and does not give us any information.

In this work, we consider three cases: source terminates, diverges or panics. See Fig. 1 that sketches a logical relation for each case. TERMINATE: if the source e terminates within less than k steps, then the target E terminates as well where the number of evaluation steps do not matter. DIVERGE/PANIC: if the source e evaluates to e' in less than k steps and e' diverges/panics, then so does target E. The detour via e' in the last two cases is required to prove that source e and its translation E are related. Taken together, the three cases yield a much stronger characterization of the semantic relation between source and target programs compared to our earlier work.

We use the convention that $\equiv$ relates values whereas $\approx$ relates expressions. The step index in the relation for values, see $v \equiv V \in [\![t]\!]_{k-k'}$, seems unnecessary but is important to guarantee that the definition of logical relations is well-founded (c.f. Sect. 5)

Ill-Founded Without Step Index. Consider the example from above where Int{1} of type Eq translates to (1,eqInt). We expect Int{1} $\equiv$ (1,eqInt) $\in$ $[\![Eq]\!]$ to hold; that is, FG value Int{1} is equivalent to target value (1,eqInt) when viewed at FG type Eq.

The following reasoning steps try to verify this claim. We deliberately ignore the step index to show that without a step index we run into some issue.

    (1) Int{1} $\equiv$ (1,eqInt) $\in$ $[\![Eq]\!]$

  if (2) Int{1} $\equiv$ 1 $\subset$ $[\![Int]\!]$

  and (3) **func** (x Int) eq(y Eq) bool {e'} $\approx$ eqInt $\in$ $[\![eq(y\ Eq)\ bool]\!]$

Statement (1) reduces to statements (2) and (3). (2) states that the underlying values are related at struct type Int. This clearly holds, we omit the details. (3) requires a bit more thought. Function eqInt is part of the dictionary. Hence, eqInt must have the same behavior as method eq defined on receiver type Int. This is the intention of statement (3). Compared to the earlier notation of the example, the function body has been replaced by some expression e'.

How can we establish (3)? It must hold that when applied to related argument values, eqInt and method eq defined on receiver type Int behave the same. Thus, establishing (3) requires (4):

  (4) $\forall v \equiv V \in [\![Int]\!], v' \equiv V' \in [\![Eq]\!]. \langle x \mapsto v, y \mapsto v' \rangle e' \approx eqInt\ V\ V' \in [\![bool]\!]$

where we write $\langle x \mapsto v, y \mapsto v' \rangle$e' to denote the substitution of arguments by values in the function body.

---

[1] We defer all formal and missing definitions to Sects. 3, 4 and 5. For now, we appeal to intuition.

There is an issue. One of the arguments is of interface type Eq. Hence, for any values v', V' we require $v' \equiv V' \in [\![\text{Eq}]\!]$. This leads to a cyclic dependency as a statement of the form $\cdot \equiv \cdot \in [\![\text{Eq}]\!]$ relies on a statement $\cdot \equiv \cdot \in [\![\text{Eq}]\!]$. See (1) and (4). This would mean that the definition of our logical relation is ill-founded.

Rule schemes parameterized by some binary ordering relation $\blacktriangleleft$:

METHOD-$\blacktriangleleft$

$$\frac{\forall k', v, v', V, V'.k' \blacktriangleleft k \wedge v \equiv V \in [\![\text{Int}]\!]_{k'} \wedge v' \equiv V' \in [\![\text{Eq}]\!]_{k'}}{\textbf{func} \ (\text{x Int}) \ \text{eq(y Eq) bool} \ \{\text{e'}\} \approx \text{eq} \in [\![\text{eq(y Eq) bool}]\!]_k}$$
$$\implies \langle \text{x} \mapsto v, \text{y} \mapsto v' \rangle \text{e'} \approx \text{eq} \ V \ V' \in [\![\text{bool}]\!]_{k'}$$

IFACE-$\blacktriangleleft$

$$\frac{\forall k_1.k_1 \blacktriangleleft k \implies v \equiv V \in [\![\text{Int}]\!]_{k_1}}{\forall k_2.k_2 \blacktriangleleft k \implies \textbf{func} \ (\text{x Int}) \ \text{eq(y Eq) bool} \ \{\text{e'}\} \approx V' \in [\![\text{eq(y Eq) bool}]\!]_{k_2}}{v \equiv (V, V') \in [\![\text{Eq}]\!]_k}$$

Logical relation properties:

LR-STEP $e \approx E \in [\![t]\!]_k \wedge e' \longrightarrow^1 e \wedge E' \longrightarrow^* E \implies e' \approx E' \in [\![t]\!]_{k+1}$

LR-MONO $e \approx E \in [\![t]\!]_k \wedge k' \leq k \implies e \approx E \in [\![t]\!]_{k'}$

Fig. 2. Getting the step index right

Step Indices to the Rescue. FG interfaces can have cyclic dependencies similar to recursive types, see interface Eq. To guarantee well-foundedness we include a step index in the definition of our logical relations. There is in fact a second reason for a step index. Method definitions may be recursive similar to recursive functions. There is no well-foundedness issue here. But to apply an inductive proof method where semantic preservation for expressions is lifted to method definitions require a step-index.

Step indices in case of recursive types and recursive functions have been studied before [2]. What makes our setting interesting is a subtle interaction between (recursive) interfaces and (recursive) methods. Figure 2 specifies the logical relation rules for methods and interfaces that we have used in the above reasoning steps (1–4). The rule for interfaces relies on the rule for methods and the rule for methods relies on the rule for interfaces (in case of recursive interfaces). For brevity, we omit rules for struct types such as Int.

Rules METHOD-$\blacktriangleleft$ and IFACE-$\blacktriangleleft$ are parameterized by some binary ordering relation $\blacktriangleleft$. Why not simply replace $\blacktriangleleft$ by $<$, the less than relation? Rule instances METHOD-$<$ and IFACE-$<$ are clearly well-founded.

Failed Proof Attempt in Case of METHOD-< *and* IFACE-<. Via our running example we illustrate that the proof of semantic preservation for expressions will not go through. Recall that

```
i.e.q(i) of type bool   translates to   case j of (x,eq) -> eq x j
i = Int{1} of type Eq                    j = (1, eqInt)
```

For values i and j, we may assume (1) $\mathtt{Int\{1\}} \equiv \mathtt{(1,eqInt)} \in [\![\mathtt{Eq}]\!]_k$ for some k. To verify that the translation yields related expressions, we must show

$$(2)\ \mathtt{i.e.q(i)} \approx \mathbf{case}\ \mathtt{j}\ \mathbf{of}\ \mathtt{(x,eq)}\ \mathtt{->}\ \mathtt{eq}\ \mathtt{x}\ \mathtt{j} \in [\![\mathtt{bool}]\!]_k$$

From (1), via reverse application of rule IFACE-<, we can derive

$$(3)\ \mathbf{func}\ \mathtt{(x\ Int)}\ \mathtt{eq(y\ Eq)}\ \mathtt{bool}\ \mathtt{\{e'\}} \approx \mathtt{eqInt} \in [\![\mathtt{eq(y\ Eq)}\ \mathtt{bool}]\!]_{k-1}$$

From (3) we get the implication in the premise of rule METHOD-<. The left-hand side of this implication can be satisfied for $k - 2 < k - 1$ via LR-MONO from Fig. 2 and (1) and the fact that $\mathtt{Int\{1\}} \equiv 1 \in [\![\mathtt{Int}]\!]_k$. Thus, we can derive the right-hand side $\langle \mathtt{x} \mapsto \mathtt{i}, \mathtt{y} \mapsto \mathtt{i} \rangle \mathtt{e'} \approx \mathtt{eqInt}\ 1\ \mathtt{j} \in [\![\mathtt{bool}]\!]_{k-2}$. From this we get

$$(5)\ \mathtt{i.e.q(i)} \approx \mathbf{case}\ \mathtt{j}\ \mathbf{of}\ \mathtt{(x,eq)}\ \mathtt{->}\ \mathtt{eq}\ \mathtt{x}\ \mathtt{j} \in [\![\mathtt{bool}]\!]_{k-1}$$

via property LR-STEP in Fig. 2 and the following evaluation steps:

$$\mathtt{i.e.q(i)} \longrightarrow^1 \langle \mathtt{x} \mapsto \mathtt{i}, \mathtt{y} \mapsto \mathtt{i} \rangle \mathtt{e'}$$
$$\mathbf{case}\ \mathtt{j}\ \mathbf{of}\ \mathtt{(x,eq)}\ \mathtt{->}\ \mathtt{eq}\ \mathtt{x}\ \mathtt{j} \longrightarrow^* \mathtt{eqInt}\ 1\ \mathtt{j}$$

The issue is that from (5) we cannot deduce (2). Property LR-STEP allows us to bump up the step index in case of source reduction steps. Target reductions have no impact. Hence, we end up being one step short.

Fixing the Proof by Turning < into ≤. The solution is to turn one < into ≤. Then, we can derive (5) $\mathtt{i.eq(i)} \approx \mathbf{case}\ \mathtt{j}\ \mathbf{of}\ \mathtt{(x,eq)}\ \mathtt{->}\ \mathtt{eq}\ \mathtt{x}\ \mathtt{j} \in [\![\mathtt{bool}]\!]_k$ and the proof of semantic equivalence for expressions goes through. It seems that we have a choice between (A) rule instances METHOD-≤ and IFACE-< and (B) rule instances METHOD-< and IFACE-≤. We pick choice (B) because under (A) the proof of semantic preservation for (possibly recursive) method definitions will not go through. See the proof of the upcoming Lemma 2 in Sect. 5.

Comparison to Our Earlier Work [26]. The logical relation introduced in our earlier work [26] is more limited in that semantic preservation is only stated under the assumption that both expressions, source and target programs, terminate. Recall Fig. 1 that shows that the logical relation $\approx_{APLAS} \in [\![]\!]$ also takes into account source as well as target steps. Under this stronger assumption it is easier to get the step index right as we can derive the following more general variant of property LR-STEP

$$e \approx_{APLAS} E \in [\![t]\!]_k \wedge e' \longrightarrow^{k_1} e \wedge E \longrightarrow^{k_2} E' \implies e' \approx_{APLAS} E' \in [\![t]\!]_{k+k_1+k_2}$$

That is, we can bump up the step index based on target reductions as well. This provides for more flexibility, even with rule instances METHOD-< and IFACE-<, the proofs go through. As highlighted above, more care is needed for the logical relations that we introduce in this work.

Next, we introduce the semantics of Featherweight Go and give the details of the typed-directed translation scheme followed by our semantic preservation results.

3   Featherweight Go

Featherweight Go (FG) [6] is a tiny fragment of Go containing only structs, methods and interfaces. Figure 3 gives its syntax and the dynamic semantics. Overbar notation $\bar{s}^n$ denotes the sequence $s_1 \dots s_n$ for some syntactic construct s, where in some places commas separate the sequence items. If irrelevant, we omit the n and simply write $\bar{s}$. Using the index variable i under an overbar marks the parts that vary from sequence item to sequence item; for example, $\overline{s' s_i}^n$ abbreviates $s' s_1 \dots s' s_n$ and $\overline{s_j}^q$ abbreviates $s_{j1} \dots s_{jq}$.

A FG program P consists of declarations $\overline{D}$ and a main function. A declaration is either a type declaration for a struct or an interface, or a method declaration. Such a method declaration **func** $(x\ t_S)\ mM\ \{\textbf{return } e\}$ makes method of name m and signature M available for receiver type t_S, where the body e may refer to the receiver as x. Expressions e consist of variables x, method calls $e.m(\bar{e})$, struct literals $t_S\{\bar{e}\}$ with field values $\bar{e}$, access to a struct's field $e.f$, and dynamic type assertions $e.(t)$. For convenience, we use disjoint sets of identifiers for structs t_S and interfaces t_I.

FG is a statically typed language. For brevity, we omit a detailed description of the FG typing rules as they appear in [6] and will show up in slightly different form in the type-directed translation in Sect. 4. However, we state the following conditions that must be satisfied by a FG program:

FG1: Structs must be non-recursive.
FG2: For each struct, field names must be distinct.
FG3: For each interface, method names must be distinct.
FG4: Each method declaration is uniquely identified by the receiver type and method name.

The execution of dynamic type assertions in FG relies on structural subtyping. The relation $\overline{D} \vdash_{FG} t <: u$ denotes that under declarations $\overline{D}$ type t is a subtype of type u (see Fig. 3). A struct t_S is a subtype of an interface t_I if t_S implements all the methods specified by t_I. An interface t_I is a subtype of another interface u_I if the methods specified by t_I are a superset of the methods specified by u_I.

The dynamic semantics of FG is given in the bottom part of Fig. 3 as structural operational semantics rules. The relation $\overline{D} \vdash_{FG} e \longrightarrow e'$ denotes that expression e reduces to expression e' under the sequence $\overline{D}$ of declarations. Rule FG-CONTEXT makes use of evaluation contexts $\mathcal{E}$ with holes $\square$ to apply a reduction

Field name	f			
Method name	m		Expression	$d,e ::=$
Variable name	x,y		Variable	x	
Struct type name	t_S, u_S		Method call	$e.m(\overline{e})$	
Interface type name	t_I, u_I		Struct literal	$t_S\{\overline{e}\}$	
Type name	$t,u ::= t_S \mid t_I$		Select	$e.f$	
Method signature	$M ::= (\overline{x_i\ t_i})\ t$		Type assertion	$e.(t)$
Method specification	$R,S ::= mM$			

Type literal $L ::=$			Declaration $D ::=$	
Struct	$\mathbf{struct}\ \{\overline{f\ t}\}$		Type	$\mathbf{type}\ t\ L$	
Interface	$\mathbf{interface}\ \{\overline{S}\}$		Method	$\mathbf{func}\ (x\ t_S)\ mM\ \{\mathbf{return}\ e\}$

$$\text{Program}\ P ::= \overline{D}\ \mathbf{func}\ \mathrm{main}()\{\_ = e\}$$

$\boxed{\overline{D} \vdash_{\mathsf{FG}} t <: u}$ *Subtyping*

METHODS-STRUCT
$$\mathsf{methods}(\overline{D}, t_S) = \{mM \mid \mathbf{func}\ (x\ t_S)\ mM\ \{\mathbf{return}\ e\} \in \overline{D}\}$$

METHODS-IFACE
$$\frac{\mathbf{type}\ t_I\ \mathbf{interface}\ \{\overline{S}\} \in \overline{D}}{\mathsf{methods}(\overline{D}, t_I) = \{\overline{S}\}}$$

SUB-STRUCT-REFL
$$\frac{}{\overline{D} \vdash_{\mathsf{FG}} t_S <: t_S}$$

SUB-IFACE
$$\frac{\mathsf{methods}(\overline{D}, t) \supseteq \mathsf{methods}(\overline{D}, u_I)}{\overline{D} \vdash_{\mathsf{FG}} t <: u_I}$$

$\boxed{\overline{D} \vdash_{\mathsf{FG}} e \longrightarrow e}$ *Reductions*

Value	$v ::= t_S\{\overline{v}\}$
Evaluation context	$\mathcal{E} ::= \Box \mid t_S\{\overline{v}, \mathcal{E}, \overline{e}\} \mid \mathcal{E}.f \mid \mathcal{E}.(t) \mid \mathcal{E}.m(\overline{e}) \mid v.m(\overline{v}, \mathcal{E}, \overline{e})$
Substitution (FG values)	$\Phi_v ::= \langle \overline{x_i \mapsto v_i}\rangle$

FG-CONTEXT
$$\frac{\overline{D} \vdash_{\mathsf{FG}} e \longrightarrow e'}{\overline{D} \vdash_{\mathsf{FG}} \mathcal{E}[e] \longrightarrow \mathcal{E}[e']}$$

FG-FIELD
$$\frac{\mathbf{type}\ t_S\ \mathbf{struct}\ \{\overline{f\ t}\} \in \overline{D}}{\overline{D} \vdash_{\mathsf{FG}} t_S\{\overline{v}\}.f_i \longrightarrow v_i}$$

FG-CALL
$$\frac{v = t_S\{\overline{v}\} \qquad \mathbf{func}\ (x\ t_S)\ m(\overline{x\ t})\ l\ \{\mathbf{return}\ e\} \in \overline{D}}{\overline{D} \vdash_{\mathsf{FG}} v.m(\overline{v}) \longrightarrow \langle x \mapsto v, \overline{x_i \mapsto v_i}\rangle e}$$

FG-ASSERT
$$\frac{v - t_S\{\overline{v}\} \qquad \overline{D} \vdash_{\mathsf{FG}} t_S <: t}{\overline{D} \vdash_{\mathsf{FG}} v.(t) \longrightarrow v}$$

Fig. 3. Featherweight Go (FG)

inside an expression. Values, ranged over by v, are struct literals whose components are all values. A capture-avoiding substitution $\Phi_v = \langle \overline{x_i \mapsto v_i}\rangle$ replaces variables x_i with values v_i, applying a substitution Φ_v to an expression e is written $\Phi_v e$.

Rule FG-FIELD deals with field access. Condition FG2 guarantees that field name lookup is unambiguous. Rule FG-CALL reduces method calls. Condition FG4 guarantees that method lookup is unambiguous. The method call is reduced to the method body e where we map the receiver argument to a concrete value v and method arguments x_i to concrete values v_i. Rule FG-ASSERT covers type assertions. We need to check that the type t_S of value v is consistent with the type t asserted in the program text. This check can be carried out by checking that t_S and t are in a structural subtype relation.

We write $\overline{D} \vdash_{\mathsf{FG}} e \longrightarrow^k e'$ to denote that e reduces to e' in exactly k steps. We write $\overline{D} \vdash_{\mathsf{FG}} e \longrightarrow^* e'$ to denote that there exists some $k \in \mathbb{N}$ with $e \longrightarrow^k e'$. We assume that $\mathbb{N}$ includes zero. If e reduces ad infinitum, we say that e diverges, written $\overline{D} \Uparrow_{\mathsf{FG}} e$. Formally, $\overline{D} \Uparrow_{\mathsf{FG}} e$ if $\forall k \in \mathbb{N}.\exists e'.\overline{D} \vdash_{\mathsf{FG}} e \longrightarrow^k e'$.

FG enjoys type soundness [6]. A well-typed program either reduces to a value, diverges, or it panics by getting stuck on a failed type assertion. The predicate $\mathsf{panic}_{\mathsf{FG}}(\overline{D}, e)$ formalizes panicking:

$$\frac{\neg\ \overline{D} \vdash_{\mathsf{FG}} t_S <: t}{\mathsf{panic}_{\mathsf{FG}}(\overline{D}, \mathcal{E}[t_S\{\overline{v}\}.(t)])}\ \text{FG-PANIC}$$

4   Type Directed Translation

We specify a type-directed translation from FG to an untyped lambda-calculus extended with recursive let-bindings, constructors, and pattern matching. The translation itself has already been specified elsewhere [26], but there only a weak form of semantic equivalence between source and target programs was given. The goal of the article at hand is to prove a much stronger form of semantic equivalence (see Sect. 5).

4.1   Target Language

Figure 4 specifies the syntax and dynamic semantics of our target language (TL). We use capital letters for constructs of the target language. Target expressions E include variables X, Y, data constructors K, function application, lambda abstraction and case expressions to pattern match against constructors. In a case expression with only one pattern clause, we often omit the brackets. If a case expressions has more than one clause $\overline{[Pat \to E]}$, we assume that the constructors in Pat are distinct. A program consists of a sequence of (mutually recursive) function definitions and a (main) expression. The function definitions are the result of translating FG method definitions.

We assume data constructors for tuples up to some fixed but arbitrary size. The syntax $(\overline{E}^n)$ constructs an n-tuple when used as an expression, and deconstructs it when used in a pattern context. At some places, we use nested patterns as an abbreviation for nested case expressions. The notation $\lambda Pat.E$ stands for $\lambda X.\mathbf{case}\ X\ \mathbf{of}\ Pat \to E$, where X is fresh.

$$\begin{array}{llll}
\text{Expression} & E ::= \\
\quad\text{Variable} & X \mid Y & \mid & \text{Pattern clause} \quad Cls ::= Pat \to E \\
\quad\text{Constructor} & K & \mid & \text{Pattern} \quad\quad\quad\ Pat ::= K\ \overline{X} \\
\quad\text{Application} & E\ E & \mid & \text{Program} \quad\quad\ Prog ::= \mathbf{let}\ \overline{Y_i = \lambda X_i.E_i} \\
\quad\text{Abstraction} & \lambda X.E & \mid & \quad\quad\quad\quad\quad\quad\quad \mathbf{in}\ E \\
\quad\text{Pattern case} & \mathbf{case}\ E\ \mathbf{of}\ [\overline{Cls}]
\end{array}$$

$$\begin{array}{lll}
\text{TL values} & V & ::= K\ \overline{V} \mid \lambda X.E \mid X \\
\text{TL evaluation context} & \mathcal{R} & ::= \square \mid \mathbf{case}\ \mathcal{R}\ \mathbf{of}\ [\overline{Pat \to E}] \mid \mathcal{R}\ E \mid V\ \mathcal{R} \\
\text{Substitution (TL values)} & \Phi_\mathsf{V} & ::= \langle \overline{X \mapsto V} \rangle \\
\text{Substitution (TL methods)} & \Phi_\mathsf{m} & ::= \langle \overline{Y \mapsto \lambda X.E} \rangle
\end{array}$$

$\boxed{\Phi_\mathsf{m} \vdash_\mathsf{TL} E \longrightarrow E'}$ $\qquad\qquad\qquad\qquad\qquad\qquad$ *TL expression reductions*

TL-CONTEXT
$$\frac{\Phi_\mathsf{m} \vdash_\mathsf{TL} E \longrightarrow E'}{\Phi_\mathsf{m} \vdash_\mathsf{TL} \mathcal{R}[E] \longrightarrow \mathcal{R}[E']}$$

TL-LAMBDA
$$\Phi_\mathsf{m} \vdash_\mathsf{TL} (\lambda X.E)\ V \longrightarrow \langle X \mapsto V \rangle E$$

TL-CASE
$$\frac{K\ \overline{X_i}^n \to E' \in \overline{Cls}}{\Phi_\mathsf{m} \vdash_\mathsf{TL} \mathbf{case}\ K\ \overline{V_i}^n\ \mathbf{of}\ [\overline{Cls}] \longrightarrow \langle \overline{X_i \mapsto V_i}^n \rangle E'}$$

TL-METHOD
$$\Phi_\mathsf{m} \vdash_\mathsf{TL} Y\ V \longrightarrow \Phi_\mathsf{m}(Y)\ V$$

$\boxed{\vdash_\mathsf{TL} Prog \longrightarrow Prog'}$ $\qquad\qquad\qquad\qquad\qquad\qquad\qquad$ *TL reductions*

TL-PROG
$$\frac{\langle \overline{Y_i \mapsto \lambda X_i.E_i} \rangle \vdash_\mathsf{TL} E \longrightarrow E'}{\vdash_\mathsf{TL} \mathbf{let}\ \overline{Y_i = \lambda X_i.E_i}\ \mathbf{in}\ E \longrightarrow \mathbf{let}\ \overline{Y_i = \lambda X_i.E_i}\ \mathbf{in}\ E'}$$

Fig. 4. Target Language (TL)

Target values V consist of constructors, lambda expressions, and variables. A variable may be a value if it is bound in a **let** at the top-level; that is, it refers to a method from FG. A constructor value $K\ \overline{V}^n$ is short for $(\ldots (K\ V_1) \ldots)\ V_n$.

The structural operational semantics employs two types of substitutions. Value substitutions Φ_V records the bindings resulting from pattern matching and function applications. Method substitutions Φ_m records the bindings for translated method definitions (i.e. top-level let-bindings). Reduction of programs is mapped to reduction of expressions under a method substitution, see rule TL-PROG. A variable Y applied to a value V reduces to $\Phi_\mathsf{m}(Y)\ V$ via TL-METHOD. The remaining reduction rules are standard.

We write $\Phi_\mathsf{m} \vdash_\mathsf{TL} E \longrightarrow^k E'$ to denote that E reduces to E' with exactly k steps, and $\Phi_\mathsf{m} \vdash_\mathsf{TL} E \longrightarrow^* E'$ for some finite number of steps. If E reduces an arbitrary number of steps, we say that E *diverges*, written $\Phi_\mathsf{m} \Uparrow_\mathsf{TL} E$. Formally, $\Phi_\mathsf{m} \Uparrow_\mathsf{TL} E$ iff $\forall k \in \mathbb{N}.\exists E'.\Phi_\mathsf{m} \vdash_\mathsf{TL} E \longrightarrow^k E'$.

In the source language FG, evaluation might panic by getting stuck on a failed type assertion. The translation to the target language preserves panicking, so we need to formalize panic. A target language expression panics if it is stuck on a **case**-expression and there is no matching clause.

$$\frac{K \; \overline{X_i}^n \to E' \notin \lceil \overline{Cls} \rceil}{\mathsf{panic}_{\mathsf{TL}}(\Phi_{\mathsf{m}}, \mathcal{R}[\mathbf{case} \; K \; \overline{V_i}^n \; \mathbf{of} \; \lceil \overline{Cls} \rceil])} \quad \text{TL-PANIC}$$

4.2 Translation

The specification of the translation spreads out over three figures. Figure 5 gives the translation of expressions, relying on Fig. 6 to define auxiliary relations for translating structural subtyping and type assertions. Finally, Fig. 7 translates method declarations and programs.

Before explaining the translation rules, we establish the following conventions (see also the top of Fig. 5). We assume that each FG variable x translates to the TL variable X. FG variables introduced in method declarations are assumed to be distinct. This guarantees that there are no name clashes in environment Γ. For each struct t_S we introduce a TL constructor K_{t_S}, and for each interface t_I we introduce a TL constructor K_{t_I}. For each method declaration **func** $(x \; t_S) \; mM \; \{\mathbf{return} \; e\}$ we introduce a TL variable X_{m,t_S}, thereby relying on condition FG4 which guarantees that m and t_S uniquely identify this declaration. We write Γ to denote typing environments where we record the types of FG variables. The notation $[n]$ is a short-hand for the set $\{1, \ldots, n\}$.

The overall idea of the translation is to choose the TL-representation of an FG-value $v = t_S\{\overline{v}\}$ based on the type t that v is used at:

- If t is a struct type t_S, then the representation of v is $K_{t_S} \; (\overline{V})$, where each V_i is the representation of v_i, so $(\overline{V})$ is a tuple for the struct fields.
- If t is an interface type, then the representation of v is an *interface-value* $K_{t_I} \; (V, \overline{X_{m_i,t_S}})$, where V is the representation of v at struct type t_S and $\overline{X_{m_i,t_S}}$ is a dictionary [7] containing all methods $\overline{m_i}$ of interface t_I. The translation makes each method **func** $(x \; t_S) \; m_iM \; \{\mathbf{return} \; e\}$ available as a top-level binding **let** $X_{m_i,t_S} = E$. An interface value $K_{t_I} \; (V, \overline{X_{m_i,t_S}})$ bears close resemblance to an existential type [12], as it hides the concrete representation of the value V.

Convention for mapping source to target terms

$$x \rightsquigarrow X \quad t_S \rightsquigarrow K_{t_S} \quad t_I \rightsquigarrow K_{t_I} \quad \textbf{func } (x\ t_S)\ mM\ \{\textbf{return } e\} \rightsquigarrow X_{m,t_S}$$

$$\text{FG environment } \Gamma ::= \{\} \mid \{x : t\} \mid \Gamma \cup \Gamma$$

$\boxed{\langle \overline{D}, \Gamma \rangle \vdash_{\mathsf{exp}} e : t \rightsquigarrow E}$ *Translating expressions*

TD-VAR
$$\frac{(x : t) \in \Gamma}{\langle \overline{D}, \Gamma \rangle \vdash_{\mathsf{exp}} x : t \rightsquigarrow X}$$

TD-STRUCT
$$\frac{\textbf{type } t_S \textbf{ struct } \{\overline{f\ t}^n\} \in \overline{D} \qquad \langle \overline{D}, \Gamma \rangle \vdash_{\mathsf{exp}} e_i : t_i \rightsquigarrow E_i \quad (\forall i \in [n])}{\langle \overline{D}, \Gamma \rangle \vdash_{\mathsf{exp}} t_S\{\overline{e}^n\} : t_S \rightsquigarrow K_{t_S}\ (\overline{E}^n)}$$

TD-ACCESS
$$\frac{\langle \overline{D}, \Gamma \rangle \vdash_{\mathsf{exp}} e : t_S \rightsquigarrow E \qquad \textbf{type } t_S \textbf{ struct } \{\overline{f\ t}^n\} \in \overline{D}}{\langle \overline{D}, \Gamma \rangle \vdash_{\mathsf{exp}} e.f_i : t_i \rightsquigarrow \textbf{case } E \textbf{ of } K_{t_S}\ (\overline{X}^n) \rightarrow X_i}$$

TD-CALL-STRUCT
$$\frac{m(\overline{x\ t}^n)\ t \in \mathsf{methods}(\overline{D}, t_S) \qquad \langle \overline{D}, \Gamma \rangle \vdash_{\mathsf{exp}} e : t_S \rightsquigarrow E \qquad \langle \overline{D}, \Gamma \rangle \vdash_{\mathsf{exp}} e_i : t_i \rightsquigarrow E_i \quad (\forall i \in [n])}{\langle \overline{D}, \Gamma \rangle \vdash_{\mathsf{exp}} e.m(\overline{e}^n) : t \rightsquigarrow X_{m,t_S}\ E\ (\overline{E}^n)}$$

TD-CALL-IFACE
$$\frac{\langle \overline{D}, \Gamma \rangle \vdash_{\mathsf{exp}} e : t_I \rightsquigarrow E \qquad \textbf{type } t_I \textbf{ interface } \{\overline{S}\} \in \overline{D} \qquad S_j = m(\overline{x\ t}^n)\,t \qquad \langle \overline{D}, \Gamma \rangle \vdash_{\mathsf{exp}} e_i : t_i \rightsquigarrow E_i \quad (\forall i \in [n]) \qquad X, \overline{X}^q \text{ fresh}}{\langle \overline{D}, \Gamma \rangle \vdash_{\mathsf{exp}} e.m(\overline{e}^n) : t \rightsquigarrow \textbf{case } E \textbf{ of } K_{t_I}\ (X, \overline{X}^q) \rightarrow X_j\ X\ (\overline{E}^n)}$$

TD-ASSERT
$$\frac{\langle \overline{D}, \Gamma \rangle \vdash_{\mathsf{exp}} e : t_I \rightsquigarrow E_2 \qquad u \text{ defined in } \overline{D} \qquad \overline{D} \vdash_{\mathsf{iDestr}} t_I \searrow u \rightsquigarrow E_1}{\langle \overline{D}, \Gamma \rangle \vdash_{\mathsf{exp}} e.(u) : u \rightsquigarrow E_1\ E_2}$$

TD-SUB
$$\frac{\langle \overline{D}, \Gamma \rangle \vdash_{\mathsf{exp}} e : t \rightsquigarrow E_2 \qquad \overline{D} \vdash_{\mathsf{iCons}} t <: u \rightsquigarrow E_1}{\langle \overline{D}, \Gamma \rangle \vdash_{\mathsf{exp}} e : u \rightsquigarrow E_1\ E_2}$$

Fig. 5. Translation of expressions

The translation rules for expressions (Fig. 5) are of the form $\langle \overline{D}, \Gamma \rangle \vdash_{\mathsf{exp}} e : t \rightsquigarrow E$ where $\overline{D}$ refers to the sequence of FG declarations, Γ refers to type binding of local variables, e is the to be translated FG expression, t its type and E the resulting target term. Rule TD-VAR translates variables and follows our convention that x translates to X. Rule TD-STRUCT translates a struct creation. The translated field elements E_i are collected in a tuple and tagged via the constructor K_{t_S}. Rule TD-ACCESS uses pattern matching to capture field access in the translation.

Method calls are dealt with by rules TD-CALL-STRUCT and TD-CALL-IFACE. Rule TD-CALL-STRUCT covers the case that the receiver e is of the struct type t_S. The first precondition guarantees that an implementation for this specific method call exists. (See Fig. 3 for the auxiliary methods.) Hence, we can assume that we have available a corresponding definition for X_{m,t_S} in our translation. The method call then translates to applying X_{m,t_S} first on the translated receiver E, followed by the translated arguments collected in a tuple $(\overline{E}^n)$.

Rule TD-CALL-IFACE assumes that receiver e is of interface type t_I, so e translates to interface-value E. Hence, we pattern match on E to access the underlying value and the desired method in the dictionary. We assume that the order of methods in the dictionary corresponds to the order of method declarations in the interface. The preconditions guarantee that t_I provides a method m as demanded by the method call, where j denotes the index of m in interface t_I.

To explain the two remaining rules for expressions (TD-ASSERT and TD-SUB), we first introduce the two auxiliary relations defined in Fig. 6. The relation $\overline{D} \vdash_{\mathsf{iCons}} t <: u_I \rightsquigarrow E$ constructs an interface-value for u_I. Thus, the resulting expression E is a λ-expression taking the representation of a value at type t and yields its representation at type u_I.

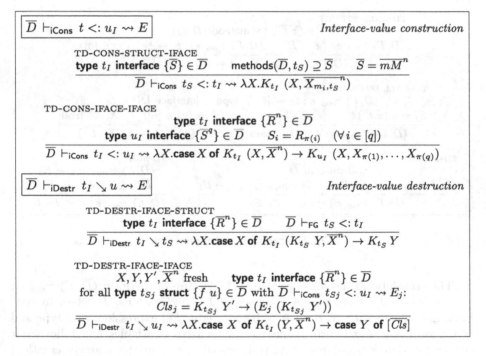

Fig. 6. Translation of structural subtyping and type assertions

The preconditions in rule TD-CONS-STRUCT-IFACE check that struct t_S implements the interface. This guarantees the existence of method definitions X_{m_i,t_S}. Hence, we can construct the desired interface-value. The preconditions in rule TD-CONS-IFACE-IFACE check that t_I's methods are a superset of u_I's methods. This is done via the total function $\pi : \{1,\ldots,q\} \rightarrow \{1,\ldots,n\}$ that matches each (wanted) method in u_I against a (given) method in t_I. We use pattern matching over the t_I's interface-value to extract the wanted methods. Recall that dictionaries maintain the order of method as specified by the interface.

The relation $\overline{D} \vdash_{\mathsf{iDestr}} t_I \searrow u \rightsquigarrow E$ destructs an interface-value. The λ-expression E takes a representation at type t_I and converts it to the representation at type u. This conversion might fail, resulting in a pattern-match error.

Rule TD-DESTR-IFACE-STRUCT deals with the case that the target type u is a struct type t_S. Hence, we find the precondition $\overline{D} \vdash_{\mathsf{FG}} t_S <: t_I$. We pattern match over the interface-value that represents t_I to check that the underlying value matches t_S and extract the value. It is possible that some other value has been used to implement the interface-value that represents t_I. In such a case, the pattern match fails and we experience run-time failure.

Rule TD-DESTR-IFACE-IFACE deals with the case that the target type u is an interface type u_I. The outer case expression extracts the value Y underlying interface-value t_I (this case never fails). We then check if we can construct an interface-value for u_I via Y. This is done via an inner case expression. For each struct t_{Sj} implementing u_I, we have a pattern clause Cls_j that matches against the constructor $K_{t_{Sj}}$ of the struct and then constructs an interface-value for u_I. There are two reasons for run-time failure here. First, Y (used to implement t_I) might not implement u_I; that is, none of the pattern clauses Cls_j match. Second, $\overline{[Cls]}$ might be empty because no receiver at all implements u_I. This case is rather unlikely and could be caught statically.

We now come back explaining the two remaining translation rules for expressions (Fig. 5). Rule TD-ASSERT translates a type assertion $e.(u)$ by destructing e's interface-value, potentially yielding a representation at type u. The type of e must be an interface type because only conversions from an interface type to some other type must be checked dynamically. Rule TD-SUB translates structural subtyping by constructing an appropriate interface-value. This rule could be integrated as part of the other rules to make the translation more syntax-directed. For clarity, we prefer to have a stand-alone subtyping rule.

The translation of programs and methods (Fig. 7) boils down to the translation of expressions involved. Rule TD-METHOD translates a specific method declaration, rule TD-PROG collects all method declarations and also translates the

---

$$\boxed{\overline{D} \vdash_{\mathsf{meth}} \mathbf{func}\ (x\ t_S)\ m(\overline{x\ t})\ t \rightsquigarrow E} \qquad \textit{Translating method declarations}$$

$$\text{TD-METHOD} \quad \frac{\langle \overline{D}, \{x : t_S, \overline{x_i : t_i}^n\}\rangle \vdash_{\mathsf{exp}} e : t \rightsquigarrow E}{\overline{D} \vdash_{\mathsf{meth}} \mathbf{func}\ (x\ t_S)\ m(x\ t^n)\ t\ \{\mathbf{return}\ e\} \rightsquigarrow \lambda X.\lambda(\overline{X}^n).E}$$

$$\boxed{\vdash_{\mathsf{prog}} P \rightsquigarrow Prog} \qquad \textit{Translating programs}$$

TD-PROG
$$\frac{\text{all types used in } \overline{D} \text{ are defined in } \overline{D} \qquad \langle \overline{D}, \{\}\rangle \vdash_{\mathsf{exp}} e : t \rightsquigarrow E}{\vdash_{\mathsf{prog}} \overline{D}\ \mathbf{func}\ \text{main}()\{\_ = e\} \rightsquigarrow \mathbf{let}\ \overline{X_{m_i, t_{S_i}} = E_i}^n\ \mathbf{in}\ E}$$
$$\overline{D} \vdash_{\mathsf{meth}} D_i' \rightsquigarrow E_i \qquad D_i' = \mathbf{func}\ (x_i\ t_{S_i})\ m_i M_i\ \{\mathbf{return}\ e_i\}$$
$$(\text{for all } i \in [n], \text{where } \overline{D'}^n \text{ are the } \mathbf{func} \text{ declarations in } \overline{D})$$

Fig. 7. Translation of methods and programs

main expression. The type system induced by the translation rules is equivalent to the original type system of Featherweight Go. See the Appendix.

5 Semantic Preservation

We establish correctness of the type-directed translation scheme by showing that source and target behave the same. Figure 8 introduces the details of the logical relations that are discussed in the earlier Sect. 2. We assume that step indices k are natural numbers starting with 0.

The relation $e \approx E \in [\![t]\!]_k^{\langle \overline{D}, \Phi_{\mathsf{m}} \rangle}$ specifies how an FG expression e and TL expression E are related at FG type t. The three cases TERMINATE, DIVERGE and PANIC from Fig. 1 are combined in one rule RED-REL-EXP.

The relation $v \equiv V \in [\![t]\!]_k^{\langle \overline{D}, \Phi_{\mathsf{m}} \rangle}$ specifies when FG value v and TL value V are equivalent at FG type t. Rule RED-REL-STRUCT covers struct values by ensuring that the constructor tag matches and all field values are equivalent. Rule RED-REL-IFACE generalizes IFACE-$\leq$ from Fig. 2. The auxiliary methodLookup retrieves the method declaration for some method name and receiver type:

$$\frac{\mathsf{func}\ (x\ t_S)\ mM\ \{\mathsf{return}\ e\} \in \overline{D}}{\mathsf{methodLookup}(\overline{D}, (m, t_S)) = \mathsf{func}\ (x\ t_S)\ mM\ \{\mathsf{return}\ e\}}$$

Rule RED-REL-METHOD relates methods, generalizing METHOD-$<$ from Sect. 2. Rules RED-REL-VB and RED-REL-DECLS lift the logical relation to environments and declarations.

Thanks to the step index our logical relations are well-founded. In the definitions in Fig. 8, the relations $e \approx E \in [\![t]\!]_k^{\langle \overline{D}, \Phi_{\mathsf{m}} \rangle}$ and $v \equiv V \in [\![t]\!]_k^{\langle \overline{D}, \Phi_{\mathsf{m}} \rangle}$ form a cycle. But either the step index k decreases or it stays constant but the size of the target value V decreases in recursive calls. Several other basic properties hold, such as LR-STEP and LR-MONO from the earlier Fig. 2. Details are given in the appendix. These properties are vital to establish the following results.

We can prove that target expressions resulting from FG expressions are semantically equivalent to the source.

Lemma 1 (Expression Equivalence). *Let* $\langle \overline{D}, \Gamma \rangle \vdash_{\mathsf{exp}} e : t \rightsquigarrow E$ *and* $\Phi_{\mathsf{v}}, \Phi_{\mathsf{V}}, \Phi_{\mathsf{m}}$ *such that* $\langle \overline{D}, \Phi_{\mathsf{m}}, \Gamma \rangle \vdash_{\mathsf{rr}}^{k} \Phi_{\mathsf{v}} \approx \Phi_{\mathsf{V}}$ *and* $\vdash_{\mathsf{rr}}^{k} \overline{D} \approx \Phi_{\mathsf{m}}$ *for some* k. *Then, we find that* $\Phi_{\mathsf{v}}(e) \approx \Phi_{\mathsf{V}}(E) \in [\![t]\!]_k^{\langle \overline{D}, \Phi_{\mathsf{m}} \rangle}$.

$$\boxed{e \approx E \in [\![t]\!]_k^{\langle \overline{D}, \Phi_{\mathsf{m}} \rangle}} \qquad\qquad\qquad \textit{FG versus TL expressions}$$

RED-REL-EXP
$$\left(\forall k' < k, v \,.\, \overline{D} \vdash_{\mathsf{FG}} e \longrightarrow^{k'} v \implies \exists V.\Phi_{\mathsf{m}} \vdash_{\mathsf{TL}} E \longrightarrow^* V \wedge v \equiv V \in [\![t]\!]_{k-k'}^{\langle \overline{D}, \Phi_{\mathsf{m}} \rangle} \right)$$
$$\wedge$$
$$\left(\forall k' < k, e' \,.\, \overline{D} \vdash_{\mathsf{FG}} e \longrightarrow^{k'} e' \wedge \overline{D} \Uparrow_{\mathsf{FG}} e' \implies \Phi_{\mathsf{m}} \Uparrow_{\mathsf{TL}} E \right)$$
$$\wedge$$
$$\left(\forall k' < k, e' \,.\, \overline{D} \vdash_{\mathsf{FG}} e \longrightarrow^{k'} e' \wedge \mathsf{panic}_{\mathsf{FG}}(\overline{D}, e') \implies \mathsf{panic}_{\mathsf{TL}}(\Phi_{\mathsf{m}}, E) \right)$$
$$\overline{e \approx E \in [\![t]\!]_k^{\langle \overline{D}, \Phi_{\mathsf{m}} \rangle}}$$

$$\boxed{v \equiv V \in [\![t]\!]_k^{\langle \overline{D}, \Phi_{\mathsf{m}} \rangle}} \qquad\qquad\qquad \textit{FG versus TL values}$$

RED-REL-STRUCT
$$\frac{\textbf{type } t_S \textbf{ struct } \{\overline{f\ t}^n\} \in \overline{D} \qquad \forall i \in [n].v_i \equiv V_i \in [\![t_i]\!]_k^{\langle \overline{D}, \Phi_{\mathsf{m}} \rangle}}{t_S\{\overline{v}^n\} \equiv K_{t_S}\ (\overline{V}^n) \in [\![t_S]\!]_k^{\langle \overline{D}, \Phi_{\mathsf{m}} \rangle}}$$

RED-REL-IFACE
$$\frac{\begin{array}{c} V = K_{u_S}\ V' \qquad \forall k_1 \le k.v \equiv V \in [\![u_S]\!]_{k_1}^{\langle \overline{D}, \Phi_{\mathsf{m}} \rangle} \qquad \mathsf{methods}(\overline{D}, t_I) = \{\overline{mM}^n\} \\ \forall k_2 \le k, i \in [n].\mathsf{methodLookup}(\overline{D}, (m_i, u_S)) \approx Y_i \in [\![m_i M_i]\!]_{k_2}^{\langle \overline{D}, \Phi_{\mathsf{m}} \rangle} \end{array}}{v \equiv K_{t_I}\ (V, \overline{Y}^n) \in [\![t_I]\!]_k^{\langle \overline{D}, \Phi_{\mathsf{m}} \rangle}}$$

$$\boxed{\textbf{func } (x\ t_S)\ mM\ \{\textbf{return } e\} \approx Y \in [\![mM]\!]_k^{\langle \overline{D}, \Phi_{\mathsf{m}} \rangle}} \qquad \textit{FG versus TL methods}$$

RED-REL-METHOD
$$\frac{\begin{array}{c} \forall k' < k, v', V', \overline{v_i}^n, \overline{V_i}^n.(v' \equiv V' \in [\![t_S]\!]_{k'}^{\langle \overline{D}, \Phi_{\mathsf{m}} \rangle} \wedge (\forall i \in [n].v_i \equiv V_i \in [\![t_i]\!]_{k'}^{\langle \overline{D}, \Phi_{\mathsf{m}} \rangle})) \\ \longrightarrow \langle x \mapsto v', \overline{x_i \mapsto v_i}^n \rangle e \approx (Y\ V')\ (\overline{V}^n) \in [\![t]\!]_{k'}^{\langle \overline{D}, \Phi_{\mathsf{m}} \rangle} \end{array}}{\textbf{func } (x\ t_S)\ m(\overline{x\ t}^n)\ t\ \{\textbf{return } e\} \approx Y \in [\![m(\overline{x\ t}^n)\ t]\!]_k^{\langle \overline{D}, \Phi_{\mathsf{m}} \rangle}}$$

$$\boxed{\langle \overline{D}, \Phi_{\mathsf{m}}, \Gamma \rangle \vdash_{\mathsf{rr}}^k \Phi_{\mathsf{v}} \approx \Phi_{\mathsf{V}}} \qquad \textit{FG environments versus TL value substitutions}$$

RED-REL-VB
$$\frac{\forall (x : t) \in \Gamma.\Phi_{\mathsf{v}}(x) \approx \Phi_{\mathsf{V}}(X) \in [\![t]\!]_k^{\langle \overline{D}, \Phi_{\mathsf{m}} \rangle}}{\langle \overline{D}, \Phi_{\mathsf{m}}, \Gamma \rangle \vdash_{\mathsf{rr}}^k \Phi_{\mathsf{v}} \approx \Phi_{\mathsf{V}}}$$

$$\boxed{\vdash_{\mathsf{rr}}^k \overline{D} \approx \Phi_{\mathsf{m}}} \qquad\qquad \textit{FG declarations versus TL method substitutions}$$

RED-REL-DECLS
$$\frac{\begin{array}{c} \forall \textbf{func } (x\ t_S)\ mM\ \{\textbf{return } e\} \in \overline{D} : \\ \textbf{func } (x\ t_S)\ mM\ \{\textbf{return } e\} \approx X_{m,t_S} \in [\![mM]\!]_k^{\langle \overline{D}, \Phi_{\mathsf{m}} \rangle} \end{array}}{\vdash_{\mathsf{rr}}^k \overline{D} \approx \Phi_{\mathsf{m}}}$$

Fig. 8. Relating FG to TL Reduction

As motivated in Sect. 2, for the proof to go through, one of the rules RED-REL-IFACE and RED-REL-METHOD must use $<$ and the other $\leq$. In our case, we use $\leq$ in rule RED-REL-IFACE and $<$ in rule RED-REL-METHOD. The lengthy proof is given in the online version of this paper.[2]

Based on the above result, we can establish semantic equivalence for method definitions. For this proof to go through it is essential that we find $\leq$ in rule RED-REL-IFACE and $<$ in rule RED-REL-METHOD.

Lemma 2 (Method Equivalence). *Let $\overline{D}$ and Φ_{m} such that for each* **func** $(x\ t_S)\ m(\overline{x\ t}^n)\ t\ \{$**return** $e\}$ *in* $\overline{D}$ *we have* $\Phi_{\mathsf{m}}(X_{m,t_S}) = \lambda X.\lambda(\overline{X}^n).E$ *where* $\overline{D}\ \vdash_{\mathsf{meth}}$ **func** $(x\ t_S)\ m(\overline{x\ t}^n)\ t\ \{$**return** $e\} \rightsquigarrow \lambda X.\lambda(\overline{X}^n).E$. *Then, we find that* $\vdash_{\mathsf{rr}}^k \overline{D} \approx \Phi_{\mathsf{m}}$ *for any* k.

Proof. To verify (1) $\vdash_{\mathsf{rr}}^k \overline{D} \approx \Phi_{\mathsf{m}}$ for each **func** $(x\ t_S)\ m(\overline{x_i\ t_i}^n)\ t\ \{$**return** $e\}$ in $\overline{D}$ we have to show based on rules RED-REL-DECLS and RED-REL-METHOD that

$$\forall k' < k, v, V, \overline{v}^n, \overline{V}^n.(v \approx V \in [\![t_S]\!]_{k'}^{\langle \overline{D}, \Phi_{\mathsf{m}}\rangle} \wedge (\forall i \in [n].v_i \approx V_i \in [\![t_i]\!]_{k'}^{\langle \overline{D}, \Phi_{\mathsf{m}}\rangle}))$$
$$\implies (2)\ \langle x \mapsto v, \overline{x_i \mapsto v_i}^n\rangle e \approx (X_{m,t_S}\ V)\ (\overline{V}^n) \in [\![t]\!]_{k'}^{\langle \overline{D}, \Phi_{\mathsf{m}}\rangle}$$

We verify the result by induction on k.

- **Case** $k = 0$ or $k = 1$: Holds immediately. See rule RED-REL-EXP.
- **Case** $k \implies k + 1$: Suppose $k' < k + 1$ and (3) $v \approx V \in [\![t_S]\!]_{k'}^{\langle \overline{D}, \Phi_{\mathsf{m}}\rangle}$ and (4) $v_i \approx V_i \in [\![t_i]\!]_{k'}^{\langle \overline{D}, \Phi_{\mathsf{m}}\rangle}$ for some v, V, v_i, V_i for $i \in [n]$. Define $\Phi_{\mathsf{v}} = \langle x \mapsto v, \overline{x_i \mapsto v_i}^n\rangle$ and $\Phi_{\mathsf{V}} = \langle X \mapsto V, \overline{X_i \mapsto V_i}^n\rangle$ and $\Gamma = \{x : t_S, \overline{x_i : t_i}^n\}$.

  (5) $\langle \overline{D}, \Phi_{\mathsf{m}}, \Gamma\rangle \vdash_{\mathsf{rr}}^{k'} \Phi_{\mathsf{v}} \approx \Phi_{\mathsf{V}}$ via (3) and (4).

  (6) $\vdash_{\mathsf{rr}}^{k'} \overline{D} \approx \Phi_{\mathsf{m}}$ by induction.

  (7) $\langle \overline{D}, \Gamma\rangle \vdash_{\mathsf{exp}} e : t \rightsquigarrow E$ from the assumption and rule TD-METHOD.

  (8) $\Phi_{\mathsf{v}}e \approx \Phi_{\mathsf{V}}E \in [\![t]\!]_{k'}^{\langle \overline{D}, \Phi_{\mathsf{m}}\rangle}$ via (5), (6), (7), and Lemma 1.

  (9) $\Phi_{\mathsf{m}} \vdash_{\mathsf{TL}} (X_{m,t_S}\ V)\ (\overline{V}^n) \longrightarrow^* \Phi_{\mathsf{V}}E$
      via the assumption that $\Phi_{\mathsf{m}}(X_{m,t_S}) = \lambda X.\lambda(\overline{X}^n).E$.

  (10) $\Phi_{\mathsf{v}}e \approx (X_{m,t_S}\ V)\ (\overline{V}^n) \in [\![t]\!]_{k'}^{\langle \overline{D}, \Phi_{\mathsf{m}}\rangle}$
       via (8), (9) and because target reductions do not affect the step index

Statement (10) corresponds to (2). Thus, we can establish (1). □

If we would find $\leq$ instead of $<$ in rule RED-REL-METHOD, the proof would not go through. We would then need to establish the implication at the beginning of the proof for $k' \leq k$, but the induction hypothesis gives us only $\vdash_{\mathsf{rr}}^{k'-1} \overline{D} \approx \Phi_{\mathsf{m}}$ in (6).

We state our main result that the dictionary-passing translation preserves the dynamic behavior of FG programs.

Theorem 1 (Program Equivalence). *Let* $\vdash_{\mathsf{prog}} \overline{D}$ **func** $\mathsf{main}()\{\_ = e\} \rightsquigarrow$ **let** $\overline{X_{m_i,t_{S_i}} = E_i}^n$ *in* E *where we assume that e has type t. Let* $\Phi_{\mathsf{m}} = \langle \overline{X_{m_i,t_{S_i}} \mapsto E_i}^n\rangle$. *Then, we find that* $e \approx E \in [\![t]\!]_k^{\langle \overline{D}, \Phi_{\mathsf{m}}\rangle}$ *for any* k.

Proof. Follows from Lemmas 1 and 2. □

---

[2] https://arxiv.org/abs/2206.09980.

6   Related Work

Logical relations have a long tradition of proving properties of typed programming languages. Such properties include termination [25,28], type safety [24], and program equivalence [18, Chapters 6, 7]. A logical relation (LR) is often defined inductively, indexed by type. If its definition is based on an operational semantics, the LR is called syntactic [5,20]. With recursive types, a step-index [2,3] provides a decreasing measure to keep the definition well-founded. See [15, Chapter 8] and [24] for introductions to the topic.

LRs are often used to relate two terms of the same language. For our translation, the two terms are from different languages, related at a type from the source language. Benton and Hur [4] prove correctness of compiler transformations. They used a step-index LR to relate a denotational semantics of the λ-calculus with recursion to configurations of a SECD-machine. The setup relies on biorthogonality [11,14,21,22] to allow for compositionality and extensionality of equivalences.

Hur and Dreyer [9] build on this idea to show equivalence between an expressive source language (polymorphic λ-calculus with references, existentials, and recursive types) and assembly language. Their biorthogonal, step-indexed Kripke LR does not directly relate the two languages but relies on abstract language specifications. The Kripke part of the LR [19] allows reasoning about the shape of the heap.

Our setting is different in that we consider a source language with support for overloading. Besides structured data and functions, we need to cover interface values. This then leads to some challenges to get the step index right. Recall Fig. 2 and the discussion in Sect. 2.

Simulation or bisimulation (see e.g. [27]) is another common technique for showing program equivalences. In our setting, using this technique amounts to proving that reduction and translation commutes: if source term e reduces to e' and translates to target term E, then e' translates to E' such that E reduces to E'' (potentially in several steps) with $E' = E''$. One challenge is that two target terms E' and E'' are not necessarily syntactically equal but only semantically. With LR, we abstract away certain details of single step reductions, as we only compare values not intermediate results. A downside of the LR is that getting the step index right is sometimes not trivial.

Paraskevopoulou and Grover [17] combine simulation and an untyped, step-indexed LR [1] to relate the translation of a reduced expression (the E' from the preceding paragraph) with the reduction result of the translated expression (the E''). They use this technique to prove correctness of CPS transformations using small-step and big-step operational semantics. Resource invariants connect the number of steps a term and its translation might take, allowing them to prove that divergence and asymptotic runtime is preserved by the transformation. Our LR does not support resource invariants but includes a case for divergence directly.

Hur and coworkers [10] as well as Hermida and coworkers [8] also blend bisimulation with LRs, building on previous results [9].

7   Conclusion

In this work, we established a strong semantic preservation result for a type-directed translation scheme of Featherweight Go. To achieve this result, we rely on syntactic, step-indexed logical relations. There are some subtle corners and we gave a detailed discussion of how to get the definition of logical relations right so that the proofs will go through. The proofs are still hand-written where all cases are worked out in detail. To formalize the proofs in a proof assistant we yet need to mechanize the source and target semantics. This is something we plan to pursue in future work.

We believe that the methods developed in this work will be useful in other language settings that employ a type-directed translation scheme for a form of overloading, e.g. consider Haskell type classes [7] and traits in Scala [29] and Rust [23]. This is another topic for future work. In another direction, we plan to adapt our translation scheme and proof method to cover Featherweight Go extended with generics [6].

Acknowledgments. We thank the MPC'22 reviewers for their comments.

References

1. Acar, U.A., Ahmed, A., Blume, M.: Imperative self-adjusting computation. In: Proceedings of POPL. ACM (2008). https://doi.org/10.1145/1328438.1328476
2. Ahmed, A.: Step-indexed syntactic logical relations for recursive and quantified types. In: Sestoft, P. (ed.) ESOP 2006. LNCS, vol. 3924, pp. 69–83. Springer, Heidelberg (2006). https://doi.org/10.1007/11693024_6
3. Appel, A.W., McAllester, D.A.: An indexed model of recursive types for foundational proof-carrying code. ACM Trans. Program. Lang. Syst. **23**(5) (2001). https://doi.org/10.1145/504709.504712
4. Benton, N., Hur, C.: Biorthogonality, step-indexing and compiler correctness. In: Proceedings of SIGPLAN. ACM (2009). https://doi.org/10.1145/1596550.1596567
5. Crary, K., Harper, R.: Syntactic logical relations for polymorphic and recursive types. Electron. Notes Theor. Comput. Sci. **172** (2007). https://doi.org/10.1016/j.entcs.2007.02.010
6. Griesemer, R., et al.: Featherweight Go. Proc. ACM Program. Lang. **4**(OOPSLA) (2020). https://doi.org/10.1145/3428217
7. Hall, C.V., Hammond, K., Peyton Jones, S.L., Wadler, P.L.: Type classes in Haskell. ACM Trans. Program. Lang. Syst. **18**(2) (1996). https://doi.org/10.1145/227699.227700
8. Hermida, C., Reddy, U., Robinson, E., Santamaria, A.: Bisimulation as a logical relation. Math. Struct. Comput. Sci. (2022)
9. Hur, C., Dreyer, D.: A Kripke logical relation between ML and assembly. In: Proceedings of POPL. ACM (2011). https://doi.org/10.1145/1926385.1926402
10. Hur, C., Dreyer, D., Neis, G., Vafeiadis, V.: The marriage of bisimulations and Kripke logical relations. In: Proceedings of POPL. ACM (2012). https://doi.org/10.1145/2103656.2103666
11. Jaber, G., Tabareau, N.: The journey of biorthogonal logical relations to the realm of assembly code. In: Workshop LOLA 2011, Syntax and Semantics of Low Level Languages. Toronto, Canada, June 2011. https://hal.archives-ouvertes.fr/hal-00594386
12. Läufer, K., Odersky, M.: Polymorphic type inference and abstract data types. ACM Trans. Program. Lang. Syst. **16**(5) (1994). https://doi.org/10.1145/186025.186031, https://doi.acm.org/10.1145/186025.186031
13. Leijen, D.: A type directed translation of MLF to system F. In: Proceedings of ICFP 2007. ACM (2007)

14. Melliès, P., Vouillon, J.: Recursive polymorphic types and parametricity in an operational framework. In: Proceedings of LICS. IEEE Computer Society (2005). https://doi.org/10.1109/LICS.2005.42
15. Mitchell, J.C.: Foundations for Programming Languages. Foundation of Computing Series, MIT Press, Cambridge (1996)
16. Morrisett, G.: Compiling with Types. Ph.D. thesis, CMU (1995)
17. Paraskevopoulou, Z., Grover, A.: Compiling with continuations, correctly. Proc. ACM Program. Lang. 5(OOPSLA) (2021). https://doi.org/10.1145/3485491
18. Pierce, B.: Advanced Topics in Types and Programming Languages. The MIT Press, Cambridge (2004)
19. Pitts, A., Stark, I.: Operational reasoning for functions with local state. In: Higher Order Operational Techniques in Semantics. Cambridge University Press (1998)
20. Pitts, A.M.: Existential types: logical relations and operational equivalence. In: Larsen, K.G., Skyum, S., Winskel, G. (eds.) ICALP 1998. LNCS, vol. 1443, pp. 309–326. Springer, Heidelberg (1998). https://doi.org/10.1007/BFb0055063
21. Pitts, A.M.: Parametric polymorphism and operational equivalence. Math. Struct. Comput. Sci. 10(3) (2000). https://journals.cambridge.org/action/displayAbstract?aid=44651
22. Pitts, A.M.: Step-indexed biorthogonality: a tutorial example. In: Modelling, Controlling and Reasoning About State. Dagstuhl Seminar Proceedings, vol. 10351. Schloss Dagstuhl - Leibniz-Zentrum für Informatik, Germany (2010). https://drops.dagstuhl.de/opus/volltexte/2010/2806/
23. https://www.rust-lang.org/d (2021)
24. Skorstengaard, L.: An introduction to logical relations (2019). https://arxiv.org/abs/1907.11133
25. Statman, R.: Logical relations and the typed lambda-calculus. Inf. Control. 65(2/3) (1985). https://doi.org/10.1016/S0019-9958(85)80001-2
26. Sulzmann, M., Wehr, S.: A dictionary-passing translation of featherweight go. In: Oh, H. (ed.) APLAS 2021. LNCS, vol. 13008, pp. 102–120. Springer, Cham (2021). https://doi.org/10.1007/978-3-030-89051-3_7
27. Sumii, E., Pierce, B.C.: A bisimulation for type abstraction and recursion. J. ACM 54(5) (2007). https://doi.org/10.1145/1284320.1284325
28. Tait, W.W.: Intensional interpretations of functionals of finite type I. J. Symb. Log. 32(2) (1967). https://doi.org/10.2307/2271658
29. https://www.scala-lang.org/ (2021)

Streams of Approximations, Equivalence of Recursive Effectful Programs

Niccoló Veltri[ID] and Niels Voorneveld[✉][ID]

Department of Software Science, Tallinn University of Technology, Tallinn, Estonia
{niccolo,niels}@cs.ioc.ee

Abstract. Behavioural equivalence for functional languages with algebraic effects and general recursion is often difficult to formalize. When modelling the behaviour of higher-order programs, one often needs to employ multiple coinductive structures simultaneously. In this paper, we aim to simplify the issue with a single external stream monad dealing with recursion, and deal with the structures for modelling higher-order types in a purely inductive (finite) manner. We take a page from classical domain theory, modelling recursive programs as limits of increasing sequences of "finite" denotational elements. We carry around a single relation which contains all relevant information of behaviour: self-related elements are considered correct according to the denotational semantics, and two elements that are related both ways are considered equivalent. We implement equivalence of effectful programs using a relation lifting, creating a notion of behavioural equivalence for approximations. This is lifted to behavioural equivalence for recursive programs modelled by sequences of approximations, using a relator implementing a notion of weak similarity. We apply this to a fragment of call-by-push-value lambda calculus with algebraic effects, and establish a denotational equivalence which is sound with respect to an operational semantics, and sound with respect to contextual equivalence.

Keywords: Program equivalence · Algebraic effects · Call-by-push-value · Agda

1 Introduction

Equivalence of programs is a very useful tool for establishing when it is safe to replace one program with another. This can be checked by embedding a programming language into a more abstract mathematical domain which captures the right notions of behaviour. Two programs can then be deemed equivalent if they are given the same interpretation. More generally, the denotational domain allows the verification of properties of programs by exhibiting an equivalence between the program interpretation and a more abstract design specification.

The authors were supported by the ESF funded Estonian IT Academy research measure (project 2014–2020.4.05.19–0001). Veltri was also supported by the Estonian Research Council grant PSG749.

© The Author(s), under exclusive license to Springer Nature Switzerland AG 2022
E. Komendantskaya (Ed.): MPC 2022, LNCS 13544, pp. 198–221, 2022.
https://doi.org/10.1007/978-3-031-16912-0_8

In this work, we are interested in capturing the behaviour of a particular collection of programming features: *higher-order functional programs, general recursion, and algebraic effects*. Various techniques and abstract theories have been developed in the past decades to formulate notions of program equivalence for languages with these features. The formalization of such equivalences typically depends on the preceding formalization of a large volume of background mathematical theory. In this paper, we attempt a more direct approach to denotational semantics of effectful higher-order programs. We present a new denotational model for a variant of Levy's call-by-push-value (CBPV) paradigm [12], a theoretical functional language equipped with general recursion and algebraic effects [21]. Using this model, we formalize a *congruent* program equivalence, capturing appropriate notions of behaviour for all the interesting programming features of this language. Let us take a closer look at these features.

General Recursion. In order to make the language Turing complete, CBPV can include a notion of recursion which, as typical in a functional setting, takes the form of a *fixpoint operator*. This unlocks the Pandora's box of *divergence* and *undecidable termination*. Denotations of potentially diverging programs are typically formalized in proof assistants such as Agda and Coq using *coinductive types*. In its purest form, i.e. in the absence of side effects, possible non-termination can be captured using Capretta's *delay monad* [5] or, more extensionally in homotopy type theory, employing the *partiality monad* [2,6]. Other techniques include putting guards around each recursive unfolding, as done e.g. in *guarded/clocked type theory* [3,4].

In this paper, the mathematical structures employed for modelling general recursion are directly inspired by *domain theory* [1,9]. In domain theory, coinductive structures such as possible non-terminating computations and infinite trees are typically represented as limits of certain sequences of approximations, where the approximating elements are finite, belonging to inductively defined sets of structures. In our work we take a more *intensional* approach, representing infinite structures directly as sequences (streams) of approximations. The behaviour of these approximations is captured by a notion of *improvement order*, which allows us to state when an approximation is able to simulate all the behaviours of another approximation. These denotations are more intensional than normal domain denotations, since different sequences may approximate the same infinite object. As such, the collection of approximations needs to be equipped with a notion of *weak similarity*: a sequence r weakly simulates another sequence l if each element belonging to l is improved upon by some element belonging to r.

Algebraic Effects. Besides possible divergence, we capture a multitude of different effects by equipping our language with a collection of *algebraic effect operations* [21]. These implement some form of interaction between a program and the environment, which has an effect on how the program is evaluated. Key examples include *nondeterminism*, where program evaluation is influenced by some unknowable decider. Our semantic treatment of nondeterminism is inspired by the domain-theoretic *lower powerdomain* construction [18]. A second example is given by *stateful effects*, where operations are handled [22] by some deterministic decision process with a persistent state. These can be modelled by *stateful runners* [25].

In this work, such effects are modelled by taking the set of finite approximations to be an inductive set of terms generated by a collection of effect operations. More precisely, this set consists of finite trees where the branching is specified by effect operations and leaves can either be denotations of values or a fixed "bottom" element, representing a position in which the infinite structure that the finite tree is approximating has been pruned. Relations on values are lifted to relations on these finite trees using a *relator* [13,24]. Relators are a flexible tool for relational reasoning, used in [11] to formulate a notion of applicative bisimilarity on effectful lambda-calculi. To each effect we associate an appropriate relator implementing its behaviour.

Higher-Order. To capture the behaviour of a variety of functional languages, we study a variant of Levy's call-by-push-value language [12]. This variant subsumes the *PCF language* [19] for describing computable functions on natural numbers. CBPV captures both *call-by-name* and *call-by-value* evaluation strategies, by separating *values* from *computations* in a *fine-grained* manner [14]. The denotational semantics of our language associates to each type of the language an inductive set of approximations, and a transitive relation specifying the improvement order. Programs are then modelled by sequences (streams) of elements from these sets. Two programs are considered equivalent if their approximation sequences weakly simulate each other, i.e. they are weakly bisimilar.

We establish a variety of properties of this notion of equivalence. Firstly, using the improvement order we can show that the interpretation of each program in the model is *correct* in the following sense: 1) approximations of functional programs are modelled by functions which preserve the improvement order on correct arguments, 2) the sequence of approximations modelling each program are increasing with respect to the improvement order. The proofs of these facts follow arguments from the theory of *logical relations*, as we encode this notion of correctness within the improvement order: a model is correct if it improves upon itself. Using this notion of correctness as a base, we can prove that program equivalence is a *congruence*. This is a technical way of saying that weak bisimilarity is preserved under the language construction rules. As a direct corollary, we obtain that program equivalence is sound with respect to *contextual equivalence* [15,17], which is the largest congruent relation which still distinguishes between behaviourally distinct basic programs.

We also show that program equivalence is sound wrt. A small-step operational semantics. First, we show that program equivalence is preserved under *syntactic substitution* as used by the β-reduction of lambda terms. We then describe the operational semantics using evaluation stacks [8,30] capturing functional continuations of our programs, after which we establish the soundness result.

Formalisation in Agda. Results from this paper have been completely formalized in the Agda proof assistant: https://github.com/Voorn/Stream-Equivalence.

Many of the choices of definitions in this paper were made for ease of formalization. As such, the main contribution is the relatively direct and intensional implementation of the results, which can be theoretically motivated by abstract theory from the programming language literature. Moreover, the techniques presented in this paper give a more hands-on approach. It does not take a lot of work to define a model of a program, as it is given by a concrete approximation. This concrete approximation is then easier to investigate. Hence it may not be necessary to resort to specified equivalence-proving techniques, such as applicative bisimilarity, as are often employed for other more traditional denotational models. Another main difference between this and the domain theoretic approach, is that in domain theory results like soundness and congruence are due to intrinsic properties of the model, whereas here they are due to externally identified properties. This is simply a shift in proof obligations, and not a shift in complexity.

Lastly, it should be noted that the resulting notion of program equivalence is slightly more fine-grained than other notions, such as contextual equivalence and applicative bisimilarity. This is a necessary consequence, due to the uniform way in which recursion is treated, with a singular external constructor. This difference is not unreasonable however; it distinguishes programs with a constant time complexity from those with an unbounded time complexity.

Structure of the Paper. We start by discussing some general theory on streams and spaces of approximation in Sect. 2. In Sect. 3, we introduce the syntactic constructs of the functional call-by-push-value language with general recursion and effect operations, together with their models. In Sect. 4 we specify the right improvement orders for our programs, specifically implementing the right notion of effect behaviour. These construct our notion of program equivalence, whose properties are proven in Sect. 5. Lastly, we discuss some final thoughts in Sect. 6.

2   Recursion Streams

In a programming language with general recursion, programs may call upon themselves without any restriction. This makes it possible to meet a wide variety of specifications, going beyond the bounds of what is possible in decidable or primitive recursive languages. However, this simultaneously introduces the possibility of divergence. Not only that, this divergence is undecidable due to the Halting Problem.

A common solution to safeguarding such programs is to avoid modelling the complete evaluation, and instead work with finite approximations. One may bound the evaluation of a program by number of reduction steps, or number of problematic recursive calls. This gives a function from natural numbers to some space of approximations.

In some instances, it is sufficient to use the *delay monad*. Elements of this monad expose whether the evaluation of a program is ready now, or whether it takes at least one more step. This monad can be defined as $DX = \nu C.X + C$, the final coalgebra of the functor $C \mapsto X + C$ which chooses between providing a result in X, or continuing with one more step. This "one more step" is often used to implement a *guard* on the evaluation of the program.

There are however two complications which make it difficult to work with, and which we attempt to avoid in our models:

1. The delay monad is inherently *coinductive*, and its behaviour depends on how this coinduction is implemented in the meta-language.
2. In general, higher-order structures such as functions cannot be given a complete denotation in a finite amount of time, hence they do not *distribute* over the delay monad. A similar problem arises with effectful computations.

It is important to note that it is not impossible to overcome these complications with the delay monad. Solutions are however not always straightforward: one needs to make sure that each functional programming feature interacts well with recursion, i.e. as modelled by the delay monad. In this paper, we would like to make more concrete how to deal with recursion such that it readily composes with higher-order structures in a more uniform way.

In particular, to solve the second problem, we use *streams of approximations*. This model is built on the *reader monad* $RX = X^{\mathbb{N}}$. An element of RX reads a natural number describing the bound of the program evaluation, which we call *fuel*, and gives a corresponding approximation from X. The unit $\eta_X^R : X \to RX$ and multiplication $\mu_X^R : RRX \to RX$ are given by

$$\eta_X^R(x) = \lambda n.x, \qquad \mu_X^R(d) = \lambda n.d(n)(n). \tag{1}$$

We may describe sequenced programs using the *bind* operation $\kappa_{X,Y}^R : RX \to (X \to RY) \to RY$ given by $\kappa_{X,Y}^R(s)(f) = \lambda n.f(s(n))(n)$. In other words, when composing programs, we give each program the same amount of fuel.

2.1   Approximations

We would like to equip the reader monad with additional suitable structure that describes streams of approximations. To do this, we first need to specify a structure on the set to which we apply the monad R.

Definition 1. *An* approximation space X *is a pair* $(|X|, \leq_X)$ *given by:*

– *A set* $|X|$, *called the* carrier *of* X.
– *A transitive relation* $\leq_X$ *on* X, *which we call the* improvement order *of* X.

We often use the same notation for an approximation space and its carrier, i.e. we write X in place of $|X|$.

First some notes on the structure of an approximation space, or more precisely its lack of structure. It would be reasonable to require that the improvement order is also *reflexive*. However, this is not a priori necessary since we can always limit ourselves to the subset $\{x \in |X| \mid x \leq_X x\}$ of self-related elements of X, for which $\leq_X$ gives a reflexive and transitive relation. We call $x \in |X|$ *correct* if $x \leq_X x$. For reasons we will go into later, we do sometimes require our order to satisfy the extra property: $\forall x, y \in X. \ x \leq_X y$ implies $x \leq_X x$, which we call *quasi reflexivity*.

Secondly, one may suppose that the relation should be *anti-symmetric*, saying that if two elements improve each other, they should be equal. This is also not strictly necessary, since we can in principle take the *quotient* of X over the symmetrisation of the improvement order. So it is always possible to construct a reflexive, transitive and anti-symmetric relation.

The reason we do not build this into the structure itself is mainly to ease the formalization of these structures in Agda.

For the denotation of a program, we use an inductive set with a single relation which we use for *relational reasoning*, reminding ourselves we can always take the appropriate subset and quotient to get to a more structured abstract model.

Definition 2. *Given two approximation spaces X and Y, we define the approximation space of functions Y^X as:*

- *Carrier $|Y^X| = |X| \to |Y|$.*
- *$f \leq_{Y^X} g$ if: $\forall x, x' \in X. \ x \leq_X x \wedge x \leq_X x' \Rightarrow f(x) \leq_Y g(x')$.*

Proposition 1. *The relation $\leq_{Y^X}$ is transitive.*

Proof. Suppose $f \leq_{Y^X} g, g \leq_{Y^X} h, x \leq_X x$, and $x \leq_X x'$. Then $x \leq_X x \wedge x \leq_X x$ implies $f(x) \leq_Y g(x)$ and $x \leq_X x \wedge x \leq_X x'$ implies $g(x) \leq_Y h(x')$. Hence $f(x) \leq_Y h(x')$ by transitivity of $\leq_Y$.

If X is quasi reflexive, then the order of Y^X can be simplified to:

$$f \leq_{Y^X} g \iff \forall x, x' \in X. \ x \leq_X x' \Rightarrow f(x) \leq_Y g(x'). \tag{2}$$

In this case, $f \in |Y^X|$ is correct if and only if it is *monotone*.

As a concrete example consider the domain $\omega = (\mathbb{N}, \leq)$, which is an approximation space with underlying set $\mathbb{N}$ with $\leq$ the standard ordering on natural numbers, which is reflexive. For each approximation space X, we define the approximation space of streams over X as given by the function space X^ω. Though the set contains any possible infinite sequence of elements, it does hold that if $s \leq_{X^\omega} s$, then $s(0) \leq_X s(1) \leq_X s(2) \leq_X \dots$, hence correctness of s implies that s is an increasing sequence of elements.

The mapping $X \mapsto X^\omega$ can be used as a basis for a monad, using the structure of a *reader monad*. Given a function $f : X \to Y$, $f^\omega : X^\omega \to Y^\omega$ is given by $f^\omega(s)(n) = f(s(n))$, and unit and multiplication are as in (1). We call this reader monad the *stream monad*, and it has the following properties.

Lemma 1. *The monad structure of the stream monad preserves the improvement order:*

- *If $x \leq_X y$ then $\eta_X^R(x) \leq_{X^\omega} \eta_Y^R(y)$.*

– If $d \leq_{(X^\omega)^\omega} e$ then $\mu_X^R(d) \leq_{X^\omega} \mu_Y^R(e)$.

Given a set X, let $X_\perp$ be the approximation space with carrier $X + \{\perp\}$ and improvement order the relation generated by $\perp \leq_{X_\perp} x$ and $x \leq_{X_\perp} x$, for all $x \in X$. Then one can prove that the elements $s \in |X_\perp^\omega|$ such that $s \leq_{X^\omega} s$ are in one-to-one correspondence with elements from the delay monad DX [26].

2.2 Relating Streams

When relating two streams, we do not want to simply check whether they are related at each stage of the approximation. It is not always the case that an external observer of a program can see how much fuel the evaluation of a program needs. Hence, programs which take different amounts of fuel to get to the same result should still be considered the same. So we would like to relate any two streams if they can be synchronized in the following way.

Definition 3. *Given a relation* $\mathcal{R} \subseteq X \times Y$ *between* X *and* Y, *we define the relation of* weak similarity *over* $\mathcal{R}$ *as* $\Omega(\mathcal{R}) \subseteq X^\omega \times Y^\omega$ *such that:*

$$s\,\Omega(\mathcal{R})\,z \quad \Longleftrightarrow \quad \forall n.\ \exists m.\ s(n)\,\mathcal{R}\,z(m)$$

The above relation lifting preserves reflexivity and transitivity.

Weak similarity is the non-symmetric variant of weak bisimilarity, which relates programs regardless of the number of steps that are needed to evaluate them. In our case, this means that we disregard how far into the approximation we are, and only care about the existence of related approximations. As such, weak similarity relates more terms than standard (strong) similarity.

How well does this behave with respect to approximation spaces? A relation between two approximation spaces X and Y is given by a relation $\mathcal{R} \subseteq X \times Y$ such that: $(\leq_X; \mathcal{R}) \subseteq \mathcal{R}$ and $(\mathcal{R}; \leq_Y) \subseteq \mathcal{R}$ (here the semicolon denotes sequential composition of relations). Relations between approximation spaces are closed under composition, and each approximation space X has an identity relation on itself given by its approximation order $\leq_X$.

Proposition 2. *Let* X *and* Y *be approximation spaces and let* $\mathcal{R}$ *be a relation between them. The following properties hold:*

1. *for all* $x, y \in |X^\omega|$, *if* $x \leq_{X^\omega} y$ *then* $x\,\Omega(\leq_X)\,y$,
2. *for all* $x \in |X|, y \in |Y|$, *if* $x\,\mathcal{R}\,y$ *then* $\eta_X^R(x)\,\Omega(\mathcal{R})\,\eta_Y^R(y)$,
3. *for all* $d \in |(X^\omega)^\omega|, e \in |(Y^\omega)^\omega|$, *if* $d\,\Omega(\Omega(\mathcal{R}))\,e$ *and* $e \leq_{(Y^\omega)^\omega} e$, *then* $\mu_X^R(d)\,\Omega(\mathcal{R})\,\mu_Y^R(e)$.

3   Higher-Order Programs

We want to use streams to approximate coinductive structures, so that the n-th element in a stream represents the n-th approximation of a program denotation. In this section, we describe the space of approximations used for modelling higher-order functional programs, using a theoretical programming language.

We look at a fragment of *call-by-push-value* extended with a type of natural numbers, a fixpoint operator and algebraic effect operations. Call-by-push-value is a variation on simply-typed lambda calculus, which captures both call-by-value and call-by-name evaluation strategies. In this section we focus on the functional aspects of the language, leaving the interpretation of algebraic effects for the next section. In call-by-push-value, programs are distinguished between *values* and *computations*. Values are "passive" arguments of functions, and can be substituted for variables. Computations are "active" terms which can be normalized and potentially raise effects. We use α as variable ranging over value types, β as variable ranging over computation type and γ as variable ranging over arbitrary types. We define the types inductively as follows:

$$\textit{Values Types:} \quad \alpha := \mathbf{N} \mid \mathbf{U}\beta, \qquad \textit{Computation Types:} \quad \beta := \alpha \to \beta \mid \mathbf{F}\alpha$$

Value types contain a type of natural numbers $\mathbf{N}$, which is a base type. Natural numbers are inductively generated with zero and successor. The second value type is a *thunk type* $\mathbf{U}\beta$, which contains computations of type β, but considers them as values that can be given as arguments to functions.

Computation types contain a type of functions $\alpha \to \beta$, which consists of programs which accept value arguments of type α and return computations of type β. The second computation type is a *producer* type $\mathbf{F}\alpha$ of computations which, when evaluated, return a value of type α.

3.1   Algebraic Effect Operations

Computations may invoke operations whose behaviour are dependent on the environment and situation. Such operations are called algebraic effect operations. We collect these using a *signature* $S = (S_o, S_a)$ containing a set of names for operations S_o and a function designating the arity of each operation $S_a : S_o \to \mathbf{N}$, i.e. $S_a(\sigma)$ is the number of arguments of the operation $\sigma \in S_o$. We consider programs which may invoke operations from S.

When modelling the evaluation of computations which may invoke effect operations, we aim to abstract away the known deterministic reduction steps, leaving only the operations. What is left is a tree, known as an algebraic term.

Definition 4. *Given a set X, the set of S-terms (or trees) over X is the set $T_S X$ whose elements are inductively defined as follows:*

- $\mathtt{leaf}(x) \in T_S X$, *for any $x \in X$.*
- $\mathtt{node}(\sigma)(t_1, \dots, t_{S_a(\sigma)}) \in T_S X$, *for any $\sigma \in S_o$, and $(t_1, \dots, t_n) \in (T_S X)^{S_a(\sigma)}$.*
- $\mathtt{bott} \in T_S X$.

Here, $\mathtt{leaf}(x)$ describes the end of the evaluation, returning some value x. The tree $\mathtt{node}(\sigma)(t_1, \dots, t_n)$ expresses the invocation of the effect operation σ, which can be resolved in $S_a(\sigma)$-many possible ways. To each of these resolutions, a continuation t_i of the evaluation is assigned. If $S_a(\sigma) = 0$, no continuation is possible. In the Agda formalization, we use finite sets to describe finite tuples.

Given a natural number $n \in \mathbb{N}$, we write $[n]$ for the set $\{0, 1, \ldots, n - 1\}$. Then for a function $f : [S_a(\sigma)] \to T_S X$, we can write $\mathsf{node}(\sigma)(f)$ for the tree $\mathsf{node}(\sigma)(f(0), f(1), \ldots, f(n-1))$. Lastly, $T_S X$ includes a special designated *bottom* element bott, which is used as an end-of-approximation marker. It tells us that we do not know how the evaluation of the computation continues given the current approximation of our program. Concisely, T_S corresponds to the free monad wrt. the signature S extended with the 0-ary bottom operation.

Example 1. Let us consider first the situation in which there are no extra effects, besides non-termination. This can be modelled using the empty signature, and the monad of $\emptyset$-terms $T_\emptyset$ is then equivalent to the *maybe* monad.

Example 2. A signature S can be used to specify *input/output* style operations. Each operation σ outputs a unique message to the screen, for example a question, and the program user may respond with an input number between 1 and $S_a\sigma$.

Example 3. We can also consider the presence of a global memory. Depending on the state of the global memory, operations are resolved in a deterministic way, and the state may change in the process. In case the operation cannot be resolved, we raise an error represented by our bottom token bott. We capture the result with the maybe monad $T_\emptyset$.

Definition 5. *A stateful runner θ on a signature S is given by a state set M, and for each operation $\sigma \in S$ a function $\theta_\sigma : M \to T_\emptyset([S_a(\sigma)] \times M)$.*

The function θ_σ tells us that, if we encounter an operation σ and the current state is m, then when θ_σ returns a pair $\mathsf{leaf}(i, m')$ the following two things happen:

1. The evaluation of the program continues picking the i-th element as continuation.
2. The global state changes to m'.

We consider two examples of runners:

- *Global store*: Assume given a finite set of memory states M with n elements, and a signature S where $S_o = \{\mathsf{lookup}\} \cup \{\mathsf{update}_m \mid m \in M\}$ with arities $S_a(\mathsf{lookup}) = n$ and $S_a(\mathsf{update}_m) = 1$. The lookup operation reads the current state of the memory, and passes it to the program. The update_m operation changes the state of the memory to m. This is implemented with the runner on state space M:

$$\theta_{\mathsf{lookup}}(m) = \mathsf{leaf}(m, m), \qquad \theta_{\mathsf{update}_k}(m) = \mathsf{leaf}(0, k).$$

- *Cost*: Consider a signature S of cost operations, where $S_o = \{\mathsf{cost}_m \mid m \in \mathbb{N}\}$ and $S_a(\mathsf{cost}_m) = 1$. We use a global memory to keep track of how much we can still afford to pay. We define a runner θ on state space $\mathbb{N}$, where

$$\theta_{\mathsf{cost}_m}(k) = \begin{cases} \mathsf{leaf}(0, k - m) & \text{if } k \leq m \\ \mathsf{bott} & \text{otherwise} \end{cases}$$

3.2   Call-by-Push-Value

We now define the terms (i.e. the programs) of our fragment of call-by-push-value [12] with natural numbers, algebraic effect operations and a fixpoint operator. We assume given a countable set of *variables*. Variable contexts are given by sequences of pairs of variables and value types:

$$\textit{Contexts:}\quad \Gamma := \varepsilon \mid \Gamma; (x : \alpha)$$

Two variables appearing in the same context are always assumed to be distinct. We write $(x : \alpha) \in \Gamma$ to say that the pair $(x : \alpha)$ appears somewhere in the context Γ. For a term P, we write $\Gamma \vdash P : \gamma$ to indicate that term P has type γ and free variables in context Γ. We may mark the turnstile $\vdash$ with either v or c, to specify that the term is respectively a value or computation. Terms are inductively defined, following the judgements from Fig. 1.

$$\frac{(x : \alpha) \in \Gamma}{\Gamma \vdash_v \mathbf{var}(x) : \alpha} \quad \frac{\Gamma \vdash_c P : \alpha \to \beta \quad \Gamma \vdash_v V : \alpha}{\Gamma \vdash_c \mathbf{app}(P)(V) : \beta} \quad \frac{\Gamma; (x : \alpha) \vdash_c P : \beta}{\Gamma \vdash_c \mathbf{lam}_x(P) : \alpha \to \beta}$$

$$\frac{}{\Gamma \vdash_v \mathbf{Z} : \mathbf{N}} \quad \frac{\Gamma \vdash_v V : \mathbf{N}}{\Gamma \vdash_v \mathbf{S}(V) : \mathbf{N}} \quad \frac{\Gamma \vdash_v V : \mathbf{N} \quad \Gamma \vdash_c P : \beta \quad \Gamma; (x : \mathbf{N}) \vdash_c Q : \beta}{\Gamma \vdash_c \mathbf{case}\ V\ \mathbf{of}\ \{\mathbf{Z} \mapsto P;\ \mathbf{S}(x) \mapsto Q\} : \beta}$$

$$\frac{\Gamma \vdash_v V : \alpha}{\Gamma \vdash_c \mathbf{return}(V) : \mathbf{F}\alpha} \quad \frac{\Gamma \vdash_c P : \beta}{\Gamma \vdash_v \mathbf{thunk}(P) : \mathbf{U}\beta} \quad \frac{\Gamma \vdash_v V : \mathbf{U}\beta}{\Gamma \vdash_c \mathbf{force}(V) : \beta}$$

$$\frac{\Gamma \vdash_v V : \alpha \quad \Gamma; (x : \alpha) \vdash_c P : \beta}{\Gamma \vdash_c \mathbf{let}\ x\ \mathbf{be}\ V\ \mathbf{in}\ P : \beta} \quad \frac{\Gamma \vdash_c P : \mathbf{F}\alpha \quad \Gamma; (x : \alpha) \vdash_c Q : \beta}{\Gamma \vdash_c P\ \mathbf{to}\ x\ \mathbf{in}\ Q : \beta}$$

$$\frac{\sigma \in S_o \quad \forall i.\ \Gamma \vdash_c P_i : \beta}{\Gamma \vdash_c \mathbf{op}(\sigma)(P_1, \ldots, P_{S_a \sigma}) : \beta} \quad \frac{\Gamma \vdash_c P : \mathbf{U}\beta \to \beta}{\Gamma \vdash_c \mathbf{fix}(P) : \beta}$$

Fig. 1. Term judgements

For each type γ, we define a set $||\gamma||$ of approximations inductively as follows:

$$||\mathbf{N}|| = \mathbb{N}$$
$$||\mathbf{U}\beta|| = ||\beta||$$
$$||\alpha \to \beta|| = ||\alpha|| \to ||\beta||$$
$$||\mathbf{F}\alpha|| = T_S(||\alpha||)$$

A context $\Gamma = e_1; e_2; \ldots; e_n$ with $e_i = (x_i : \alpha_i)$ has as denotation set the product $||\Gamma|| = ||\alpha_1|| \times ||\alpha_2|| \times \cdots \times ||\alpha_n||$. For each $(x : \alpha) \in \Gamma$, there is a projection $\pi_{(x:\alpha) \in \Gamma} : ||\Gamma|| \to ||\alpha||$.

We denote approximations of each term $\Gamma \vdash P : \gamma$ using functions $||\Gamma \vdash \gamma|| = ||\Gamma|| \to ||\gamma||$. Without the inclusion of the fixpoint operation, which implements general recursion, the term can be denoted by a single function. However, once recursion is a possibility, we cannot always find a full denotation inductively. Instead, we make an approximation in terms of a function from the natural numbers. These approximations are monotone with respect to the order on the natural numbers and an improvement order on $||\Gamma \vdash \gamma||$ which will be defined in Sect. 4.1. For each $\Gamma \vdash P : \gamma$ and $n \in \mathbb{N}$, we define a denotation $||P||_n \in ||\Gamma \vdash \gamma||$ by mutual induction on both terms P and natural numbers n, given $\bar{e} \in ||\Gamma||$:

$$||\text{var}(x)||_n(\bar{e}) = \pi_{(x:\alpha)\in\Gamma}(\bar{e})$$
$$||\text{app}(P)(V)||_n(\bar{e}) = ||P||_n(\bar{e})(||V||_n(\bar{e}))$$
$$||\text{lam}_x(P)||_n(\bar{e}) = \lambda e'. \, ||P||_n(\bar{e}, e')$$
$$||\text{Z}||_n(\bar{e}) = 0$$
$$||\text{S}(V)||_n(\bar{e}) = ||V||_n(\bar{e}) + 1$$
$$||\text{case } V \text{ of } \{\text{Z} \mapsto P; \ \text{S}(x) \mapsto Q\}||_n(\bar{e}) = \begin{cases} ||P||_n & \text{if } ||V||_n(\bar{e}) = 0 \\ ||Q||_n(\bar{e}, e') & \text{if } ||V||_n(\bar{e}) = e' + 1 \end{cases}$$
$$||\text{return}(V)||_n(\bar{e}) = \text{leaf}(||V||_n(\bar{e}))$$
$$||\text{thunk}(P)||_n(\bar{e}) = ||P||_n(\bar{e})$$
$$||\text{force}(V)||_n(\bar{e}) = ||V||_n(\bar{e})$$
$$||\text{let } x \text{ be } V \text{ in } P||(\bar{e}) = ||P||_n(\bar{e}, ||V||_n(\bar{e}))$$
$$||P \text{ to } x \text{ in } Q||_n(\bar{e}) = \kappa_\beta(||P||_n(\bar{e}))(\lambda v.||Q||_n(\bar{e}, v))$$
$$||\text{op}(\sigma)(i \mapsto P_i)||_n(\bar{e}) = \text{node}_\beta(\sigma)(\lambda i.||P_i||_n(\bar{e}))$$
$$||\text{fix}(P)||_0(\bar{e}) = \text{bott}_\beta$$
$$||\text{fix}(P)||_{n+1}(\bar{e}) = ||P||_n(\bar{e}, ||\text{fix}(P)||_n(\bar{e}))$$

Above we have employed the special operations $\kappa_\beta : T_S X \to (X \to ||\beta||) \to ||\beta||$, $\text{node}_\beta : (\sigma \in S_o) \to (S_a(\sigma) \to ||\beta||) \to ||\beta||$ and $\text{bott}_\beta \in ||\beta||$ which are inductively defined as follows:

$$\kappa_{\mathbf{F}\alpha} = \kappa^{T_S}, \qquad\qquad \kappa_{\alpha\to\beta}(t)(f) = \lambda v. \ \kappa_\beta(t)(f(v)).$$
$$\text{node}_{\mathbf{F}\alpha}(\sigma)(f) = \text{node } \sigma \ f, \qquad \text{node}_{\alpha\to\beta}(\sigma)(f) = \lambda v. \ \text{node}_\beta(\sigma)(f(v)).$$
$$\text{bott}_{\mathbf{F}\alpha} = \text{bott}, \qquad\qquad \text{bott}_{\alpha\to\beta} = \lambda v. \ \text{bott}_\beta.$$

Crucially, the only situation in which the fuel n decreases in the definition of $||P||_n$ is when the fixpoint operator gets unfolded. If n is zero at the time of unfolding, we bind an end-of-approximation marker bott to the denotation.

The denotations implement the behaviour of terms, not their explicit evaluation. In the next section, we will associate to the denotation spaces an improvement order depending on the behaviour of effects. The program denotation will be increasing with respect to this order. In Sect. 5, we will see that these denotations are sound with respect to the standard evaluation strategy of computations.

4 Effectful Behaviour

In order to associate an improvement order to approximations, we need to specify what constitutes an improvement on effectful S-terms. This depends on the behaviour of the effect operations, which can be characterized using the notion of *relator* [13,24]. We follow the literature in using Γ for denoting relators, which should not be confused with variable contexts.

Definition 6. *A relator Γ on S-terms is a function that takes a relation $\mathcal{R}$ between sets X and Y to a relation $\Gamma(\mathcal{R})$ between $T_S X$ and $T_S Y$, such that:*

- $=_{T_S X} \subseteq \Gamma(=_X)$.
- $\Gamma(\mathcal{R}); \Gamma(\mathcal{S}) \subseteq \Gamma(\mathcal{R}; \mathcal{S})$.
- *If $\mathcal{R} \subseteq \mathcal{S}$ then $\Gamma(\mathcal{R}) \subseteq \Gamma(\mathcal{S})$.*
- *Given $f : X \to X'$, $g : Y \to Y'$, and $\mathcal{R} \subseteq X \times X'$, then, for all $a \in T_S X$ and $b \in T_S Y$, $a \, \Gamma(\{(x,y) \mid f(x) \, \mathcal{R} \, g(y)\}) \, b$ if and only if $T_S(f)(a) \, \Gamma(\mathcal{R}) \, T_S(g)(b)$.*

The first two properties assert that a relator should behave well with respect to the unit relation and relation composition. The third property states that the relator is monotone with respect to the inclusion order. The fourth property entails a sort of naturality, which is not directly necessary for the results of this paper, given some extra assumptions made later. However, it is a useful reasoning tool, and it holds for all the main examples of signatures and relators. As a consequence of the above properties, we see that a relator preserves both reflexivity and transitivity of relations. Hence, it can be used to lift an approximation space $(X, \leq_X)$ to an approximation space $(T_S(X), \Gamma(\leq_X))$.

We additionally require relators to respect the monadic structure of S-terms and we ask bott to be the bottom element of the lifted relation.

Definition 7. *A relator Γ is said to be* sufficient[1] *if it additionally satisfies the three following properties:*

- *If $x \, \mathcal{R} \, y$, then $\mathtt{leaf}(x) \, \Gamma(\mathcal{R}) \, \mathtt{leaf}(y)$.*
- *Given $a \in T_S X$, $b \in T_S X'$, $f : X \to T_S X'$, $g : Y \to T_S Y'$, $\mathcal{R} \subseteq X \times Y$, and $\mathcal{S} \subseteq X' \times Y'$ such that $a \, \Gamma(\mathcal{R}) \, b$ and, for any $x \, \mathcal{R} \, y$, $f(x) \, \Gamma(\mathcal{S}) \, g(y)$, then $\kappa^S(a)(f) \, \Gamma(\mathcal{S}) \, \kappa^S(b)(g)$.*
- *For any $t \in T_S Y$, $\mathtt{bott} \, \Gamma(\mathcal{R}) \, t$.*

There always exists a canonical *minimal* sufficient relator, which separates different effect operations.

Definition 8. *The* syntactic relator *Δ^S on S-terms is inductively defined as follows, given a relation $\mathcal{R} \subseteq X \times Y$:*

- *If $x \, \mathcal{R} \, y$, then $\mathtt{leaf}(x) \, \Delta^S(\mathcal{R}) \, \mathtt{leaf}(y)$.*
- *If $\forall i. \, l_i \, \Delta^S(\mathcal{R}) \, r_i$, then $\mathtt{node}(\sigma)(l_1, \ldots, l_n) \, \Delta^S(\mathcal{R}) \, \mathtt{node}(\sigma)(r_1, \ldots, r_n)$.*
- *$\mathtt{bott} \, \Delta^S(\mathcal{R}) \, r$ for any $r \in T_S Y$.*

The syntactic relator is called as such since it leaves the operations uninterpreted. It relates the least number of terms out of all possible sufficient relators.

---

[1] In [11] these would be called *inductive relators for T_S*, though in our case without the inductive property requiring closure under limits since our approximation spaces are not closed under limits. To avoid confusion, we would like to use the word "sufficient", which is not a technical term. It simply encapsulates a collection of properties that are sufficient for achieving the results presented later in the paper.

Lemma 2. *The syntactic relator Δ^S is sufficient. Moreover, for any sufficient relator Γ on S-terms and any relation $\mathcal{R}$, $\Delta^S(\mathcal{R}) \subseteq \Gamma(\mathcal{R})$.*

Other sufficient relators can be seen as quotients over the syntactic relator, and can be defined for instance by adding equations between terms. We now look at several different types of relators for different kind of algebraic effects.

Example 4 (Example 1 ctd). In case there are no extra effects besides non-termination, the syntactic relator $\Delta^\emptyset$ from Definition 8 gives an appropriate notion of behaviour, where $a\ \Delta^\emptyset(\mathcal{R})\ b$ holds iff, whenever a terminates giving result x, then b terminates giving some result y such that $x\ \mathcal{R}\ y$.

Example 5 (Example 2 Ctd.). Consider the input/output effect over some signature S. A user of a program may navigate to any location in the input/output tree using a precise series of inputs. As such, external observers can figure out the precise shape of the tree, and differentiate between different trees. So the syntactic relator Δ^S is an appropriate model of behaviour in this situation.

Example 6 (Example 3 ctd). A stateful runner θ specifies a natural transformation $\widehat{\theta}_X : T_S X \times M \rightarrow T_\emptyset(X \times M)$, with additional properties related to the monadic structure of both T_S and $T_\emptyset$. Important to our purposes however is that we can construct a relator on T_S using a runner. This should implement the fact that two trees are equivalent if for any starting state, they evaluate to equivalent results and have the same final state remaining.

Definition 9. *The stateful relator Γ_θ for θ is the relator lifting a relation $\mathcal{R} \subseteq X \times Y$ to the relation $\Gamma_\theta(\mathcal{R}) \subseteq T_S X \times T_S Y$, where:*

$$a\ \Gamma_\theta(\mathcal{R})\ b \iff \forall m \in M.\ \widehat{\theta}_X(a, m)\ \Delta^\emptyset(\mathcal{R} \times (=_M))\ \widehat{\theta}_Y(b, m)$$

In other words, $\Gamma_\theta(\mathcal{R})$ relates S-terms a and b iff, for any starting state m, whenever a evaluates to a result x with final state m', then b evaluates to a result y such that $x\ \mathcal{R}\ y$, ending with the same final state m'.

Lemma 3. *For any stateful runner θ, Γ_θ is a sufficient relator on T_S.*

Example 7. The *nondeterministic relator* Γ_{nd}^S on S-terms implements the idea that operations are resolved nondeterministically. This compares the set of leaves of two terms, ignoring node operations. This can be inductively defined as follows:

- If $x\ \mathcal{R}\ y$ then $\texttt{leaf}(x)\ \Gamma_{nd}^S(\mathcal{R})\ \texttt{leaf}(y)$.
- For $\sigma \in S_o$, $\texttt{leaf}(x)\ \Gamma_{nd}^S(\mathcal{R})\ \texttt{node}(\sigma)(a_1, \ldots, a_n)$ if $\exists i.\ \texttt{leaf}(x)\ \Gamma_{nd}^S(\mathcal{R})\ a_i$.
- For $\sigma \in S_o$, $\texttt{node}(\sigma)(a_1, \ldots, a_n)\ \Gamma_{nd}^S(\mathcal{R})\ b$ if $\forall i.\ a_i\ \Gamma_{nd}^S(\mathcal{R})\ b$.
- $\texttt{bott}\ \Gamma_{nd}^S(\mathcal{R})\ a$.

Informally, $\Gamma_{nd}^S(\mathcal{R})$ relates terms a and b if for any $\texttt{leaf}(x)$ of a there is a $\texttt{leaf}(y)$ of b such that $x\ \mathcal{R}\ y$.

Lemma 4. *For any effect signature S, Γ_{nd}^S is a sufficient relator on T_S.*

4.1 Improvement Orders

Suppose given a sufficient relator Γ on S-terms, we associate the following improvement orders to the denotations of types:

Type γ	Denotation set $\|\|\gamma\|\|$	Improvement order $a \leq_\gamma b$
N	$\mathbb{N}$	$a = b$
$\mathbf{U}\beta$	$\|\|\beta\|\|$	$a \leq_\beta a \,\wedge\, a \leq_\beta b$
$\alpha \to \beta$	$\|\|\alpha\|\| \to \|\|\beta\|\|$	$\forall v, w \in \|\|\alpha\|\|.\ v \leq_\alpha w \;\Rightarrow\; a(v) \leq_\beta b(w)$
$\mathbf{F}\alpha$	$T_S\|\|\alpha\|\|$	$a\,\Gamma(\leq_\alpha)\,b$

The definition of $a \leq_{\mathbf{U}\beta} b$ includes the requirement $a \leq_\beta a$ to ensure the following property.

Lemma 5. *For any value type α, the relation $\leq_\alpha$ is quasi reflexive.*

The improvement order for functions is taken from (2) which, by the above lemma, is transitive as shown in Proposition 1. Hence, since every relator preserves transitivity of relations, we can conclude the following:

Lemma 6. *For any type γ, $\leq_\gamma$ is transitive, hence $(\|\|\gamma\|\|, \leq_\gamma)$ is an approximation space.*

Remark 1. Before we got to the currently presented definition, we tried to use Definition 2 directly as the improvement order $\leq_{\alpha\to\beta}$ of function denotations, to ensure its transitivity. In order to make this work well with relators, the second property of Definition 7 regarding the κ-bind operation would need to be strengthened. However, this stronger property is very stringent and unsatisfactory, and it is not satisfied by the nondeterministic relator from Example 7. This is due to the fact that self-related trees do not necessarily have self-related leaves. So we use the current formulation instead.

The improvement order on type denotations can be extended to context denotations $\|\|\Gamma\|\|$ by combining the orders on the underlying value types:

$$(v_1, \ldots, v_n) \leq_\Gamma (v_1', \ldots, v_n') \iff \forall i.v_i \leq_{\alpha_i} v_i'.$$

Notice that this relation inherits quasi reflexivity. Finally, the improvement order on type and context denotations can be extended to judgement denotations $\|\|\Gamma \vdash \gamma\|\|$ as follows:

$$f \leq_{\Gamma\vdash\gamma} g \iff \forall e, e' \in \|\|\Gamma\|\|.\ e \leq_\Gamma e' \;\Rightarrow\; f(e) \leq_\gamma g(e')$$

From Lemma 6 and properties of sufficient relators, we can show the following main result.

Proposition 3. *For any term $\Gamma \vdash P : \gamma$, and $n, m \in \mathbb{N}$ such that $n \leq m$, $\|\|P\|\|_n \leq_{\Gamma\vdash\gamma} \|\|P\|\|_m$.*

As discussed before, improvement orders are not required to be reflexive, and in fact they are not reflexive for most of the denotation spaces. For example, denotations of functions are only related to themselves if they are monotone with respect to the improvement order. One important consequence of the above proposition is that for any $n \in \mathbb{N}$, $||P||_n$ is related to itself, and hence each approximation is *correct* according to the improvement order $\leq_{\Gamma \vdash \gamma}$.

5   Full Program Denotations and Equivalence

The full denotation of a program will be given by a stream of approximations. We call this the ω-denotation, so-called after ω-chains from domain theory, reflecting the fact that they are increasing sequences of elements. For a context Γ and a type γ, this full denotation is given by $[\![\Gamma \vdash \gamma]\!] = ||\Gamma \vdash \gamma||^\omega$. For any term $\Gamma \vdash P : \gamma$, we give its full denotation $[\![P]\!] \in [\![\Gamma \vdash \gamma]\!]$ as $\lambda n.||P||_n$. Proposition 3 implies that $[\![P]\!] \leq_{[\![\Gamma \vdash \gamma]\!]} [\![P]\!]$ for any $\Gamma \vdash P : \gamma$, hence the ω-denotation of P is correct according to the improvement order $\leq_{[\![\Gamma \vdash \gamma]\!]}$.

There is however one problem that still needs to be solved. The full denotation is sensitive to the current stage of the approximation. Consider for instance the fixpoint case, where $||\mathtt{fix}(P)||_{n+1} = ||\mathtt{app}(P)(\mathtt{thunk}(\mathtt{fix}(P)))||_n$. We would like to say that these two terms are indistinguishable, but it does not hold that $[\![\mathtt{app}(P)(\mathtt{thunk}(\mathtt{fix}(P)))]\!] \leq_{[\![\Gamma \vdash \beta]\!]} [\![\mathtt{fix}(P)]\!]$. This discrepancy leaks into all aspects of the program denotations, blocking us from proving soundness of operational semantics with respect to the improvement order.

This issue can be overcome by implementing a type of *weak* relation, which ignores any finite difference in fuel. To do this, we use the stream relator Ω for weak similarity from Definition 3.

Definition 10. *For any Γ and γ, the behavioural relation $\sqsubseteq_{\Gamma \vdash \gamma}$ on $[\![\Gamma \vdash \gamma]\!]$ is defined as:*

$$a \sqsubseteq_{\Gamma \vdash \gamma} b \quad \Longleftrightarrow \quad a\,\Omega(\leq_{||\Gamma \vdash \gamma||})\,b.$$

We simply write $\sqsubseteq$ in place of $\sqsubseteq_{\Gamma \vdash \gamma}$ when the judgement $\Gamma \vdash \gamma$ is clear from context. The behavioural relation also gives a relation on programs P, Q of type γ in context Γ: $P \sqsubseteq Q$ if and only if $[\![P]\!] \sqsubseteq [\![Q]\!]$. We write $P \equiv Q$ if both $P \sqsubseteq Q$ and $Q \sqsubseteq P$.

The behavioural relation is weaker than the improvement order, because $a \leq_{[\![\Gamma \vdash \gamma]\!]} b$ implies $a \sqsubseteq_{\Gamma \vdash \gamma} b$, hence the former gives a viable proof technique for establishing the latter. We will study the properties of the behavioural relation as a relation on programs.

First and foremost, we establish that the relation is preserved over the term judgements of Fig. 1, which makes it a *precongruence*.

Definition 11. *A typed relation on programs is a family of relations $\mathcal{R}$ consisting of, for each pair of context Γ and type γ, a relation $\mathcal{R}_{\Gamma \vdash \gamma}$ between terms of type γ in context Γ. A typed relation $\mathcal{R}$ is a precongruence if for any judgement $\frac{\Gamma_1 \vdash P_1 : \gamma_1 \ldots \Gamma_n \vdash P_n : \gamma_n}{\Gamma \vdash M(P_1, \ldots, P_n) : \gamma}$ from Fig. 1, it holds that, for any tuple of related programs $Q_i \mathcal{R}_{\Gamma_i \vdash \gamma_i} R_i$, we have $M(Q_1, \ldots, Q_n) \mathcal{R}_{\Gamma \vdash \gamma} M(R_1, \ldots, R_n)$.*

Theorem 1 (precongruence). *The behavioural relation $\sqsubseteq$ is a precongruence.*

Proof. We can establish a stronger result by translating each typing rule of Fig. 1 into a function $m : [\![\Gamma_1 \vdash \gamma_1]\!] \times \cdots \times [\![\Gamma_n \vdash \gamma_n]\!] \to [\![\Gamma \vdash \gamma]\!]$ within the denotational spaces. It can then be established that, given pairs $p_i, q_i \in [\![\Gamma_i \vdash \gamma_i]\!]$ such that the three statements $p_i \sqsubseteq q_i$, $p_i \leq p_i$ and $q_i \leq q_i$ hold, then the elements constructed via m are related, i.e. $m(p_1, \ldots, p_n) \sqsubseteq m(q_1, \ldots, q_n)$.

As a direct corollary, we can say that the behavioural relation is sound with respect to *contextual relation*. This can be made precise in the following way. Consider a *closed program context* $C[-]$ of type β (not to be confused with variable contexts), which is a program in the empty variable context with a hole of some other computation type β'. We can simulate such contexts using thunk types: simply replace the hole of C with $\texttt{force}(\texttt{var}(x))$, where $x : \mathbf{U}\beta'$, creating a program $(x : \mathbf{U}\beta') \vdash_c C' : \beta$. For a program $\varepsilon \vdash_c P : \beta'$, we simulate the substitution of P into $C[-]$ as $C[P] = \texttt{let } x \texttt{ be thunk}(P) \texttt{ in } C'$.

Corollary 1. *For any context C of type β with hole of type β', and any pair of programs $\varepsilon \vdash_c P, Q : \beta$ such that $P \sqsubseteq Q$, then $C[P] \sqsubseteq C[Q]$.*

One way of defining the contextual relation is to first define a base relation on programs of *ground producer types*, which in this case are programs of type **FN**. This base relation should capture externally observable behaviour, and in our case it is given by $\Gamma(=_\mathbb{N})$. Then we say that two programs $\varepsilon \vdash_c P, Q : \beta$ are contextually related if for any context C of type **FN** with hole of type β, $C[P]$ and $C[Q]$ are related via the base relation. By the above corollary, our behavioural relation is sound with respect to the contextual relation.

5.1 The Subtlety of Approximation

As seen in Corollary 1, equivalence in our model implies contextual equivalence. However, the reverse direction does not hold, which is partially due to similar issues in the domain-theoretic approach, and we will discuss some reasons for this lack of *full abstraction* in the conclusive Sect. 6. It should however be said that the notion of equivalence constructed here is even more fine-grained than traditional denotational equivalences and applicative (bi)similarities, due to dealing with recursion completely externally. This difference does have a practical motivation with regards to time complexity.

Example 8. Consider the constantly zero function $\varepsilon \vdash_c M : \mathbf{N} \to \mathbf{FN}$ given by $M = \texttt{lam}_x(\texttt{return}(\mathtt{Z}))$. For any $n \in \mathbb{N}$, the approximation $||M||_n : \mathbb{N} \to T_S\mathbb{N}$ is given by $m \mapsto \texttt{leaf}(0)$. Consider the following alternative $\varepsilon \vdash_c N : \mathbf{N} \to \mathbf{FN}$ given by:

$$\texttt{fix}(\texttt{lam}_c(\texttt{lam}_n(\texttt{case } n \texttt{ of } \{\mathtt{Z} \mapsto \mathtt{Z};\ \mathtt{S}(m) \mapsto \texttt{app}(\texttt{force}(c))(m)\})))$$

which counts down its argument using recursion, until it reaches zero. We left out applications of $\texttt{return}$ and $\texttt{var}$ for readability's sake. For any $n \in \mathbb{N}$, $||N||_n :$

$\mathbb{N} \to T_S\mathbb{N}$ denotes the function sending any $m < n$ to $\text{leaf}(m)$, and any $m \geq n$ to bott.

In domain theory, both these terms would denote the same constantly zero function. In our model though, given a reasonable relator (see below), the two are distinguishable. Since, for any $n \in \mathbb{N}$, $||N||_n \leq_{\varepsilon \vdash \mathbf{N} \to \mathbf{FN}} ||M||_n$, and therefore $[\![N]\!] \sqsubseteq_{\varepsilon \vdash \mathbf{N} \to \mathbf{FN}} [\![M]\!]$. However, $[\![M]\!] \not\sqsubseteq_{\varepsilon \vdash \mathbf{N} \to \mathbf{FN}} [\![N]\!]$, since there is no approximation $n \in \mathbb{N}$ of N which fully captures the first approximation of M.

The above example works in any situation where we use a relator Γ for which $\text{leaf}(x)\Gamma(\mathcal{R})\text{bott}$ never holds, which is a perfectly reasonable assumption since otherwise the equivalence becomes rather trivial. Moreover, alternative examples can be constructed in any case when there is an infinitary input, for instance using a runner (Definition 5) with an infinitary state space M.

In general, our notion of program equivalence asserts a sort of *uniform boundedness* on infinitely wide input spaces. This is due to the fact that programs need to be related on the level of approximation, and hence these approximations need to be related when instantiated with any possible input. Another way of looking at it is that the equivalence separates programs with a constant time complexity from those with a non-constant time complexity.

5.2   The Substitution Lemma

We are working towards a result of soundness for the behavioural relation with respect to the operational semantics. We have not yet specified an operational semantics for the language in Fig. 1 however, and to do so we need to first look at term substitution.

Consider the term $\text{app}(\text{lam}_x(P))(V)$, which should reduce to $P[V/x]$ according to standard lambda calculus β-reduction. Here, $P[V/x]$ stands for substituting V for every instance of $\text{var}(x)$ in P. This substitution can be defined by induction on terms, though one needs to be careful of how to deal with variable names. In the Agda formalization, this is dealt with using *De Bruijn indices*.

It is important to analyse the difference between the denotations $[\![P[V/x]]\!]$ and $[\![\text{app}(\text{lam}_x(P))(V)]\!]$, which is determined by the amount of fuel each of them gives to V.

- $[\![\text{app}(\text{lam}_x(P))(V)]\!](n)(e) = ||\text{app}(\text{lam}_x(P))(V)||_n(e) = ||P||_n(e, ||V||_n(e))$, gives to V the same amount of fuel n as it gives to P.
- $[\![P[V/x]]\!](n)(e) = ||P[V/x]||_n(e)$ may give to V a lower amount of fuel since we may have fixpoint reduction steps before reaching V.

We can say that $[\![P[V/x]]\!] \leq [\![\text{app}(\text{lam}_x(P))(V)]\!]$ but not the other way around. However, we can establish that $[\![\text{app}(\text{lam}_x(P))(V)]\!] \sqsubseteq [\![P[V/x]]\!]$. We actually prove a more general form of these latter statements. First, we make explicit how the denotational semantics deals with substitution.

Definition 12. *Given a context* $\Gamma = e_1; \ldots; e_n$ *with* $e_j = (x_j : \alpha_j)$, *and an index* $1 \leq i \leq n$. *We define* $\Gamma \setminus i := e_1; \ldots; e_{i-1}; e_{i+1}; \ldots; e_n$ *and* $\Gamma \ominus i := e_1; \ldots; e_{i-1}$. *Given* $\overline{v} \in ||\Gamma \setminus i||$ *and* $w \in ||\Gamma \ominus i \vdash \alpha_i||$, *we define* $\overline{v}\{w\} \in ||\Gamma||$ *as:*

$$\overline{v}\{w\} = (v_1, \ldots, v_{i-1}, w(v_1, \ldots, v_{i-1}), v_{i+1}, \ldots, v_n)$$

Given $p \in ||\Gamma \vdash \gamma||$, *we define* $p[w/i] \in ||\Gamma \setminus i \vdash \gamma||$ *as* $p[w/i] = \lambda e.p(e\{w\})$.

We call $p[v/i]$ the *substitution* of v for i in p. As an example, if $i = n$ as in the case of β-reduction $\mathtt{app}(\mathtt{lam}_x(P))(V)$, we have that $p[v/i](e) = p(e, v)$. The following result shows soundness of denotational substitution with respect to syntactic substitution. This is the corner-stone of soundness of denotations with respect to the operational semantics.

Lemma 7 (substitution lemma). *Given a context* $\Gamma = (x_1 : \alpha_1); \ldots; (x_n : \alpha_n)$, *an index* $1 \leq i \leq n$ *and two programs* $\Gamma \vdash P : \gamma$ *and* $\Gamma \ominus i \vdash V : \alpha_i$. *Then:*

1. $[\![P[V/x_i]]\!] \leq_{\Gamma \setminus i \vdash \gamma} \lambda n.||P||_n[||V||_n/i]$.
2. $[\![P[V/x_i]]\!] \equiv_{[\![\Gamma \setminus i \vdash \gamma]\!]} \lambda n.||P||_n[||V||_n/i]$.

Proof. The first statement can be shown by simultaneous induction on P and n. The only non-standard case is that of the fixpoint operator, which is done by case analysis on n. If $n = 0$, the left is $\mathtt{bott}$ which we know can be improved by any other element. If $n = m + 1$, both sides unfold to almost the same thing, except that the substituted argument $||V||$ is given fuel m on the left-hand-side, and fuel $m+1$ on the right-hand-side. The statement follows from the correctness of $||V||$ (Proposition 3).

The left-to-right direction of the second statement is directly implied by the first statement. The right-to-left direction cannot be shown directly by induction. Instead, we need to first show that for any $k \subset \mathbb{N}$:

$$(\lambda n.||P||_n[||V||_k/i]) \sqsubseteq_{[\![\Gamma \setminus i \vdash \gamma]\!]} [\![P[V/x_i]]\!]. \tag{3}$$

This requires an induction on P and n, where in the base case of $P = \mathtt{var}(i)$, we need to choose m to be k. All other cases are relatively straightforward. We can subsequently show $(\lambda n.||P||_n[||V||_n/i]) \sqsubseteq_{[\![\Gamma \setminus i \vdash \gamma]\!]} [\![P[V/x_i]]\!]$ by instantiating $k = n$ in (3), for each n.

5.3   Operational Semantics and Soundness

We specify a small step operational semantics for our language in Fig. 1. This will have to deal with the following problem: given an application $\mathtt{app}(P)(V)$, the first term P need not be in normal form. So when evaluating $\mathtt{app}(P)(V)$, we will need to first focus on evaluating P until it reduces to a lambda term $\mathtt{lam}_x(Q)$, after which we can perform the substitution $Q[V/x]$. Similarly, to reduce P to x in Q, we need to reduce P to a $\mathtt{return}(V)$ before continuing with $Q[V/x]$. Moreover, whilst evaluating P we may encounter effect operations.

We solve this issue by defining *stacks* for implementing evaluation contexts [8,30]. To focus our evaluation on a sub-term, we unfold the rest of the term to the stack. Once the sub-term has been fully evaluated, we retrieve from the stack how the evaluation should proceed. Stacks are defined by the grammar:

$$\text{Stacks:} \quad S \quad := \quad \varepsilon \mid \text{ap } S \ V \mid \text{to } S \ Q$$

Here, $\text{ap } S \ V$ is an *application stack*, which stores an argument V of a function, while $\text{to } S \ Q$ is a *continuation stack*, which stores a continuation Q for a producer type $\mathbf{F}\alpha$. A stack can be typed by a pair of computation types $S : \beta \rightarrowtail \beta'$, and this typing is defined inductively:

- $\varepsilon : \beta \rightarrowtail \beta$ for any computation type β.
- If $S : \beta \rightarrowtail \beta'$ and $\varepsilon \vdash_v V : \alpha$, then $\text{ap } S \ V : (\alpha \to \beta) \rightarrowtail \beta'$.
- If $S : \beta \rightarrowtail \beta'$ and $(x : \alpha) \vdash_c Q : \beta$, then $\text{to } S \ Q : \mathbf{F}\alpha \rightarrowtail \beta'$.

A *stack-pair* is a pair (S, Q) where S is a stack of some type $\beta' \rightarrowtail \beta$, and Q is a closed term $\varepsilon \vdash_c Q : \beta'$. Let $ST(\beta)$ be the set of stack-pairs (S, Q) such that $S : \beta' \rightarrowtail \beta$ for some β'. Given a stack-pair $(S, Q) \in ST(\beta)$, we define the term $\varepsilon \vdash S\{Q\} : \beta$ recursively as follows:

$$\varepsilon\{Q\} = Q$$
$$(\text{ap } S \ V)\{Q\} = S\{\text{app}(Q)(V)\}$$
$$(\text{to } S \ P)\{Q\} = S\{P \text{ to } x \text{ in } Q\}$$

We define the operational semantics in terms of stack-pairs, where a pair (S, Q) signifies that we are evaluating $S\{Q\}$, and are currently focussing on evaluating Q. We consider the following evaluation steps:

$$
\begin{aligned}
(S, \text{case } Z \text{ of } \{Z \mapsto P; \ S(x) \mapsto Q\}) &\rightsquigarrow (S, P) \\
(S, \text{case } S(V) \text{ of } \{Z \mapsto P; \ S(x) \mapsto Q\}) &\rightsquigarrow (S, Q[V/x]) \\
(S, \text{app}(P)(V)) &\rightsquigarrow (\text{ap } S \ V, P) \\
(\text{ap } S \ V, \text{lam}_x(P)) &\rightsquigarrow (S, P[V/x]) \\
(S, P \text{ to } x \text{ in } Q) &\rightsquigarrow (\text{to } S \ Q, P) \quad (4) \\
(\text{to } S \ P, \text{return}(V)) &\rightsquigarrow (S, P[V/x]) \\
(S, \text{force}(\text{thunk}(P))) &\rightsquigarrow (S, P) \\
(S, \text{let } x \text{ be } V \text{ in } P) &\rightsquigarrow (S, P[V/x]) \\
(S, \text{fix}(P)) &\rightsquigarrow (S, \text{app}(P)(\text{thunk}(\text{fix}(P))))
\end{aligned}
$$

There are three special cases which do not have a direct reduction in (4). When evaluation reaches $(\varepsilon, \text{return}(V))$ or $(\varepsilon, \text{lam}_x(P))$, we are done since both terms are completely normalized. The last missing case is when we encounter an effect operation, i.e. the program is of the form $\text{op}(\sigma)(P_1, \ldots, P_n)$. To deal with this case, we define the inductive set $F_S X$, where X is a set and S here is a signature of effects, which has two constructors:

- $\text{step}(x) \in F_S X$ for any $x \in X$.
- $\sigma(x_1, \ldots, x_{S_a(\sigma)}) \in F_S X$ for any $\sigma \in S_o$ and $x_1, \ldots, x_{S_a(\sigma)} \in X$.

Elements of the set $F_S X$ specify whether the next evaluation step is deterministic or results in an effect operation.

We define the general evaluation step as a function $\rho : ST(\beta) \to F_S(ST(\beta))$,

$$\rho(S, P) = \mathtt{step}(S', Q) \qquad\quad \text{if } (S, P) \rightsquigarrow (S', Q)$$
$$\rho(\varepsilon, \mathtt{lam}_x(P)) = \mathtt{step}(\varepsilon, \mathtt{lam}_x(P))$$
$$\rho(\varepsilon, \mathtt{return}(V)) = \mathtt{step}(\varepsilon, \mathtt{return}(V))$$
$$\rho((S, \mathtt{op}(\sigma)(P_1, \ldots, P_n))) = \sigma((S, P_1), \ldots, (S, P_n))$$

Let $Terms(\beta) = \{P \mid \varepsilon \vdash_c P : \beta\}$ be the collection of closed computations of type β. Then we have a function $\phi : F_S(ST(\beta)) \to Terms(\beta)$ which extracts the appropriate terms associated to results of a general evaluation step.

$$\phi(\mathtt{step}((S, P))) = S\{P\}$$
$$\phi(\sigma((S_1, P_1), \ldots, (S_n, P_n))) = \mathtt{op}(\sigma)(S_1\{P_1\}, \ldots, S_n\{P_n\})$$

Given the above definitions, we can state soundness with respect to the operational semantics with the following concise statement.

Theorem 2 (soundness). *For any* (S, P), $S\{P\} \equiv \phi(\rho(S, P))$.

6   Discussion and Conclusion

Connection to Domain Theory. Streams of approximations are used to represent coinductive objects via a concrete sequence of inductive objects. At their core, streams need not satisfy any additional property. But if a stream is correct, as is the case for our program denotations, we can say that it adequately approximates some unbounded element. Theoretically, these unbounded elements can be gathered together to form a domain (in the sense of domain theory). We give a sketch of this construction, though this has not been formalized in Agda yet. Given an approximation space X, we define the domain over X as follows:

- The carrier of the domain is the set $[X] = \{[f] \mid f \in X^\omega, f \leq_{X^\omega} f\}$ where $[f] \subseteq X^\omega$ is the equivalence class of f induced by (the symmetrisation of) the weak similarity relation $\Omega(\leq_X)$.
- The order of the domain is a relation $\preceq$ where $[f] \preceq [g]$ iff $f\Omega(\leq_X)g$.

Proving that this is a domain is not straightforward, considering one has to show that any sequence of streams which is increasing according to the $\preceq$ order has a unique limit. A helpful lemma for achieving this result is showing that for any $[f] \preceq [g]$, there is a stream $h \in X^\omega$ such that $f \leq_{X^\omega} h$, $h\,\Omega(\leq_X)\,g$ and $g\,\Omega(\leq_X)\,h$.

We can look at the examples of effects discussed in Sect. 4 through this domain-theoretic lens. Starting from the approximation space of S-terms and the syntactic relator, the above construction retrieves the partiality monad (in Example 4) and the tree monad (in Example 5) of domains. More interestingly, Example 7 corresponds to an implementation of the *lower powerdomain* [18]. Example 6, taking the global store sub-example, gives rise to the *state monad*.

Towards Full Abstraction? One disadvantage of the syntactic approach of this paper is that not all elements of denotation spaces are *finite*. This means that there exist elements $x \in |X|$ for which the set $\{y \in |X| \mid y \leq_X x\}$ is infinite. As such, if this x is approximated by a sequence $x_0 \leq_X x_1 \leq_X x_2 \leq_X \dots$ of elements not equal to x, then the stream $x_0, x_1, x_2, \dots$ is not necessarily equivalent (wrt. the symmetrisation of $\leq_{X^\omega}$) to the constant stream $x, x, x, \dots$ even though they "should" be the same.

This issue arises specifically when looking at function spaces. Effectively, there is a separation between programs which are bounded across the width of their codomain and programs that are unbounded. This is one way which separates the program equivalence of this paper from contextual equivalence, and gets in the way of *full abstraction*. However, one can motivate this discrepancy by considering possible *infinite variable contexts*, capable of evaluating an infinite number of programs in parallel. One potential solution is to only relate finite substructures of approximations in the formulation of the stream relator. This will have to be investigated further in future work.

Another way in which our program equivalence differs from contextual equivalence is by its inclusion of denotational elements which do not model any existing program. Hence contextually equivalent functional programs may still be considered different according to our program equivalence, if they behave differently on "virtual" arguments, i.e. semantic elements which are not in the image of the program evaluation function. Solutions for this kind of problem are widespread, and include forcing lambda-definability with logical relations [20], or limiting the denotation space using game semantics strategies [10].

Earlier Work. The program equivalence from this paper has both inductive and coinductive predicates built in. The statement $a\,\Omega(\mathcal{R})\,b$ checks for every approximation of a, whether there is an approximation of b which is related to a via $\mathcal{R}$. In the case of nondeterminism presented in Example 7, this entails showing, for any leaf encountered in a, whether there exists a leaf in b which is $\mathcal{R}$-related to it. Viewing a and b as infinite (coinductive) trees, this implements a coinductive test on a followed by an inductive test on b. Using this perspective, we can give a logical specification of our program equivalence using inductive and coinductive predicates, following the approach of [28]. Such a logical specification constructs for each type a collection of predicates capturing behavioural properties. In particular, these use *modalities* [23] for lifting predicates on values to predicates on trees over such values.

As seen in this paper, we can model a wide variety of effect examples. One interesting example from [11,23] which is theoretically possible but difficult to formalize, is that of probabilistic programs. Formalizing a relator for this effect would be cumbersome, as proofs of composability often require more advanced mathematical methods, such as Riemann integration. We leave the implementation of such a relator as a future goal.

Coinductive Types. A reader of this paper may reasonably ask: Agda has support for coinductive types, why did you not employ them in your work? First of all, the provided support for corecursive definitions is relatively limited, since all corecursive functions must satisfy very stringent syntactic guardedness conditions in order to be approved by Agda's productivity checker. This issue is practically overcome by the employment of *sizes* in the specification of coinductive types, which turn productivity checks into termination checks and give more flexibility in the construction of corecursive functions [7].

To the best of our knowledge, sized coinductive types have not been used for the purpose of denotational semantics of programming languages in the presence of higher-order functional programs and effects. In fact, it is not immediately clear to us what should be, in this specific case, the correct treatment of sizes in the construction of the semantic domains. All our attempts at defining a denotational domain for our variant of CBPV (or even call-by-value PCF) in Agda using sized coinductive types pointed to a specific direction: the type of denotational values, not only the denotational model of computations, should be parametrised by a size, and should moreover appropriately preserve the ordering of sizes (technically speaking, it has to be a contravariant presheaf on the thin category of sizes).

This is a very pervasive requirement, which would have forced us to work semantically in a category in which every type is sized, plus every semantic construction is required to be monotone wrt. sizes. Interestingly, this would be equivalent to working in a model of guarded/clocked type theory [29]. The complications that arose from our attempt using sized types initiated the search for alternative solutions, which eventually led to the very intensional approach using stream of approximations that we have presented in this paper.

The development of a more extensional and fully-abstract denotational model of our variant of CBPV is still an open problem and we leave it to future work. We foresee that the appropriate framework for this endeavour would be Guarded/Clocked Cubical Agda [16,27].

References

1. Abramsky, S.: Domain theory in logical form. Ann. Pure Appl. Log. **51**(1–2), 1–77 (1991). https://doi.org/10.1016/0168-0072(91)90065-T
2. Altenkirch, T., Danielsson, N.A., Kraus, N.: Partiality, Revisited. In: Esparza, J., Murawski, A.S. (eds.) FoSSaCS 2017. LNCS, vol. 10203, pp. 534–549. Springer, Heidelberg (2017). https://doi.org/10.1007/978-3-662-54458-7_31
3. Bahr, P., Grathwohl, H.B., Møgelberg, R.E.: The clocks are ticking: no more delays! In: Proceedings of 32nd Annual ACM/IEEE Symposium on Logic in Computer Science, LICS 2017, pp. 1–12. IEEE Computer Society (2017). https://doi.org/10.1109/LICS.2017.8005097
4. Bizjak, A., Grathwohl, H.B., Clouston, R., Møgelberg, R.E., Birkedal, L.: Guarded dependent type theory with coinductive types. In: Jacobs, B., Löding, C. (eds.) FoSSaCS 2016. LNCS, vol. 9634, pp. 20–35. Springer, Heidelberg (2016). https://doi.org/10.1007/978-3-662-49630-5_2

5. Capretta, V.: General recursion via coinductive types. Log. Methods Comput. Sci. **1**(2) (2005). https://doi.org/10.2168/LMCS-1(2:1)2005
6. Chapman, J., Uustalu, T., Veltri, N.: Quotienting the delay monad by weak bisimilarity. Math. Struct. Comput. Sci. **29**(1), 67–92 (2019). https://doi.org/10.1017/S0960129517000184
7. Danielsson, N.A.: Up-to techniques using sized types. Proc. ACM Program. Lang. **2**(POPL), 1–28 (2018). https://doi.org/10.1145/3158131
8. Felleisen, M., Hieb, R.: The revised report on the syntactic theories of sequential control and state. Theor. Comput. Sci. **103**, 235–271 (1992). https://doi.org/10.1016/0304-3975(92)90014-7
9. Gierz, G., Hofmann, K.H., Keimel, K., Lawson, J., Mislove, M., Scott, D.S.: Continuous Lattices and Domains. Cambridge University Press, Cambridge (2003)
10. Hyland, M., Ong, L.: On full abstraction for PCF: I II and III. Inf. Comput. **163**(2), 285–408 (2000). https://doi.org/10.1006/inco.2000.2917
11. Lago, U.D., Gavazzo, F., Levy, P.B.: Effectful applicative bisimilarity: monads, relators, and Howe's method. In: Proceedings of 32nd Annual ACM/IEEE Symposium on Logic in Computer Science, LICS 2017, pp. 1–12. IEEE Computer Society (2017). https://doi.org/10.1109/LICS.2017.8005117
12. Levy, P.: Call-by-push-value: decomposing call-by-value and call-by-name. Higher-Order Symb. Comput. **19**, 377–414 (2006). https://doi.org/10.1007/s10990-006-0480-6
13. Levy, P.B.: Similarity quotients as final coalgebras. In: Hofmann, M. (ed.) FoSSaCS 2011. LNCS, vol. 6604, pp. 27–41. Springer, Heidelberg (2011). https://doi.org/10.1007/978-3-642-19805-2_3
14. Levy, P., Power, J., Thielecke, H.: Modelling environments in call-by-value programming languages. Inf. Comput. **185**(2), 182–210 (2003). https://doi.org/10.1016/S0890-5401(03)00088-9
15. Milner, R.: Fully abstract models of typed lambda-calculi. Theor. Comput. Sci. **4**, 1–22 (1977). https://doi.org/10.1016/0304-3975(77)90053-6
16. Møgelberg, R.E., Vezzosi, A.: Two guarded recursive powerdomains for applicative simulation. In: Sokolova, A. (ed.) Proceedings of 37th Conference on Mathematical Foundations of Programming Semantics, MFPS 2021. Electron. Proceedings in Theoretical Computer Science, vol. 351, pp. 200–217 (2021). https://doi.org/10.4204/EPTCS.351.13
17. Morris, J.H.: Lambda-calculus models of programming languages, Ph.D. thesis, Massachusetts Institute of Technology (1969). https://dspace.mit.edu/handle/1721.1/64850
18. Plotkin, G.D.: A powerdomain construction. Siam J. Comput. **5**(3), 452–487 (1976). https://doi.org/10.1137/0205035
19. Plotkin, G.D.: LCF considered as a programming language. Theor. Comput. Sci. **5**(3), 223–255 (1977). https://doi.org/10.1016/0304-3975(77)90044-5
20. Plotkin, G.D.: Lambda-definability in the full type hierarchy. In: Seldin, J.P., Hindley, J.R. (eds.) To H. B. Curry: Essays on Combinatory Logic, Lambda Calculus and Formalism, pp. 363–374. Academic Press (1980)
21. Plotkin, G.D., Power, J.: Adequacy for algebraic effects. In: Honsell, F., Miculan, M. (eds.) FoSSaCS 2001, LNCS, vol. 2030, pp. 1–24 (2001). https://doi.org/10.1007/3-540-45315-6_1
22. Plotkin, G.D., Pretnar, M.: Handling algebraic effects. Log. Methods Comput. Sci. **9**(4), 1–36 (2013). https://doi.org/10.2168/lmcs-9(4:23)2013

23. Simpson, A., Voorneveld, N.: Behavioural equivalence via modalities for algebraic effects. ACM Trans. Program. Lang. Syst. **42**(1), 1–45 (2020). https://doi.org/10.1145/3363518

24. Thijs, A.M.: Simulation and fixpoint semantics, Ph.D. thesis, University of Groningen (1996). https://research.rug.nl/en/publications/simulation-and-fixpoint-semantics

25. Uustalu, T.: Stateful runners of effectful computations. Electron. Notes Theor. Comput. Sci. **319**, 403–421 (2015). https://doi.org/10.1016/j.entcs.2015.12.024

26. Uustalu, T., Veltri, N.: The delay monad and restriction categories. In: Hung, D.V., Kapur, D. (eds.) ICTAC 2017. LNCS, vol. 10580, pp. 32–50. Springer (2017). https://doi.org/10.1007/978-3-319-67729-3_3

27. Veltri, N., Vezzosi, A.: Formalizing π-calculus in Guarded Cubical Agda. In: Blanchette, J., Hritcu, C. (eds.) Proceedings of 9th ACM SIGPLAN International Conference on Certified Programs and Proofs, CPP 2020, pp. 270–283. ACM (2020). https://doi.org/10.1145/3372885.3373814

28. Veltri, N., Voorneveld, N.F.W.: Inductive and coinductive predicate liftings for effectful programs. In: Sokolova, A. (ed.) Proceedings of 37th Conference on Mathematical Foundations of Programming Semantics, MFPS 2021. Electronic Proceedings in Theoretical Computer Science, vol. 351, pp. 260–277 (2021). https://doi.org/10.4204/EPTCS.351.16

29. Veltri, N., van der Weide, N.: Guarded recursion in Agda via sized types. In: Geuvers, H. (ed.) Proceedings of 4th International Conference on Formal Structures for Computation and Deduction, FSCD 2019. LIPIcs, vol. 131, pp. 1–19. Dagstuhl Publishing (2019). https://doi.org/10.4230/LIPIcs.FSCD.2019.32

30. Wright, A.K., Felleisen, M.: A syntactic approach to type soundness. Inf. Comput. **115**(1), 38–94 (1994). https://doi.org/10.1006/inco.1994.1093

Fantastic Morphisms and Where to Find Them
A Guide to Recursion Schemes

Zhixuan Yang[✉] and Nicolas Wu

Imperial College London, London, UK
{s.yang20,n.wu}@imperial.ac.uk

Abstract. *Structured recursion schemes* have been widely used in constructing, optimizing, and reasoning about programs over inductive and coinductive datatypes. Their plain forms, *catamorphisms* and *anamorphisms*, are restricted in expressivity. Thus many generalizations have been proposed, which further led to several unifying frameworks of structured recursion schemes. However, the existing work on unifying frameworks typically focuses on the categorical foundation, and thus is perhaps inaccessible to practitioners who are willing to apply recursion schemes in practice but are not versed in category theory. To fill this gap, this expository paper introduces structured recursion schemes from a practical point of view: a variety of recursion schemes are motivated and explained in contexts of concrete programming examples. The categorical duals of these recursion schemes are also explained.

Keywords: Recursion schemes · Generic programming · (Un)Folds · (Co)Inductive datatypes · Equational reasoning · Haskell

1 Introduction

Among the wilderness of recursive functions, there exists a taxonomy of tame functions, each with its own character and behaviour that is more predictable than the other wilder functions. The first function to be tamed was the *catamorphism*, so-named by Meertens in 1988 [43] who wanted to capture and more closely study the unique function that arises as a homomorphism from an initial algebra. Such functions had previously been studied in the context of category theory, but this identification marked the beginning of the appreciation of such functions as valuable companions in the menagerie of functional programmers. They were appreciated for their many benefits to programming: by expressing recursive programs as a recursion schemes such as a catamorphism, the structure of a program is made obvious; the recursion is ensured to terminate; and the program can be reasoned about using the calculational properties.

These benefits motivated a whole research agenda concerned with identifying and classifying *structured recursion schemes* that capture the pattern of many other recursive functions that did not quite fit as catamorphisms. Just

E. Komendantskaya (Ed.): MPC 2022, LNCS 13544, pp. 222–267, 2022.
https://doi.org/10.1007/978-3-031-16912-0_9

as with catamorphisms, these structured recursion schemes attracted attention since they make termination or productivity manifest, and enjoy many useful calculational properties which would otherwise have to be established afresh for each new application.

In the early days, and in keeping the Bird-Meertens formalism, also known as Squiggol due to its lavish use of squiggly notation, the identification of a new species came both with an exotic name, as well as exotic notation to describe such recursion schemes. Soon there came a whole zoo of other interesting species, and this paper attempts to document its main inhabitants.

1.1 Diversification

The first variation on the catamorphisms was paramorphisms [44], about which Meertens talked at the 41st IFIP Working Group 2.1 (WG2.1) meeting in Burton, UK (1990). Paramorphisms describe recursive functions in which the body of structured recursion has access to not only the (recursively computed) subresults of the input, but also the original subterms of the input.

Then came the zoo of morphisms. *Mutumorphisms* [14], which are pairs of mutually recursive functions; *zygomorphisms* [41], which consist of a main recursive function and an auxiliary one on which it depends; *monadic catamorphisms* [13], which are recursive functions that also cause computational effects; so-called *generalized folds* [6], which use polymorphic recursion to handle nested datatypes; *histomorphisms* [50], in which the body has access to the recursive images of all subterms, not just the immediate ones; and then there were *generic accumulations* [48], which keep intermediate results in additional parameters for later stages in the computation.

While catamorphisms focused on terminating programs based on initial algebra, the theory also generalized in the dual direction: *anamorphisms*. These describe productive programs based on final coalgebras, that is, programs that progressively output structure, perhaps indefinitely. As variations on anamorphisms, there are *apomorphisms* [53], which may generate subterms monolithically rather than step by step; *futumorphisms* [50], which may generate multiple levels of a subterm in a single step, rather than just one; and many other anonymous schemes that dualize better known inductive patterns of recursion.

Recursion schemes that combined the features of inductive and coinductive datatypes were also considered. A *hylomorphism* [45] arises when an anamorphism is followed by a catamorphism, and a *metamorphism* [16] is when they are the other way around. A more sophisticated recursion scheme gives *dynamorphisms* [37] which encodes dynamic programming algorithms, where a lookup table is coinductively constructed in an inductive computation over the input.

1.2 Unification

The many divergent generalizations of catamorphisms can be bewildering to the uninitiated, and there have been attempts to unify them. One approach is the identification of recursion schemes from comonads (RSFCs for short) by Uustalu et al. [52]. Comonads capture the general idea of 'evaluation in context' [51], and this scheme makes contextual information available to the body of the recursion. It was used to subsume both zygomorphisms and histomorphisms.

Another attempt by Hinze [23] used adjunctions as the common thread. Adjoint folds arise by inserting a left adjoint functor into the recursive characterization, thereby adapting the form of the recursion; they subsume accumulating folds, mutumorphisms, zygomorphisms, and generalized folds. Later, it was observed that adjoint folds could be used to subsume RSFCs [28].

Thus far, the unifications had dealt largely with generalizations of catamorphisms and anamorphisms separately. The job of putting combinations of these together and covering complex beasts such as dynamorphisms was first achieved by Hinze and Wu [26], which was then generalized by Hinze et al.'s *conjugate hylomorphisms* [29], which WG2.1 dubbed *mamamorphisms*. This worked by viewing all recursion schemes as specialized forms of hylomorphisms, and showing that they are well-defined hylomorphisms using adjunctions and conjugate natural transformations.

1.3   Overview

The existing literature [28, 29, 51] on unifying accounts to structured recursion schemes has focused on the categorical foundation of recursion schemes rather than their motivations or applications, and thus is perhaps not quite useful for practitioners who would like to learn about recursion schemes and apply them in practice. To fill the gap, this paper introduces the zoo of recursion schemes by putting them in programming contexts. This paper provides a survey of many recursion schemes that have been explored, and is organized as follows.

- Section 2 explains the idea of modelling (co)inductive datatypes as fixed points of functors, which makes generic recursion schemes possible.
- Section 3 explains the three fundamental recursion schemes: *catamorphisms*, which compute values by consuming inductive data; *anamorphisms*, which build coinductive data from values; and their common generalization, *hylomorphisms*, which build data from values and consume them.
- Section 4 introduces structured recursion with an accumulating parameter.
- Section 5 is about mutual recursion on inductive datatypes, known as *mutumorphisms*, and their duals *comutumorphisms*, which build mutually defined coinductive datatypes from a single value.
- Section 6 talks about primitive recursion, known as *paramorphisms*, featuring the ability to access both the original subterms and the corresponding output in the recursive function. Their corecursive counterpart, *apomorphisms*, and a generalization, *zygomorphisms*, are also shown.
- Section 7 discusses the so-called course-of-values recursion, *histomorphisms*, featuring the ability to access the results of all direct and indirect subterms in the body of recursive function, which is typically necessary in dynamic programming. Several related schemes, *futumorphisms*, *dynamorphisms*, and *chronomorphisms* are briefly discussed.

- Section 8 introduces recursion schemes that cause computational effects.
- Section 9 explains recursion schemes on nested datatypes and GADTs.
- Section 10 briefly demonstrates how one can do equational reasoning about programs using calculational properties of recursion schemes.
- Finally, Sect. 11 discusses two general recipes for finding more recursion schemes and concludes.

The recursion schemes that we will see in this paper are summarized in Table 1. Sections 3–9 are loosely ordered by their complexity, rather than by the order in which they appeared in the literature, and these sections are mutually independent so can be read in an arbitrary order. A common pattern in these sections is that we start with a concrete programming example, from which we distil a recursion scheme, followed by more examples. Where appropriate, we also consider their dual corecursion scheme and hylomorphic generalization.

Table 1. Recursion schemes explored in this paper

Scheme	Type signature	Usage
Catamorphism	$(f\ a \to a) \to \mu\ f \to a$	Consume inductive data
Anamorphism	$(c \to f\ c) \to c \to \nu\ f$	Generate coinductive data
Hylomorphism	$(f\ a \to a) \to (c \to f\ c) \to c \to a$	Generate then consume data
Accumulation	$(\forall x.f\ x \to p \to f\ (x,p)) \to$ $(f\ a \to p \to a) \to \mu\ f \to p \to a$	Recursion with an accumulating parameter
Mutumorphism	$(f\ (a,b) \to a) \to (f\ (a,b) \to b)$ $\to (\mu\ f \to a, \mu\ f \to b)$	Mutual recursion on inductive data
Comutumorphism	$(c \to f\ c\ c) \to (c \to g\ c\ c)$ $\to c \to (\nu_1\ f\ g, \nu_2\ f\ g)$	Generate mutually defined coinductive data
Paramorphism	$(f\ (\mu\ f, a) \to a) \to \mu\ f \to a$	Primitive recursion, i.e. access to original input
Apomorphism	$(c \to f\ (Either\ (\nu\ f)\ c))$ $\to c \to \nu\ f$	Early termination of generation
Zygomorphism	$(f\ (a,b) \to a) \to (f\ b \to b)$ $\to \mu\ f \to a$	Recursion with auxiliary information
Histomorphism	$(f\ (Cofree\ f\ a) \to a) \to \mu\ f \to a$	Access to all sub-results
Dynamorphism	$(f\ (Cofree\ f\ a) \to a)$ $\to (c \to f\ c) \to c \to a$	Dynamic programing
Futumorphism	$(c \to f\ (Free\ f\ c)) \to c \to \nu\ f$	Generate multiple layers
Monadic catamorphism	$(\forall x.f\ (m\ x) \to m\ (f\ x))$ $\to (f\ a \to m\ a) \to \mu\ f \to m\ a$	Recursion causing computational effects
Indexed catamorphism	$(f\ a \overset{\cdot}{\to} a) \to \dot\mu\ f \overset{\cdot}{\to} a$	Consume nested datatypes and GADTs

2   Datatypes and Fixed Points

This paper assumes basic familiarity with Haskell as we use it to present all examples and recursion schemes, but we do not assume any knowledge of category theory. In this section, we briefly review the prerequisite of recursion schemes—recursive datatypes, viewed as fixed points of functors.

Datatypes. *Algebraic data types* (ADTs) in Haskell allow the programmer to create new datatypes from existing ones. For example, the type *List a* of lists of elements of type *a* can be declared as follows:

$$\textbf{data } List\ a = Nil\ |\ Cons\ a\ (List\ a) \tag{1}$$

which means that an element of *List a* is exactly *Nil* or *Cons x xs* for all $x :: a$ and $xs :: List\ a$. Similarly, the type *Tree a* of binary trees whose nodes are labelled with *a*-elements can be declared as follows:

$$\textbf{data } Tree\ a = Empty\ |\ Node\ (Tree\ a)\ a\ (Tree\ a) \tag{2}$$

In definitions like *List a* and *Tree a*, the datatypes being defined also appear on the right-hand side of the declaration, so they are *recursive types*. Moreover, *List a* and *Tree a* are among a special family of recursive types, called *inductive datatypes*, meaning that they are *least* fixed points of functors.

Functors and Algebras. Let us recall how endofunctors, or simply functors, in Haskell are type constructors $f :: * \rightarrow *$ instantiating the following type class:

$$\textbf{class } Functor\ f\ \textbf{where } fmap :: (a \rightarrow b) \rightarrow f\ a \rightarrow f\ b$$

Additionally, *fmap* is expected to satisfy two functor laws:

$$fmap\ id = id \qquad fmap\ (h \circ g) = fmap\ h \circ fmap\ g$$

for all functions $g :: a \rightarrow b$ and $h :: b \rightarrow c$.

Given a functor f, we call a function of type $f\ a \rightarrow a$, for some type a, an *f-algebra*, and a function of type $a \rightarrow f\ a$ an *f-coalgebra*. In either case, type a is called the *carrier* of the (co)algebra.

Fixed Points. Given a functor f, a fixed point for f is a type p such that p is isomorphic to $f\ p$. In the set theoretic semantics, a functor may have more than one fixed point: the *least fixed point*, denoted by $\mu\ f$, is the set of f-branching trees of *finite* depths, while the *greatest fixed point*, denoted by $\nu\ f$, is intuitively the set of f-branching trees of *possibly infinite* depths.

However, due to the fact that Haskell is a lazy language with general recursion, the least and greatest fixed points of a Haskell functor f *coincide* as the following datatype of possibly infinite f-branching trees:

$$\textbf{newtype } Fix\ f = In\ \{\ out :: f\ (Fix\ f)\}$$

This notation introduces the constructor $In :: f\ (Fix\ f) \rightarrow Fix\ f$ to create fixed point, and its inverse $out :: Fix\ f \rightarrow f\ (Fix\ f)$.

Although Haskell allows general recursion, the point of using structural recursion is precisely avoiding general recursion whenever possible, since general recursion is typically tricky to reason about. Hence in this paper we use Haskell as if it is a total programming language, by making sure all recursive functions that we use are structurally recursive as much as possible. Thus we distinguish the least and greatest fixed points as two datatypes:

$$\textbf{newtype } \mu\, f = In\, (f\, (\mu\, f)) \qquad \textbf{newtype } \nu\, f = Out^{\circ}\, (f\, (\nu\, f))$$

While these two datatypes $\mu\, f$ and $\nu\, f$ are the same datatype declaration, we mentally understand $\mu\, f$ as the type of *finite* f-branching trees, and $\nu\, f$ as the type of *possibly infinite* ones, as in the set-theoretic semantics. Making such a nominal distinction is not entirely pointless: the type system at least ensures that we never accidentally misuse an element of $\nu\, f$ as an element of $\mu\, f$, unless we make an explicit conversion. But it is our own responsibility to make sure that we never construct an infinite element in $\mu\, f$ using general recursion.

Example 1. The datatypes (1) and (2) that we saw earlier are isomorphic to fixed points of functors *ListF* and *TreeF* defined as follows (with the evident *fmap* that can be derived by GHC automatically[1]):

```
data ListF a x = Nil    | Cons a x   deriving Functor
data TreeF a x = Empty | Node x a x deriving Functor
```

The type $\mu\, (ListF\ a)$ represents finite lists of a elements and $\mu\, (TreeF\ a)$ represents finite binary trees carrying a elements. Correspondingly, $\nu\, (ListF\ a)$ and $\nu\, (TreeF\ a)$ are possibly infinite lists and trees respectively.

As an example, the correspondence between $\mu\, (ListF\ a)$ and finite elements of $[a]$ is evidenced by the following isomorphism.

$$
\begin{array}{ll}
conv_{\mu} :: [a] \quad \rightarrow \mu\, (ListF\ a) & conv_{\mu}^{\circ} :: \mu\, (ListF\ a) \quad \rightarrow [a] \\
conv_{\mu}\, [] \quad = In\ Nil & conv_{\mu}^{\circ}\, (In\ Nil) \quad = [] \\
conv_{\mu}\, (a:as) = In\ (Cons\ a\ (conv_{\mu}\ as)) & conv_{\mu}^{\circ}\, (In\ (Cons\ a\ as)) = a : conv_{\mu}^{\circ}\ as
\end{array}
$$

Supposing that there is a function computing the length of a list,

$$length :: \mu\, (ListF\ a) \rightarrow Integer$$

The type checker of Haskell will then ensure that we never pass a value of $\nu\, (ListF\ a)$ to this function.

Initial and Final (Co)Algebra. The constructor $In :: f\, (\mu\, f) \rightarrow \mu\, f$ is an f-algebra with carrier $\mu\, f$, and it has an inverse $in^{\circ} :: \mu\, f \rightarrow f\, (\mu\, f)$ defined as

---

[1] It requires the `DeriveFunctor` extension of GHC to derive functors automatically.

$$in^{\circ} \, (In \ x) = x$$

which is an f-coalgebra thta witnesses the isomorphism between $\mu \ f$ and $f \ (\mu \ f)$, a fact known as Lambek's Lemma [40]. Conversely, the constructor $Out^{\circ} :: f \ (\nu \ f) \rightarrow \nu \ f$ is an f-algebra with carrier $\nu \ f$, and its inverse $out :: \nu \ f \rightarrow f \ (\nu \ f)$ defined as

$$out \ (Out^{\circ} \ x) = x$$

is an f-coalgebra with carrier $\nu \ f$.

What is special with In and out is that In is the so-called *initial algebra* of f, in the sense that it has the nice property that for any f-algebra $alg :: f \ a \rightarrow a$, there is exactly one function $h :: \mu \ f \rightarrow a$ such that

$$h \circ In = alg \circ fmap \ h \tag{3}$$

Dually, out is called the *final coalgebra* of f since for any f-coalgebra $coalg :: c \rightarrow f \ c$, there is exactly one function $h :: c \rightarrow \nu \ f$ such that

$$out \circ h = fmap \ h \circ coalg \tag{4}$$

The h's in (3) and (4) are precisely the two fundamental recursion schemes, *catamorphisms* and *anamorphisms*, which we will talk about in the next section.

3   Fundamental Recursion Schemes

Most if not all programs are about processing data, and as Hoare [30] noted, 'there are certain close analogies between the methods used for structuring data and the methods for structuring a program which processes that data.' In essence, *data structure determines program structure* [11,18]. The determination is abstracted as recursion schemes for programs processing recursive datatypes.

In this section, we look at the three fundamental recursion schemes: catamorphisms, in which the program is structured by its input; anamorphisms, in which the program is structured by its output; and hylomorphisms, in which the program is structured by an internal recursive call structure.

3.1   Catamorphisms

We start our journey with programs whose structure follows their input. As the first example, consider the program computing the length of a list:

```
length :: [a]      → Integer
length   []        = 0
length   (x : xs) = 1 + length xs
```

In Haskell, a list is either the empty list $[\,]$ or $x : xs$, an element x prepended to list xs. This structure of lists is closely reflected by the program *length*, which is defined by two cases too, one for the empty list $[\,]$ and one for the recursive case $x : xs$. Additionally, in the recursive case *length* $(x : xs)$ is solely determined by *length* xs without further usage of xs.

List Folds. The pattern in *length* is called *structural recursion* and is expressed by the function *foldr* in Haskell:

$$foldr :: (a \rightarrow b \rightarrow b) \rightarrow b \rightarrow [a] \rightarrow b$$
$$foldr\ f\ e\ [\,] \qquad\quad = e$$
$$foldr\ f\ e\ (x : xs) = f\ x\ (foldr\ f\ e\ xs)$$

which is very useful in list processing. As a fold, $length = foldr\ (\lambda\_\ l \rightarrow 1 + l)\ 0$. The frequently used function *map* is also a fold:

$$map :: (a \rightarrow b) \rightarrow [a] \rightarrow [b]$$
$$map\ f = foldr\ (\lambda x\ xs \rightarrow f\ x : xs)\ [\,]$$

Another example is the function flattening a list of lists into a list:

$$concat :: [[a]] \rightarrow [a]$$
$$concat = foldr\ (\mathbin{+\!\!+})\ [\,]$$

By expressing structural recursive functions as folds, their structure becomes clearer, similarly in spirit to the well accepted practice of structuring programs with if-conditionals and for-/while-loops in imperative languages.

Recursion Scheme 1 (*cata*). Folds on lists can be readily generalized to the generic setting, where the shape of the datatype is determined by a functor [12,20,42]. Such functions are called *catamorphisms*, and come from the following recursion scheme:

$$cata :: Functor\ f \Rightarrow (f\ a \rightarrow a) \rightarrow \mu f \rightarrowtail a$$
$$cata\ alg = alg \circ fmap\ (cata\ alg) \circ in^{\circ}$$

Intuitively, *cata alg* gradually breaks down the inductively defined input data, computing the result by replacing constructors with the given algebra *alg*.

The name *cata* dubbed by Meertens [43] is from Greek κατά meaning 'downwards along' or 'according to'. A notation for *cata alg* is the so-called banana bracket $(\!|\ alg\ |\!)$ but we will not use this style of notation in this paper, as there will not be enough squiggly brackets for all the different recursion schemes.

Example 2. By converting the builtin list type $[a]$ to the initial algebra of *ListF* as in Example 1, we can recover *foldr* from *cata* as follows:

$$foldr :: (a \rightarrow b \rightarrow b) \rightarrow b \rightarrow [a] \rightarrow b$$
$$foldr\ f\ e = cata\ alg \circ conv_\mu\ \textbf{where}$$
$$\quad alg\ Nil \quad\quad = e$$
$$\quad alg\ (Cons\ a\ x) = f\ a\ x$$

Now we can also fold datatypes other than lists, such as binary trees:

$$size :: \mu\ (TreeF\ e) \rightarrow Integer$$
$$size = cata\ alg\ \textbf{where}$$
$$\quad alg :: TreeF\ a\ Integer \rightarrow Integer$$
$$\quad alg\ Empty \quad\quad = 0$$
$$\quad alg\ (Node\ l\ e\ r) = l + 1 + r$$

Example 3 (Interpreting DSLs*).* The 'killer application' of catamorphisms is using them to implement *domain-specific languages* (DSLs) [19,33]. The abstract syntax of a DSL can usually be modelled as an inductive datatype, and then the (denotational) semantics of the DSL can be given as a catamorphism. The semantics given in this way is *compositional*, meaning that the semantics of a program is determined by the semantics of its immediate sub-parts—exactly the pattern of catamorphisms.

As a small example here, consider a mini language of mutable memory consisting of three language constructs: *Put* (i, x) k writes value x to memory cell of address i and then executes program k; *Get* $i\ k$ reads memory cell i, letting the result be s, and then executes program $k\ s$; and *Ret* a terminates the execution with return value a. The abstract syntax of the language can be modelled as the initial algebra $\mu\ (ProgF\ s\ a)$ of the following functor:

$$\textbf{data}\ ProgF\ s\ a\ x = Ret\ a \mid Put\ (Int, s)\ x \mid Get\ Int\ (s \rightarrow x)$$

where s is the type of values stored by memory cells and a is the type of values finally returned. An example of a program in this language is

$$p_1 :: \mu\ (ProgF\ Int\ Int)$$
$$p_1 = In\ (Get\ 0\ (\lambda s \rightarrow (In\ (Put\ (0, s + 1)\ (In\ (Ret\ s)))))))$$

which reads the 0-th cell, increments it, and returns the old value. The syntax is admittedly clumsy because of the repeating *In* constructors, but they can be eliminated if 'smart constructors' such as $ret = In \circ Ret$ are defined.

The semantics of a program in this mini language can be given as a value of type *Map Int* $s \rightarrow a$, and the interpretation is a catamorphisms:

$interp :: \mu \, (ProgF \, s \, a) \rightarrow (Map \, Int \, s \rightarrow a)$
$interp = cata \, handle$ **where**
$\quad handle \, (Ret \, a) \qquad = \lambda\_ \rightarrow a$
$\quad handle \, (Put \, (i, x) \, k) = \lambda m \rightarrow k \, (update \, m \, i \, x)$
$\quad handle \, (Get \, i \, k) \qquad = \lambda m \rightarrow k \, (m \, ! \, i) \, m$

where $update \, m \, i \, x$ is the map m with the value at i changed to x, and $m \, ! \, i$ looks up i in m. Then we can use it to run programs:

$\quad * > \quad interp \, p_1 \, (fromList \, [(0, 100)]) \quad$ -- outputs 100

3.2   Anamorphisms

In catamorphisms, the structure of a program mimics the structure of the input. Needless to say, this pattern is insufficient to cover all programs in the wild. Imagine a program returning a record:

data $Person = Person \, \{ name :: String, addr :: String, phone :: [Int] \}$
$mkEntry :: StaffInfo \rightarrow Person$
$mkEntry \, i = Person \, n \, a \, p$ **where** $n = ...; a = ...; p = ...$

The structure of the program more resembles the structure of its output—each field of the output is computed by a corresponding part of the program. Similarly, when the output is a recursive datatype, a natural pattern is that the program generates the output recursively, called *(structural) corecursion* [18]. Consider the following program generating evenly spaced numbers over an interval.

$linspace :: RealFrac \, a \Rightarrow a \rightarrow a \rightarrow Integer \rightarrow [a]$
$linspace \, s \, e \, n = gen \, s$ **where**
$\quad step = (e - s) \, / \, fromIntegral \, (n + 1)$
$\quad gen \, i$
$\quad\quad | \, i < e \qquad = i : gen \, (i + step)$
$\quad\quad | \, otherwise = [\,]$

The program gen does not mirror the structure of its numeric input at all, but it follows the structure of its output, which is a list: for the two cases of a list, $[\,]$ and $(:)$, gen has a corresponding branch generating it.

List Unfolds. The pattern of generating a list in the example above is abstracted as the Haskell function $unfoldr$:

$unfoldr :: (b \rightarrow Maybe \, (a, b)) \rightarrow b \rightarrow [a]$
$unfoldr \, g \, s =$ **case** $g \, s$ **of**

$$(Just\ (a, s')) \rightarrow a : unfoldr\ g\ s'$$
$$Nothing \quad\quad \rightarrow [\,]$$

in which g either produces *Nothing* indicating the end of the output or produces from a seed s the next element a of the output together with a new seed s' for generating the rest of the output. Thus we can rewrite *linspace* as

$$linspace\ s\ e\ n = unfoldr\ gen\ s\ \textbf{where}$$
$$step = (e - s)\ /\ fromIntegral\ (n + 1)$$
$$gen\ i = \textbf{if}\ i < e\ \textbf{then}\ Just\ (i, i + step)\ \textbf{else}\ Nothing$$

Note that the list produced by *unfoldr* is not necessarily finite. For example,

$$from :: Integer \rightarrow [\,Integer\,]$$
$$from = unfoldr\ (\lambda n \rightarrow Just\ (n, n + 1))$$

generates the infinite list of all integers from n.

Recursion Scheme 2 (*ana*). In the same way that *cata* generalizes *foldr*, *unfoldr* can be generalized from lists to arbitrary coinductive datatypes. Functions arising from this (co)recursion scheme are called *anamorphisms*:

$$ana :: Functor\ f \Rightarrow (c \rightarrow f\ c) \rightarrow c \rightarrow \nu\ f$$
$$ana\ coalg = Out^\circ \circ fmap\ (ana\ coalg) \circ coalg$$

The name *ana* is from the Greek word ανά means 'upwards', dual to *cata* meaning 'downwards'.

Example 4. Modulo the isomorphism between $[a]$ and $\nu\ (ListF\ a)$, *unfoldr* produces an anamorphism:

$$unfoldr :: (b \rightarrow Maybe\ (a, b)) \rightarrow b \rightarrow [a]$$
$$unfoldr\ g = conv^\circ_\nu \circ ana\ coalg\ \textbf{where}$$
$$coalg\ b = \textbf{case}\ g\ b\ \textbf{of}\ Nothing \quad\quad \rightarrow Nil$$
$$(Just\ (a, b)) \rightarrow Cons\ a\ b$$

Example 5. A more interesting example of anamorphisms is merging a pair of ordered lists:

$$merge :: Ord\ a \Rightarrow (\nu\ (ListF\ a), \nu\ (ListF\ a)) \rightarrow \nu\ (ListF\ a)$$
$$merge = ana\ c\ \textbf{where}$$
$$c\ (x, y)$$
$$|\ null_\nu\ x \wedge null_\nu\ y = Nil$$

$$| \; null_\nu \; y \lor head_\nu \; x < head_\nu \; y$$
$$= Cons \; (head_\nu \; x) \; (tail_\nu \; x, y)$$
$$| \; otherwise = Cons \; (head_\nu \; y) \; (x, tail_\nu \; y)$$

where $null_\nu$, $head_\nu$ and $tail_\nu$ are the corresponding list functions for ν (*ListF a*).

3.3   Hylomorphisms

Catamorphisms consume data and anamorphisms produce data, but some algorithms are more complex than playing a single role—they produce and consume data at the same time. Taking the quicksort algorithm for example, a (not-in-place, worst-case complexity $\mathcal{O}(n^2)$) implementation is:

```
qsort :: Ord a ⇒ [a] → [a]
qsort []      = []
qsort (a : as) = qsort l ++ [a] ++ qsort r where
  l = [b | b ← as, b < a]
  r = [b | b ← as, b ⩾ a]
```

Although the input $[a]$ is an inductive datatype, *qsort* is not a catamorphism as the recursion is not performed on the sub-list *as*. Neither is it an anamorphism, since the output is not produced in the head-and-recursion manner.

Felleisen et al. [11] referred to this form of recursive programs as *generative recursion* since the input $a : as$ is used to generate a set of sub-problems, namely l and r, which are recursively solved, and their solutions are combined to solve the overall problem $a : as$. The structure of computing *qsort* is manifested in the following rewrite of *qsort*:

```
qsort' :: Ord a ⇒ [a] → [a]
qsort' = combine ∘ fmap qsort' ∘ partition

partition :: Ord a ⇒ [a] → TreeF a [a]
partition []      = Empty
partition (a : as) = Node [b | b ← as, b < a] a [b | b ← as, b ⩾ a]

combine :: TreeF a [a] → [a]
combine Empty      = []
combine (Node l x r) = l ++ [x] ++ r
```

The functor *TreeF a x = Empty | Node x a x* governs the recursive call structure, which is a binary tree. The (*TreeF a*)-coalgebra *partition* divides a problem (if not trivial) into two sub-problems, and the (*TreeF a*)-algebra *combine* concatenates the results of sub-problems to form a solution to the whole problem.

It is worth noting that, quicksort, as well as many other sorting algorithms such as merge sort can be understood as the combination of catamorphisms and anamorphisms in various ways, leading to numerous dualities between various sorting algorithms [24, 25], but we will not explore that further here.

Recursion Scheme 3 (*hylo*). Abstracting the pattern of divide-and-conquer algorithms like *qsort* results in the recursion scheme for *hylomorphisms*:

$$hylo :: Functor\ f \Rightarrow (f\ a \rightarrow a) \rightarrow (c \rightarrow f\ c) \rightarrow c \rightarrow a$$
$$hylo\ a\ c = a \circ fmap\ (hylo\ a\ c) \circ c$$

The name is due to Meijer et al. [45] and is a term from Aristotelian philosophy that objects are compounded of matter and form, where the prefix hylo- (Greek ὕλη) means 'matter'.

Hylomorphisms are highly expressive. In fact, all recursion schemes in this paper can be defined as special cases of hylomorphisms, and Hu et al. [32] showed a mechanical way to transform almost all recursive functions in practice into hylomorphisms. In particular, hylomorphisms subsume both catamorphisms and anamorphisms: for all $alg :: f\ a \rightarrow a$ and $coalg :: c \rightarrow f\ c$, we have

$$cata\ alg = hylo\ alg\ in^{\circ} \qquad and \qquad ana\ coalg = hylo\ Out^{\circ}\ coalg.$$

However, the expressiveness of *hylo* comes at a cost: even when both $alg :: f\ a \rightarrow a$ and $coalg :: c \rightarrow f\ c$ are total functions, *hylo alg coalg* may not be total (in contrast, *cata alg* and *ana coalg* are always total whenever *alg* and *coalg* are). Intuitively, it is because the coalgebra *coalg* may infinitely generate sub-problems while the algebra *alg* may require all subproblems solved to solve the whole problem.

Example 6. As an instance of the problematic situation, consider a coalgebra

$$geo :: Integer \rightarrow ListF\ Double\ Integer$$
$$geo\ n = Cons\ (1\ /\ fromIntegral\ n)\ (2*n)$$

which generates the geometric sequence $[\frac{1}{n}, \frac{1}{2n}, \frac{1}{4n}, \frac{1}{8n}, ..]$, and an algebra

$$sum :: ListF\ Double\ Double \rightarrow Double$$
$$sum\ Nil \qquad\quad = 0$$
$$sum\ (Cons\ n\ p) = n + p$$

which sums a sequence. Both *geo* and *sum* are total Haskell functions, but the function $zeno = hylo\ sum\ geo$ diverges for all input $i :: Integer$. (It does not mean that Achilles can never overtake the tortoise—*zeno* diverges because it really tries to add up an infinite sequence rather than taking the limit.)

Recover Totality. One way to tame the well-definedness of *hylo* is to consider coalgebras $coalg :: c \rightarrow f\ c$ with the special properties that the equation

$$h = alg \circ fmap\ h \circ coalg \qquad\qquad\qquad (5)$$

has a unique solution $h :: c \to a$ for *all* algebras $alg :: f\ a \to a$. Such coalgebras are called *recursive coalgebras*. Dually, one can also consider *corecursive algebras* alg that make (5) have a unique solution for all *coalg*. For example, the coalgebra $in^\circ :: \mu\ f \to f\ (\mu\ f)$ is recursive, since the equation

$$h = alg \circ fmap\ h \circ in^\circ \quad \iff \quad h \circ In = alg \circ fmap\ h$$

has a unique solution by property (3) of the initial algebra. Dually, $Out^\circ ::$ $f\ (\nu\ f) \to \nu\ f$ is a corecursive algebra by (4).

Besides these two basic examples, quite some effort has been made in searching for more recursive coalgebras (and corecursive algebras): Capretta et al. [9] first show that it is possible to construct new recursive coalgebras from existing ones using comonads, and later Hinze et al. [29] show a more general technique using adjunctions and conjugate pairs. With these techniques, all recursion schemes on (co)inductive datatypes presented in this paper can be uniformly understood as hylomorphisms with a recursive coalgebra or corecursive algebra. However, we shall not emphasize this perspective in this paper since it sometimes involves non-trivial category theory to massage a recursion scheme into a hylomorphism with a recursive coalgebra (or a corecursive algebra).

Example 7. The coalgebra $partition :: [a] \to TreeF\ a\ [a]$ above is recursive (when only finite lists are allowed as input). This can be proved by an easy inductive argument: for any total $alg :: TreeF\ a\ b \to b$, suppose that $h :: [a] \to b$ satisfies

$$h = alg \circ fmap\ h \circ partition. \tag{6}$$

Given any finite list xs, we show $h\ xs$ is determined by alg by an induction on xs. For the base case $xs = [\,]$, we have

$$h\ [\,] = alg\ (fmap\ h\ (partition\ [\,])) = alg\ (fmap\ h\ Empty) = alg\ Empty.$$

For the inductive case $xs = y : ys$, we have

$$\begin{aligned}
h\ (y : ys) &= alg\ (fmap\ h\ (partition\ (y : ys))) \\
&= alg\ (fmap\ h\ (Node\ ls\ y\ rs)) \\
&= alg\ (Node\ (h\ ls)\ y\ (h\ rs))
\end{aligned}$$

where $ls = [l \mid l \leftarrow ys, l < y]$ and $rs = [r \mid r \leftarrow ys, r \geqslant a]$ are strictly smaller than $xs = y : ys$, and thus $h\ ls$ and $h\ rs$ are uniquely determined by alg. Consequently, $h\ (y : ys)$ is uniquely determined by alg. Thus we conclude that h satisfying the hylo equation (6) is unique.

Aside: Metamorphisms. If we separate the producing and consuming phases of a hylomorphism *hylo alg coalg* for some recursive *coalg*, we have the following equations (both follow from the uniqueness of the solution to hylomorphism equations with recursive coalgebra *coalg*):

$$\begin{aligned}
hylo\ alg\ coalg &= cata\ alg \circ hylo\ In\ coalg \\
&= cata\ alg \circ \nu2\mu \circ ana\ coalg
\end{aligned}$$

where $\nu 2\mu = hylo\ In\ out :: \nu\ f \to \mu\ f$ is the *partial* function that converts the subset of finite elements of a coinductive datatype into its inductive counterpart. Thus, loosely speaking, a *hylo* is a *cata* after an *ana*. The opposite direction of composition can also be considered:

$$meta :: (Functor\ f, Functor\ g) \Rightarrow (c \to g\ c) \to (f\ c \to c) \to \mu\ f \to \nu\ g$$
$$meta\ coalg\ alg = ana\ coalg \circ cata\ alg$$

which produces functions called *metamorphisms* by Gibbons [16] because they *metamorphose* data represented by functor f to g. Unlike hylomorphisms, the producing and consuming phases in metamorphisms cannot be straightforwardly fused into a single recursive function. Gibbons [16,17] gives conditions for doing this when f is *ListF*, but we will not expand on this in this paper.

4   Accumulations

Accumulating parameters are a well known technique for optimizing recursive functions. An example is optimizing the following *reverse* function:

$$reverse :: [a] \to [a]$$
$$reverse\quad [\,] \qquad = [\,]$$
$$reverse\quad (x : xs) = reverse\ xs \mathbin{+\!\!+} [x]$$

This can be transformed from running in quadratic time (due to the fact that $xs \mathbin{+\!\!+} ys$ runs in $\mathcal{O}(length\ xs)$ time) to linear time by first generalizing the function with an additional parameter—an *accumulating parameter* ys:

$$revCat :: [a] \to [a] \to [a]$$
$$revCat\ ys\ [\,] \qquad = ys$$
$$revCat\ ys\ (x : xs) = revCat\ (x : ys)\ xs$$

This specializes to *reverse* by letting $reverse = recCat\ [\,]$. This pattern of scanning a list from left to right and accumulating a parameter at the same time is abstracted as the Haskell function *foldl*:

$$foldl :: (b \to a \to b) \to b \to [a] \to b$$
$$foldl\ f\ e\ [\,] \qquad = e$$
$$foldl\ f\ e\ (x : xs) = foldl\ f\ (f\ e\ x)\ xs$$

which specializes to *revCat* for $f = \lambda ys\ x \to x : ys$. Similar to *foldr*, *foldl* follows the structure of the input—a base case for $[\,]$ and an inductive case for $x : xs$. What differs is that *foldl* has an argument e varied during the recursion.

The pattern of accumulation is not limited to lists. For example, consider writing a program that transforms a binary tree labelled with integers to the tree whose nodes are relabelled with the *sum* of the labels along the path from the root in the original tree. A natural idea is to keep an accumulating parameter for the sum of labels from the root:

$relabel :: \mu \ (TreeF \ Integer) \rightarrow Integer \rightarrow \mu \ (TreeF \ Integer)$
$relabel \ (In \ Empty) \qquad s = In \ Empty$
$relabel \ (In \ (Node \ l \ e \ r)) \ s = In \ (Node \ (relabel \ l \ s') \ s' \ (relabel \ r \ s'))$
   where $s' = s + e$

In the *Node* case, the current accumulating parameter s is updated to s' for both of the subtrees, but we can certainly accumulate the parameter for the subtrees using other accumulating strategies. In general, an accumulating strategy can be captured as a function of type

$$\forall x. TreeF \ Integer \ x \rightarrow Integer \rightarrow TreeF \ Integer \ (x, Integer)$$

For example, the strategy for *relabel* is

$st_{relabel} \ Empty \ s \qquad = Empty$
$st_{relabel} \ (Node \ l \ e \ r) \ s = Node \ (l, s') \ e \ (r, s') \ \textbf{where} \ s' = s + e$

Notice that the type above is polymorphic over x, which means that the accumulation cannot depend on the subtrees. This is not strictly necessary, but it reflects the pattern of most accumulations in practice.

Recursion Scheme 1 (*accu*). Abstracting the idea for a generic initial algebra, we obtain the recursion scheme for *accumulations* [15,31,48][2]:

$accu :: Functor \ f \Rightarrow (\forall x.f \ x \rightarrow p \rightarrow f \ (x,p))$
$\qquad \rightarrow (f \ a \rightarrow p \rightarrow a) \rightarrow \mu \ f \rightarrow p \rightarrow a$
$accu \ st \ alg \ (In \ t) \ p = alg \ (fmap \ (uncurry \ (accu \ st \ alg)) \ (st \ t \ p)) \ p$

Using the recursion scheme, the *relabel* function can be rewritten as

$relabel' :: \mu \ (TreeF \ Integer) \rightarrow Integer \rightarrow \mu \ (TreeF \ Integer)$
$relabel' = accu \ st_{relabel} \ alg \ \textbf{where}$
   $alg \ Empty \qquad s = In \ Empty$
   $alg \ (Node \ l \ \_ \ r) \ s = In \ (Node \ l \ s \ r)$

---

[2] The recursion scheme requires the GHC extension RankNTypes since the first argument involves a polymorphic function.

Example 8. In Example 3, the semantics function *interp* is written as a cata-morphism into a function type *Map Int s* → *a*. With a closer look, we can see that the *Map Int s* parameter is an accumulating parameter, so we can more accurately express *interp* using *accu*:

$$interp' :: \mu \ (ProgF \ s \ a) \to Map \ Int \ s \to a$$
$$interp' = accu \ st \ alg \ \textbf{where}$$
$$\quad st :: ProgF \ s \ a \ x \to Map \ Int \ s \to ProgF \ s \ a \ (x, Map \ Int \ s)$$
$$\quad st \ (Ret \ a) \qquad m = Ret \ a$$
$$\quad st \ (Put \ (i, x) \ k) \ m = Put \ (i, x) \ (k, update \ m \ i \ x)$$
$$\quad st \ (Get \ i \ k) \qquad m = Get \ i \ (\lambda x \to (k \ x, m))$$

$$\quad alg :: ProgF \ s \ a \ a \to Map \ Int \ s \to a$$
$$\quad alg \ (Ret \ a) \quad m = a$$
$$\quad alg \ (Put \ \_ \ k) \ m = k$$
$$\quad alg \ (Get \ i \ k) \ m = k \ (m \ ! \ i)$$

Compared to the previous version *interp* in Example 3, this version *interp'* singles out *st*, which controls how the memory *m* is altered by each operation, whereas *alg* shows how each operation continues.

5 Mutual Recursion

This section is about *mutual recursion* in two forms: mutually recursive func-tions and mutually recursive datatypes. Mutually recursive functions are called mutumorphisms, and we will discuss their categorical dual, which turns out to be corecursion generating elements of mutually recursive datatypes.

5.1 Mutumorphisms

In Haskell, function definitions can not only be recursive but also be *mutually* recursive—two or more functions are defined in terms of each other. A sim-ple example is *isOdd* and *isEven* determining the parity of a natural number:

```
data NatF a = Zero | Succ a          type Nat = μ NatF
isEven :: Nat → Bool                 isOdd :: Nat → Bool
isEven (In Zero)      = True         isOdd (In Zero)      = False
isEven (In (Succ n)) = isOdd n       isOdd (In (Succ n)) = isEven n
```

Here we are using an inductive definition of natural numbers: *Zero* is a natural number and *Succ n* is a natural number whenever *n* is. Both *isEven* and *isOdd* are very much like a catamorphism: they have a non-recursive definition for the base case *Zero*, and a recursive definition for the inductive case *Succ n* in terms of the substructure *n*, except that their recursive definitions depend on the recursive result for *n* of the other function, instead of their own, making them not a catamorphism.

Another example of mutual recursion is the following way of computing the Fibonacci number F_i (i.e. $F_0 = 0$, $F_1 = 1$, and $F_n = F_{n-1} + F_{n-2}$ for $n \geqslant 2$):

$fib :: Nat \rightarrow Integer$	$aux :: Nat \rightarrow Integer$
$fib\ (In\ Zero) = 0$	$aux\ (In\ Zero) = 1$
$fib\ (In\ (Succ\ n)) = fib\ n + aux\ n$	$aux\ (In\ (Succ\ n)) = fib\ n$

The value $aux\ n$ is defined to be equal to the $(n-1)$-th Fibonacci number F_{n-1} for $n \geqslant 1$, and $aux\ 0$ is chosen to be $F_1 - F_0 = 1$. Consequently, $fib\ 0 = F_0$,

$$fib\ 1 = fib\ 0 + aux\ 1 = F_0 + (F_1 - F_0) = F_1,$$

and $fib\ n = fib\ (n-1) + fib\ (n-2)$ for $n >= 2$, which matches the definition of Fibonacci sequence.

Well-Definedness. The recursive definitions of the examples above are well-defined, in the sense that there is a unique solution to each group of recursive definitions regarded as a system of equations. For the example of fib and aux, the values at $Zero$ are uniquely determined for both functions:

$$\langle fib\ 0, aux\ 0 \rangle = \langle 0, 1 \rangle$$

Then the values at $Succ\ Zero$ are uniquely determined for both functions too, according to their inductive cases: $\langle fib\ 1, aux\ 1 \rangle = \langle 1, 0 \rangle$, and so on for all inputs:

$$\langle fib\ 2, aux\ 2 \rangle = \langle 1, 1 \rangle, \quad \langle fib\ 3, aux\ 3 \rangle = \langle 2, 1 \rangle, \quad \langle fib\ 4, aux\ 4 \rangle = \langle 3, 2 \rangle, \quad \ldots$$

The same line of reasoning applies too when we generalize this pattern to mutual recursion on a generic inductive datatype.

Recursion Scheme 5. Two mutually recursive functions on an inductive datatype are called *mutumorphisms* [12], and arise from the recursion scheme that defines them both at once:[3]

$$mutu :: Functor\ f \Rightarrow (f\ (a, b) \rightarrow a) \rightarrow (f\ (a, b) \rightarrow b) \rightarrow (\mu f \rightarrow a, \mu f \rightarrow b)$$
$$mutu\ alg_1\ alg_2 = (fst \circ h, snd \circ h)$$
$$\mathbf{where}\ h\quad = cata\ alg$$
$$alg\ x = (alg_1\ x, alg_2\ x)$$

in which $alg :: f\ (a, b) \rightarrow (a, b)$ makes use of alg_1 and alg_2 to compute the results of the two functions being defined, from the sub-results of both functions.

For example, using $mutu$, fib and aux can be expressed as

---

[3] The name *mutumorphism* is a bit special in the zoo of recursion schemes: the prefix mutu- is from Latin rather than Greek.

$fib, aux :: Nat \rightarrow Integer$
$(fib, aux) = mutu\ f\ g$ **where**

$f\ Zero = 0$ $g\ Zero = 1$
$f\ (Succ\ (n, m)) = n + m$ $g\ (Succ\ (n, \_)) = n$

In the unifying theory of recursion schemes of conjugate hylomorphisms, a mutu-morphism $mutu\ alg_1\ alg_2 :: (\mu\ f \rightarrow a, \mu\ f \rightarrow b)$ is the left-adjunct of a catamorphism of type $\mu\ f \rightarrow (a, b)$ via the adjunction $\Delta \dashv \times$ between the product category $C \times C$ and some base category C [27] (In the setting of this paper, $C = \textbf{Set}$). The same adjunction also underlies a dual corecursion scheme that we explain below.

5.2 Dual of Mutumorphisms

Since mutumorphisms are two or more mutually recursive functions folding one inductive datatype, we can consider the dual situation—unfolding a seed to two or more mutually-defined coinductive datatypes. An instructive example is recovering an expression from a Gödel number that encodes the expression. Consider the grammar of a simple family of arithmetic expressions:

data $Expr = Add\ Expr\ Term \mid Minus\ Expr\ Term \mid FromT\ Term$
data $Term = Lit\ Integer \mid Neg\ Term \mid Paren\ Expr$

which is a pair of mutually-recursive datatypes. A Gödel numbering of this grammar *invertibly* maps an $Expr$ or a $Term$ to a natural number, for example:

$encE\ (Add\ e\ t) = 2^{encE\ e} * 3^{encT\ t}$ $encT\ (Lit\ n) = 2^{encLit\ n}$
$encE\ (Minus\ e\ t) = 5^{encE\ e} * 7^{encT\ t}$ $encT\ (Neg\ t) = 3^{encT\ t}$
$encE\ (FromT\ t) = 11^{encT\ t}$ $h\ (Paren\ e) = 5^{encE\ e}$

where $encLit\ n = $ **if** $n \geqslant 0$ **then** $2 * n + 1$ **else** $2 * (-n)$ invertibly maps any integer to a positive integer. Although the encoding functions $encE$ and $encT$ clearly hint at a recursion scheme (of folding mutually-recursive datatypes to the same type), in this section we are interested in the opposite decoding direction:

$decE :: Integer \rightarrow Expr$
$decE\ n = $ **let** $(e_2, e_3, e_5, e_7, e_{11}) = factorize11\ n$
 in if $e_2 > 0 \vee e_3 > 0$ **then** $Add\ (decE\ e_2)\ (decT\ e_3)$
  else if $e_5 > 0 \vee e_7 > 0$
    then $Minus\ (decE\ e_5)\ (decT\ e_7)$
     else $FromT\ (decT\ e_{11})$

$decT :: Integer \rightarrow Term$
$decT\ n = \textbf{let}\ (e_2, e_3, e_5, \_, \_) = factorize11\ n$
    $\textbf{in if}\ e_2 > 0\ \textbf{then}\ Lit\ (decLit\ e_2)$
       $\textbf{else if}\ e_3 > 0\ \textbf{then}\ Neg\ (decT\ e_3)$
          $\textbf{else}\ Paren\ (decE\ e_5)$

where $factorize11\ n$ computes the exponents for $2, 3, 5, 7$ and 11 in the prime factorization of n, and $decLit$ is the inverse of $encLit$. Functions $decT$ and $decE$ can correctly recover the encoded expression/term because of the fundamental theorem of arithmetic (i.e. the unique-prime-factorization theorem).

In the definitions of $decE$ and $decT$, the choice of $decE$ or $decT$ when making a recursive call must match the type of the substructure at that position. It would be convenient, if the correct choice (of $decE$ or $decT$) can be automatically made based on the types—we can let a recursion scheme do the job for us.

For the generality of our recursion scheme, let us first generalize $Expr$ and $Term$ to an arbitrary pair of mutually recursive datatypes, which we model as fixed points of two bifunctors f and g given by the $Bifunctor$ class:

class $Bifunctor\ f$ **where**
    $bimap :: (a \rightarrow a') \rightarrow (b \rightarrow b') \rightarrow f\ a\ b \rightarrow f\ a'\ b'$

A bifunctor $f\ a\ b$ can be understood as a functor whose domain is the product category. A valid instance must respect the following laws:

$bimap\ id\ id = id$
$bimap\ (h \circ g)\ (k \circ j) = bimap\ h\ k \circ bimap\ g\ j$

These laws correspond to the usual identity and composition laws of functors.

The least fixed point models finite inductive data, and the greatest fixed point models possibly infinite coinductive data. Here we are interested in the latter, specialized to bifunctors:

newtype $\nu_1\ f\ g$ **where**   **newtype** $\nu_2\ f\ g$ **where**
  $Out_1^\circ :: f\ (\nu_1\ f\ g)\ (\nu_2\ f\ g) \rightarrow \nu_1\ f\ g$ $Out_2^\circ :: g\ (\nu_1\ f\ g)\ (\nu_2\ f\ g) \rightarrow \nu_2\ f\ g$

For instance, $Expr$ is isomorphic to $\nu_1\ ExprF\ TermF$ and $Term$ is isomorphic to $\nu_2\ ExprF\ TermF$:

data $ExprF\ e\ t = Add'\ e\ t \mid Minus'\ e\ t \mid FromT'\ t$
data $TermF\ e\ t = Lit'\ Int \mid Neg'\ t \mid Paren'\ e$

Recursion Scheme 6 (*comutu*). Now we can define a recursion scheme that generates a pair of elements of mutually recursive datatypes from a single seed:

$$comutu :: (Bifunctor\ f, Bifunctor\ g) \Rightarrow (c \to f\ c\ c) \to (c \to g\ c\ c)$$
$$\to c \to (\nu_1\ f\ g, \nu_2\ f\ g)$$
$$comutu\ c_1\ c_2\ s = (x\ s, y\ s)\ \textbf{where}$$
$$x = Out_1^{\circ} \circ bimap\ x\ y \circ c_1$$
$$y = Out_2^{\circ} \circ bimap\ x\ y \circ c_2$$

which remains unnamed in the literature, and so we will call this the recursion scheme for *comutumorphisms*, because of its relationship to mutumorphisms.

Example 9. The *comutu* scheme renders our decoding example to become

$$decExprTerm :: Integer \to (\nu_1\ ExprF\ TermF, \nu_2\ ExprF\ TermF)$$
$$decExprTerm = comutu\ genExpr\ genTerm\ \textbf{where}$$

    $genExpr :: Integer \to ExprF\ Integer\ Integer$
    $genExpr\ n =$
      let $(e_2, e_3, e_5, e_7, e_{11}) = factorize11\ n$
      in if $e_2 > 0 \vee e_3 > 0$ **then** $Add'\ e_2\ e_3$
        else if $e_5 > 0 \vee e_7 > 0$
            then $Minus'\ e_5\ e_7$ **else** $FromT'\ e_{11}$

    $genTerm :: Integer \to TermF\ Integer\ Integer$
    $genTerm\ n =$
      let $(e_2, e_3, e_5, \_, \_) = factorize11\ n$
      in if $e_2 > 0$ **then** $Lit'\ (decLit\ e_2)$
        else if $e_3 > 0$ **then** $Neg'\ e_3$ **else** $Paren'\ e_5$

Comparing to the direct definitions of *decE* and *decT*, *genTerm* and *genExpr* are simpler as they just generate a new seed for each recursive position and recursive calls of the correct type is invoked by the recursion scheme *comutu*.

Theoretically, *comutu* is the adjoint unfold from the adjunction $\Delta \dashv \times$: *comutu* $c_1\ c_2 :: c \to (\nu_1\ f\ g, \nu_2\ f\ g)$ is the right-adjunct of an anamorphism of type $(c \to \nu_1\ f\ g, c \to \nu_2\ f\ g)$ in the product category $C \times C$. A closely related adjunction $+ \dashv \Delta$ also gives two recursion schemes for mutual recursion. One is an adjoint fold that consumes mutually recursive datatypes, of which an example is the encoding function of Gödel numbering discussed above, and dually an adjoint unfold that generates $\nu\ f$ from seed *Either* $c_1\ c_2$, which captures *mutual corecursion*. Although attractive and practically important, we forgo an exhibition of these two recursion schemes here.

6   Primitive (Co)Recursion

In this section, we investigate the pattern in recursive programs in which the original input is directly involved besides the recursively computed results, resulting in a generalization of catamorphisms—*paramorphisms*. We also discuss a generalization, *zygomorphisms*, and the categorical dual *apomorphisms*.

6.1 Paramorphisms

A wide family of recursive functions that are not directly covered by catamorphisms are those in which the original substructures are directly used in addition to their images under the function being defined. An example is one of the most frequently demonstrated recursive function *factorial*, where *Nat* has been given a suitable *Num* instance:

$$
\begin{aligned}
&factorial :: Nat \to Nat \\
&factorial\ (In\ Zero) \quad = 1 \\
&factorial\ (In\ (Succ\ n)) = In\ (Succ\ n) * factorial\ n
\end{aligned}
$$

In the second case, besides the recursively computed result *factorial n*, the substructure n itself is also used, but it is not directly provided by *cata*. A slightly more practical example is counting the number of words (more accurately, maximal sub-sequences of non-space characters) in a list of characters:

$$
\begin{aligned}
&wc :: \mu\ (ListF\ Char) \to Integer \\
&wc\ (In\ Nil) \qquad = 0 \\
&wc\ (In\ (Cons\ c\ cs)) = \textbf{if}\ isNewWord\ \textbf{then}\ wc\ cs + 1\ \textbf{else}\ wc\ cs \\
&\quad \textbf{where}\ isNewWord = \neg\ (isSpace\ c) \wedge (null\ cs \vee isSpace\ (head\ cs))
\end{aligned}
$$

Again in the second case, *cs* is used besides *wc cs*, making it not a direct instance of catamorphisms either.

To express *factorial* and *wc* with a structural recursion scheme, we can use mutumorphisms by understanding *factorial* and *wc* as mutually defined with the identity function. For example,

$$
\begin{aligned}
&factorial' = fst\ (mutu\ alg\ alg_{id})\ \textbf{where} \\
&\quad alg\ Zero \qquad\qquad = 1 \\
&\quad alg\ (Succ\ (fn, n)) \quad = (In\ (Succ\ n)) * fn \\
&\quad alg_{id}\ Zero \qquad\qquad = In\ Zero \\
&\quad alg_{id}\ (Succ\ (\_, n)) = In\ (Succ\ n)
\end{aligned}
$$

Better is to use a recursion scheme that captures this common pattern.

Recursion Scheme 7. Functions given by structured recursion with access to the original sub-parts of the input are called *paramorphisms*, and are described by the following scheme:

$$
\begin{aligned}
&para :: Functor\ f \Rightarrow (f\ (\mu\ f, a) \to a) \to \mu\ f \to a \\
&para\ alg = alg \circ fmap\ (id \bigtriangleup para\ alg) \circ in^{\circ}\ \textbf{where} \\
&\quad (f \bigtriangleup g)\ x = (f\ x, g\ x)
\end{aligned}
$$

The prefix para- is derived from Greek παρά, meaning 'beside'.

Example 10. With *para*, *factorial* is defined neatly:

$$factorial'' = para\ alg\ \textbf{where}$$
$$alg\ Zero\qquad\quad = 1$$
$$alg\ (Succ\ (n, fn)) = In\ (Succ\ n) * fn$$

Compared with *cata*, *para* also supplies the original substructures besides their images to the algebra. However, *cata* and *para* are interdefinable in Haskell. Every catamorphism is simply a paramorphism that makes no use of the additional information:

$$cata\ alg = para\ (alg \circ fmap\ snd)$$

Conversely, every paramorphism together with the identity function is a mutumorphism, which in turn is a catamorphism for a pair type (a, b), or directly:

$$para\ alg = snd \circ cata\ ((In \circ fmap\ fst) \triangle alg)$$

Sometimes the recursion scheme of paramorphisms is called *primitive recursion*. However, functions definable with paramorphisms in Haskell are beyond primitive recursive functions in computability theory because of the presence of higher order functions. Indeed, the canonical example of non-primitive recursive function, the Ackermann function, is definable with *cata* and thus *para*:

$$ack :: Nat \to Nat \to Nat$$
$$ack = cata\ alg\ \textbf{where}$$
$$\quad alg :: NatF\ (Nat \to Nat) \to (Nat \to Nat)$$
$$\quad alg\ Zero\qquad = In \circ Succ$$
$$\quad alg\ (Succ\ a_n) = cata\ alg'\ \textbf{where}$$
$$\qquad alg' :: NatF\ Nat \to Nat$$
$$\qquad alg'\ Zero = a_n\ (In\ (Succ\ (In\ Zero)))$$
$$\qquad alg'\ (Succ\ a_{n+1,m}) = a_n\ a_{n+1,m}$$

6.2   Apomorphisms

Paramorphisms can be dualized to corecursion. The algebra of a paramorphism has type $f\ (\mu\ f, a) \to a$, in which $\mu\ f$ is dual to $\nu\ f$, and the pair type is dual to the *Either* type. Thus the coalgebra of the dual recursion scheme should have type $c \to f\ (Either\ (\nu\ f)\ c)$.

Recursion Scheme 8. The following recursion scheme gives rise to *apomorphisms* [50,53]. The prefix apo- comes from Greek απο meaning 'apart from'.

$$apo :: Functor\ f \Rightarrow (c \rightarrow f\ (Either\ (\nu\ f)\ c)) \rightarrow c \rightarrow \nu\ f$$
$$apo\ coalg = Out^\circ \circ fmap\ (either\ id\ (apo\ coalg)) \circ coalg$$

which is sometimes called *primitive corecursion*.

Similar to anamorphisms, the coalgebra of an apomorphism generates a layer of f-structure in each step, but for substructures, it either generates a new seed of type c for corecursion as in anamorphisms, or a complete structure of $\nu\ f$ and stop the corecursion there.

In the same way that *cata* and *para* are interdefinable, *ana* and *apo* are interdefinable in Haskell too, but *apo* are particularly suitable for corecursive functions in which the future output is fully known at some step. Consider a function *maphd* from Vene and Uustalu [53] that applies a function f to the first element (if there is) of a coinductive list.

$$maphd :: (a \rightarrow a) \rightarrow \nu\ (ListF\ a) \rightarrow \nu\ (ListF\ a)$$

As an anamorphism, it is expressed as

```
maphd f = ana c ∘ Left where
  c (Left (Out° Nil))          = Nil
  c (Right (Out° Nil))         = Nil
  c (Left (Out° (Cons x xs)))  = Cons (f x) (Right xs)
  c (Right (Out° (Cons x xs))) = Cons x    (Right xs)
```

in which the seed for generation is of type *Either* $(\nu\ (ListF\ a))\ (\nu\ (ListF\ a))$ to distinguish if the head element has been processed. This function is more intuitively an apomorphism since the future output is instantly known when the head element gets processed:

```
maphd' f = apo coalg where
  coalg (Out° Nil) = Nil
  coalg (Out° (Cons x xs)) = Cons (f x) (Left xs)
```

Moreover, this definition is more efficient than the previous one because it avoids deconstructing and reconstructing the tail of the input list.

Example 11. Another instructive example of apomorphisms is inserting a value into an ordered (coinductive) list:

```
insert :: Ord a ⇒ a → ν (ListF a) → ν (ListF a)
insert y = apo c where
  c (Out° Nil)   = Cons y (Left (Out° Nil))
  c xxs@(Out° (Cons x xs))
```

$$| \; y \leqslant x \quad\;\; = Cons \; y \; (Left \; xxs)$$
$$| \; otherwise = Cons \; x \; (Right \; xs)$$

In both cases, an element y or x is emitted, and $Left \; xxs$ makes xxs the rest of the output, whereas $Right \; xs$ continues the corecursion to insert y into xs.

6.3 Zygomorphisms

When computing a recursive function on a datatype, it is usually the case that some auxiliary information about substructures is needed in addition to the images of substructures under the recursive function being computed. For instance, when determining if a binary tree is a perfect tree—a tree in which all leaf nodes have the same depth and all interior nodes have two children—by structural recursion, besides checking that the left and right subtrees are both perfect, it is also needed to check that they have the same depth:

$$perfect :: \mu \; (TreeF \; e) \quad \to Bool$$
$$perfect \; (In \; Empty) \quad\;\; = True$$
$$perfect \; (In \; (Node \; l \_ r)) = perfect \; l \wedge perfect \; r \wedge (depth \; l \equiv depth \; r)$$

$$depth :: \mu \; (TreeF \; e) \quad\;\; \to Integer$$
$$depth \; (In \; Empty) \quad\;\;\;\; = 0$$
$$depth \; (In \; (Node \; l \_ r)) \;\; = 1 + max \; (depth \; l) \; (depth \; r)$$

The function $perfect$ is not directly a catamorphism because the algebra is not provided with $depth \; l$ and $depth \; r$ by the $cata$ recursion scheme. However we can define $perfect$ as a paramorphism:

$$perfect' = para \; alg \; \textbf{where}$$
$$\quad alg \; Empty = True$$
$$\quad alg \; (Node \; (l, p_l) \_ (r, p_r)) = p_l \wedge p_r \wedge (depth \; l \equiv depth \; r)$$

But this is inefficient because the depth of a subtree is computed repeatedly at each of its ancestor nodes, despite the fact that $depth$ can be computed structurally too. Thus we need a generalization of paramorphisms in which instead of the original structure being kept and supplied to the algebra, some auxiliary information (that can be computed structurally) is maintained along the recursion and supplied to the algebra, which leads to the following recursion scheme.

Recursion Scheme 9. A structurally recursive function with auxiliary information is called a *zygomorphism* [41]:

$$zygo :: Functor \; f \Rightarrow (f \; (a, b) \to a) \to (f \; b \to b) \to \mu \; f \to a$$
$$zygo \; alg_1 \; alg_2 = fst \; (mutu \; alg_1 \; (alg_2 \circ fmap \; snd))$$

Here alg_1 computes the function of interest from the recursive results together with auxiliary information of type b, and alg_2 maintains the auxiliary information. Malcolm [41] called zygomorphisms 'yoking together of paramorphisms and catamorphisms' and prefix 'zygo-' is from Greek ζυγόν meaning 'yoke'.

Example 12. As we said, *zygo* is a generalization of paramorphisms: *para alg =* *zygo alg In*. And the above *perfect* is *zygo p d* where

$p :: TreeF\ e\ (Bool, Integer) \rightarrow Bool$
$p\ Empty \qquad\qquad\quad = True$
$p\ (Node\ (p_l, d_l) \_ (p_r, d_r)) = p_l \wedge p_r \wedge (d_l \equiv d_r)$
$d :: TreeF\ e\ Integer \rightarrow Integer$
$d\ Empty \qquad\qquad\quad = 0$
$d\ (Node\ d_l \_ d_r) \qquad = 1 + (max\ d_l\ d_r)$

Note that although zygomorphisms are special cases of mutumorphisms, the recursion scheme *zygo* is not a special case of *mutu*, precisely because of the projection *fst*. In the unifying framework by means of adjunctions, zygomorphisms arise from an adjunction between the slice category $C \downarrow b$ and the base category C [27]. The same adjunction also leads to the dual of zygomorphisms—the recursion scheme in which a seed is unfolded to a value of a recursive datatype that is defined with some auxiliary datatype.

7   Course-of-Value (Co)Recursion

This section is about the patterns in dynamic programming algorithms, in which a problem is solved based on solutions to subproblems just as in catamorphisms. But in dynamic programming algorithms, subproblems are largely shared among problems, and thus a common implementation technique is to memoize solved subproblems with a table. This section shows the recursion scheme for functions that capture dynamic programming called *histomorphisms*, a generalization called *dynamorphisms*, the corecursive dual *futumorphisms*, and a further generalization *chronomorphisms*.

7.1   Histomorphisms

A powerful generalization of catamorphisms is to provide the algebra with all the recursively computed results of direct and indirect substructures rather than only the *immediate* substructures. Consider the longest increasing subsequence (LIS) problem: given a sequence of integers, its subsequences are obtained by deleting some (or none) of its elements and keeping the remaining elements in its original order, and the problem is to find (the length of) longest subsequences in which the elements are in increasing order. For example, the longest increasing subsequences of $[1, 6, -5, 4, 2, 3, 9]$ have length 4 and one of them is $[1, 2, 3, 9]$.

A way to find LIS follows the observation that an LIS of $x : xs$ is either an LIS of xs, or a subsequence beginning with the head element x and whose tail is also an LIS (or the whole LIS could be longer). This idea is implemented by the program below.

$$lis = snd \circ lis'$$
$$lis' :: Ord\ a \Rightarrow [a] \rightarrow (Integer, Integer)$$
$$lis'\ [\,] \qquad = (0, 0)$$
$$lis'\ (x : xs) = (a, b)\ \textbf{where}$$
$$\quad a = 1 + maximum\ [fst\ (lis'\ sub)\ |\ sub \leftarrow tails\ xs, null\ sub \vee x < head\ sub]$$
$$\quad b = max\ a\ (snd\ (lis'\ xs))$$

where the first component of $lis'\ (x : xs)$ is the length of the longest increasing subsequence that is restricted to begin with the first element x, and the second component is the length of LIS without this restriction and thus $lis = snd \circ lis'$.

Unfortunately this implementation is very inefficient because lis' is recursively applied to possibly all substructures of the input, leading to exponential running time with respect to the length of the input. The inefficiency is mainly due to redundant recomputation of lis' on substructures: when computing $lis'\ (xs +\!\!\!+ ys)$, for each x in xs, $lis'\ ys$ is recomputed although the results are identical. A technique to speed up the algorithm is to memoize the results of lis' on substructures and skip recomputing the function when identical input is encountered, a technique called *dynamic programming*.

To implement dynamic programming, what we want is a scheme that provides the algebra with a table of the results for all substructures that have been computed. A table is represented by the *Cofree* comonad

data *Cofree f a* **where**
$\qquad (\triangleleft) :: a \rightarrow f\ (Cofree\ f\ a) \rightarrow Cofree\ f\ a$

which can be intuitively understood as a (coinductive) tree whose branching structure is determined by functor f and all nodes are tagged with a value of type a, which can be extracted with

$$extract :: Cofree\ f\ a \rightarrow a$$
$$extract\ (x \triangleleft \_) = x$$

Recursion Scheme 10. The recursion scheme *histomorphism* [50] is:

$$histo :: Functor\ f \Rightarrow (f\ (Cofree\ f\ a) \rightarrow a) \rightarrow \mu f \rightarrow a$$
$$histo\ alg = extract \circ cata\ (\lambda x \rightarrow (alg\ x) \triangleleft x)$$

which is a catamorphism computing a memo-table of type *Cofree f a* followed by extracting the result for the whole structure. The name histo- follows that the entire computation history is passed to the algebra. It is also called *course-of-value* recursion.

Example 13. The dynamic programming implementation of *lis* is then:

$$lis'' :: Ord\ a \Rightarrow \mu\ (ListF\ a) \to Integer$$
$$lis'' = snd \circ histo\ alg$$
$$alg :: Ord\ a \Rightarrow ListF\ a\ (Cofree\ (ListF\ a)\ (Integer, Integer))$$
$$\to (Integer, Integer)$$
$$alg\ Nil \qquad\qquad = (0,0)$$
$$alg\ (Cons\ x\ table) = (a,b)\ \textbf{where}$$
$$a = 1 + findNext\ x\ table$$
$$b = max\ a\ (snd\ (extract\ table))$$

where *findNext* searches in the rest of the list for the element that is greater than x and begins a longest increasing subsequence:

$$findNext :: Ord\ a \Rightarrow a \to Cofree\ (ListF\ a)\ (Integer, Integer) \to Integer$$
$$findNext\ x\ ((a,\_) \lhd Nil) \qquad\qquad = a$$
$$findNext\ x\ ((a,\_) \lhd (Cons\ y\ table')) = \textbf{if}\ x < y\ \textbf{then}\ max\ a\ b\ \textbf{else}\ b$$
$$\textbf{where}\ b = findNext\ x\ table'$$

which improves the time complexity to quadratic time because *alg* runs in linear time for each element and *alg* is computed only once for each element.

In the unifying theory of recursion schemes by adjunctions, histomorphisms arise from the adjunction $U \dashv Cofree_F$ [26] where $Cofree_F$ sends an object to its cofree coalgebra in the category of F-coalgebras, and U is the forgetful functor. As we have seen, cofree coalgebras are used to model the memo-table of computation history in histomorphisms, but an oddity here is that (the carrier of) the cofree coalgebra is a possibly infinite structure, while the computation history is in fact finite because the input is a finite inductive structure. A remedy for this imprecision is to replace cofree coalgebras with *cofree para-recursive coalgebras* in the construction, and the *Cofree f a* comonad in *histo* is replaced by its para-recursive counterpart, which is exactly *finite* trees whose branching structure is f and nodes are tagged with a-values [29].

7.2 Dynamorphisms

Histomorphisms require the input to be an initial algebra, and this is inconvenient in applications whose structure of computation is determined on the fly while computing. An example is the following program finding the length of *longest common subsequences* (LCS) of two sequences [2].

$$lcs :: Eq\ a \Rightarrow [a] \rightarrow [a] \rightarrow Integer$$
$$lcs\ []\ \_ = 0$$
$$lcs\ \_\ [] = 0$$
$$lcs\ xxs@(x : xs)\ yys@(y : ys)$$
$$\quad |\ x \equiv y \qquad = lcs\ xs\ ys + 1$$
$$\quad |\ otherwise = max\ (lcs\ xs\ yys)\ (lcs\ xxs\ ys)$$

This program runs in exponential time but it is well suited for optimization with dynamic programming because a lot of subproblems are shared across recursion. However, it is not accommodated by *histo* because the input, a pair of lists, is not an initial algebra. Therefore it is handy to generalize *histo* by replacing $in°$ with a user-supplied recursive coalgebra:

Recursion Scheme 11. A *dynamorphism* (evidently the name is derived from *dyna*mic programming) introduced by Kabanov and Vene [37] is given by:

$$dyna :: Functor\ f \Rightarrow (f\ (Cofree\ f\ a) \rightarrow a) \rightarrow (c \rightarrow f\ c) \rightarrow c \rightarrow a$$
$$dyna\ alg\ coalg = extract \circ hylo\ (\lambda x \rightarrow alg\ x \triangleleft x)\ coalg$$

in which the recursive coalgebra *coalg* breaks a problem into subproblems, which are recursively solved, and the algebra *alg* solves a problem with solutions to all direct and indirect subproblems.

Because the subproblems of a dynamic programming algorithm together with the dependency relation of subproblems form an acyclic graph, an appealing choice of the functor f in *dyna* is *ListF* and the coalgebra c generates subproblems in a topological order of the dependency graph of subproblems, so that a subproblem is solved exactly once when it is needed by bigger problems.

Example 14. Continuing the example of LCS, the set of subproblems of $lcs\ s_1\ s_2$ are all pairs (x, y) for x and y being suffixes of s_1 and s_2 respectively. An ordering of subproblems that respects their computing dependency is:

$$g :: ([a], [a]) \rightarrow ListF\ ([a], [a])\ ([a], [a])$$
$$g\ ([], []) = Nil$$
$$g\ (x, y)\ = \textbf{if}\ null\ y\ \textbf{then}\ Cons\ (x, y)\ (tail\ x, s_2)$$
$$\qquad\qquad\qquad \textbf{else}\quad Cons\ (x, y)\ (x, tail\ y)$$

The algebra a solves a problem with solutions to subproblems available:

$$a :: ListF\ ([a], [a])\ (Cofree\ (ListF\ ([a], [a]))\ Integer) \rightarrow Integer$$
$$a\ Nil = 0$$
$$a\ (Cons\ (x, y)\ table)$$
$$\quad |\ null\ x \lor null\ y\ = 0$$
$$\quad |\ head\ x \equiv head\ y = index\ table\ (offset\ 1\ 1) + 1$$

$$| \; otherwise \qquad = max \; (index \; table \; (offset \; 1 \; 0))$$
$$(index \; table \; (offset \; 0 \; 1))$$

where *index t n* extracts the *n*-th entry of the memo-table *t*:

$$index :: Cofree \; (ListF \; a) \; p \rightarrow Integer \rightarrow p$$
$$index \; t \; 0 \qquad\qquad = extract \; t$$
$$index \; (\_ \lhd (Cons \_ \; t')) \; n = index \; t' \; (n - 1)$$

The tricky part is computing the indices for entries to subproblems in the memo-table. Because subproblems are enumerated by *g* in the order that reduces the second sequence first, thus the entry for $(drop \; n \; x, drop \; m \; y)$ in the memo-table when computing (x, y) is:

$$offset \; n \; m = n * (length \; s_2 + 1) + m - 1$$

Putting them together, we get the dynamic programming solution to LCS:

$$lcs' \; s_1 \; s_2 = dyna \; a \; g \; (s_1, s_2)$$

which improves the exponential running time of specification *lcs* to $\mathcal{O}(|s_1||s_2|^2)$, yet slower than the $\mathcal{O}(|s_1||s_2|)$ array-based implementation of dynamic programming because of the cost of indexing the list-structured memo-table.

7.3   Futumorphisms

Histomorphisms are generalized catamorphisms that can inspect the history of computation. The dual generalization is anamorphisms that can *control the future*. As an example, consider the problem of decoding the *run-length encoding* of a sequence: the input is a list of elements (n, x) of type (Int, a) and $n > 0$ for all elements. The output is a list $[a]$ and each (n, x) in the input is interpreted as *n* consecutive copies of *x*. As an anamorphism, it is expressed as

$$rld :: [(Int, a)] \rightarrow \nu \; (ListF \; a)$$
$$rld = ana \; c \; \textbf{where}$$
$$c \; [] = Nil$$
$$c \; ((n, x) : xs)$$
$$| \; n \equiv 1 \qquad = Cons \; x \; xs$$
$$| \; otherwise = Cons \; x \; ((n - 1, x) : xs)$$

This is slightly awkward because anamorphisms can emit only one layer of the structure in each step, while in this example it is more natural to emit *n* copies of *x* in a batch. This can be done if the recursion scheme allows the coalgebra to generate more than one layer in a single step—in a sense controlling the future of the computation.

Multiple layers of a structure given by a functor f are represented by the *Free* monad:

data *Free f a* = *Ret a* | *Op* (*f* (*Free f a*))

which is the type of (inductive) trees whose branching is determined by f and leaf nodes are a-values. Free algebras subsume initial algebras as *Free f Void* $\cong \mu f$ where *Void* is the bottom type, and *cata* for μf is replaced by

$$eval :: Functor\ f \Rightarrow (f\ b \rightarrow b) \rightarrow (a \rightarrow b) \rightarrow Free\ f\ a \rightarrow b$$
$$eval\ alg\ g\ (Ret\ a) = g\ a$$
$$eval\ alg\ g\ (Op\ k)\ = alg\ (fmap\ (eval\ alg\ g)\ k)$$

Recursion Scheme 12. With these constructions, the recursion scheme for *futumorphisms* [50] is defined by:

$$futu :: Functor\ f \Rightarrow (c \rightarrow f\ (Free\ f\ c)) \rightarrow c \rightarrow \nu f$$
$$futu\ coalg = ana\ coalg' \circ Ret\ \textbf{where}$$
$$\quad coalg'\ (Ret\ a) = coalg\ a$$
$$\quad coalg'\ (Op\ k)\ = k$$

Example 15. We can redefine *rld* as a futumorphism:

$$rld' :: [(Int, a)] \rightarrow \nu\ (ListF\ a)$$
$$rld' = futu\ dec$$
$$dec\ [\ ]\qquad\quad = Nil$$
$$dec\ ((n, c) : xs) = \textbf{let}\ (Op\ g) = rep\ n\ \textbf{in}\ g\ \textbf{where}$$
$$\quad rep\ 0\ = Ret\ xs$$
$$\quad rep\ m = Op\ (Cons\ c\ (rep\ (m - 1)))$$

Note that *dec* assumes $n > 0$ because *futu* demands that the coalgebra generate at least one layer of f-structure.

Theoretically, futumorphisms are adjoint unfolds from the adjunction $Free_F \dashv U$ where $Free_F$ maps object a to the free algebra generated by a in the category of F-algebras. In the same way that dynamorphisms generalize histomorphisms, futumorphisms can be generalized by replacing $(\nu\ F, Out^\circ)$ with a user-supplied corecursive F-algebra.

A broader generalization is to combine futumorphisms and histomorphisms in a similar way to hylomorphisms combining anamorphisms and catamorphisms:

$$chrono :: Functor\ f \Rightarrow (f\ (Cofree\ f\ b) \to b)$$
$$\to (a \to f\ (Free\ f\ a))$$
$$\to a \to b$$
$$chrono\ alg\ coalg = extract \circ hylo\ alg'\ coalg' \circ Ret\ \textbf{where}$$
$$alg'\ x = alg\ x \lhd x$$
$$coalg'\ (Ret\ a) = coalg\ a$$
$$coalg'\ (Op\ k)\ = k$$

These were dubbed *chronomorphisms* by Kmett [38] (prefix chrono- from Greek χρόνος meaning 'time'), because they subsume both histo- and futumorphisms.

8   Monadic Structural Recursion

Up to now we have been working in the world of pure functions. It is certainly possible to extend the recursion schemes to the non-pure world where computational effects are modelled with monads.

8.1   Monadic Catamorphism

Let us start with a straightforward example of printing a tree with the IO monad:

$$printTree :: Show\ a \Rightarrow \mu\ (TreeF\ a) \to IO\ ()$$
$$printTree\ (In\ Empty) \qquad = return\ ()$$
$$printTree\ (In\ (Node\ l\ a\ r)) = \textbf{do}\ printTree\ l; printTree\ r; print\ a$$

The reader may have recognized that it is already a catamorphism:

$$printTree' :: Show\ a \Rightarrow \mu\ (TreeF\ a) \to IO\ ()$$
$$printTree' = cata\ printAlg\ \textbf{where}$$
$$printAlg :: Show\ a \Rightarrow TreeF\ a\ (IO\ ()) \to IO\ ()$$
$$printAlg\ Empty \qquad = return\ ()$$
$$printAlg\ (Node\ ml\ a\ mr) = \textbf{do}\ ml; mr; print\ a$$

Thus a straightforward way of abstracting 'monadic catamorphisms' is to restrict *cata* to monadic values.

Recursion Scheme 13 (*cataM*). We call the morphisms given by the following recursion scheme *catamorphisms on monadic values*:

$$cataM :: (Functor\ f, Monad\ m) \Rightarrow (f\ (m\ a) \to m\ a) \to \mu\ f \to m\ a$$
$$cataM\ algM = cata\ algM$$

which is the second approach to monadic catamorphisms in [49].

However, *cataM* does not fully capture our intuition for 'monadic catamorphism' because the algebra $algM :: f\ (m\ a) \to m\ a$ is allowed to combine computations from subparts arbitrarily. For a more precise characterization, we decompose $algM :: f\ (m\ a) \to m\ a$ in *cataM* into two parts: a function $alg :: f\ a \to m\ a$ which (monadically) computes the result for the whole structure given the results of substructures, and a polymorphic function

$$seq :: \forall x.f\ (m\ x) \to m\ (f\ x)$$

called a *sequencing* of f over m, which combines computations for substructures into one monadic computation. The decomposition reflects the intuition that a monadic catamorphism processes substructures (in the order determined by *seq*) and combines their results (by *alg*) to process the root structure:

$$algM\ r = seq\ r \ggg alg.$$

Example 16. Binary trees *TreeF* can be sequenced from left to right:

$lToR :: Monad\ m \Rightarrow TreeF\ a\ (m\ x) \to m\ (TreeF\ a\ x)$
$lToR\ Empty \qquad\quad = return\ Empty$
$lToR\ (Node\ ml\ a\ mr) = \mathbf{do}\ l \leftarrow ml; r \leftarrow mr; return\ (Node\ l\ a\ r)$

and also from right to left:

$rToL :: Monad\ m \Rightarrow TreeF\ a\ (m\ x) \to m\ (TreeF\ a\ x)$
$rToL\ Empty \qquad\quad = return\ Empty$
$rToL\ (Node\ ml\ a\ mr) = \mathbf{do}\ r \leftarrow mr; l \leftarrow ml; return\ (Node\ l\ a\ r)$

Recursion Scheme 14 (*mcata*). A *monadic catamorphism* [13,49] is given by the following recursion scheme:

$mcata :: (Monad\ m, Functor\ f) \Rightarrow (\forall x.f\ (m\ x) \to m\ (f\ x))$
$\qquad\quad \to (f\ a \to m\ a) \to \mu\ f \to m\ a$
$mcata\ seq\ alg = cata\ ((\ggg alg) \circ seq)$

Example 17. The program *printTree* above is a monadic catamorphism:

$printTree'' :: Show\ a \Rightarrow \mu\ (TreeF\ a) \to IO\ ()$
$printTree'' = mcata\ lToR\ printElem\ \mathbf{where}$
$\quad printElem\ Empty \qquad = return\ ()$
$\quad printElem\ (Node\ \_\ a\ \_) = print\ a$

Note that *mcata* is strictly less expressive than *cataM* because *mcata* requires all subtrees processed before the root.

Distributive Conditions. In the literature [13, 27, 49], the sequencing of a monadic catamorphism is required to satisfy a *distributive law* of functor f over monad m, which means that $seq :: \forall x.f\ (m\ x) \rightarrow m\ (f\ x)$ satisfies two conditions:

$$seq \circ fmap\ return = return \tag{7}$$

$$seq \circ fmap\ join = join \circ fmap\ seq \circ seq \tag{8}$$

Intuitively, condition (7) prohibits *seq* from inserting additional computational effects when combining computations for substructures, which is a reasonable requirement. Condition (8) requires *seq* to be commutative with monadic sequencing. These requirements are theoretically elegant, because they allow functor f to be lifted to the Kleisli category of m and consequently *mcata seq alg* is also a catamorphism in the Kleisli category (*mcata* by definition is a catamorphism in the base category)—giving us nicer calculational properties.

Unfortunately, condition (8) is usually too strong in practice. For example, neither *lToR* nor *rToL* in Example 16 satisfies condition (8) when m is the *IO* monad. To see this, let

$$c = Node\ (putStr\ \texttt{"A"} \gg return\ (putStr\ \texttt{"C"}))\ ()$$
$$(putStr\ \texttt{"B"} \gg return\ (putStr\ \texttt{"D"}))$$

Then $(lToR \circ fmap\ join)\ c$ prints $\texttt{"ACBD"}$ but $(join \circ fmap\ lToR \circ lToR)\ c$ prints $\texttt{"ABCD"}$. In fact, there is no distributive law of *TreeF* a over a monad unless it is commutative, excluding the *IO* monad and *State* monad. Thus we drop the requirement for *seq* being a distributive law in our definition of monadic catamorphism.

8.2   More Monadic Recursion Schemes

As we mentioned above, *mcata* is the catamorphism in the Kleisli category provided *seq* is a distributive law. No doubt, we can replay our development of recursion schemes in the Kleisli category to get the monadic version of more recursion schemes. For example, we have *monadic hylomorphisms* [47, 49]:

$$mhylo :: (Monad\ m, Functor\ f) \Rightarrow (\forall x.f\ (m\ x) \rightarrow m\ (f\ x))$$
$$\rightarrow (f\ a \rightarrow m\ a) \rightarrow (c \rightarrow m\ (f\ c)) \rightarrow c \rightarrow m\ a$$
$$mhylo\ seq\ alg\ coalg\ c = \textbf{do}\ x \leftarrow coalg\ c$$
$$y \leftarrow seq\ (fmap\ (mhylo\ seq\ alg\ coalg)\ x)$$
$$alg\ y$$

which specializes to *mcata* by *mhylo seq alg* $(return \circ in^\circ)$ and *monadic anamorphisms* by

$$mana :: (Monad\ m, Functor\ f) \Rightarrow (\forall x.f\ (m\ x) \rightarrow m\ (f\ x))$$
$$\rightarrow (c \rightarrow m\ (f\ c)) \rightarrow c \rightarrow m\ (\nu\ f)$$
$$mana\ seq\ coalg = mhylo\ seq\ (return \circ Out^\circ)\ coalg$$

Other recursion schemes discussed in this paper can be devised in the same way.

Example 18. Generating a random binary tree of some depth with *randomIO* :: *IO Int* is a monadic anamorphism:

ranTree :: *Integer* → *IO* (*ν* (*TreeF Int*))
ranTree = *mana lToR gen* **where**
    gen :: *Integer* → *IO* (*TreeF Int Integer*)
    gen 0 = *return Empty*
    gen n = **do** *a* ← *randomIO* :: *IO Int*
                return (*Node* (*n* − 1) *a* (*n* − 1))

9 Structural Recursion on GADTs

So far we have worked exclusively with (co)inductive datatypes, but they do not cover all algebraic datatypes and *generalized algebraic datatypes* (GADTs). An example of algebraic datatypes that is not (co)inductive is the datatype for purely functional *random-access lists* [46]:

data *RList a* = *Null* | *Zero* (*RList* (*a, a*)) | *One a* (*RList* (*a, a*))

The recursive occurrences of *RList* in constructor *Zero* and *One* are *RList* (*a, a*) rather than *RList a*, and consequently we cannot model *RList a* as *μ f* for some functor *f* as we did for lists. Algebraic datatypes such as *RList* whose defining equation has on the right-hand side any occurrence of the declared type applied to parameters different from those on the left-hand side are called *non-regular* datatypes or *nested* datatypes [7, 34, 36].

Nested datatypes are covered by a broader range of datatypes called *generalized algebraic datatypes* (GADTs) [21, 35]. In terms of the **data** syntax in Haskell, the generalization of GADTs is to allow the parameters *P* supplied to the declared type *D* on the left-hand side of an defining equation **data** *D P* = ... to be more complex than type variables. GADTs have a different syntax from that of ADTs in Haskell[4]. For example, as a GADT, *RList* is

data *RList* :: * → * **where**
    Null :: *RList a*
    Zero :: *RList* (*a, a*) → *RList a*
    One :: *a* → *RList* (*a, a*) → *RList a*

in which each constructor is directly declared with a type signature. With this syntax, allowing parameters on the left-hand side of an ADT equation to be not just variables means that the finally returned type of constructors of a GADT *G* can be more complex than *G a* where *a* is a type variable. A classic example

---

[4] Support of GADTs is turned on by the extension **GADTS** in GHC.

is fixed length vectors of a-values: first we define two datatypes **data** Z' and **data** S' n with no constructors, then the GADT for vectors is

> **data** $Vec\ (a :: *) :: * \rightarrow *$ **where**
> Nil $:: Vec\ a\ Z'$
> $Cons :: a \rightarrow Vec\ a\ n \rightarrow Vec\ a\ (S'\ n)$

in which types Z' and S' n encode natural numbers at the type level, thus it does not matter what their term constructors are.

GADTs are a powerful tool to ensure program correctness by indexing datatypes with sophisticated properties of data, such as the size or shape of data, and then the type checker can check these properties statically. For example, the following program extracting the first element of a vector is always safe because the type of its argument guarantees it is non-empty.

> $safeHead :: Vec\ a\ (S'\ n) \rightarrow a$
> $safeHead\ (Cons\ a\ \_)$ $= a$

GADTs as Fixed Points. As we mentioned earlier, nested datatypes and GADTs cannot be modelled as fixed points of Haskell functors in general, making them out of the reach of the recursion schemes that we have seen so far. However, there are other ways to view them as fixed points. Let us look at the $RList$ datatype again,

> **data** $RList\ a = Null\ |\ Zero\ (RList\ (a, a))\ |\ One\ a\ (RList\ (a, a))$

instead of viewing it as defining a type $RList\ a :: *$, we can alternatively understand it as defining a functor $RList :: * \rightarrow *$, where $*$ is the category of Haskell types, such that $RList$ satisfies the fixed point equation $RList \cong RListF\ RList$ for a *higher-order* functor $RListF :: (* \rightarrow *) \rightarrow (* \rightarrow *)$ defined as

> **data** $RListF\ f\ a = NullF\ |\ ZeroF\ (f\ (a, a))\ |\ OneF\ a\ (f\ (a, a))$

In this way, nested datatypes are still fixed points, but of higher-order functors, rather than usual Haskell functors [7, 34].

This idea applies to GADTs as well, but with a caveat: consider the GADT G defined as follows:

> **data** $G\ a$ **where**
> $Leaf :: a \rightarrow G\ a$
> $Prod :: G\ a \rightarrow G\ b \rightarrow G\ (a, b)$

then G *cannot* be a functor at all, let alone a fixed point of some higher-order functor. The problem is defining *fmap* for the *Prod* constructor:

$$fmap\ f\ (Prod\ ga\ gb) = \_ :: G\ c$$

However, we have no way to construct a $G\ c$ given $f :: (a, b) \to c$, $ga :: G\ a$ and $gb :: G\ b$. Luckily, Johann and Ghani [35] shows how to fix this problem. In fact, all we need to do is to give up the expectation that a GADT $G::* \to *$ is functorial in its domain. In categorical terminology, we view GADTs as functors from the *discrete category* $| * |$ of Haskell types to the category $*$ of Haskell types, rather than functors from $*$ to $*$. In other words, a GADT $G :: * \to *$ is then merely a type constructor in Haskell, without necessarily a *Functor* instance. A *natural transformation* between two functors a and b from $| * |$ to $*$ is a polymorphic function $\forall i.a\ i \to b\ i$, which we give a type synonym $a \overset{.}{\to} b$[5]:

type $(\overset{.}{\to})\ a\ b = \forall i.a\ i \to b\ i$

And a higher-order endofunctor (on the functor category $*^{|*|}$) is f instantiating the following type class, which is analogous to the *Functor* type class of Haskell:

    class *HFunctor* $(f :: (* \to *) \to (* \to *))$ **where**
      hfmap $:: (a \overset{.}{\to} b) \to (f\ a \overset{.}{\to} f\ b)$

in which *fmap*'s counterpart *hfmap* maps a natural transformation $a \overset{.}{\to} b$ to another natural transformation $f\ a \overset{.}{\to} f\ b$. On top of these, the least-fixed-point operator for an *HFunctor* is

    data $\dot{\mu} :: ((* \to *) \to (* \to *)) \to (* \to *)$ **where**
      $\dot{In} :: f\ (\dot{\mu}\ f)\ i \to \dot{\mu}\ f\ i$

Example 19. Fixed-length vectors *Vec e* are isomorphic to $\dot{\mu}\ (VecF\ e)$ where

    data *VecF* $:: * \to (* \to *) \to (* \to *)$ **where**
      NilF $:: VecF\ e\ f\ Z'$
      ConsF $:: e \to f\ n \to VecF\ e\ f\ (S'\ n)$

which has *HFunctor* instance

    instance *HFunctor* (*VecF e*) **where**
      hfmap phi NilF   = *NilF*
      hfmap phi (*ConsF e es*) = *ConsF e* (*phi es*)

---

[5] It requires the `RankNTypes` extension of GHC.

Recursion Scheme 15 (*icata*). With the machinery above, we can devise the structural recursion scheme for $\dot{\mu}$, which we call *indexed catamorphisms*:

$$icata :: HFunctor\ f \Rightarrow (f\ a \overset{.}{\to} a) \to \dot{\mu}\ f \overset{.}{\to} a$$
$$icata\ alg\ (\dot{In}\ x) = alg\ (hfmap\ (icata\ alg)\ x)$$

Example 20. Just like list processing functions such as *map* are catamorphisms, their counterparts for vectors can also be written as indexed catamorphisms:

$$vmap :: \forall a\ b.(a \to b) \to \dot{\mu}\ (VecF\ a) \overset{.}{\to} \dot{\mu}\ (VecF\ b)$$
$$vmap\ f = icata\ alg\ \textbf{where}$$
$$\quad alg :: VecF\ a\ (\dot{\mu}\ (VecF\ b)) \overset{.}{\to} \dot{\mu}\ (VecF\ b)$$
$$\quad alg\ NilF \qquad\quad = \dot{In}\ NilF$$
$$\quad alg\ (ConsF\ a\ bs) = \dot{In}\ (ConsF\ (f\ a)\ bs)$$

Example 21. Terms of untyped lambda calculus with de Bruijn indices can be modelled as the fixed point of the following higher-order functor [8]:

$$\textbf{data}\ LambdaF :: (* \to *) \to (* \to *)\ \textbf{where}$$
$$\quad Var :: a \to LambdaF\ f\ a$$
$$\quad App :: f\ a \to f\ a \to LambdaF\ f\ a$$
$$\quad Abs :: f\ (Maybe\ a) \to LambdaF\ f\ a$$

Letting a be some type, inhabitants of $\dot{\mu}\ LambdaF\ a$ are precisely the lambda terms in which free variables range over a. Thus $\dot{\mu}\ LambdaF\ Void$ is the type of closed lambda terms where *Void* is the type has no inhabitants. Note that the constructor *Abs* applies the recursive placeholder f to *Maybe a*, providing the inner term with exactly one more fresh variable *Nothing*.

The free variables of a lambda term can be extracted into a list quite easily, by converting from $\dot{\mu}\ LambdaF\ a$ to $[a]$ for any type a:

$$vars :: \dot{\mu}\ LambdaF \overset{.}{\to} []$$
$$vars = icata\ alg\ \textbf{where}$$
$$\quad alg :: LambdaF\ [] \overset{.}{\to} []$$
$$\quad alg\ (Var\ v) \qquad = [v]$$
$$\quad alg\ (App\ fvs\ xvs) = fvs + \!\!+\ xvs$$
$$\quad alg\ (Abs\ vs) \qquad = [v \mid Just\ v \leftarrow vs]$$

This obtains all the free variables without attempting to remove duplicates.

The size of a lambda term can also be computed structurally. However, what we get from *icata* is always an arrow $\dot{\mu}\ LambdaF \overset{.}{\to} a$ for some $a :: * \to *$. If we want to compute just an integer, we need to wrap it in a constant functor:

newtype K a $x = K$ $\{unwrap :: a\}$

Computing the size of a term is done by

$size :: \mu$ $LambdaF \overset{\cdot}{\to} K$ $Integer$
$size = icata$ alg **where**
  $alg :: LambdaF$ $(K$ $Integer) \overset{\cdot}{\to} K$ $Integer$
  alg $(Var \_)$ $= K$ 1
  alg $(App$ $(K$ $n)$ $(K$ $m)) = K$ $(n + m + 1)$
  alg $(Abs$ $(K$ $n))$ $= K$ $(n + 1)$

Example 22. An indexed catamorphism $icata$ alg is a function $\forall i. \mu$ f $i \to a$ i polymorphic in index i. However, we might be interested in GADTs and nested datatypes applied to some monomorphic index. Consider the following program summing up a random-access list of integers.

$sumRList :: RList$ $Integer \to Integer$
$sumRList$ $Null$ $= 0$
$sumRList$ $(Zero$ $xs)$ $= sumRList$ $(fmap$ $(uncurry$ $(+))$ $xs)$
$sumRList$ $(One$ x $xs) = x + sumRList$ $(fmap$ $(uncurry$ $(+))$ $xs)$

Does it fit into an indexed catamorphism from μ $RListF$? The answer is yes, with the clever choice of the continuation monad $Cont$ $Integer$ a as the result type of $icata$.

newtype $Cont$ r $a = Cont$ $\{runCont :: (a \to r) \to r\}$
$sumRList' :: \mu$ $RListF$ $Integer \to Integer$
$sumRList'$ $x = runCont$ $(h$ $x)$ id **where**
  $h :: \mu$ $RListF \overset{\cdot}{\to} Cont$ $Integer$
  $h = icata$ sum **where**
    $sum :: RListF$ $(Cont$ $Integer) \overset{\cdot}{\to} Cont$ $Integer$
    sum $NullF$ $= Cont$ $(\lambda k \to 0)$
    sum $(ZeroF$ $s)$ $= Cont$ $(\lambda k \to runCont$ s $(fork$ $k))$
    sum $(OneF$ a $s) = Cont$ $(\lambda k \to k$ $a + runCont$ s $(fork$ $k))$
    $fork :: (y \to Integer) \to (y, y) \to Integer$
    $fork$ k $(a, b) = k$ $a + k$ b

Historically, structural recursion on nested datatypes applied to a monomorphic type was thought as falling out of $icata$ and led to the development of *generalized folds* [1,6]. Later, Johann and Ghani [34] showed $icata$ is in fact expressive enough by using right Kan extensions as the result type of $icata$, of which $Cont$ used in this example is a special case.

10 Equational Reasoning with Recursion Schemes

We have talked about a handful of recursion schemes, which are recognized common patterns in recursive functions. Recognizing common patterns help programmers understand a new problem and communicate their solutions with others. Better still, recursion schemes offer rigorous and formal *calculational properties* with which the programmer can manipulate programs in a way similar to manipulate standard mathematical objects such as numbers and polynomials. In this section, we briefly show some of the properties and an example of reasoning about programs using them. We refer to Bird and de Moor [4] for a comprehensive introduction to this subject and Bird [3] for more examples of reasoning about and optimizing algorithms in this approach.

We focus on *hylomorphisms*, as almost all recursion schemes are a hylomorphism in a certain category. The fundamental property is the unique existence of the solution to a hylo equation given a recursive coalgebra c (or dually, a corecursive algebra a): for any x,

$$x = a \circ fmap\ x \circ c \iff x = hylo\ a\ c \qquad \text{(HyloUniq)}$$

which directly follows the definition of a recursive coalgebra. Instantiating x to $hylo\ a\ c$, we get the defining equation of $hylo$

$$hylo\ a\ c = a \circ fmap\ (hylo\ a\ c) \circ c \qquad \text{(HyloComp)}$$

which is sometimes called the *computation law*, because it tells how to compute $hylo\ a\ c$ recursively. Instantiating x to id, we get

$$id = a \circ c \iff id = hylo\ a\ c \qquad \text{(HyloRefl)}$$

called the *reflection law*, which gives a necessary and sufficient condition for $hylo\ a\ c$ being the identity function. Note that in this law, $c :: r \to f\ r$ and $a :: f\ r \to r$ share the same carrier type r. Furthermore this law entails that the algebra a is surjective, and the coalgebra c is injective. A direct consequence of HyloRefl is $cata\ In = id$ because $cata\ a = hylo\ a\ in^\circ$ and $id = In \circ in^\circ$. Dually, we also have $ana\ Out = id$.

An important consequence of HyloUniq is the following *fusion law*. It is easier to describe diagrammatically: The HyloUniq law states that there is exactly one x, i.e. $hylo\ a\ c$, such that the following diagram commutes (i.e. all paths with the same start and end points give the same result when their edges are composed together):

$$
\begin{array}{ccc}
ta & \xleftarrow{\ x\ } & tc \\
a\uparrow & & \downarrow c \\
f\ ta & \xleftarrow[fmap\ x]{} & f\ tc
\end{array}
$$

If we put another *commuting* square beside it,

$$
\begin{array}{ccccc}
tb & \xleftarrow{\;h\;} & ta & \xleftarrow{\;x\;} & tc \\
{\scriptstyle b}\big\uparrow & & {\scriptstyle a}\big\uparrow & & \big\downarrow{\scriptstyle c} \\
f\,tb & \xleftarrow[fmap\ h]{} & f\,ta & \xleftarrow[fmap\ x]{} & f\,tc
\end{array}
\qquad (9)
$$

the outer rectangle (with top edge $h \circ x$) also commutes, and it is also an instance of HYLOUNIQ with coalgebra c and algebra b. Because HYLOUNIQ states $hylo\ c\ b$ is the only arrow making the outer rectangle commute, thus $hylo\ c\ b = h \circ x = h \circ hylo\ a\ c$. In summary, the fusion law is:

$$ h \circ hylo\ a\ c = hylo\ b\ c \iff h \circ a = b \circ fmap\ h \qquad \text{(HYLOFUSION)} $$

and its dual version for corecursive algebra a is

$$ hylo\ a\ c \circ h = hylo\ a\ d \iff c \circ h = fmap\ h \circ d \qquad \text{(HYLOFUSIONCO)} $$

where $d :: td \to f\ td$. Fusion laws combine a function after or before a hylomorphism into one hylomorphism, and thus they are is widely used for optimization [10].

We demonstrate how these calculational properties can be used to reason about programs with an example.

Example 23. Suppose some $f :: Integer \to Integer$ such that for all $a, b :: Integer$,

$$ f\,(a+b) = f\,a + f\,b \quad \wedge \quad f\,0 = 0 \qquad (10) $$

and *sum* and *map* are the familiar Haskell functions defined with *hylo*:

```
type List a = μ (ListF a)

sum :: List Integer → Integer          map :: (a → b) → List a → List b
sum = hylo plus in° where              map f = hylo app in° where
  plus Nil        = 0                    app Nil         = In Nil
  plus (Cons a b) = a + b                app (Cons a bs) = In (Cons (f a) bs)
```

Let us prove $sum \circ map\ f = f \circ sum$ with the properties of *hylo*.

Proof. Both $sum \circ map\ f$ and $f \circ sum$ are in the form of a function after a hylomorphism, and thus we can try to use the fusion law to establish

$$ sum \circ map\ f = hylo\ g\ in° = f \circ sum $$

for some g. The correct choice of g is

$g :: ListF\ Integer \to Integer$
$g\ Nil \qquad = f\ 0$
$g\ (Cons\ x\ y) = f\ x + y$

First, $sum \circ map\ f = sum \circ hylo\ app\ in°$, and by HYLOFUSION,

$$sum \circ hylo\ app\ in° = hylo\ g\ in°$$

is implied by

$$sum \circ app = g \circ fmap\ sum \qquad (11)$$

Expanding sum on the left-hand side, it is equivalent to

$$(plus \circ fmap\ sum \circ in°) \circ app = g \circ fmap\ sum \qquad (12)$$

which is an equation of functions

$$ListF\ Integer\ (\mu\ (ListF\ Integer)) \to Integer$$

and it can be shown by a case analysis on the input. For Nil, the left-hand side of (12) equals to

$plus\ (fmap\ sum\ (in°\ (app\ Nil)))$
$= plus\ (fmap\ sum\ (in°\ (In\ Nil)))$
$= plus\ (fmap\ sum\ Nil)$
$= plus\ Nil \qquad\qquad\qquad\qquad$ (by definition of $fmap$ for $ListF$)
$= 0$

and the right-hand side of (12) equals to

$$g\ (fmap\ sum\ Nil) = g\ Nil = g\ 0 = f\ 0$$

and by assumption (10) about f, $f\ 0 = 0$. Similarly when the input is $Cons\ a\ b$, we can calculate that both sides equal to $f\ a + sum\ b$. Thus we have shown (11), and therefore $sum \circ hylo\ app\ in° = hylo\ g\ in°$.

Similarly, by HYLOFUSION, $f \circ sum = hylo\ g\ in°$ is implied by

$$f \circ plus = g \circ fmap\ f$$

which can be verified by case analysis on the input: When the input is Nil, both sides equal to $f\ 0$. When the input is $Cons\ a\ b$, the left-hand side equals to $f\ (a + b)$ and the right-hand side is $f\ a + f\ b$. By assumption (10) on f, $f\ (a + b) = f\ a + f\ b$.

11   Closing Remarks and Further Reading

We have shown a handful of structural recursion schemes and their applications by examples. We hope that this paper can be an accessible introduction to this subject and a quick reference when functional programmers hear about some *morphism* with an obscure Greek prefix. We end this paper with some remarks on general approaches to find more *fantastic morphisms* and some pointers to further reading about the theory and applications of recursion schemes.

From Categories and Adjunctions. As we have seen, recursion schemes live with categories and adjunctions, so whenever we see a new category, it is a good idea to think about catamorphisms and anamorphisms in this category, as we did for the Kleisli category, where we obtained *mcata*, and the functor category $*^{|*|}$, where we obtained *icata*, etc. Also, whenever we encounter an adjunction $L \dashv R$, we can think about if functions of type $L\ c \to a$, especially $L\ (\mu\ f) \to a$, are anything interesting. If they are, there might be interesting conjugate hylomorphisms from this adjunction.

Composing Recursion Schemes. Up to now we have considered recursion schemes in isolation, each of which provides an extra functionality compared with *cata* or *ana*, such as mutual recursion, accessing the original structure, accessing the computation history. However, when writing larger programs in practice, we probably want to combine the functionalities of recursion schemes. For example, if we want to define two mutually recursive functions with historical information, we need a recursion scheme of type

$$mutuHist :: Functor\ f \Rightarrow (f\ (Cofree\ f\ (a, b)) \to a)$$
$$\to (f\ (Cofree\ f\ (a, b)) \to b) \to (\mu\ f \to a, \mu\ f \to b)$$

Theoretically, *mutuHist* is the composite of *mutu* and *accu* in the sense that the adjunction $U \dashv Cofree_F$ underlying *hist* and the adjunction $\Delta \dashv \times$ underlying *mutu* can be composed to an adjunction inducing *mutuHist* [23]. Unfortunately, our Haskell implementations of *mutu* and *hist* are not composable. A composable library of recursion schemes in Haskell would require considerable machinery for doing category theory in Haskell, and how to do it with good usability is a question worth exploring.

Further Reading. The examples in this paper are fairly small ones, but recursion schemes are surely useful in real-world programs and algorithms. For the reader who wants to see recursion schemes in real-world algorithms, we recommend books by Bird [3] and Bird and Gibbons [5]. Their books provide a great deal of examples of proving correctness of algorithms using properties of recursion schemes, which we only briefly showcased in Sect. 10.

We have only glossed over the category theory of the unifying theories of recursion schemes. For the reader interested in them, a good place to start is Hinze's lecture notes [22] on adjoint folds and unfolds, and then Uustalu et al.'s paper [52] on recursion schemes from comonads, which are less general than adjoint folds, but they have generic implementations in Haskell [39]. Finally, Hinze et al.'s conjugate hylomorphisms [29] are the most general framework of recursion schemes so far.

Acknowledgements. Particular thanks are due to Jeremy Gibbons for his numerous suggestions and comments. We would also like to thank the reviewers for the efforts in helping us to improve this paper.

We dedicate this paper to the memory of Richard Bird.

References

1. Abel, A., Matthes, R., Uustalu, T.: Iteration and coiteration schemes for higher-order and nested datatypes. Theoret. Comput. Sci. **333**(1–2), 3–66 (2005). https://doi.org/10.1016/j.tcs.2004.10.017
2. Bergroth, L., Hakonen, H., Raita, T.: A survey of longest common subsequence algorithms. In: Proceedings Seventh International Symposium on String Processing and Information Retrieval. SPIRE 2000, pp. 39–48, September 2000. https://doi.org/10.1109/SPIRE.2000.878178
3. Bird, R.: Pearls of Functional Algorithm Design. Cambridge University Press, Cambridge (2010)
4. Bird, R., de Moor, O.: Algebra of Programming, London (1997)
5. Bird, R., Gibbons, J.: Algorithm Design with Haskell. Cambridge University Press, Cambridge (2020). http://www.cs.ox.ac.uk/publications/books/adwh/
6. Bird, R., Paterson, R.: Generalised folds for nested datatypes. Formal Aspects Comput. **11**(2), 200–222 (1999). https://doi.org/10.1007/s001650050047
7. Bird, R., Meertens, L.: Nested datatypes. In: Jeuring, J. (ed.) MPC 1998. LNCS, vol. 1422, pp. 52–67. Springer, Heidelberg (1998). https://doi.org/10.1007/BFb0054285
8. Bird, R.S., Paterson, R.: de Bruijn notation as a nested datatype. J. Funct. Program. **9**(1), 77–91 (1999). https://doi.org/10.1017/S0956796899003366
9. Capretta, V., Uustalu, T., Vene, V.: Recursive coalgebras from comonads. Inf. Comput. **204**(4), 437–468 (2006). https://doi.org/10.1016/j.ic.2005.08.005
10. Coutts, D., Leshchinskiy, R., Stewart, D.: Stream fusion: from lists to streams to nothing at all. In: Proceedings of the 12th ACM SIGPLAN International Conference on Functional Programming. ICFP 2007, pp. 315–326. Association for Computing Machinery, New York (2007). https://doi.org/10.1145/1291151.1291199
11. Felleisen, M., Findler, R.B., Flatt, M., Krishnamurthi, S.: How to Design Programs: An Introduction to Programming and Computing. The MIT Press, Cambridge (2018)
12. Fokkinga, M.: Law and order in algorithmics. Ph.D. thesis, University of Twente, 7500 AE Enschede, Netherlands, February 1992
13. Fokkinga, M.: Monadic maps and folds for arbitrary datatypes. Memoranda Informatica 94–28, Department of Computer Science, University of Twente, June 1994. http://doc.utwente.nl/66622/
14. Fokkinga, M.M.: Tupling and mutumorphisms. Squiggolist **1**(4), 81–82 (1990)
15. Gibbons, J.: Generic downwards accumulations. Sci. Comput. Program. **37**(1–3), 37–65 (2000). https://doi.org/10.1016/S0167-6423(99)00022-2
16. Gibbons, J.: Metamorphisms: streaming representation-changers. Sci. Comput. Program. **65**(2), 108–139 (2007). https://doi.org/10.1016/j.scico.2006.01.006
17. Gibbons, J.: Coding with asymmetric numeral systems. In: Hutton, G. (ed.) MPC 2019. LNCS, vol. 11825, pp. 444–465. Springer, Cham (2019). https://doi.org/10.1007/978-3-030-33636-3_16
18. Gibbons, J.: How to design co-programs. J. Funct. Program. **31**, e15 (2021). https://doi.org/10.1017/S0956796821000113
19. Gibbons, J., Wu, N.: Folding domain-specific languages: deep and shallow embeddings (functional pearl). In: Proceedings of the 19th ACM SIGPLAN International Conference on Functional Programming, Gothenburg, Sweden, 1–3 September 2014, pp. 339–347. ACM (2014). https://doi.org/10.1145/2628136.2628138

20. Hagino, T.: Category theoretic approach to data types. Ph.D. thesis, University of Edinburgh (1987)
21. Hinze, R.: Fun with phantom types. The fun of programming, pp. 245–262 (2003)
22. Hinze, R.: Generic programming with adjunctions. In: Gibbons, J. (ed.) Generic and Indexed Programming. LNCS, vol. 7470, pp. 47–129. Springer, Heidelberg (2012). https://doi.org/10.1007/978-3-642-32202-0_2
23. Hinze, R.: Adjoint folds and unfolds–an extended study. Sci. Comput. Program. **78**(11), 2108–2159 (2013). https://doi.org/10.1016/j.scico.2012.07.011
24. Hinze, R., James, D.W.H., Harper, T., Wu, N., Magalhães, J.P.: Sorting with bialgebras and distributive laws. In: Löh, A., Garcia, R. (eds.) Proceedings of the 8th ACM SIGPLAN workshop on Generic programming, WGP@ICFP 2012, Copenhagen, Denmark, 9–15 September 2012, pp. 69–80. ACM (2012). https://doi.org/10.1145/2364394.2364405
25. Hinze, R., Magalhães, J.P., Wu, N.: A duality of sorts. In: Achten, P., Koopman, P. (eds.) The Beauty of Functional Code. LNCS, vol. 8106, pp. 151–167. Springer, Heidelberg (2013). https://doi.org/10.1007/978-3-642-40355-2_11
26. Hinze, R., Wu, N.: Histo- and dynamorphisms revisited. In: Proceedings of the 9th ACM SIGPLAN Workshop on Generic Programming. WGP 2013, New York, NY, USA, pp. 1–12 (2013). https://doi.org/10.1145/2502488.2502496
27. Hinze, R., Wu, N.: Unifying structured recursion schemes: an extended study. J. Funct. Program. **26**, e1 (2016). https://doi.org/10.1017/S0956796815000258
28. Hinze, R., Wu, N., Gibbons, J.: Unifying structured recursion schemes. In: Proceedings of the 18th ACM SIGPLAN International Conference on Functional Programming, ICFP 2013. New York, NY, USA, pp. 209–220 (2013). https://doi.org/10.1145/2500365.2500578
29. Hinze, R., Wu, N., Gibbons, J.: Conjugate hylomorphisms - or: the mother of all structured recursion schemes. In: Proceedings of the 42nd Annual ACM SIGPLAN-SIGACT Symposium on Principles of Programming Languages, POPL 2015, pp. 527–538. ACM, New York (2015). https://doi.org/10.1145/2676726.2676989
30. Hoare, C.A.R.: Chapter II: Notes on Data Structuring, pp. 83–174. Academic Press Ltd., GBR (1972)
31. Hu, Z., Iwasaki, H., Takeichi, M.: Calculating accumulations. N. Gener. Comput. **17**(2), 153–173 (1999)
32. Hu, Z., Iwasaki, H., Takeichi, M.: Deriving structural hylomorphisms from recursive definitions. ACM SIGPLAN Not. **31** (1999). https://doi.org/10.1145/232629.232637
33. Hutton, G.: Fold and unfold for program semantics. In: Proceedings of the Third ACM SIGPLAN International Conference on Functional Programming. ICFP 1998, pp. 280–288. Association for Computing Machinery, New York (1998). https://doi.org/10.1145/289423.289457
34. Johann, P., Ghani, N.: Initial algebra semantics is enough! In: Della Rocca, S.R. (ed.) TLCA 2007. LNCS, vol. 4583, pp. 207–222. Springer, Heidelberg (2007). https://doi.org/10.1007/978-3-540-73228-0_16
35. Johann, P., Ghani, N.: Foundations for structured programming with GADTs. SIGPLAN Not. **43**(1), 297–308 (2008). https://doi.org/10.1145/1328897.1328475
36. Johann, P., Ghani, N.: A principled approach to programming with nested types in Haskell. High.-Order Symb. Comput. **22**(2), 155–189 (2009). https://doi.org/10.1007/s10990-009-9047-7
37. Kabanov, J., Vene, V.: Recursion schemes for dynamic programming. In: Uustalu, T. (ed.) MPC 2006. LNCS, vol. 4014, pp. 235–252. Springer, Heidelberg (2006). https://doi.org/10.1007/11783596_15

38. Kmett, E.: Time for chronomorphisms. http://comonad.com/reader/2008/time-for-chronomorphisms/ (2008), accessed: 2020-06-15
39. Kmett, E.: Recursion-schemes: representing common recursion patterns as higher-order functions (2011). https://hackage.haskell.org/package/recursion-schemes
40. Lambek, J.: A fixpoint theorem for complete categories. Math. Z. **103**, 151–161 (1968)
41. Malcolm, G.: Algebraic data types and program transformation. Ph.D. thesis, University of Groningen (1990)
42. Malcolm, G.: Data structures and program transformation. Sci. Comput. Program. **14**(2–3), 255–280 (1990). https://doi.org/10.1016/0167-6423(90)90023-7
43. Meertens, L.: First Steps Towards the Theory of Rose Trees. CWI, Amsterdam (1988)
44. Meertens, L.: Paramorphisms. Formal Aspects Comput. **4**(5), 413–424 (1992)
45. Meijer, E., Fokkinga, M., Paterson, R.: Functional programming with bananas, lenses, envelopes and barbed wire. In: Hughes, J. (ed.) 5th ACM Conference on Functional Programming Languages and Computer Architecture. FPCA 1991, vol. 523, pp. 124–144 (1991). https://doi.org/10.1007/3540543961_7
46. Okasaki, C.: Purely functional random-access lists. In: Proceedings of the Seventh International Conference on Functional Programming Languages and Computer Architecture. FPCA 1995, pp. 86–95. Association for Computing Machinery, New York (1995). https://doi.org/10.1145/224164.224187
47. Pardo, A.: Monadic corecursion -definition, fusion laws, and applications-. Electron. Notes Theor. Comput. Sci. **11**(C), 105–139 (1998). https://doi.org/10.1016/S1571-0661(04)00055-6
48. Pardo, A.: Generic accumulations. In: Gibbons, J., Jeuring, J. (eds.) Generic Programming: IFIP TC2/WG2.1 Working Conference on Generic Programming. International Federation for Information Processing, vol. 115, pp. 49–78. Kluwer Academic Publishers (2002). https://doi.org/10.1007/978-0-387-35672-3_3
49. Pardo, A.: Combining datatypes and effects. In: Vene, V., Uustalu, T. (eds.) AFP 2004. LNCS, vol. 3622, pp. 171–209. Springer, Heidelberg (2005). https://doi.org/10.1007/11546382_4
50. Uustalu, T., Vene, V.: Primitive (co)recursion and course-of-value (co)iteration, categorically. Informatica **10**(1), 5–26 (1999). https://doi.org/10.3233/INF-1999-10102
51. Uustalu, T., Vene, V.: Comonadic notions of computation, **203**(5), 263–284 (2008). https://doi.org/10.1016/j.entcs.2008.05.029
52. Uustalu, T., Vene, V., Pardo, A.: Recursion schemes from comonads. Nordic J. Comput. **8**(3), 366–390 (2001)
53. Vene, V., Uustalu, T.: Functional programming with apomorphisms (corecursion). Proc. Estonian Acad. Sci. Phys. Math. **47**(3), 147–161 (1998)

Author Index